IT TAKES
A PILLAGE

IT TAKES
A PILLAGE

Behind the Bailouts, Bonuses, and Backroom Deals from Washington to Wall Street

---

Nomi Prins

WILEY

John Wiley & Sons, Inc.

For general information about our other products and services, please contact our Customer Care Department within the United States at (800) 762-2974, outside the United States at (317) 572-3993 or fax (317) 572-4002.

Wiley also publishes its books in a variety of electronic formats. Some content that appears in print may not be available in electronic books. For more information about Wiley products, visit our web site at www.wiley.com.

ISBN: 978-0-470-52959-1

Printed in the United States of America
10   9   8   7   6   5   4   3   2   1

CONTENTS

ACKNOWLEDGMENTS

To write a book in four months on a subject that's such a moving target is intimidating. When data are not always readily available and those most involved with handling the crisis rarely say what they mean or act on what they say, it makes the endeavor especially daunting.

I would not have been able to complete this task without the support of, yes, a small village of people. First of all, I would like to express my heartfelt gratitude for the invaluable research work provided by Sara Abbas, Clark Merrefield, Don McAdam, and Krisztina Ugrin, who all clocked exceedingly long hours over the course of this project. In particular, Krisztina's compilation of the bailout numbers was vital to my understanding the breadth of the Pillage. Clark's sharp eye for detail and consummate editorial skills were critical in shaping the book through every stage, especially in the face of the constant barrage of information. Thanks also to Theresa Diamond and Ed Cole for their research work. Thanks to David Lobenstein, whose editorial advice during the earlier stages of this book was crucial. Thanks to my dear friend and agent, Mark Suroff, for always being there.

My special thanks to my editor, Eric Nelson at John Wiley & Sons, who reached out to me at the end of 2008 to write this book and whose outrage matched my own. I am also grateful to the rest of the fabulous team at Wiley, including production editor Rachel Meyers and freelance copy editor Patricia Waldygo. Thanks to my publicist, Celeste

Balducci, for all of her dedication, as well as to the rest of Monteiro & Company.

My gratitude to Demos for all the support they've provided since I left Wall Street in 2002 and for the important contributions they make every day, especially Miles Rapoport, David Callahan, Tammy Draut, Carol Villano, Bob Kuttner, Lew Daly, and the man who never seems to sleep, Tim Rusch.

I've been fortunate to have the backing, inspiration and friendship of some wonderful people—writers, editors, and thinkers—over the years. Thanks to Megan Kiefer, Margaret Bustell, Viv Shelton, Deborah Dor, Francesca Lieb, Jessica Weizman, Karen Meola, Matt Suroff, Lynne Roberts, Robin Lentz, Marna Bunger, Doug Henwood, John Dizard, Michael Deibert, Tracy Quan, Colin Robinson, Andy Robinson, Monika Bauerlein, David Corn, Alleen Barber, Betsy Reed, Esther Kaplan, Andy Serwer, Michael Pollack, Suzi Weissman, Neil Weinberg, Walt Pavlo, Don Hazen, Amy Rowe, Jay Kramer, Natalie Schwartzberg, Tom Mackell, Harry Phillips, Jed Wallace, Jon Elliott, Ralph Nader, and Greg "the navigator" Della Stua. Thanks to my friends on the Street who remain in contact and keep me abreast of what's going on.

My love and appreciation to my fiancé, Lukas Serafin, for being so supportive and reading through the many versions of this book with love and attention. Thanks to my family for putting up with my long hours, absences, and constant tirades about the subject matter.

Introduction
The More Wall Street Changes, the More It Stays the Same

If the thought of the government spending trillions of dollars on Wall Street's screwups pisses you off, you're not crazy. Can't you think of a zillion better uses for the ridiculous sums of money that have been dumped into the laps of financial firms, whose execs made more in a minute than you do in a year, to support the system that they trashed? You're not alone. You are living in the most costly and reckless period of American history. You have every right to understand how the quasi-legal extortion happened and who was behind it. But it doesn't stop there: you also deserve to know how to ensure this kind of pillaging stops and never happens again. You can and must demand a complete overhaul of the banking industry's status quo. Our country wasn't founded so that we, the people, could indefinitely support them, the banks.

Welcome to what I call the Second Great Bank Depression. Why that name? Because this period of economic chaos, loss, and global financial destruction was manufactured by the men who shaped the banking

1

sector. They had help, of course. But this debacle is as man-made and avoidable as the Great Depression was. If anyone in the Oval Office, in Congress, at the Federal Reserve, in the Treasury Department, or in the offices of any regulatory agency had done any serious preventative work, had exposed the murky Wall Street practices before they blew up in our collective faces, had contained reckless trading and borrowing activities, or had rendered financial firms smaller and more transparent—if any of these people had *cared*—the crash could have been avoided, or at least would have been less severe. Millions of jobs and trillions of dollars would have been spared. Billions of dollars of bonuses wouldn't have rewarded the mostly legal but ridiculously risky practices that had such devastating effects.

The deluge of money pouring from all orifices of Washington into the banks gives tacit approval to the backward culture of banking—a world based on crazy compensation, counterproductive competition, and loosely regulated practices and laws. Yet it was all pushed by a select group of Wall Street power players, who move back and forth with all too much ease between our nation's capital and the gilded realm of finance.

If it seems as if the culture of Goldman Sachs pervades the halls of Washington, that's because the people of Goldman Sachs pervade the halls of Washington. That's why, despite all the talk in Washington about reforming the system, the same execs who orchestrated its failures were the ones hobnobbing with the political leaders of both the Bush and the Obama administrations. In fact, Obama is even closer to the financial execs than Bush was. In early spring of 2009, Obama called a meeting with Wall Street's heads to ask them to accept responsibility for causing the crisis *and* to commit to helping mitigate it.[1] As if that admission would change the rules of their game.

That's why we still have a bizarre and misplaced faith that huge corporations—which are designed for the sole purpose of making profits—are somehow able to act ethically and restrain themselves. That's why the Federal Reserve continues to operate in cloak-and-dagger mode, after it covertly and easily orchestrated the largest transfer of wealth from the American people to the banking system in the nation's history. That's why, as Henry M. Paulson left his treasury secretary post on January 20, 2009, he concluded that most of his "major decisions were right"—despite all of the losses that the banks had racked up and all of the lives that were hurt as a result.[2]

Unfortunately, no one prevented our collective disaster, even though many people, from economist Dean Baker to Senator Byron Dorgan to yours truly, called it correctly. Worse, despite a spew of indignation for the media's cameras, Washington has collectively and in a bipartisan manner demonstrated the most knee-jerk and expensive approach to groping toward financial stability in human history.

President Obama's treasury secretary, Timothy F. Geithner, built on Paulson's bailout notions when he had every opportunity to behave differently. The plan that Geithner first announced in a February 10, 2009, speech and unveiled in more detail six weeks later, on March 23, 2009, underscored the mentality of Washington's disconnect from the public and attachment to Big Finance.[3] The strategy he came up with to "fix" the financial system was to ask its most reckless and opaque companies—the ones that shirked the most taxes and took the most selfish and irresponsible risks—to buy up Wall Street's junkiest assets in order to rid the system of its own clutter.

The worst part? The government would front them most of the money to do it.

Even without examining the plan's details (short version: if the assets gain value, these companies win. If they lose value, the public covers the loss), there's a greater insanity to this strategy. The firms that the government is asking to buy assets for the "common good" are dedicated to keeping transparency and regulations at a minimum in order to stack the deck in their favor to buy assets for the "common good." Yes, the Treasury Department wants the shadiest operators to somehow make the system cleaner.

A friend of mine, who is a former partner at Goldman Sachs, once commented that finance is one of the few disciplines "based on the creation of absolutely nothing." And that's very true. *Finance is based on the principle of continuously pushing nothing for something throughout the system as long as someone else is around to pay for it*. Passing the buck comes in the form of extreme profits and bonuses during economic upswings, and it has continued afterward with the unprecedented bailouts that began in 2008. I know from experience that most of the people on Wall Street view making money as a game, one that is less (if you can imagine) about colossal paychecks and more about winning—status, position, and power. No one is ever "happy" about his or her bonus. If you admit you're happy, senior management assumes it overpaid you. The rules that govern this competition have much more to do with internal politics than with anything related to the outside world. Pushing highly profitable transactions is merely a means toward an end. So what if, in practice, churning trillions of dollars of fabricated securities can take down the whole economy? That thinking comes into play only if it affects pay. Otherwise, what goes on inside a Wall Street investment bank on a day-to-day basis simply doesn't take ordinary people into account.

But if we don't admit that these pay standards are manifested by a system that condones them, even when it pretends to be horrified, we will be missing the opportunity to tame and reconstruct the entire nature of Big Finance. If we don't restructure Wall Street, there will always be lower economic lows for the public and greater financial highs for those who pillage from society.

The first step in the twelve-step program for addicts is to admit "that we were powerless over our addiction, that our lives had become unmanageable."[4] If that doesn't happen, the program says, chances of recovery are bleak.

But Wall Street is not only addicted to money. Unconscionable bonuses and ethics abound because its titans are also addicted to winning. They possess a hyper-competitive instinct that propels them to lead their firms to become ever bigger—in profits, and in sheer size. This notion of manifest pecking order on the Street spurs irresponsible actions. Big bonuses for certain CEOs mean they're beating out the other CEOs. The same goes for big mergers. Nowhere does size matter as much as it does on Wall Street. That always has and always will be true. That's why external counterbalances are needed.

The Second Great Bank Depression took out two of the five major investment banks: the 85-year-old Bear Stearns in March 2008 and the 158-year-old Lehman Brothers six months later.[5] A third, Merrill Lynch, survived with $10 billion of government aid (from which it paid out $3.6 billion in bonuses) in a shotgun merger with Bank of America.[6] Goldman Sachs and Morgan Stanley avoided the same fate with an even more cunning move—they each got $10 billion of bailout money and overnight permission from the federal government to become "bank holding companies," which, as we'll see, is the financial crisis version of a get-out-of-fail-free card. Worse, the Second Great Bank Depression led to the very expensive and largely nontransparent $13 trillion bailout of the financial industry, while leaving the banking and investment structures intact.[7]

Wait? More than $13 trillion in the bailout? If you thought this bailout was only about a $700 billion thing called the Troubled Asset Relief Program, which is what the banks, the Treasury Department, and the Federal Reserve want you to believe, you really need this book.

Of course, a few people and firms have paid the price (aside from the American taxpayer).

Some companies exist no longer. Lehman Brothers, with a record $4 billion in profits, and Bear Stearns, with a record $2.1 billion in 2006, were dead and gone by 2008.[8] And a few scapegoats will head to prison, though they did not create the financial system that condones risk and excess, they merely took advantage of it. But rolling a few heads won't lead to reform.

Merely focusing our anger on these minor characters in the multi-trillion dollar scheme of things is a deflection from the deeper and very legal bilking that Wall Street and Washington accomplished—which involved a great deal more money than Wall Street produced in the lead up to the crisis, generated in a fraction of the time. The bloodlust reserved for Bernard L. "Bernie" Madoff and the other new villains ultimately only serves to cloak larger systemic crimes: specifically, the $13 trillion that the federal government doled out from the Federal Reserve, the Treasury Department, and the Federal Deposit Insurance Corporation (FDIC) to back the biggest players on Wall Street.[9]

As you watch these events play out in this book and in real life, you should keep a couple of points in mind. The first is that this bailout was never meant to help consumers. As we'll see, if the government wanted to get the money to consumers, it could have given them bailout assistance directly, or at least directed it to banks that were eager to give out or renegotiate loans. Second, for all of the money that we threw at the problem, we still got the worst-case scenario: barely solvent and under-regulated institutions. This, in a more concentrated playing field, where bigger firms have more control.

Finally, there's no way you and I will make it out of this unscathed. If any money is made from the bailout, Wall Street will not let it end up back in the government till.

I'm writing about some of these bankers that orchestrated expensive life jackets in a sea of their financial debris, because I used to traverse their world. As a managing director at Goldman Sachs, who was responsible for, among other things, the group that provided credit derivatives analytics, and a senior managing director at Bear, Stearns International (R.I.P.) in charge of the group that provided numbers behind all sorts of securitized deals, I had an upfront and global seat for a lot of the internal politics and power plays that drive the external pillaging.

The acquisition of power comes through the consolidation of money on Wall Street. You need to have a big appetite for power to be truly successful there. I think that when you live outside this world, it's hard to understand the motivation to act in ways that seem, and often are, so disconnected from reality. As much as their actions are about hoarding money, their strategy is more about consolidating power and influence. Money is a marker. Power is a drug of choice.

The Causes of the Crisis

As we get to know these delightful characters and the institutions that they have run into the ground and recapitalized with our money, we will also put together the pieces of the pillage, the specific acts of economic irresponsibility and borderline illegality that got us into this mess.

We'll look closer at the full story in later chapters, but for now there are six primary roots of the crisis, each one related to the other and dangerous in its own right:

- risky loans that benefitted lenders over borrowers
- layered securities consisting of complex combinations of those loans
- the immense amount of borrowing, or leverage, taken on by the financial system using those loans and securities as collateral

- the greed for money and positioning that propelled Wall Street titans to extract immense bonuses while they bent the ears and filled the pockets of the politicians who changed the rules to enable institutions to become too big to fail
- the repeal of the Glass-Steagall Act of 1933, which had separated financial institutions into commercial banks (consumer oriented) and investment banks (speculative), plus other acts of deregulation that resulted in an inappropriately structured financial system (covering all types of banks, insurance companies, private equity, and hedge funds) monitored by lax regulators who sided more with Wall Street than Main Street

These are, of course, not the only reasons why some of us won't be able to retire until sometime in the twenty-second century. The financial industry, after all, prides itself on being painfully complex, so there are endless strands to this story—and, more often than not, they are tangled together in a knotty mess. But we can isolate certain strands that have helped along our unraveling, and particular practices and "products" that have combined to create the perfect financial storm.

The financial hysteria that surfaced in 2008 started with the fall of the housing market and the barrage of foreclosures that followed. But before the fall came the rise. Once Alan Greenspan finished his 2001–2003 cycle of interest rate cuts from 6.50 to 1.25 percent, money was so cheap that Wall Street was naturally inclined to take advantage.[10]

Homeowners, and their mortgages, provided the means to a profitable end, simply because they were convenient targets. Wall Street pushed lenders. Lenders pushed borrowers. That's how it worked. Don't let anyone tell you otherwise. If you can borrow at 1 percent and loan it out at 6 or 8 or 13 percent, you can make money. Even the squirrels in my backyard can make money on that play.

To Wall Street, individual loans were like carbs. When you're hungry it doesn't matter whether you eat doughnuts or pizza or fries, you fill up with what you can easily get at that moment. Loans were easy. If Wall Street didn't want them, they would not have been issued in massive volumes. Their collapse wouldn't have triggered an economic crisis. The demand was from the top down, never from the bottom up.

The more Wall Street could package the loans that Americans took out, the more loans could be extended, and the more the Street profited from reselling the packages to investors. Bernie Madoff might be the single individual associated with the most evil scams, but the legal ones of the banking sector, abetted by the government, eclipsed his crimes.

Lenders started lending *a lot* to anyone because Wall Street wizards could spin these loans, good or bad, into new packages, or securities, stamped AAA, or "best," by rating agencies. The agencies fed these securities through mathematical formulas (based on delusion) that pronounced them completely safe. The agencies got hefty fees for these validations. Wall Street then did two things. First, they borrowed heavily against these "safe securities," because they could. Then they pawned them off to countless investors—from understaffed state pension funds, to savvy hedge funds, to European insurers—who went on and borrowed even more money against them. That insatiable demand required further supply, which spurred mortgage brokers to push loans to buy homes, which couldn't be built fast enough to satisfy all of the borrowers. Not without major real estate developers overborrowing, which they did, too, as their stocks quadrupled between 2002 and late 2005.[11]

The result? National average home prices skyrocketed.[12] The reckoning that followed began in 2006, when the housing boom slowed.[13] People were hurting, but Wall Street was rolling in record amounts of dough.

Meanwhile, the Fed was raising rates to combat inflation, due in large part to rising oil prices.[14] This interest rate policy certainly slowed inflation, but it had unintended consequences that led to the Second Great Bank Depression. As rates rose, so did reset values on adjustable rate mortgages, meaning that people had to cough up more money for their monthly mortgage payments. This led to defaults, foreclosures, and opening up the Pandora's box of reckless Wall Street practices that trashed the economy. Don't say Alan Greenspan never did anything for you.

Inflation also meant that borrowing money was no longer cheap. It would be the least of the Fed's concerns two years later. Rates on loans for citizens, as well as among Wall Street firms, started to rise. The credit that had slicked the wheels of the economy ceased to flow as freely. There was no slack in the system to make up for the devaluing of the assets used as collateral for credit. Eventually, the system came to a halt.

With credit harder to come by, buying on credit slowed down. As a result, according to the S&P/Case-Schiller index, the period between fall of 2007 and fall of 2008 registered a 16.5 percent (average) drop in prices.[15]

The stock market, always a good inverse indicator of the real economic condition of ordinary people, followed along, with a little lag. At first, the market was oblivious to the plateau and the signs of loan and credit problems that began to percolate for homeowners. The Dow and the S&P 500 reached all-time highs of 14,164.53 and 1,565.15, respectively, on October 9, 2007, on news that the Fed would make it even cheaper to borrow money and would cut rates.[16] Bonuses for Wall Street in 2007 were concurrently very good; it was the second-best year ever for the Street, after 2006.[17]

But as we learned in physics class, what goes up must come down. Rates rose from 2.28 to 5.24 percent from the beginning of 2005 to the end of 2006.[18] Banks started to feel the pressure from these hikes as much as citizens did. Money wasn't as cheap for them to lend anymore or to borrow in order to leverage assets, so they tried to increase their production of asset-backed securities instead. That led to a frenzy of packaging deteriorating loans and the highest production of what would become known as toxic assets.

Just eighteen months later, indices were flirting with twelve-year lows, with the Dow dropping to 6,763.29 by March 3, 2009, a record 52 percent from its high.[19]

The economy functions only if people and institutions can borrow money; we can borrow only if we can put something up as collateral—a tangible asset that acts as a guarantee that the money will be paid back. During the housing boom, nearly any type of asset could be used as collateral to concoct securities. From 2002 to 2006, subprime and other risky home loans were the main form of collateral. The restrictions that could have stopped those loans from being used as collateral to create so much systemic debt, which later introduced so much systemic risk, were ripped apart in 2004 through a dangerous Securities and Exchange Commission rules revision.

Banks soon found numerous off-book hiding places to take on debt without holding extra cash against the debt in case things got bad. Entities called structured investment vehicles (SIV), particularly at the large supermarket commercial banks such as Citigroup, became convenient places to conceal the true health of the bank. SIVs became part of the reason Citigroup had more than a trillion dollars of risky assets off its book.[20]

When the assets in SIVs stopped producing income, the SIVs started to default and investors pulled out. As Citigroup and others struggled to back their SIVs with money from other areas in the bank—Get it? On-book money to fund off-book risk?—Treasury Secretary Henry Paulson was eager to help.

Toward the end of 2007, he wanted to form a $100 billion fund to bail out the banks.[21] This ultimately didn't happen, but it gave way to a much broader, more costly bank bailout, which included the $700 billion Troubled Asset Relief Program (TARP), as part of the Emergency Economic Stabilization Act (EESA) of 2008.[22] SIVs weren't the only off-book way of stockpiling risky assets and borrowing money against them. There were variations, but the names aren't the point.

The FDIC was in the uncomfortable role of having to back commercial bank deposits (our deposits), no matter what dumb and risky things banks did with those deposits.[23] The agency always had transparency concerns about asset-backed securities (ABS), a technology developed by Wall Street in the 1980s that bundled bunches of loans and sold bonds that were constructed using the payments from those loans. But the agency caught on way too late that it didn't quite have its head around the more complex securities packages. "Standardization and transactional transparency for more exotic forms of securitization, such as structured investment vehicles (SIVs) and collateralized debt obligations (CDOs), remains inadequate," the FDIC admitted in December 2007.[24]

The Borrowing Chain

Like everything else on Wall Street, the credit crisis is based on reincarnating a lucrative financial gimmick from the past, in this case from the 1980s junk bond era. It was Michael Milken who constructed the first CDO in 1987 at the now-extinct investment bank Drexel Burnham Lambert.[25] This CDO was basically a security made up of a bunch of junk bonds. In the late 1990s, the same security was stuffed with high-yield (a nice name for junk bonds) and emerging-market (Latin American, Pan-Asian, and Eastern European) bonds. In 2003, the stuffing was subprime loans.

After Drexel's bankruptcy and the implosion of the junk bond market, the use of CDOs went dormant for nearly a decade. But the stuffing, slicing, and dicing of any security that contained credit risk—the possibility that a person or a company might default on payments—into another one reemerged as a highly profitable business in the late 1990s. The stuffing was the emerging-market and high-yield bonds. The four years from 2002 to 2006 saw a third wave of stuffing using subprime and otherwise risky mortgages. It was leveraging these subprime-backed CDOs to the hilt that became a catastrophe.

In essence, CDOs are fabricated assets, which means that they are concocted from a little bit of reality and a lot of fakery. They are bonds whose value is backed by loans and promises rendered by a chain of interested parties in finance, from rating agencies that rake in fees every time a new CDO is created to insurance and reinsurance companies. Although the idea sounds absurd, we must remember that financial folks are used to dealing with things that often don't really exist. So a CDO is just a natural extension of the abstractions inherent to finance. In the late 1990s, the fabricated assets consisting of emerging-market and high-yield bonds paid higher commissions than any other product, which made pushing them very desirable. My foray into international investment banking began with Bear Stearns in 1993 in London. I ran the European analytics group. Bear Stearns differentiated itself from its more established competitors by concentrating on the more analytically intense products, such as mortgage-backed securities, the very first CDO consisting of emerging-market bonds in 1996, and high-yield bonds (formerly known as junk bonds) in 1998.

From 1996 on, it was part of my job to introduce these new CDOs to European companies. I lived and breathed these bizarre concoctions and other securitized products until I left to return to the United States and a job at Goldman Sachs in 2000.

The CDO market, which was largely dormant for almost a decade after Drexel's fall, wound up climbing from nearly nothing in 1996 to become a $2 trillion global disaster by 2008.[26] Those same types of securities were still the talk of the town except with, as I mentioned, subprime loans as the stuffing. And this time, they would bring outrageous profits for a few short years and then just as fast would help cause the downfall of Bear Stearns, unravel Wall Street, and unleash a global recession. But not before a few people made a lot of money.

I was one of the lucky ones who had no stock in Bear at the time of their demise (I sold it to support my writing habit), except for a retirement plan that had shriveled down to $3,000. My other remaining connection was with former colleagues and friends.

People began e-mailing me whom I hadn't heard from in a decade, as if some close relative had died. A couple of the internal hedge funds at Bear Stearns had undergone explosive growth, based on overleveraging subprime and other risky securities, which were spun into high-quality assets and blessed by the various rating agencies. Once demand dried up for these types of securities, their values plummeted. This meant that their value as collateral for borrowing also shrunk. Creditors started to ask for more collateral to be posted to make up for this difference. At the same time, investors were pulling out. The only way to come up with extra money to post as collateral was to sell the assets at bargain prices, which decreased the value of the funds further. The funds were running low on money to pay the borrowing costs, also known as margin calls, they had incurred. In the end, the funds ran out of cash completely and the largely, federally orchestrated demise of Bear Stearns followed. Bear had found itself in a similar situation as the people who couldn't make their mortgage payments or get new mortgages to make up for that shortfall because of the declining value of their soon-to-be foreclosed homes.

Besides off-book bank shenanigans and complex securities, forces outside the traditional investment bank world have also aided our financial crisis. Recently, the number of hedge and private equity funds and the pool of money they control in the market have grown substantially. These funds were unregulated and enjoyed special tax advantages, such as paying the IRS at the capital gains rate of 15 percent, instead of at the normal person or corporate rate of 35 percent of the profits they made.[27]

According to finance historian Niall Ferguson, "there were just 610 hedge and equity funds with $39 billion in assets in 1990. By the end of 2006, there were 9,462 of such funds with $1.5 trillion in assets under management."[28] That's a lot of money acting with no rules. Plus, those hedge funds can borrow, or leverage, substantially against their assets. In addition, hedge fund head honchos make 20 percent of all returns and charge 20 percent fees simply for the privilege of taking investor money.

I've always wanted to know exactly how much leverage is out there, but there's no good source. The company Hedge Fund Research is considered the authority in the hedge fund field, so I thought it might know. But it turns out that this firm doesn't. The only leverage information it has is culled directly from a particular fund's strategy. Hedge Fund Research doesn't have the information to compile an overall leverage figure for the industry.

In other words, the hedge fund managers don't even let the experts know how much they borrow, using whatever assets they have as collateral. It's part of their "strategy." If they told, maybe all of their customers would know their secret and put their money somewhere else. And the government has never requested this information. So, there we are, with another pocket of borrowing and no transparency.

In 2007, more than $194.5 billion in capital flowed into the unregulated hedge fund business, setting a new record and bringing total assets under management to $1.87 trillion.[29] The amount of assets slowed slightly in 2006 but chugged along again the following year.[30] The scary part wasn't even the total assets under management, it was the secret—and still unknown—leverage behind them.

Expensive Failure

By summer of 2009, the price tag for the federal government's bailout of the banks (including all federal loans, capital injections, and government loan guarantees) stood at approximately $13.3 trillion, roughly dividing into $7.6 trillion from the Fed, $2.5 trillion from the Treasury (not including additional interest payments), $1.5 trillion from the FDIC (including a $1.4 trillion Temporary Liquidity Guarantee program

[TLGP] initiated in October 2008 to help banks continue to provide lending to consumers), a $1.4 trillion joint effort and a $300 billion housing bill.[31] This number is so huge, it is almost meaningless. But by comparison, $13.3 trillion is more money than the combined costs of every major U.S. war (including the American Revolution, the War of 1812, the Civil War, the Spanish-American War, World War I, World War II, Korea, Vietnam, Iraq, and Afghanistan), whose total price tag, adjusted for inflation, is $7.2 trillion. Plus, according to Olivier Garret, the CEO of Casey Research, who studied this war-versus-bank-bailout comparison, "World War II was financed by savings, the American people's savings, when Americans bought war bonds. . . . today, families are in debt and the government is in debt."[32] Lots and lots of debt.

Meanwhile, $50 trillion in global wealth was erased between September 2007 and March 2009, including $7 trillion in the U.S. stock market and $6 trillion in the housing market.[33] In addition, the total amount of retirement and household wealth trashed was $7.5 trillion in pension plans and household portfolios, $2.0 trillion in lost income in 401(k)s and individual retirement accounts (IRAs), $1.9 trillion in traditional defined-benefit plans, and $3.6 trillion in nonpension assets.[34] Job losses, too, have skyrocketed. Between January 2008 and June 2009, the number of unemployed Americans rose from 7.5 to 14.7 million. The unemployment rate shot from 4.8 to 9.5 percent.[35] So, reckless banking practices cost the world $65 trillion in losses, plus $13 trillion in various forms of bailout, a total of $78 trillion—and we still have no clue what losses continue to fester in the industry. Stress tests administered by the government and concocted by the industry indicated that ten banks in the United States were short $75 billion in capital, which Treasury Secretary Timothy Geithner declared "reassuring." I don't buy that—not the reassuring bit or the fact that with another $75 billion in capital, the industry will be stabilized. You won't buy it either, after you read this book.

Even while banks were getting bailed out, their bad loans increased. According to a March 2009 report put out jointly by MSNBC.com and the Investigative Reporting Workshop at American University, which followed 8,198 banks over the two-year period from the beginning of 2007 through the end of 2008, the total amount of troubled assets rose to $235.3 billion by the end of 2008, from $94.62 billion a year earlier, an increase of 149 percent. Nearly 71 percent of the banks had a higher troubled-asset ratio at the end of 2008 than they did in 2007. Only 1,974 banks, or 24 percent, had fewer troubled assets.[36] During the first quarter of 2009, the amount of delinquent or defaulting bank loans increased by another 22 percent. Plus six out of ten banks were less prepared to sustain further loan losses than they had been during the end of 2008.

What do all of these disheartening statistics mean? They mean that the bailout is not working. They mean that our government is trying to sustain fundamentally flawed institutions, ignoring a system that is itself fundamentally flawed. Though few of us want to admit it, the failures of the bailout reveal the extent of the problem. We cannot simply patch up the banks with some capital and loans and pretend that everything works fine. We will get out of this mess only if we recognize the incestuous relationship between Wall Street and Washington and see how the economic instability that it manifests affects us all. We need to understand how the addiction to making money in the short term with limited regulation and constraint hinders America's long-term economic stability. We need to stop this pillaging. And we need to totally reconstruct Big Finance in the process, so that it benefits the many, instead of the few.

1

Where'd the Bailout Money Go, Exactly?

Behind every great fortune, there is a crime.

—*Honoré de Balzac*

Once President George W. Bush took office on January 20, 2001, he appointed a string of his buddies to the treasury secretary position.[1] The first was Paul H. O'Neill, the former chairman and CEO of the aluminum producer Alcoa, who served during the mini-recession between 2001 and 2002.[2] Then came John Snow, the former chairman and CEO of the transportation company CSX, who served from February 2003 to June 2006.[3] These men were rarely seen doing very much of anything.

Treasury Secretary Paul O'Neill basically played the role of the administration's optimist during a spate of corporate scandals. On February 5, 2002, right smack between the Enron and WorldCom scandals, O'Neill testified before the Senate Finance Committee on how to strengthen the economy. Even as the country was in the midst of a recession, he said, "I believe we always have untapped potential that can be unleashed to spread prosperity throughout the nation. Never has that been more true than right now."[4] O'Neill was later pushed out of his job because he spoke out against Bush's tax cuts and war policy.

John William Snow spent his time extolling free market virtues and supporting Bush's tax cuts. He rode into his post on the wave of a unanimous Senate confirmation on February 3, 2003.[5] Back then, the economy looked rosy—on its shell. Gross domestic product was bustling again, up 6.1 percent in the last half of 2003, the fastest growth rate in two decades. That's what war, rising oil prices, and a burgeoning housing-loan bubble will do for you![6] Snow enthused, "This country's free market system is strong, and the envy of the world."[7]

But it takes a banker to make a real difference—to really misuse the country's money with appropriate flair and deception.

That's what former Goldman Sachs chairman and CEO Henry (aka Hank) Paulson did. Though politically on the other side of the aisle from the likes of Robert Rubin, he was part of the same Goldman fraternity and espoused its free-market, deregulatory, competitive-to-the-point-of-destruction philosophy. Which goes to show you that money trumps political party affiliation, and Wall Street heritage trumps both.

At Paulson's confirmation hearing on June 27, 2006, he addressed "some of the steps that could be taken to achieve a stronger and more competitive U.S. economy." (Note: When Paulson and his ilk use the word *competitive*, they mean reckless business practices and the absence of cumbersome restrictions on their viability. In reality, competition between financial institutions drives them to make profits out of the most esoteric securities and behaviors, while merging to dangerous levels of concentration.)

In addition to "maintaining and enhancing the flexibility of our capital and labor markets," Paulson promised to prevent "creeping regulatory expansion from driving jobs and capital overseas."[8] He was good, that Paulson. Regulation equals jobs going overseas. No one wants to lose his or her job. Ergo, no one should want regulation. Good thing he prevented us from losing our flexibility, jobs, and capital.

His actions helped create the economic crisis that began a couple of years later, when deregulated banks leveraged their solid assets, such as citizen deposits, into oblivion, all in the name of competition. But at least his friends on Wall Street were freed from the shackles of regulation.

Paulson Loves Small Government for Big Reasons

Hank Paulson was confirmed for the Treasury post during a three-hour Senate hearing love-fest, which followed a unanimous Senate Finance Committee voice vote, on June 28, 2006.[9] "In the world of finance and international markets there's simply no equal to Hank," cooed Senator Charles Schumer (D-NY).[10]

On July 10, 2006, Paulson was sworn in as treasury secretary.[11] It wasn't his first time in Washington. Paulson had been there before he joined Goldman in 1974.[12] After completing Dartmouth College and then Harvard Business School, he went to work in the Nixon administration as Staff Assistant to the Assistant Secretary of Defense at the Pentagon from 1970 to 1972 and was Staff Assistant to John Ehrlichman (the man who masterminded Watergate) from 1972 to 1973.[13] The *Guardian*, for one, was impressed by the young Paulson's propensity for good timing: "Not only was he well connected enough to get the job, but well connected enough to resign in the thick of the Watergate scandal without ever getting caught up in the fallout."[14] Though Paulson's initial run in D.C. was brief, it endowed him with a trait that would come in handy later: the ability to make a mess (or at least be a part of one), and not be held responsible.

Walter Minnick, one of Paulson's closest friends, described Paulson during those years as "a bulldog, very much like a young Dick Cheney. . . . Hank is a salesman's salesman, and this combination of being tenacious as well as enthusiastic made him very effective."[15] Now if a friend of mine compared me with Dick Cheney, I'd have to find a new friend. But I'm guessing Paulson took it as a compliment.

Even after decades on Wall Street with Goldman Sachs and a successful turn at running the über-powerful investment bank, Paulson had reservations about the Treasury post.[16] He was concerned about taking a position that wouldn't have enough of a central policy-making role (read: power).[17]

John Snow, Paulson's predecessor, never had much sway. Mostly, he just championed the Bush policies that gave a disproportionate tax break to the wealthiest people in the nation and lavished the largest corporate tax breaks in two decades.[18] The Senate passed a $70 billion tax-cut package, mostly along party lines, which extended tax breaks on capital gains and dividends through 2010, as well as Bush's 2003 tax cuts.[19]

Paulson, of course, would have been a private-sector advocate of Bush's dividend tax cut in 2003. With it, he saved about $2 million per year in taxes on the Goldman stock he owned at the time.[20] But the best tax coup came from his new job and left every other Wall Street executive's sign-on bonus in the dust. There is a little loophole in the tax code that enables government officers to defer capital gains taxes on assets they had to sell based on divestiture requirements for the post, as long as the money received from the sale of those assets was put directly into U.S. Treasury securities or a list of acceptable mutual funds within sixty days.[21] The intent is to prevent the anointed from not taking a public post, for fear of suffering a tax hit.

By leaving Goldman for the Treasury position, Paulson saved himself about $100 million in immediate tax payments, a handsome chunk of change for taking a job that pays only $183,500 per year in salary.[22] All that he needed to bank the money was a "certificate of divestiture" from the Office of Government Ethics, which he got just before he sold 3.23 million shares of Goldman stock on June 29, 2006, worth nearly half a billion dollars.[23] The sale remains completely tax-free until the day the U.S. securities get resold.[24]

Paulson was surely unaware of what he signed up for regarding the looming economic implosion. In a way, that lack of awareness underscored the disconnect between the moneyed-powerful and the rest of the world. Any car-assembly workers or schoolteachers or tour guides in the country could have told you they were feeling inordinately pinched (as I found out while researching my previous book, *Jacked*, from late 2005 through early 2006) and were maxing out on credit cards to pay for essentials like food, medicine, and health care.[25] Or perhaps Paulson knew but didn't want to admit it. Maybe he thought the signs of strain would simply go away. Which is why, as the economy started slipping and banks began to post losses, he insisted that things were fine.

On January 29, 2007, Paulson told a roundtable discussion of big-business types what he thought of the U.S. economy: "One of the very pleasant surprises I had coming to government has been the strong economy we have today. I can't take a lot of credit for it but I'm still very, very pleased about it."[26]

Seven months and a Fed rate cut later, on August 21, 2007,[27] Paulson had a slight change of heart, in an interview with CNBC, noting that the economy was "stressed":

> We've been seeing stress and strains in a—strains in a number of capital markets but this is against the backdrop of a strong global economy, a very healthy U.S. economy, and the reason I start by making this point is that markets ultimately follow the economy. I've been through periods of stress, turbulence in the market for over the course of my career, various times, and never in any of those other periods have we had the advantage of a strong economy underpinning the markets.[28]

His choice of words was a little odd, implying that the economy just needed a good massage and then everything would be fine, but at least he was starting to acknowledge that the capital markets weren't perfect.

But as we all know, the economy "underpinning the markets" tanked about a year after he made that statement. The reasons were numerous, as we've discussed, but they were largely because of practices that took place before Paulson left Wall Street for Washington. We can't, after all, give him all of the credit for our financial ruin; however, he did encourage raising leverage limits for investment banks to dangerous levels and had a feverish hunger for deregulation at Goldman and later at the Treasury Department.

Paulson Discovers Big Government for Little Friends

As things got worse, Paulson eventually came to terms with the idea that protecting the general economy's health was kind of, like, his job, and that he should probably do something about it. So, he had some fire-drill meetings to discuss the fall of Bear Stearns and how the Federal Reserve would help JPMorgan Chase acquire the fallen investment bank in March 2008, a subject we'll return to soon enough. But that didn't halt the economic conflagration, and the autumn of 2008 would bring another set of disasters. On the evening of Friday, September 12, 2008, Paulson, New York Federal Reserve President and CEO Timothy Geithner, and Securities and Exchange Commission chairman Chris Cox held an emergency meeting with a few of the heavy hitters of the financial world: Morgan Stanley CEO John Mack, Merrill Lynch CEO John Thain, JPMorgan Chase CEO Jamie Dimon, Goldman Sachs CEO Lloyd Blankfein, and Citigroup Inc. CEO Vikram Pandit.[29] They were all scared about the market conditions but even more about their own books. None wanted to be seen as weak. None wanted to be the next to fail. Shockingly enough (well, no, not really, I'm just saying that), no official records of their conversations have ever been—or probably ever will be—released.

Notably absent from the meeting was Lehman Brothers CEO Dick Fuld. At that point, there were two potential buyers for Lehman as it tottered on the brink of extinction: Bank of America and London-based Barclays. Neither stepped up.

Two days later Fuld was facing the demise of his firm, but his phone calls to Paulson, Geithner, and Cox had met a cold reception.[30] As treasurer and designer of the federal bailout program, Paulson had ascended to become the arbiter of who lived and died on Wall Street. Though he had help from Geithner on the Bear Stearns deal and subsequent deals, Paulson wasn't the kind of guy to play second fiddle. There were no buyers for Lehman and no money from the Fed in return for Lehman's toxic assets. It was over. Paulson pressed the firm to bite the bullet late Sunday night, September 14. Early Monday morning, Lehman became the biggest corporate bankruptcy in U.S. history. The next day, Barclays came back, and for $250 million in cash, it bought Lehman's core assets, worth $72 billion, and $68 billion worth of liabilities.[31] Barclays didn't even have to pick up Lehman's toxic real estate–backed assets.[32] By stepping away from the table just days earlier, Barclays ended up with a sweet deal, while the Lehman name was no more.

It would have been insane for any suitor to buy Lehman outright, with its impending mammoth losses. With stunningly convenient timing, it dawned on Thain that since Lehman was toast, his firm would be next on the chopping block. Merrill Lynch was in need of a buyer ASAP, and Bank of America was over Lehman. So, Thain put in a call to Bank of America CEO Ken Lewis but was unsure about proceeding with a Bank of America–Merrill merger. Paulson, on the other hand, knew exactly what had to be done, and he spelled it out for Thain. Thain had to cut a deal, quickly, or Merrill would take its last breath.[33]

That wasn't exactly Thain's version. He told the *Financial Times* that the Fed and the Treasury "were initially focused on Lehman but grew concerned about us. They wanted to make sure I was being proactive [but] they didn't tell me to call Ken Lewis."[34]

We will probably never know the exact details, although if I had been a fly on the wall, I would have bet that whatever Paulson said was gospel. The Merrill deal, which made Bank of America the country's largest player in wealth management, was hammered out in forty-eight hours.[35] The $50 billion takeover was announced just hours after Lehman's bankruptcy, and after that, there was no way out for Ken Lewis, even when Merrill's stock kept diving.[36] What do you do when you're up against the Fed and a mini-cartel of strong-arming Goldmanites, including the treasury secretary, who have you backed up against the wall and are using your own addiction to acquisitions against you? You agree to acquire an investment bank, even though there's no way you have time to analyze it. Not to excuse the recklessness of the decision to take on a giant mess of a firm, but there's no way around the fact that Lewis was outnumbered. He wasn't the only one who sold the future of Bank of America down the river; it was all of the power brokers in that room who may never be held monetarily accountable for the decision.

Six months later, during questioning at the New York City office of Attorney General Andrew Cuomo on February 26, 2009, Lewis stated the obvious. He had been pressured by the best of the best. The Bank of America Board of Directors had strongly considered scrapping the deal in mid-December by invoking a material adverse change (MAC) clause, due to mounting losses on Merrill's balance sheet, then at $12 billion and later reaching $15 billion. Paulson would have none of it.

As Lewis recalled, he met in Washington, D.C., that evening with Paulson, Ben Bernanke, and a bunch of Treasury Department and Fed officials. "At the end we were basically told to stand down," Lewis said. After a follow-up call to Paulson that weekend, which found the treasury secretary riding his bike, Lewis got the sense that if he called for the MAC clause, he'd be out of a job.[37]

But Paulson wasn't all tough guy. He and Fed chairman Ben Bernanke promised Lewis they would provide taxpayer money to help out with the takeover of Merrill, but it had to be done in secret. "I just talked with Hank Paulson. He said there was no way the Federal Reserve and the Treasury could send us a letter of any substance without public disclosure which, of course, we do not want," Lewis wrote in an internal Bank of America e-mail released by Cuomo's office.[38] Lewis went on to tell Cuomo's office that it wasn't the threat of the government wiping out the board and management, per se, that led them to drop the MAC clause idea, but that they changed their minds because Paulson was *willing* to go that far. On July 9, 2009, Ben Bernanke would feel the heat for this episode when seventeen congresspeople sent a letter to President Obama requesting an investigation into Bernanke's role in the deal.[39]

At any rate, the Treasury had already invested $10 billion in Merrill and $15 billion in Bank of America with a first shot of TARP money in October.[40] And the money kept coming.

By December 2008, when Lewis wanted to back out of the Merrill deal, as it became clear what a turkey the firm was (shareholders would be the last to know), Paulson stressed that Merrill had to be saved and that Bank of America had to be the hero, to prevent what Lewis called "serious systemic harm."[41] Separately, Paulson called Lewis to Washington and days later informed him that he and his board would be replaced if Bank of America backed out.[42] Paulson is a consummate investment banker, and that's what they do—they persuade companies to get hitched. But Wall Street isn't interested in the follow-up or whether those companies stay married, because their fees are paid on the close of the deal. Yet the public's money kept this merger financed, even as the deal's value plummeted. So, we kept pouring money in but never collected our fees. Every time Merrill hemorrhaged, leading up to the January 1, 2009, deal closing date, the taxpayer was there.

Per the secret agreement cut between Bank of America and the government, the dough kept rolling in even after the deal closed. On January, 16, 2009, during the merger's honeymoon period, the Treasury dumped another $20 billion of TARP money into Bank of America and along with the FDIC's help, agreed to cap "unusually large losses" on $118 billion of assets, mostly from Merrill, two weeks after the deal went through.[43] To be clear, that money went to seal the Merrill deal, not to loosen credit for the public.[44] On April 29, 2009, Bank of America announced that its shareholders had demoted Lewis to president and CEO, stripping him of his duties as chairman.[45] It was a first for the shareholders of a Standard & Poors 500–listed company.[46]

Thain, meanwhile, was quite impressed with himself for keeping Merrill Lynch, the firm that lost $27 billion through 2008, from going bankrupt.[47] So he did what any investment banker would do after completing a large merger: he asked the board for a $10 million bonus. Where would that money come from if his company was drowning in red ink? Well, there was Bank of America, which had just gotten that $15 billion of TARP money six weeks earlier. He could add the bonus to the $15 million cash sign-on bonus he got when he had joined as CEO less than a year earlier.[48]

New York attorney general Andrew Cuomo sent an icy-worded letter to Merrill Lynch's directors, as well as to several other banks on October 29, 2008, saying, "We will have grave concerns if your expected bonus pool has increased in any way as a result of your receipt or expected receipt of taxpayer funds from the Troubled Asset Relief Program."[49]

Cuomo's sentiment, backed by a whole lot of negative public opinion, managed to convince Thain that requesting a $10 million bonus was a "shocking" (read: boneheaded) idea. Thain reversed course at a December 8 board meeting, suggesting that neither he nor some of the other senior execs get a bonus.

After that meeting, Merrill issued a press release, saying, basically, that Thain had thought about it again and decided he'd be okay without the extra ten mil. A few other board executives agreed that they, too, could do without their bonuses. The board was pleased and stood by their main man.

"The Board accepted Mr. Thain and his management team's request and applauded the Thain-led management team's superb performance in an exceptionally challenging environment," stated John Finnegan, the chairman of Merrill Lynch's Management, Compensation and Development Committee.[50]

Still, Merrill paid out a total of $3.6 billion worth of executive bonuses for 2008.[51] In late January, Cuomo subpoenaed Thain and Bank of America chief administrative officer J. Steele Alphin to testify about those bonuses, which were given out just before Bank of America took over Merrill.[52] Cuomo later opened a probe into the timing of Merrill's other bonuses. On February 10, 2009, he sent a letter specifically about Merrill to Barney Frank, the chairman of the House Committee on Financial Services, stating, "On October 29, 2008, we asked Merrill Lynch to detail, among other things, their plans for executive bonuses for 2008." But Merrill didn't provide any details. Instead, Thain moved up the Merrill bonus payment date to December, instead of the usual late January or early February time frame, in conjunction with a $15.3 billion fourth-quarter loss and before the Bank of America takeover.[53] The nearly $4 billion in Merrill bonuses went to only seven hundred people, the top four of whom bagged $221 million.[54] Cuomo's investigation continues as of this writing.

One Goldman Sachs vice president told me that because Thain managed to secure a bunch of money for himself and his friends at Merrill as the firm was dying, but before he sold it at its relative highs to Bank of America (whose employees did not fare quite so well), he retains kind of a hero status. It was classic mergers and acquisitions gamesmanship, the stuff the 1980s corporate raiders would have applauded.

Doesn't that kind of heroism make you feel better now that you know where your taxes are going?

Two Hundred Billion Isn't What It Used to Be

The same weekend in September 2008 that Lehman declared bankruptcy, AIG was also facing failure and couldn't get a single private bank to give it a loan. But Paulson's response to AIG was radically different from his indifference toward Lehman. He got Fed chairman Ben Bernanke to set up a meeting with House and Senate leaders to explain how he was going to rescue the company. Why? Among other things, he neglected to ever mention publicly that Goldman had $20 billion worth of credit-derivative transactions tied up with AIG.[55] This time, no one suggested a private bank taking on AIG's mess. That would have been crazy. That's what the public till was for. The meeting began at 6:30 P.M. the following Tuesday night, September 16, and in one whole hour they reached an agreement to give AIG an $85 billion bailout (which was reduced to $60 billion on November 10). It was the first of four helpings of public pie that, by June 2009, totaled roughly

$182 billion.[56] And with that, the U.S. government began backing AIG's credit bets and the corporate clients to whom it owed money.

You don't rise through the toughest trenches of investment banking without being persuasive, and Paulson is very persuasive. He knew that the best way to get what you want is to confront the person you want it from. So he did. According to documents compiled by Wharton School lecturer Ken Thomas, in response to a Freedom of Information Act request for Bernanke's calendar, Bernanke was one of the people Paulson confronted a lot. In just the first year that Paulson was in D.C., the two men met fifty-eight times. John Snow didn't have quite the same relationship with Bernanke. They met only eight times during the five months that their terms overlapped.[57] Of course, Snow didn't have the misfortune of dealing with a banking meltdown. Paulson's strategy was simple. Willing to be complicit, Bernanke held the bigger purse strings. The Fed also operated in greater secrecy, so the combination of Fed- and Treasury-sponsored bailouts would inject more money into the banking system than just the Treasury Department alone could. And the major players in the banking system were Paulson's people.

Three days after the AIG bailout began, Paulson promised the public that he was formulating a "bold plan." After going on about "the clogging of our financial markets," he said he would "spend the weekend working with members of Congress of both parties to examine approaches to alleviate the pressure of these bad loans on our system, so credit can flow once again to American consumers and companies." His hope was that Congress would use the legislative process to have the government take on troubled mortgage assets, and, as we discussed earlier, he got that wish.

It was all so bizarro Wizard of Oz. You can find your way back to Kansas, Dorothy, just as soon as I get all these assets out of your Yellow Brick Way. "The underlying weakness in our financial system today is the illiquid mortgage assets that have lost value as the housing correction has proceeded," said Paulson. "These illiquid assets are choking off the flow of credit that is so vitally important to our economy." He did not comment about the amount of leverage his former firm and others had put on top of those assets, which had always been the bigger problem.

Paulson promised that the federal government would remove these illiquid assets that were "weighing down our financial institutions and threatening our economy." As item number two on his agenda, he also vowed to provide credit relief by giving banks more money to play with, but the money never made its way to the consumer credit market.[58]

The Treasury Department thought up different ways to deal with the bad assets. The idea of having an auction was one.[59] Unfortunately, to run a proper auction you need interested buyers, and where were they going to find those? Plus, the banks would then be forced to reveal their true losses, and no bank wanted to be the first to say its assets were junk and risk the kind of balance sheet exposure it had spent years lobbying against.

The Wall Street men who'd been in the room with Paulson, Cox, and Bernanke that week in mid-September had billions of dollars of toxic assets on their books, with no buyers, and they thought it'd be great if the Treasury could buy them. So, over a weekend, Paulson put together a little three-page memo he sent to the Senate Banking Committee on September 23, 2008, outlining his plan to have the Treasury purchase those toxic mortgage-backed assets right off the books of the banks that'd made them in the first place.[60] It takes most of us more time to fill out a mortgage or student loan application.

Paulson's three-page memo was the seed of what would become known as TARP, or the Troubled Asset Relief Program, which was signed into law on October 3, 2008. By April 2009, TARP would come to be divided into twelve different programs.

It Was Never about Fixing the Crisis

Paulson summoned up his best banker-convincing-the-client skills to swindle Congress and the nation that TARP was a good thing.[61] "Let me make clear—this entire proposal is about benefiting the American people, because today's fragile financial system puts their economic well-being at risk," Paulson said before the House Committee on Financial Services on September 24, 2008.[62] Sure, there were some kinks, a few uncomfortable moments. His first incarnation of the TARP would have the government buying up these toxic assets. His friends made a series of bad bets, and now he wanted the government to cover their losses. What could be simpler?

A day earlier, Paulson and Bernanke sat in front of the Senate Banking Committee. Committee members pressed them on this idea of buying risky and toxic mortgage-backed assets, rather than capitalizing the banks. "If a company is willing to accept that risk, manage those risks themselves, they do not need a bailout," Senator Harry Reid (D-NV) said. To which Paulson resolutely replied, "Putting capital into institutions is about failure. This is about success."[63]

Why would Congress want to stand in the way of success? And so the Troubled Asset Relief Program was born. From the tiny memo that Paulson presented to Congress on September 20 sprung a 451-page piece of legislation.[64]

Let's just pause and consider this fully formed Athena for a second.[65] How could anything that long and created that fast be that good—or, more to the point, be that thoroughly read—by members of Congress? Or by the president? And how could ordinary Americans possibly absorb it, let alone have a meaningful debate about it? This was the kind of rush job that comes out of fear and an almost military strategy to strike before anyone notices what you're really doing. (Sound familiar? You'd think, after living through two terms of George Bush and the weapons of mass destruction debacle, that Congress would have been dubious of rush jobs.) But remember, Paulson's legislation was brought down from on high just four weeks before the November elections. Senators and representatives were fearful that the economy would continue to tank and, worse, that their constituents would blame them. They were right to worry. The Dow was putting in daily triple-digit dives, credit had ceased to flow, and everyone from economists to journalists to ordinary citizens was talking about the reality of this worst recession since—shudder—the Great Depression. Congress did have to do something. But throwing money at the belly of the Wall Street Beast, rather than providing credit help to citizens, from mortgage to auto and student loans, was precisely the wrong focus of money and attention. Unfortunately, detailed or patient analysis didn't take precedent over keeping a seat. The banks, not the people themselves, would get public help with their bad assets.

Here's how Naomi Klein, the author of *The Shock Doctrine*, put it to me: "I don't think the financial sector bailout has ever been about fixing the problem; it's been about using the crisis as a pretext for the greatest transfer of public wealth into private hands in monetary history. That's not to say that there isn't a crisis, just that the people in charge are less interested in fixing it than in taking care of their friends who take care of them. It's straight-up pillage, what a kleptocratic regime does when it panics."[66]

The House wasn't all that gung-ho as it considered the piece of bailout legislation the first time around. Paulson (literally) got down on bended knee before House leader Nancy Pelosi, begging her not to "blow it up" by withdrawing her party's support. The gesture would be amusing if it wasn't so sad. Drama aside, the first incarnation of TARP got rejected on September 29, 2008, which precipitated the worst single-day drop in two decades for the stock market.[67] That, in turn, scared the hell out of all of them. The market, or more precisely, the financial stocks in the market, wanted a bailout. And they were going to get one even if they had to bleed out all their share value in the process. The Senate passed nearly the exact same act two days later, adding only an increase in FDIC insurance for deposits to $500,000 from $250,000 and $150 billion in tax breaks for individuals and businesses.[68]

Senators, after all, always need more funding money for their campaigns; Wall Street, even with the mounting troubles, was still a good place to find a few bucks.[69] For the 2008 election cycle, Senate Banking Committee chairman Chris Dodd (D-CT) got $132,050 from the banking and mortgage sectors, the most of anyone not running for president that year.[70]

The market dive on September 29 and Paulson's increasing pressure for Congress to act (or else!) were enough to get another version passed by the House of Representatives on October 3. President George W. Bush signed the resulting Emergency Economic Stabilization Act of 2008 into law immediately.[71]

"By coming together on this legislation, we have acted boldly to prevent the crisis on Wall Street from becoming a crisis in communities across our country," Bush said with his typical lack of irony, less than an hour after signing the bill.[72] If you squinted, you could almost make out a "Mission Accomplished" sign behind him.

Paulson was relieved. He'd come through for his team—that is, his fellow Goldmanites and the other gilded members of Wall Street's elite. To some, he was a national hero. And he milked the notion with pointed rhetoric: "The broad authorities in this legislation, when combined with existing regulatory authorities and resources, gives us the ability to protect and recapitalize our financial system as we work through the stresses in our credit markets."[73]

Three days later, on October 6, Paulson brought in the assistant treasury secretary Neel Kashkari (who was—surprise—his former protégé and a VP at Goldman) to oversee the plan that would rescue the American economy by supporting its flailing banks.[74]

But, as we shall see, what Paulson said and what he did were very different things, although he always took advantage of the situation at hand. On October 12, 2008, he did a one-eighty on the success of buying junky assets, after attending the G7 Finance Ministers and Central Bank Governors meeting in Washington, D.C. "We can use the taxpayers' money more effectively and efficiently—get more for the taxpayer's dollar—if we develop a standardized program to buy equity in financial institutions," he said.[75] So much for fear of failure.

Wall Street was in a credit bind. Bank losses were going to be ugly. So financial firm leaders tried to play it both ways: if capital was on the table, they'd take it. But for months they'd continue to push for the elimination of their toxic assets.

A skeptical but hopeful America replied, "Really, how is this going to work?" Simple. We, the federal government, are first going to buy billions of dollars of preferred equity shares in the banking sector. "Preferred what?" said America. Preferred equity—the kind of stock that gives anyone holding it first dibs on higher dividend payments, though without the voting rights of common stock.[76] "But what about our mortgage payments?" America asked. And there was silence.

They Encouraged Banks to Sit on Their Money

In the coming months, the federal government would open its big wallet—or rather, all of our small wallets—and begin dumping money into (or capitalizing) a growing number of floundering companies. The Troubled Asset Relief Program would have its hands full before a single dime went to shoring up America's home loans. Yet no matter how much equity capital was injected into the top of the banks' balance sheets, the failure of subprime loans would continue to crumble the leveraged pyramid of securities built on them. The essence of the bailout left this most essential problem unfixed.

Paulson promised that injecting capital into the banks would "increase the flow of financing" for the country.[77] It's hard to imagine he really meant that, even though he sounded sincere at the time. You see, behind his department's words were the words within the act. The Emergency Economic Stabilization Act amended the Financial Services Regulatory Relief Act of 2006, which had extended the time the Fed had to pay interest on balances held by or on behalf of banks.[78] The reason for that extension was that paying interest on reserves reduced the annual amount of money that the Fed received from the Treasury for its Treasury securities portfolio, which before this crisis reflected the secure collateral that banks had to post in order to borrow from the Fed. In turn, the Fed gave the related interest from those treasuries back to the Treasury Department each year. Pushing this practice out to a later date was a way of helping to stabilize the growing deficit.[79] But, the Emergency Economic Stabilization Act accelerated making those reserve interest payments to October 1, 2008.

The message: It was more important to pay banks to sit on reserves than to spread money in the form of credit throughout the economy or balance the federal budget.[80] The policy of paying interest on reserves had the exact opposite effect that it was supposed to have had. Rather than easing credit for the public, as Paulson declared it would when touting the bailout plan, the policy caused banks to lend less money. On January 13, 2009, *Financial Week* wrote about Bernanke's speech at the London School of Economics, in which he admitted the problem, stating, "A huge increase in banks' excess reserves is currently stifling the Fed's monetary policy moves and, in turn, its efforts to revive private sector lending."[81]

Of course, banks were sitting on their money! Why wouldn't they? Basically, banks had two choices:

1. Hoard excess reserves and get paid interest on them.
2. Loan the excess to borrowers and take the risk of not getting paid interest on them.

It doesn't take a genius to figure this one out. In the summer of 2008, before Paulson and the Fed started dreaming up expensive acronyms for bank subsidy programs, American banks kept $44 billion in reserves with the Fed. By the end of 2008, that number soared to $821 billion. And by May 2009, it hovered just below $1 trillion.[82] Meanwhile, Americans had a hell of a time getting loans, thanks to Paulson and his powers of persuasion.[83]

They Spent It on Mergers and Paying Bills

The banks warmed quickly to the government purchasing equity stakes, providing that the Treasury wouldn't squeeze out existing shareholders by diluting their shares, and that there wouldn't be a whole lot of strings attached on things like executive pay.

Paulson, to put it bluntly, helped his pals. It helped his cause that he wasn't the only one doing it. International governments were also buying shares or injecting capital directly into their flailing banks, particularly in Britain.[84] In prepared remarks on October 10, 2008, Paulson made sure to confirm that the government would buy only "nonvoting" shares in companies,[85] meaning the government wouldn't have the right to demand anything in return. Thus, Paulson maneuvered the most expensive transfer of risk from Wall Street to Washington ever. Once again, however, his promises were empty. Why did he agree to let Washington shoulder the enormous risks of Wall Street? He said it was so that banks would be able to lend more money to the American public. But this wasn't to be the case.

The only banks that saw a noticeable increase in lending were the ones whose books were more consumer-oriented and less burdened by stupid trades, such as U.S. Bancorp and SunTrust Bank (although they were having loan-related problems anyway).[86] The bigger supermarket banks—the ones that got the most bailout money, such as Bank of America and Citigroup—posted declines in lending throughout the fall of 2008. Think about that a moment, because it is important. If we wanted the TARP money to actually go toward more loans to regular citizens, we would have given it to the banks that were more consumer-oriented or directly into consumer loan balances.

JPMorgan Chase's attitude toward TARP funds demonstrates the absurd logic behind the bailout. CEO and chairman Jamie Dimon said that his firm didn't need TARP money and didn't want to appear weak but agreed to take it in the end, in return for no rules attached.[87] He made it sound as if he was taking the $25 billion (plus issuing $40.5 billion of FDIC-backed debt) as a favor: "We did not think JPMorgan should be selfish or parochial and try to stop what is good for the system."[88]

Just four days after agreeing to take the $25 billion, Dimon admitted that the bank had no intention of using the money to lend. He said, "I would not assume that we are done on the acquisition side just because of the Washington Mutual and Bear Stearns mergers. I think there are going to be some great opportunities for us to grow in this environment, and I think we have an opportunity to use that $25 billion in that way and obviously depending on whether recession turns into depression or what happens in the future, you know, we have that as a backstop."[89]

In other words, "Thanks, taxpayers! Send me an invoice for your part of our growth. The check will be in the mail. We'll just keep getting bigger, because that strategy is working out so well for Bank of America and Citigroup. Then, we'll come back for more help."

In the end, that mismatch of intentions wasn't the main problem that melted banks and dragged down the economy. It was the lack of transparency, not only with respect to TARP, but also among banks in the financial community. They lost all trust in one another, and credit seized up completely. And no amount of government money would change that.

Then, as it turned out, Paulson had misspent the TARP money and lied about it.

They Secretly Gave Away Billions

On February 5, 2009, as banks continued to deteriorate, Elizabeth Warren, chair of the Congressional Oversight Panel for TARP, spoke about Paulson's and the Treasury Department's lack of accountability before the Senate Banking Committee.

She had sent a letter to Paulson following her panel's first report on December 10, 2008, which was the basis for her second report on January 9, 2009. All that she wanted from him were some answers to a few basic questions, such as, "What exactly did you do with the TARP money, Mr. Secretary?" He just didn't feel like answering her.

On February 5, 2009, Warren said that "many of the Treasury's answers were nonresponsive or incomplete," and that the "Treasury particularly needs to provide more information on bank accountability as well as transparency and asset valuation." She also wanted the Treasury to articulate a better strategy for dealing with foreclosures than Paulson had adopted when he was treasury secretary. It was almost as if she was expecting cooperation—from a bank leader! She clearly didn't know whom she was dealing with.

The worst part of her panel's findings was that Paulson had *overpaid* the banks with the TARP money. Yep. Not only had TARP money been used to buy preferred shares in banks that were losing value, but Paulson wound up paying more than the shares were worth.

As Paulson made his sales pitch, he had promised that all transactions using TARP funds were "made at par—that is, for every $100 injected into the banks, the taxpayer received stocks from the banks worth about $100," Warren said. That's not the way it went down, though. Warren revealed that for the first $254 billion paid out of TARP, the Treasury received assets worth only $176 billion: a shortfall of $78 billion. Republican senator Richard Shelby (R-Alabama), the only member of the GOP to vote against the Glass-Steagall repeal in 1999, asked Warren, "Isn't that a terrible way to look after the taxpayers' money and to make purchases anywhere?"

Warren replied, "Senator, Treasury simply did not do what it said it was doing."

"In other words, they misled the Congress, did they not?" Shelby asked. "The Bush administration, Secretary Paulson, Chairman Bernanke, misled the people, the Congress and the people of the United States."

"They announced one program and implemented another," Warren agreed.[90] Meaning yes, they sure did mislead Congress. The rest of us, too. But actually, they didn't simply mislead Congress, Senator Shelby—they *stole* $78 billion. It's one thing to divert public funds to TARP but quite another to give your friends double helpings. By overpaying for shares, Paulson misappropriated a chunk of public money. No sane customer would pay $254 for a $176 item.

The Congressional Oversight Panel report released on February 6 underscored Warren's testimony of the previous day. Paulson had "assured the public that the investments of TARP money were sound, given in return for full value," according to the report, "stating in October, that 'This is an investment, not an expenditure, and there is no reason to expect this program will cost taxpayers anything.'" Ha! He really got us that time, right?

The report notes that "In December he reiterated the point, 'When measured on an accrual basis, the value of the preferred stock is at or near par.'"[91]

The numbers tell a very different story. In eight of the ten biggest transactions, for each $100 the Treasury spent, it received assets worth about $78. In the other two transactions, which were with riskier banks, for each $100 spent the Treasury received assets worth approximately $41! Overall, in the top ten transactions, for each $100 spent, the Treasury received assets worth approximately $66. It overpaid by a full third. That figure doesn't even take into account the fact that the first $125 billion of transactions were down $54 billion in value by April 10, 2009. Although we were obsessed with figuring out where Madoff's money had gone, wouldn't it be even nicer to at least know where that $78 billion of our taxpayer money went? And, when we're done figuring that out, how about the fact that the rest of the Treasury's "investment" in banks had deteriorated so much after it was made?[92]

One transaction is particularly notable for its outrageous absurdity. On October 28, 2008, Goldman Sachs received a capital injection of $10 billion under the Capital Purchase Program arm of TARP. This was the third-largest one-time gift of TARP money in 2008, tied with Morgan Stanley. The congressional valuation concluded that the Treasury paid $10 billion for stock worth $7.5 billion. And these guys are supposed to be good at math. Amazingly, the discrepancy for payments to Morgan Stanley, Citigroup, and PNC was even higher. But even more amazing was that around the same time, Warren Buffett had invested $5 billion in Goldman. Except that in his case, "For each $100 that Berkshire Hathaway invested in Goldman Sachs, it received securities with a fair market value of $110."[93]

So, let's get this straight. Buffet pays $100 and gets $110 worth of stock. Paulson pays $100 and gets $75. Because no one screws with Warren Buffett, not even Goldman execs. With their old leader, however, it's perfectly okay. After all, it's only taxpayer money. And, a hell of a lot of it was at risk.

On February 24, 2009, Special Inspector General Neil Barofsky testified before the House Subcommittee on Oversight and Investigations, stating that the "total amount of money potentially at risk in these programs [new programs Treasury announced at that time, as well as the TARP related programs that are funded in part by the Fed and FDIC] was approximately $2.875 trillion. These huge investments of taxpayers' money, made over a relatively short time period, will invariably create opportunities for waste, fraud and abuse for those seeking to profit criminally and thus require strict oversight."[94]

Note: Barofsky's estimate didn't even include the $400 billion that the Treasury had spent on backing up Fannie Mae and Freddie Mac, an additional financing program to provide cash to the Federal Reserve or the Exchange Stabilization Fund, *pre TARP*. It also left out the $50 billion "special deposit" to the Federal Reserve Bank of New York on October 7, 2008 (see the bailout tally reports noted in the appendix of this book for further details).[95]

No Money for Anyone Else

Even though Paulson held a public office and many members of the public were having their homes foreclosed, throughout his tenure as treasury secretary he remained myopically focused on the banks. He even went out of his way to avoid dealing with the little people and their little homes. At a House Financial Service Committee hearing on November 11, 2008, at which committee chair Barney Frank (D-MA) attempted to get Paulson's and Bernanke's support for FDIC chair Sheila Bair's $24 billion mortgage rescue plan, Paulson expressed "reservations" about using any of the $700 billion TARP funds to directly aid homeowners. But he would "keep searching for ways to address the housing crisis." Have more comforting words ever been spoken? America's homeowners surely slept better that night.

Representative Maxine Waters (D-CA) was shocked by Paulson's callous decision and said that to "absolutely ignore the authority and the direction that this Congress had given you just amazes me."[96] Such shock, however, is so, well, Main Street. Waters never worked on Wall Street. If she had, nothing Paulson did that favored banks more than the general population would have surprised her.

Even before Paulson pushed TARP through a nervous Congress and worked with Bernanke to open the Fed's books to crappy Wall Street assets, he had little use for Main Street. On July 8, 2008, at the FDIC's Forum on Mortgage Lending to Low and Moderate Income Households, Paulson said, "There were 1.5 million foreclosures started in all of 2007, and a number of economists now estimate we will see about 2.5 million foreclosures started this year. Public policy cannot be expected to prevent these foreclosures. There is little public policymakers can, or should, do to compensate for untenable financial decisions."[97] Unless, of course, "untenable" decisions are made by banks or well-connected insurance companies that act like hedge funds. The pursuit of profit is clearly more acceptable than the pursuit of home ownership.

Just before Paulson left office, when he was asked about foreclosures in a January 12, 2009, interview on CNBC's *The Call*, he punted, "I did not think it was proper to move very quickly and to a big spending program, which is different than what the TARP had been set up for, without doing more work on the cost and the effectiveness. But beginning right from several weeks after the election, we've been consulting with the president-elect's team. And we had jointly agreed that it didn't make sense for us to, in the waning days of this administration, announce a foreclosure plan out of the TARP that would tie their hands going forward."[98] In other words, I've taken care of my banker boys, Obama—now you can deal with the plebian public.

Geithner's No Friend to Homeowners, Either

After working on the bank bailout with Paulson from his post in the New York Federal Reserve (where his boss, former chairman Stephen Friedman, had once been Chairman of Goldman Sachs), forty-seven-year-old Timothy Geithner was confirmed as President Barack Obama's treasury secretary on January 26, 2009.[99]

Geithner was touted as having experience. After all, he had been president of the New York Fed, the branch of the Fed that had always enjoyed the closest relationship to Wall Street, so close that before he resigned in May 2009, Stephen Freidman sat on Goldman's board of directors.[100] In fact, five of Geithner's mentors were or are Goldman

Sachs executives. Besides Friedman, they include former NY Federal Reserve chief Gerald Corrigan (who's now a managing director at Goldman Sachs), John Thain, and Hank Paulson himself.[101] Corrigan described his relationship with Geithner as "close," while John Thain told *Portfolio* magazine in May 2008 that he sometimes talked to Geithner "multiple times a day."[102]

Geithner's network also included his immediate predecessor at the New York Fed, William McDonough, his fifth mentor.[103] No stranger to bailouts himself, McDonough was one of the key architects of the 1998 Long-Term Capital Management bailout, which fortunately didn't rely on public money.[104] From the Fed post, McDonough went on to become a vice chairman at Merrill Lynch, which might explain why Geithner was so keen on getting on the bandwagon to shove Merrill up Bank of America's backside.[105]

McDonough brought a history of strong ties with Robert Rubin and Larry Summers, who ran the Treasury during the Clinton administration. Summers was appointed as President Obama's director of the National Economic Council on November 24, 2008.[106]

Geithner was also no stranger to the Treasury Department. He had served there in some capacity since 1988, for three different administrations, including as Rubin's and Summers's undersecretary for international affairs from 1999 to 2001.[107] Still, that Geithner and Summers were given powerful economic roles—not to mention Peter R. Orszag's appointment as Obama's budget director—showed a lineage not only to Clinton, but to Robert Rubin. They are both Rubin protégés. Geithner, I hasten to add, is careful not to shortchange Summers's formative role as well; he is so close to Summers, he told the *New York Times,* that "we can finish each other's sentences."[108] Touching, isn't it?

At Geithner's confirmation hearing on January 21, 2009, he offered vague promises about addressing the economy's problems.[109] Perhaps unsurprisingly, they sounded pretty much like the promises Paulson had made. In his address, Geithner said, "First, we must act quickly to provide substantial support for economic recovery and to get credit flowing again."

"Second, as we move quickly to get our economy back on track and to repair the financial system, we must make investments that lay the foundation for a stronger economic future."

"Third, our program to restore economic growth has to be accompanied—and I want to emphasize this—has to be accompanied by a clear strategy to get us back as quickly as possible to a sustainable fiscal position and to unwind the extraordinary interventions taken to stabilize the financial system."[110] He neglected to mention homeowners.

Like Paulson, Geithner pretty much did the banks' bidding, even when it was the wrong thing to do. The Citigroup debacle was a huge case in point. Then again, Geithner had a history of getting it wrong on Citigroup. In December 2006, he worked with the Federal Reserve to lift a reporting requirement for Citigroup that had been in place ever since the NY Fed discovered that Citigroup had helped Enron set up its off-book entities, and the Fed made the firm file quarterly reports about risk-management improvements.[111] The Fed ended that requirement about the time that Citigroup started bulking up on its own off-book hiding spots, called structured investment vehicles (SIVs).[112]

Citigroup's fall two years later was spectacular. In January 2009, Citigroup had to sell majority ownership in its Smith Barney retail brokerage unit to Morgan Stanley. Robert Rubin also announced his resignation after nearly a decade with the firm.[113]

When asked about Citigroup's woes at his confirmation hearing, Geithner did (sort of) take some responsibility for its demise, saying, "Citigroup's supervisors, including the Federal Reserve, failed to identify a number of their risk management shortcomings and to induce appropriate changes in behavior."[114]

Meanwhile, Obama's Treasury took up the toxic-asset problem where Bush's left off and for a brief interlude seemed to be considering the idea of creating some sort of government entity to scoop up the bad assets or having the government guarantee their value, instead of simply injecting capital by buying stock. In the absence of full knowledge about their potential losses, though, doing either would have been like throwing money into a big dark hole. Instead, the Treasury decided to first convert preferred shares in Citigroup to common ones, which would effectively dump more capital into the firm. Second, it developed a private-public partnership, in which private investors would be asked to use public funds to purchase toxic assets.

One of the first things you learn as a trader is *buy the rumor, sell the news*. Geithner missed that lesson. His signature blindfolded, shoot-a-dart, save-a-bank move came on Friday, February 27, 2009. After leaking the Citigroup stock idea for a few days (giving spec-traders time to scoop up shares to later dump), Geithner then announced that the Treasury would convert its preferred shares in Citigroup to common stock. This after nearly $388 billion in capital injections, and debt and loan guarantees failed to do the trick.

So, Citigroup agreed to convert the first $25 billion of its preferred stock investment (which, recall, Paulson overpaid for to begin with) to common stock, increasing the Treasury ownership stake in the flailing bank from 8 percent to 36 percent.

This pushed Citigroup's stock price down below $1 a share on March 5, 2009, and its market value, which had once been as high as $277 billion, was down to about $5 billion.[115]

The faster Citigroup's stock dove, the faster the media rushed to offer explanations, which were as painful as the stock's dive itself. The business press said that shareholders were concerned about the dilu-tion effect on their own shares: this meant that if new shares were issued to the government, existing shareholders would own propor-tionately less of the new total amount. So shareholders dumped them, contributing to the huge dip. Which wasn't the main problem. It's that shareholders still didn't know what other pitfalls lurked on Citigroup's books. The progressive press called the government's buy-in another step toward nationalization. Which it *really* wasn't. Purchasing stock in a black hole of a risk cesspool of a financial institution is not nation-alization. It's simply bad investing strategy. And the conservative press considered it a step toward the destruction of capitalism. Again, it *really* wasn't. After all, capitalism thrives on raising funds for assets that have no value.

My interpretation is that the savvier traders did the same thing they've been doing unrestrainedly throughout this crisis: they dumped or shorted Citigroup shares because they knew the government remained oblivious to the root cause of the decimation of the banking industry and wasn't asking the right questions to quantify the potential downside still out there. Without full disclosure, the market assumes the worst. In solidarity, Bank of America's stock dropped a mere 30 percent. Wells Fargo was down 16 percent. Traders trade down. Banks don't trust one another. And credit remains in a coffin. Throwing money at this situation reminds me of the bottomless pit scene in the old *Flintstones* cartoon.

And you'd think that someone in Washington might suggest a moratorium on shorting bank stocks, particularly when the federal government's buying them with public money. I mean, the move to restrict short selling would come under the allowable emergency procedures of the SEC. And yet the SEC banned the short selling of bank stocks only briefly during the Second Great Bank Depression, from September 19 to October 2, 2008.[116]

At this point, Geithner had the option of coming up with a different plan to stabilize the banking system, rather than purchasing shares in its unwieldy firms. It could have been perfect. He could have taken the mantra of change that Obama rode into the White House on and turned the banking industry inside out, beating it into submission in return for helping it survive. So, did he? No. He went back to Paulson's original plan of buying up toxic assets, with a twist. Under Geithner's public-private partnership plan, we the people wouldn't buy the assets directly and hope that they have value someday. We would be asked to loan money to private firms to buy them for us—up to $1 trillion worth.[117] If the assets have value later, those private firms will make most of the profit on them. And if they don't? Well, then we're out another trillion or so.

2

This Was Never about the Little Guy

If you owe the bank $100, that's your problem. If you owe the bank $100 million, that's the bank's problem.

—*John Paul Getty*[1]

The Second Great Bank Depression has spawned so many lies, it's hard to keep track of which is the biggest. Possibly the most irksome class of lies, usually spouted by Wall Street hacks and conservative pundits, is that we're all victims to a bunch of poor people who bought McMansions, or at least homes they had no business living in. If that was really what this crisis was all about, we could have solved it much more cheaply in a couple of days in late 2008, by simply providing borrowers with additional capital to reduce their loan principals. It would have cost about 3 percent of what the entire bailout wound up costing, with comparatively similar risk.

Just as great oaks from little acorns grow, so, too, can a Second Great Bank Depression from a tiny loan grow.[2] But so you know, it wasn't the tiny loan's fault. It was everyone and everything that piled on top. That's how a small loan in Stockton, California, can be linked to a worldwide economic collapse all the way to Iceland, through a plethora of shady financial techniques and overzealous sales pitches.[3]

Here are some numbers for you. There were approximately $1.4 trillion worth of subprime loans outstanding in the United States by the end of 2007.[4] By May 2009, there were foreclosure filings against approximately 5.1 million properties.[5] If it was only the subprime market's fault, $1.4 trillion would have covered the entire problem, right?

Yet the Federal Reserve, the Treasury, and the FDIC forked out more than $13 trillion to fix the "housing correction," as Hank Paulson steadfastly referred to the Second Great Bank Depression as late as November 20, 2008, while he was treasury secretary.[6] With that money, the government could have bought up *every* residential mortgage in the country—there were about $11.9 trillion worth at the end of December 2008—and still have had a trillion left over to buy homes for every single American who couldn't afford them, and pay their health care to boot.[7]

But there was much more to it than that: Wall Street was engaged in a very dangerous practice called leverage. Leverage is when you borrow a lot of money in order to place a big bet. It makes the payoff that much bigger. You may not be able to cover the bet if you're wrong—you may even have to put down a bit of collateral in order to place that bet—but that doesn't matter when you're sure you're going to win. It is a high-risk, high-reward way to make money, as long as you're not wrong. Or as long as you make the rules. Or as long as the government has your back.

Let's say you have a hot tip that the Lakers are going to throw their game against the Knicks tonight. You call your bookie and tell him to put down $30,000 on the Knicks, even though you don't have anything close to that much on hand. You really have about a grand. You're a longtime client of the bookie, so he doesn't ask you to front more than that. You don't worry about how you'll pay him back because, hey, you can't lose. If you win, you win bigger than you could have only using your own money. If you lose, the bookie breaks your kneecaps. Then again, if you're Citigroup, you get $388 billion of government subsidies and your extremities remain intact.

The Second Great Bank Depression wouldn't have been as tragic without a thirty-to-one leverage ratio for investment banks, and, according to the *New York Times*, a ratio that ranged from eleven to one to fifteen-to-one for the major commercial banks. Actually, it's unclear what kind of leverage the commercial banks really had, because so many of their products were off-book, or not evaluated according to what the market would pay for them.[8] Banks would have taken a hit on their mortgage and consumer credit portfolios, but the systemic credit crisis and the bailout bonanza would have been avoided. Leverage included, we're looking at a possible $140 trillion problem. That's right—$140 trillion! Imagine if the financial firms all over the globe actually exposed their piece of that leverage.

But for $1.4 trillion in subprime loans to become $140 trillion in potential losses, you need two steps in between. The most significant is a healthy dose of leverage, but leverage would not have had a platform without the help of a wondrous financial feat called securitization. Financial firms run economic models that select and package loans into new securities according to criteria such as geographic diversity, the size of the loans, and the length of the mortgages. A bunch of loans are then repackaged into an asset-backed security (ABS). This new security is backed, or collateralized, by a small number of original home loans related to the size of the security. Some securities, for example, might be 10 percent real loans and 90 percent bonds backed by those loans. Some might be 5 percent real loans. Whatever the proportion, the money the mortgage holders pay to lenders on their loans is used to make payments on new assets or securities. Those securities, in turn, pay out to their investors.

During the lead-up to the Second Great Bank Depression, the securities themselves were a much bigger problem than the loans. Between 2002 and 2007, banks in the United States created nearly 80 percent of the approximately $14 trillion worth of total global ABSs, collateralized debt obligations (CDOs), and other alphabetic concoctions or "structured" assets. Structured assets were created at triple what the rate had been from 1998 to 2002. Bankers from the rest of the world created, or "issued," the other 20 percent, around $3 trillion worth. Everyone was paid handsomely.[9] In total, issuers raked in a combined $300 billion in fees. Fees can be made for all types of securitized assets, but the more convoluted they are, the riskier and more lucrative they become. Fees ranged from 0.1 percent to 0.5 percent on standard ABS deals and up to 0.3 percent for mortgage-backed securities (MBSs) and whole business securitization (WBS) deals.[10] Fees were better for CDOs—between 1.5 and 1.75 percent for each deal, and higher for the riskier slices.[11] All told, the $2 trillion CDO market alone netted Wall Street around $30 billion before CDO values headed south.[12] Because U.S. investment banks were making huge profits from packaging churning loans and leveraging them, mortgage- and asset-backed security volume skyrocketed.

Investment banks, hedge funds, and other financial firms could use the $14 trillion of new securities as collateral against which to borrow money and incur more debt (leverage them). There is no way of knowing exactly how much was leveraged, because the players operated in an opaque system—that is, a system without proper regulatory oversight or enforcement to detect or curtail leverage. But a conservative estimate of the average amount of leverage is about ten to one, considering the roughly eleven-to-one leverage of the major commercial banks and the thirty-to-one leverage of investment banks. So, we're talking about a system that ultimately took on $140 trillion in debt on the back of $1.4 trillion of subprime loans. How insane is that? And, it happened so fast.

In 2005, the mortgage on some little home in Stockton provided the capital for two or three ill-advised loans that soon disappeared into an ABS. But it was the global banks, the insurance companies, and the pension funds—particularly in Europe—that purchased the related ABSs. Like their U.S. counterparts, European financiers bought boatloads of ABSs with borrowed money.[13] They also shoved them off-book into structured investment vehicles (SIVs) that required no capital charge and little reporting.

By the fall of 2008 those ABSs, CDOs, and all their permutations would be known as "toxic assets." They were considered by many to be the major cause of Big Finance's failures and losses. The push for TARP centered on ridding banks of these poisonous creatures. But make no mistake: toxic assets are not the same as defaulted subprime mortgage loans; loans are merely one of the ingredients that make up the assets. All the subprime loans in existence could have defaulted and the homes attached to them could have been devalued to zero (which didn't happen), but without the feat of securitization, the banks wouldn't have become nearly insolvent. Toxic assets became devoid of value, not because all the subprime loans stuffed inside them tanked, but because there was no longer demand from investors. If no one wants your Aunt Mary's antique gold-plated, diamond-encrusted starfish, for all intents and purposes, it has no monetary value at the moment. This basic supply-and-demand concept is something our government apparently didn't understand when it offered to take the toxic assets off the banks' books. And the Fed, as we'll see, doesn't seem to care that it took on trillions of dollars' worth of these assets.

Risk Models Built on Thin Air

There was a time when the quality of loans was better than it was between 2002 and 2007. Stricter lending practices made it tougher to get a mortgage and typically required a borrower to bring home four times more than her monthly mortgage payment. The idea was that lenders wanted to protect the money they lent, and borrowers wanted to make sure they were good for that money.

Plus, home loans were fairly bland. They had few bells and whistles, so it was easy to compute the behavior of borrowers. The first MBS was created in 1970 by Ginnie Mae, which is owned by the government. Another government-sponsored entity (GSE), Freddie Mac, issued its first MBS in 1971. Bank of America issued the first MBS issued by a bank in 1977.[14] Fannie Mae issued its first MBS four years later in 1981. The risk of any loan defaulting or an entire package of them defaulting was relatively easy to figure out and prepare for, or hedge.

The first adjustable-rate mortgage (ARM), also called a floating-rate mortgage, was created in the 1980s, but ARMs didn't become popular until the 1990s. They brought with them a new level of risk that had to be quantified.[15]

ARMs were more popular with the less affluent because when interest rates are lower, initial payments are also lower. ARM rates dropped steadily in the early 1990s before leveling off.[16] Lenders were offering ARMs and balloon mortgages, in which payments grew substantially during the later years of the mortgage. When these loans were packaged and subsequently cut into pieces—securitized—they became even more prevalent. Investors in securitized products were effectively providing financing for new loans. That drove more loan creation as investors began to take a more prominent role than lenders in the mortgage business. They really soared from 2002 to 2005, spurred by the rate-cut frenzy of Greenspan and securitizers on Wall Street and in Washington, including the GSEs Freddie Mac and Fannie Mae.[17] By the middle of 2007, more than half of the home mortgage market was being securitized, compared with only 10 percent in 1980 and less than 1 percent in 1970.[18]

Because ARM loans were new, they didn't come with a ready-made behavior history. Still, they were mostly made to prime borrowers whose risk of defaulting under simpler mortgages was well established, so Wall Street figured the ARMs would also be low-risk, even when extended to subprime borrowers. The lending companies that doled out these loans never had it so good, profit-wise, as they did between 2002 and 2005.

Skyrocketing home prices dominated the headlines during that lending boom, but they were nothing compared to the bubble experienced by the stock prices of the firms that made up the housing sector. From 2002 through 2005, while median home prices rose about 32 percent nationwide, the paper value of Wall Street darling companies such as Countrywide Financial, Beazer Homes U.S.A., and New Century Financial skyrocketed at least ten times as fast, with their shares posting gains of 300 to 400 percent.[19] See, that's leverage!

They were also the companies that fell first—that's the dark side of leverage. By March 27, 2007, homebuilder shares began to plummet just as the Justice Department, the U.S. Attorney's Office in Charlotte, North Carolina, the U.S. Department of Housing and Urban Development (HUD), and the Internal Revenue Service launched a criminal investigation looking into fraud at Atlanta-based Beazer Homes in its mortgage brokerage business.[20] Beazer's chief accounting officer Michael Rand was fired in June 2007 for attempting to destroy documents.[21] Ian McCarthy, who has been Beazer Homes's CEO since 1994, survived the investigation to make nearly $8 million in total compensation from 2007 to 2008.[22]

On April 2, 2007, New Century Financial, once the second-largest subprime lender in the United States, filed for Chapter 11 after it was forced to repurchase billions of dollars' worth of bad loans.[23] Melville,

New York–based American Home Mortgage, once one of the largest independent home loan lenders, filed for bankruptcy on August 6, 2007, just days after cutting its workforce down to 750; it had started the year with 7,400 employees.[24] The FBI confirmed in early October 2007 that for several weeks it had been investigating American Home Mortgage on potential conspiracy and money laundering charges, and for securities, mail, and wire fraud, all of which contributed to its collapse.[25]

Countrywide, the biggest U.S. mortgage lender, narrowly avoided bankruptcy by taking out an emergency $11.5 billion loan on August 16, 2007.[26] By October 18, 2007, the Securities and Exchange Commission (SEC) was well into an informal secret probe of Countrywide CEO Angelo R. Mozilo regarding the questionable timing of a stock sale then believed to be worth $130 million.[27]

Around the same time that the SEC started to look into Mozilo's stock sales, it joined the bevy of federal agencies investigating Beazer Homes for exaggerating its earnings since 2004. KB Home, the nation's fifth-largest homebuilder, also faced an SEC investigation over allegations that former CEO Bruce Karatz—who was paid $50 million at the boom's pinnacle in 2005—further inflated his compensation by backdating stock options.[28]

Going back a bit, the regulators and even the press maybe should have seen the subprime mess coming, at least by early 2007. A series of fraud investigations in a single industry following stupendous profits tends to foreshadow doom. On February 28, 2007, the U.S. Attorney's Office for the Central District of California told the founders of New Century Financial that they were under investigation for dumping millions of dollars' worth of stock, and on March 12, 2007, the SEC told New Century Financial that it would have to cooperate in a preliminary investigation of the company's restated financial statements.[29] All of this was leading up to the company's April 2007 bankruptcy. But New Century Financial CEO Edward F. Gotschall had the good sense to get out early, cashing in $27 million worth of stock in 2005 and 2006. He died of natural causes in January 2009 at age fifty-three, while watching football, as the Justice Department was investigating his stock sale.[30]

Going back even further, there were other investigations opened on the firms that had been subprime darlings and Wall Street lackeys

that had created the loans that Wall Street used to bundle into risky
financial packages and securities. Ameriquest reached a $325 million
settlement in January 2006 to end a two-year investigation signed off
on by all fifty state attorneys general, without admitting any fault.[31]
Nearly two years later, in December 2007, payments began to trickle
out in the tens of millions.[32] Household International reached a $484
million settlement with federal investigators in October 2002.[33] That
settlement was only a whiff of the havoc that subprime lending would
catalyze later in the decade.

In February 2009, the FBI had thirty-eight corporate fraud investigations open related to the financial crisis, with only 240 agents investigating mortgage fraud, compared to 1,000 investigators during the
Savings and Loan Crisis in the 1980s.[34] By the end of April 2009,
the FBI had 2,440 pending mortgage fraud investigations and for fiscal year 2008 there were 574 indictments that led to 354 convictions.[35]
So far, FBI investigations have yielded one high-profile criminal case
related to allegedly subprime lending—the indictment of two hedge
fund executives from Bear Stearns—which was announced along
with more than four hundred other mortgage fraud indictments on
June 19, 2008.[36]

Lazy Lending Legislation

The greedy predatory lending that fueled the Second Great Bank
Depression could have been avoided. Back in 1994, there was actually enough popular pressure to introduce legislation that would have
ushered in controls on lending and other banking activities. As is par
for the course, a handful of consumer-oriented congresspeople and
watchdog groups initially faced an uphill battle against a band of well-
funded, well-placed politicians such as Florida's Bill McCollum, Texas's
Phil Gramm, and Iowa's James Leach and Charles Grassley, who were
carrying Wall Street's torch toward deregulation.

But a burgeoning predatory lending crisis reached a very public
head in 1994 amid allegations that Fleet Finance Group had gouged
hundreds of low-income and minority consumers. Busloads of irate
anti-loan-shark-T-shirt-sporting citizens rallied through the halls of
Congress to chronicle lending abuses.

In response, just before Newt Gingrich assumed power as Speaker of the House under Democrat president Bill Clinton, the House battled for the Home Ownership and Equity Protection Act of 1994 (HOEPA) to cap the most outrageous predatory loans.[37] It was the last piece of legislation that attempted to regulate appalling lending practices. Perhaps if lending had been better regulated, subprime loans wouldn't have been the fodder for the Second Great Bank Depression. Maybe something else would have been. But that wasn't the case.

HOEPA contained several provisions that curbed "reverse redlining," in which nonbank lenders target low-income and minority borrowers. But it didn't reinstate full interest rate caps, which had been deregulated during the previous two decades, or limit fees or tighten requirements to determine the ability of borrowers to repay their loans.[38] As you can imagine, the industry and certain Republicans bitterly opposed the original House bill.

"Why can't the lenders police themselves?" Senator Richard C. Shelby (R-AL) asked.[39] Sure, and while we're at it, why not let power companies determine what's pollution and what isn't? Why not let agribusiness make the rules about what farms can do? Why not put lions in charge of your gazelle sanctuary or hire a fox to guard the henhouse? Shelby, as you may recall, later sprouted an activist streak in 2009 and took the Treasury Department to task for lying to Congress about TARP.

Even with the best intentions, HOEPA's passage had dire consequences. First, it left a huge gap between the first and second tier of rates and fees a lender could charge. If lenders didn't want to hit the new caps, they had plenty of fertile ground to play on by extending loans with rates and fees just beneath the HOEPA triggers. Because lenders would make less money from each loan, due to the reduced rates and fees, they'd have to find more borrowers to make the same profits. Voilà, the quiet birth of predatory subprime lending.

During those early and middle years of the Gingrich revolution, there was no talk of regulation. The market zoomed, and even though a spate of corporate fraud was percolating, it didn't look broke, so no one in Congress fixed it.

As the late 1990s stock market boom headed into the new millennium, there were renewed legislative attempts to rein in the lending industry. Notably, in April 2000, the dynamic duo of Representative John LaFalce (D-NY) and Senator Paul Sarbanes (D-MD) introduced the Predatory Lending Consumer Protection Act of 2000 (PLCPA) to strengthen the Truth-in-Lending Act.[40]

PLCPA would have brought down the HOEPA triggers and cut origination fees so that profit from home mortgages had to come from payments, ensuring that everyone in the chain had an interest in home-owners' ability to repay loans. Sarbanes and Senate staffer Jonathan Miller worked feverishly to line up cosponsors.

The industry attacked the bill and won, with help from McCollum and Connie Mack III (R-FL). What did pass, however, was Phil Gramm's Commodity Futures Modernization Act of 2000 (CFMA). That act ushered in tremendous growth of unregulated commodity trades through its "Enron Loophole," which allowed companies to trade energy and other commodity futures on unregulated exchanges.[41]

It also sparked growth in the unregulated credit derivative trades that bet on defaults of corporations or loans, which became the main ingredient in the hot new Wall Street financial gumbo. Credit derivatives were a type of insurance contract written against not just one corporation or loan but on investments that scarfed up bunches of subprime loans and stuffed them into the unregulated CDOs that imploded and hastened the greater lending crisis. The problem was that they weren't regulated (even half-heartedly) like insurance policies were.

Meanwhile, the quixotic Sarbanes and LaFalce soldiered on, trying to avert lending disaster through appropriate regulation. They reintroduced their bill as the Predatory Lending Consumer Protection Act of 2001, but the mortgage industry and its mouthpieces were relentless. In July 2001, Stephen W. Prough, chairman of Ameriquest Mortgage Company, said at the Senate's Banking Committee hearings, "'Predatory' is really a high-profile word with no definition."[42] In August 2001, Senate Banking Committee chairman Gramm concurred, "Some people look at subprime lending and see evil," he said. "I look at subprime lending and I see the American dream in action."[43] The 2001 version of PLCPA also died.

Down and nearly out, Sarbanes and LaFalce tried to pass their act again in May 2002.[44] It failed again and then again, for the final time, on November 21, 2003.[45] Bush's ownership society ideology was in full swing by then, and the country was at war. Any hope for regulation or transparency in the lending or banking sector was basically dead.

The culmination of years of minor and significant acts of deregulation coalesced with mortgage industry sycophants beating back solid attempts at regulation or transparency. Loans that lenders pushed on homeowners were the perfect fodder for Wall Street, which eagerly packaged the loans and profited. House prices, in turn, skyrocketed.

How Lenders Created a Risk-Free Business

Meanwhile, lending practices had gotten really wild. Alan Greenspan had chopped rates dramatically to bolster the economy following the stock market plunge in 2001 and 2002. Lower rates meant that it was cheaper for banks to borrow more money from the Fed and from one another. It also meant that lenders had more funds to play with. Because prime loan rates fell in tandem, these loans weren't funneling as much profit to lenders. To make up for it, lenders extended riskier (nonprime) loans at higher rates to more borrowers.

With cheaper money, lenders were able to fund more mortgages for those riskier borrowers. If some loans didn't go well, it wouldn't matter. Lenders bet that they could either sell the underlying homes for higher prices, which would more than cover the defaulted loans, or convince the borrowers to take out equity loans backed by the homes' presumably rising value.

That increased the risk of default and, more so, the potential loss to the lender: the same house could now back two loans instead of one, so if its value fell and the borrower couldn't pay up, both loans were screwed. Super-low teaser interest rates lasted for two or three years and begged to be refinanced (for which lenders got extra fees) before they zoomed up.[46] This added more risk to the system: loans couldn't be refinanced, and borrowers couldn't make the high rate payments. But as long as home prices kept rising as they had since at least the early 1960s, systemic loan defaults weren't a huge concern.[47]

While rates remained fairly low, there was always more cash for lenders to dole out. Lenders pushed an ongoing cycle of refinancing and new home purchases, both of which could be classified as new mortgages on their books, which was good for stock prices. Between

2002 and 2005, the stock price of the once-largest independent mortgage lender, Countrywide Financial, had tripled—well before Bank of America agreed on January 11, 2008, to buy its remains.[48] The firm created $434 billion in new loans in 2003, a 75 percent increase over 2002, securing a post in Forbes America's top twenty-five fastest-growing big companies for 2003.[49] The number-three home lender, Washington Mutual, issued $384 billion in loans that year. (Emulating Countrywide's rapid descent later in the decade, Washington Mutual lost a combined $4.44 billion in the first and second quarters of 2008, before JPMorgan Chase swooped in to buy it, with the government's help, on September 25, 2008.)[50] Wells Fargo, which hung on to buy Wachovia in October 2008, topped the charts in 2003 with $470 billion in new loans.[51] That's a combined $1.3 trillion in new home loans created by the big three mortgage lenders in 2003.

As home prices spiked amid low rates, demand increased for securitized loans, and more loans were offered. In 2003, the securitization rate of subprime loans matched that of prime loans in the mid-1990s.[52] From 2002 to 2006, subprime loan originations went from 8.6 percent of all mortgages to 20.1 percent.[53]

The more subprime loans there were in the market, the more the securities piled on top of them became exposed to the risk that a larger number of loans than expected might default. Of course, this risk was hidden until home prices started to fall and defaults started to rise. Subprime defaults decreased to 5.37 percent in 2005 (nearly half of what they'd been during the 2001 recession), right before those seeds of risk between lenders and borrowers began to sprout like Audrey II, the alien plant in *Little Shop of Horrors*.[54]

Consumer protections were simultaneously chucked. On April 20, 2005, President George W. Bush signed the 2005 Bankruptcy Abuse and Consumer Protection Act, sponsored by Senator Charles Grassley (R-IA), which worsened the quietly growing housing crisis for consumers.[55] Borrowers facing bankruptcy could no longer negotiate down the principal of their mortgages with their creditors if the market declined, meaning that they had no way to avoid foreclosure, even if they wanted to.

On September 1, 2005, two years after the final Sarbanes-LaFalce bill failed to gain traction, Office of Federal Housing Enterprise

Oversight (OFHEO) chief economist Patrick Lawler said, "There is no evidence here of prices topping out. On the contrary, house price inflation continues to accelerate, as some areas that have experienced relatively slow appreciation are picking up steam."[56]

Markets weren't yet constrained for credit. Because lenders were assured money through securitizations on Wall Street, they didn't have to worry about guidelines on individual loans. If rating agencies would certify trillions of dollars worth of collateralized packages of loans with the highest possible rating, AAA, Wall Street investment banks could sell them to a wider pool of investors, which included pension funds, university endowments, and municipalities. High-interest loan volume, which includes most subprime loans, soared to a combined $1.5 trillion between 2004 and 2006, representing 29 percent of home loans made in 2006.[57] Home equity loans bulged simultaneously. It was a loan-lending fest until adjustable rates ultimately kicked in, and prices topped out. At the same time that housing values were faltering, borrower mortgage payments jumped by 25 to 30 percent as adjustment periods began. Then the foreclosures ramped up to levels last seen during the Great Depression.

More about Making Simple Loans into Complex Securities

The first ABSs were issued in the United States in 1985 to help savings and loan associations get risky loans off their books. Credit card companies issued their first ABSs in 1987.[58] The U.S. ABS market grew steadily through the early 1990s.[59]

ABSs were stuffed with risky assets, such as subprime mortgages and subprime home equity loans, but in the beginning there weren't enough of these to make a huge difference. The financial wizardry of securitization gathered up bunches of loans, and used them as lining for new securities. These new securities were sliced into two (or more) parts. The top part was called a senior slice, or tranche. Senior slices would receive any interest payments coming from the underlying loans first. The bottom slice, called a subordinated (or "sub") tranche would protect the senior one from the risk of not receiving interest payments, if borrowers defaulted on their loans. The sub-tranche only received whatever loan payments were left after the senior investors were paid. Most ABSs had more than two tranches, but the principle worked the same. The bottom slices were like bodyguards. They took the hit of any losses, so the top ones would be assured of payment. In return for taking this extra risk that not enough payments would come in, subordinate bond holders got more interest than senior ones. This process worked only if the sub-tranche was big enough to absorb anticipated losses. If its size was miscalculated or defaults were massive, the whole security could collapse. Not only would the sub-piece not get paid, but the pieces above it might not either. As the years went on, it was common to have three, four, thirty or more tranches for each security, but no matter how many there were the hierarchy worked the same.

Prudential Securities created the first CDO obligation backed by ABSs or mortgage loans in 1999. During that time, most CDOs simply contained corporate, mostly high-yield, bonds or assets.[60] As corporate fraud was exposed and bankruptcies rose, different kinds of stuffing were needed for the CDO technology. Prudential became one of the leaders on a dangerous path that would lead the CDO market, worth $275 billion in 2000, to a value of $4.7 trillion by 2006.[61]

Fannie Mae, established in 1938, and Freddie Mac are the GSEs that originally had tight restrictions on the types and the quality of mortgages they were allowed to securitize. The credit risk for subprime loans rested just above the level these GSEs would accept, so subprime loans were off limits. Standards fell on Bill Clinton's watch. What happened was that HUD required Fannie and Freddie to buy up a certain percentage of affordable loans, and in 1995, it allowed them to purchase subprime loans to count toward that total.[62] Fannie Mae then eased its credit requirements even further in 1999.

"If they fail, the government will have to step up and bail them out the way it stepped up and bailed out the thrift industry," Peter Wallison, a resident fellow at the American Enterprise Institute, presciently told the *New York Times* in September 1999.[63]

With Wall Street profits to be made, HUD under President Bush upped the affordable loan requirement in 2004 to 56 percent of Fannie's and Freddie's total loans. Although Fannie and Freddie tried to buy loans with the least amount of risk (on the surface), they still provided capital to the entire loosely regulated subprime market.[64]

After a mess of accounting scandals—Fannie Mae was forced to correct its books by $11 billion in 2004, and Freddie Mac misreported its earnings by $5 billion from 2000 to 2002—the government mortgage darlings needed to get back into secure business, so they dove headlong into the next big thing and became the largest buyers of subprime and Alt-A mortgages from 2004 to 2007.[65] At a total of nearly half a trillion dollars, Fannie and Freddie occupied between 20 and 44 percent of the total subprime market each year during that time.[66]

As subprime and Alt-A originations in the United States rose from less than 8 percent of all mortgages in 2003 to a high of more than 20 percent in 2006, their quality also deteriorated.[67] Various metrics show that the subprime saturation might have been even worse than that—the Kansas City Federal Reserve calculated in July 2008 that nationally, the 2006 subprime loan origination alone was as high as 38 percent of the market.[68] But that didn't make a difference. If GSEs and investors had demand, lenders would make sure there was supply.

Meanwhile, investment banks were on a never-ending hunt for new profit sources. And investors were looking for a better asset class, because the stock market wasn't doing the trick anymore. Investors set their sights on subprime assets that could be scrambled up and spooned out to achieve high-quality ratings.

Based on the possibility that some part of the batch of subprime loans would default, rating agencies assigned separate ratings to the senior and the subordinate tranches. Tranches that were AAA rated were considered to be virtually risk-free. A BBB tranche had a higher chance of defaulting but, in theory, would protect the AAA tranches from losses on a default. The way that rating agency models worked, if there was a default on the BBB tranche, it didn't necessarily trigger a downgrading of the AAA tranche, although it certainly should have.[69] To make matters worse, hedge funds gradually got used to not taking on subordinated tranches at all. Their securities were selling, so why should they absorb any of the risk?[70]

Global investors were buzzing. They could buy assets that looked superior and get spreads that were higher than other similarly rated assets, such as Treasury bonds or investment-grade corporations like IBM and GE. That hunger fueled global ABS issuance, which nearly doubled, from roughly 1,600 issues in 2003 to more than 3,000 in 2006.

Companies were printing ABSs as if they were money, even though they were worth less than the paper they were printed on (metaphorically speaking).[71]

Assets were worth far less than the ratings indicated because of a risk catch. A security that might have been a perfectly good AAA, if risk assumptions were correct, could take on the risk characteristics of a BBB security if defaults increased, even though it was still called AAA. Which is what started to happen in late 2005. Credit spreads on AAA-rated ABSs were repriced as BBB corporate bonds by August 2007.[72] It wasn't long before investors realized that they'd bought a lemon, and their appetites started to sour.

Making Complex Securities into Incomprehensible Securities

To add more complexity to the mix and produce more AAA tranches, banks started to issue a new batch of securities: the CDO. Instead of simply being a scrambled mix of subprime loans backed by homes, CDOs were a rescrambled mix of ABSs and subprime loans and sometimes credit derivatives, which were unregulated securities that paid out a premium if the assets they were linked to didn't default. Somewhere in there, CDOs were backed by those same subprime home mortgages, but it was more difficult to see how.

Globally, proceeds from CDOs surged in the mid- and late-2000s. In 2003, proceeds from CDOs were at a paltry $86.5 billion, hitting a peak in 2006 of $478.8 billion and decreasing slightly in 2007 to $442.3 billion. Tragically, subprime loan packages were the fastest-growing segment of ABSs, up to 26 percent in June 2007 from 14 percent in 2000.[73] This meant that the financial products that were seeing the most growth were also the ones that contained the most inherent risk.

Demand remained insatiable through 2006. Issuing banks began to drum up synthetic CDOs backed only by credit derivatives linked to ABSs, not even by the ABSs themselves. Among other creative risk-hiding schemes, CDOs were squared, taking the most risky parts of CDOs and rescrambling them among less-risky parts. Each time the same technology was applied, the risk was amplified that the whole thing would collapse if more loans at the bottom deteriorated. That didn't stop the profit-fest.

The hedge fund community was a willing accomplice, providing equity capital to line these CDOs. Then, of course, the CDO market, along with everything else, hit rock bottom in 2008, with proceeds falling 88 percent to $52.6 billion. Growth in the CDO market ceased with a whimper, and there were no more investors to hose. CDO proceeds fell to $20 billion in the United States that year.[74]

The CDO market and the leverage taken on top of pieces of CDOs ultimately brought down Lehman Brothers, Bear Stearns, and other hedge funds. The lawsuits poured in. On March 17, 2008, Bear Stearns shareholders filed a class-action lawsuit alleging that they were misled about the firm's true financial condition leading up to its takeover by JPMorgan Chase on March 16.[75] Beverly Hills billionaire H. Roger Wang sued Bear Stearns for fraud the next month, after losing more than $5.6 million on 150,000 shares he'd bought in the weeks and days leading up to Bear's collapse.[76] Other lawsuits against Bear and other funds remain in the air.

Everyone Was Invited, Everyone RSVP'd, and Everyone Showed Up

Before the funeral, there was the party. European banks, global insurance companies and stateside pension funds, and, to a lesser extent, U.S. banks inhaled the AAA securities on the top layers of CDOs. Investors assumed that their risks were tiny. They weren't the only ones. From pension funds in Ireland to private banking and insurance specialists in Belgium, everyone was buying CDOs.[77]

The largest public pension fund in the United States, the California Public Employees' Retirement System, bought $140 million in CDO equity (the riskiest, unrated CDO slice) from Citigroup by July 2007.[78] Of all the CDO equity slices sold in the United States, 7 percent went to pension funds, endowments, and religious organizations, which bought up half a billion dollars' worth of the riskiest pieces of CDOs between 2002 and 2007.

The investors who needed to keep their money the most ended up taking the first hit when CDOs failed. In 2008, the New Mexico State Investment Council, which manages investments for twenty state agencies, including the New Mexico Retiree Health Care Authority and the New Mexico School for the Blind and Visually Impaired, had more than $500 million invested in equity tranches, while the General Retirement System of Texas had $62.8 million and the Missouri State Employees' Retirement System had a $25 million tranche.[79]

But all the investors discovered that they would face a major liquidity problem if they wanted to get rid of any of this stuff. In markets, if buyers stop buying, sellers can't sell. Demand and liquidity began to dry up in the middle of 2007. New ABS CDOs were practically halted by October 2007.[80] By February 2008, only one new CDO had been created in the United States.[81] Losses racked up.

The AAA ratings given by the major rating agencies, including Standard and Poor's, Moody's Investors Service, and Fitch Ratings, were bought and paid for by the investment banks, which were also their clients.[82] Based on a historical gauge of *default probabilities*—the likelihood that payments on loans or bonds would stop—these agencies would rate tiers of newly fashioned securities depending on whether the tier below them would default or not. If the agencies did not provide good scores, CDOs weren't created, and the agencies wouldn't get paid.

"In my view there are very few institutions that can remain objective given such a compensation scheme," Andrew Davidson, who runs a risk-management firm, told the now defunct *New York Sun* in September 2007.[83]

The rating agencies, despite having contributed to the global economic meltdown that impacted the greater public, didn't consider themselves responsible for any of it.[84]

When one of my researchers for this book called to ask one of the three major rating agencies a simple question—"What kind of fees were made on these deals?"—its response was not, "Sure, let's get that information for you ASAP." It was something along the lines of, "Tell us which company you work for, and we'll get back to you." In other words, "If you don't pay us or get us paid, we won't help you." So much for transparency. That's reason enough to nationalize rating agencies.

High ratings meant high demand everywhere in the world, so that the failed Belgian-Dutch bank Fortis and others came to own a piece of Stockton. If one Stockton home defaulted, the global effect was miniscule. But when lots of home loans went under and their interest payments stopped funneling through the massive leveraged pyramid scheme that Wall Street had created, the damage from a simple butterfly wing flap turned seismic. The SEC, late as always to every party, voted to formally propose rating agency reforms to increase transparency and constrain the practices that awarded high ratings to low assets on June 11, 2008.[85]

Three months later, on October 22, 2008, the House Committee on Oversight and Government Reform held a hearing titled, "Credit Rating Agencies and the Financial Crisis." In his opening statement, Chairman Henry Waxman (D-CA) remarked, "The credit rating agencies occupy a special place in our financial markets. Millions of investors rely on them for independent, objective assessments. The rating agencies broke this bond of trust, and federal regulators ignored the warning signs and did nothing to protect the public. The result is that our entire financial system is now at risk—just as the CEO of Moody's predicted a year ago."[86] Party over.

Making Incomprehensible Securities into Inconceivable Insurance

The orgy of toxic securities was made worse by a financial product called a credit default swap (CDS), which was invented in 1997 by JPMorgan Chase.[87] In the unregulated CDS market, the seller of a CDS gets paid a premium from the buyer, who in return gets protection from a bad credit event. In an incestuous frenzy, institutions bought and sold credit protection to one another, with money they borrowed from one another. Since 2000, the CDS market exploded from $900 billion to more than $45.5 trillion. That's about twice the size of the entire U.S. stock market.[88] The CDS boom continued until liquidity in the contracts dried up earlier this year and lenders called in their money.

The global fallout might have been manageable if banks hadn't entered this massively interconnected circle of privately negotiated CDSs. Even when banks were starting to post losses in 2007 and credit funds like those at Bear Stearns were tanking, the unregulated, over-the-counter derivatives market kept growing in the second half of 2007, particularly in the credit arena.[89] Fear seeping through Wall Street translated into a rush to buy credit protection, most notably from the American International Group (AIG), which was later on the hook for more protection than it could handle and had to ask the government for handouts.[90]

Fortunately, even though banking practices are usually shrouded in secrecy, certain whistle-blowing heroes emerged. One of them, Deepak Moorjani, an employee and a shareholder at Deutsche Bank AG, could have told you this crisis was coming. In fact, he warned his bosses of just that back in 2006. Moorjani had come out of the private equity world and had served on the boards of several small companies. It had been his job to ensure that those companies were run efficiently and honestly. When Moorjani joined the Deutsche Bank Commercial Real Estate Division, he saw that pay incentives and lack of oversight from management had led to excessive risk taking.

"I was kind of doing what I was trained to do, but you get yourself into a sort of environment like Deutsche Bank and that's not highly appreciated," he said in a phone interview.[91]

Deutsche Bank was only one of the big-name companies tied up in AIG's collapse and subsequent bailout. Insurance companies such as AIG provided insurance on CDOs through CDSs. AIG was providing insurance on securities that everyone assumed would keep churning out money, based on constantly rising housing prices. Once the CDOs, or what was inside them, started to default, AIG had to pay back these insurance claims.[92]

When the government bailed out AIG, it was really acting as the insurance company AIG had claimed to be. AIG took taxpayer money and gave $90 billion of it to fifteen of the counterparties it had promised to insure against credit defaults written on super-senior (even better then AAA) tranches of CDOs backed by mortgage securities, some of them subprime.[93]

Deutsche Bank was one of the companies AIG paid off with tax-payer billions—$1.8 billion, to be exact. That was more than 50 percent of Deutsche Bank's market capitalization at the time, according to Moorjani, who has since applied for a position with the SEC Division of Enforcement.

"If you're a bank, you can write these contracts all day long and there's no transparency," he said. The employees writing and signing off on the contracts get paid in the short term, even if, in the long term, losses from those contracts amount to a hard slap across the face of the world economy.

"You have to track managers using the company's resources for personal gain because they're not owners, they're not shareholders," he said. "It's OPM—it's other people's money—and that is the problem."[94]

The Cruelest Lie of All

There are those who blame lending, and certainly subprime lending was terribly predatory. Conservatives, however, toward the end of 2008, began to blame the people getting the subprime loans and the Democrats for pushing through the Community Reinvestment Act (CRA) in 1977, which sought to end discriminatory home-lending practices.

CRA "led to tremendous pressure on Fannie Mae and Freddie Mac—which in turn pressured banks and other lenders—to extend mortgages to people who were borrowing over their heads. That's called subprime lending. It lies at the root of our current calamity," the conservative columnist Charles Krauthammer wrote on September 26, 2008, in his nationally syndicated column. Translation: the Democrats allowed Poor People to do this. And innocent Wall Street paid the price.

Krauthammer continued, "Were there some predatory lenders? Of course. But only a fool or a demagogue—i.e., a presidential candidate—would suggest that this is a major part of the problem."[95] (Of course, maybe Krauthammer is just always reactionary. At the beginning of the Iraq War, he wrote, "Hans Blix had five months to find weapons. He found nothing. We've had five weeks. Come back to me in five months. If we haven't found any, we will have a credibility problem."[96] Credibility problem indeed.)

Since late 2008, plenty of fools and demagogues have argued and, in fact, proved Krauthammer wrong. But for a while, conservative stalwarts such as Fox News's Neil Cavuto and newspaper columnist George Will echoed the idea that it wasn't greed but a 1977 regulatory law that brought down the economy.[97] Given that the value of subprime loans in the market is overwhelmed by the amount of the full federal bailout by a factor of ten to one, that's not anywhere near reality.

The finance community's theory is one of selective Darwinism: Little people who take bad risks deserve the consequences. Companies that take bad risks are a welcome addition to the fallen competitor list. Banks that survive the chaos can reposition themselves at the top of the financial piles, and deserve all the federal bailout money, and assistance in growing even bigger, that they can get.

Indeed, after the Bear Stearns bailout, then treasury secretary Paulson said of his former competitor, "When we talk about moral hazard, I would say, 'Look at the Bear Stearns shareholder.'"[98] Blaming the bad apple and delivering some well-chosen words about America's destiny will usually mute the need for regulation. That's why current congressional packages tend to offer cosmetic financial solutions to long-term regulatory dilemmas.

No matter where the blame lies, as housing prices kept dropping and foreclosures kept rising, the feds jumped into gear late and indicted several hundred mortgage players, including former Bear Stearns credit hedge fund stars and current scapegoats Ralph Cioffe and Matt Tannin, and many lesser-known characters. The FBI and the Department of Justice targeted a slew of small and big firms after the fact, from Puerto Rico–based Doral Financial Corporation, unknown to most households, to more prominent names: AIG, Countrywide Financial, Washington Mutual, Bear Stearns, Lehman Brothers, UBS AG, New Century Financial, Freddie Mac, and Fannie Mae.

When all is forgotten and we've moved on to our next financial crisis, there will be certain fingers frozen in time pointing at the subprime loans as the cause of the calamity. Big Finance would prefer that. But the truth is that the subprime loan tragedy was merely the catalyst that exposed the mega-tiered securitizations of securitizations, the massive leverage chain derivatives attached to nothing concrete, and the ineffective regulatory restraints. All of which led us down the rabbit hole of the Second Great Bank Depression.

3

Everybody Wants to Be a Bank

When money speaks, the truth is silent.

—*Russian proverb*

An air of impending disaster pervaded Wall Street late on Sunday night, September 21, 2008. Goldman Sachs and Morgan Stanley each faced a severe capital shortage, having borrowed well beyond their means, thanks to the massive leverage ratios allowed by the Securities and Exchange Commission (SEC). The only thing these old dogs of the investment world could do at that particular moment—and it was brilliant—was flip onto their backs, muster up their cutest puppy-dog smiles (even though they should have known better than to knock over all the houseplants), and beg the federal government for a good, long scratch. Perhaps even to their own surprise, the old dogs were scratched like never before.

When we look back at that moment decades from now, it will surely seem that the very smart people at Goldman Sachs and Morgan Stanley were able to make the government's most powerful financial arbiters look foolish. How did this happen? Easy. Goldman Sachs and Morgan Stanley told the Federal Reserve exactly what it wanted to hear: We need you.

65

Two of the country's most powerful investment banks, accustomed to making huge profits and having limited government regulation, came to the Fed's doorstep, hat in hand, and asked—nay, *begged!*—for government help. They wanted the Fed to make them bank holding companies (BHCs). The proposal seemed to defy everything that Goldman Sachs and Morgan Stanley stood for. They seemed willing to relinquish their ability to speculate and leverage excessively. On the surface, anyway.

The Fed determined that emergency conditions existed because of the prevailing market chaos and because the sky had fallen on Lehman Brothers, the banks' competitor. Under "unusual and exigent circumstances," as defined in a 1932 provision in the Federal Reserve Act, the Fed could grant the changeover and allow the investment banks access to its discount lending window, effectively ensuring Morgan Stanley and Goldman Sachs easy access to massive lines of credit.[1] For those of you keeping score at home: change of status equaled river of free money. No one questioned the Fed's actions.

Morgan Stanley also applied to become a financial holding company (FHC); Goldman Sachs gave notice of its intent to do the same.[2] The BHC and FHC designations provided the best of both worlds—the investment banks got guarantees and cheap loans from the government as BHCs, plus freedom from many commercial bank regulations as FHCs. A BHC can only engage in classic commercial banking activities (such as taking deposits and extending loans), whereas an FHC has a broader mandate, in fact, one nearly identical to everything both investment banks were already doing.[3]

The Fed approved the investment banks' BHC filings that September 21 night, bypassing the regular five-day antitrust waiting period and without time or apparent inclination for any meaningful debate.[4]

So the two remaining investment bank giants, in their new BHC incarnation, craftily got access to further taxpayer backing, and they could still operate as they had before. What's more, the name change provided other avenues for the banks to bogart easy money. On October 14, 2008, the FDIC created the Temporary Liquidity Guarantee Program (TLGP), which I'll talk about more in the next chapter.[5] The TLGP allowed Goldman Sachs, Morgan Stanley, and others to mooch off money that should have been reserved for banks dealing with average consumers. With the FDIC's backing, the banks could raise capital by issuing debt with really low interest rates, as opposed to the corporate rates they would have had to pay had they not taken on the new titles. That little trick allowed Goldman Sachs to raise more than $29 billion of cheap debt and Morgan Stanley to raise nearly $24 billion.[6] Previously, neither bank had taken a dime in deposits from anyone beneath a seven-figure income bracket, and they had never acted like or had any intention of acting like consumer banks—yet they had no shame lining up at the government's vast money till. Hey, what could be better than money that was practically free? The conversion to BHCs also presented a way for Goldman Sachs and Morgan Stanley to dodge transparency. By becoming BHCs, they got around disclosing how much their assets were worth, based on market values. They could instead reclassify their assets as "held for investment," just as the big banks did.[7] In other words, don't tell, and we, the Fed, won't ask. We have yet to see how much each bank got from the Fed's loan facilities, but we'll see exactly how secretive the Fed is later.

Will They Really Be More Regulated Now?

In the aftermath of the reclassification, the Fed itself took on even more responsibility and power. It became the regulator for more U.S. financial institutions, because they were all becoming BHCs, which are under the Fed's regulatory purview. But even with their new names, Goldman Sachs and Morgan Stanley are still investment banks, just as horse manure by any other name still smells as rank. Under the rules of the Bank Holding Company Act, these newly named firms have a two-year conversion period, with the possibility of extending that grace period even further. (That's plenty of time to lobby for changes to the act, which they probably will.) See, if the Fed was serious about using this Second Great Bank Depression period to become a stricter regulator, it would not have provided this leniency. That it did shows us that the Fed will not be able to prevent a Third Depression. Indeed, it will shoulder part of the responsibility for that event.

Economist and codirector of the D.C.-based Center for Economic and Policy Research Dean Baker was skeptical from the beginning of

Goldman Sachs's and Morgan Stanley's bait, switch, and get bailed out strategy. "On principle it's a big deal that they will be regulated as commercial banks. Over the longer term, I don't know if they've thought it through and if the Fed has thought it through."[8]

I called Baker a few months after Goldman Sachs and Morgan Stanley became BHCs, and he told me, "They are going to get by as much as they can. They are first looking at survival, but they will always try to slip out of regulations. Goldman Sachs and Morgan Stanley are powerful. They are trying to make a virtue out of a necessity and will try to squirrel out of whatever they can. If they get through this, they will fight again later."[9]

Of course, public spin on the move was important. Both firms went out of their way to extol its virtues, mostly in an effort to keep nervous investors calm. "This fundamentally alters the landscape," a Goldman Sachs spokesman said. "By becoming a bank holding company and being regulated by the Federal Reserve, we have directly addressed issues that have become of mounting concern to market participants in recent weeks."[10] (Note that this "mounting concern" referred to the people who bought their stock, not to people losing their homes.)

In its SEC filing dated September 21, 2008, Goldman Sachs was equally optimistic: "In recent weeks, particularly in view of market developments, Goldman Sachs has discussed with the Federal Reserve our intention to be regulated as a bank holding company. We understand that the market views oversight by the Federal Reserve and the ability to source insured bank deposits as providing a greater degree of safety and soundness. We view regulation by the Federal Reserve Board as appropriate and in the best interests of protecting and growing our franchise across our diverse range of businesses."[11]

John J. Mack, the chairman and chief executive of Morgan Stanley, echoed his company's competitor, saying, "This new bank holding structure will ensure that Morgan Stanley is in the strongest possible position—to seize opportunities in the rapidly changing financial marketplace."[12] Don't you just love it? Not the rapidly imploding one, the rapidly *changing* one. Not to contain risk, but to seize opportunities.

Yet somehow the media pitied Goldman Sachs and Morgan Stanley, as if these once valiant warriors were forced to succumb to powers greater than themselves, only to be rendered mere commoners.

Indeed, it was unsettling that the *Wall Street Journal* bought Goldman Sachs's and Morgan Stanley's line about regulation being a necessity, with the paper concluding that Wall Street's image of investment bank gods was a thing of the past. It conjured images of dying roses, their parched stems on vines scorched by an unnatural summer heat. The financial media's empathy served to mask the true dangers behind the move these investment banks were making, one that would have lasting repercussions.

Let me just break down the first few paragraphs in the Fed's initial article on the BHC move so that you can hear the violins:

> The Federal Reserve, in an attempt to prevent the crisis on Wall Street from infecting its two premier institutions, took the extraordinary measure on Sunday night of agreeing to convert investment banks Morgan Stanley and Goldman Sachs Group Inc. into traditional bank holding companies.

In other words, the Federal Reserve is Batman and it rushed in to save Morgan Stanley and Goldman Sachs, the two most important firms in Gotham City.

> With the move, Wall Street as it has long been known—a coterie of independent brokerage firms that buy and sell securities, advise clients and are less regulated than old-fashioned banks—will cease to exist.

So, we're supposed to believe the difference between Goldman Sachs and the West Main Street Bank of Hicksville has now been erased.

> Wall Street's two most prestigious institutions will come under the close supervision of national bank regulators, subjecting them to new capital requirements, additional oversight, and far less profitability than they have historically enjoyed.[13]

So, Goldman Sachs and Morgan Stanley were not only premier, they walked on water. And now these bastions of superior finance will have to be monitored and might make less money. If you believe that it'll work out that way, I have some credit default swaps I'd like to sell you.

The Fed might not have questioned the lasting impact of its decisions to turn every capital-starved institution into a BHC, but there were other external voices of concern regarding the banks' true intentions going forward. "These are strong competitors who take advantage of loopholes," said economist Gary Dymski. "Companies may approach risk cautiously during the current economic crisis, but how is it going to be ten years from now?"[14]

Nouriel Roubini, the chairman of the RGE Monitor and a professor of economics at New York University, told the *Financial Times* that the financial supervisory system "relied on self-regulation that, in effect, meant no regulation; on market discipline that does not exist when there is euphoria and irrational exuberance; on internal risk management models that fail because—as a former chief executive of Citigroup put it—when the music is playing you gotta stand up and dance."[15]

Proof of the investment banks' slyness came six months after their BHC approvals, when Goldman Sachs announced on February 4, 2009, that it wanted to repay its $10 billion government bailout as soon as possible, because the government was cramping its style.[16]

As David Viniar, chief financial officer at Goldman Sachs, put it at a Credit Suisse Group conference in Naples, Florida, "Operating our business without the government capital would be an easier thing to do. . . . We'd be under less scrutiny and under less pressure."[17]

Investors and traders were gleeful when they heard that news. Goldman shares jumped more than 6 percent that day, which just goes to show that "the market" (meaning its speculative stock traders) will never learn from its screwups. No matter how expensive the consequences, risky practices will be rewarded more than government regulations are. It defies logic.

Indeed, as Goldman Sachs CEO Lloyd Blankfein wrote in a February 8, 2009, op-ed article for the *Financial Times*: "Taking risk completely out of the system will be at the cost of economic growth. Similarly, if we abandon, as opposed to regulate, market mechanisms created decades ago, such as securitization and derivatives, we may end up constraining access to capital and the efficient hedging and distribution of risk, when we ultimately do come through this crisis."[18] But then, no one expects Blankfein to constrain future profit potential. If you control the system, you assume you can sidestep its risks or squeeze the public to pay for the damage. It was up to the same Fed that said Goldman Sachs could step under the cheap federal assistance tent to do some regulation. But, in opening its books to extend mega-loans to these new quasi-BHCs, it demonstrated—loud and clear—that it would not.

Not Only Investment Banks Can Be Banks

The reaction of most citizens to the barrage of news about bailout bucks flying to various banks like paper clips to a desk magnet is usually, "Hey, can I get my own bailout?" No. Not a dollar, a dime or even a cent. But if you're a corporation with a good legal team, you can get an affirmative answer—as we've seen, it merely takes a little name change.

American Express was one of the first companies to follow Goldman Sachs's and Morgan Stanley's lead. On November 10, 2008, it, too, jumped on the Bank Holding Company Bailout Bandwagon.[19] Chairman and CEO Kenneth Chenault spelled out the reason for the name change in a prepared statement. "Given the continued volatility in the financial markets," he said, "we want to be best positioned to take advantage of the various programs the U.S. government has introduced or may introduce."[20]

He said this without a trace of self-consciousness, even as American Express reported a 23 percent drop in third-quarter profits and announced it would chop 10 percent of its workforce.[21] Even worse, its fourth-quarter earnings were down 72 percent versus the same quarter in 2007.[22] The move also didn't immediately help American Express's share price, which dropped a few days after the BHC announcement to its lowest value since April 1997.[23]

Still, at least American Express is sort of like a bank, in that many of its customers are normal citizens. But then there's this: its separate subsidiary, American Express Travel Related Services Co., Inc., got BHC status, too. This unit books high-class holidays, resort hotel excursions, and other *travel* activities. Its Web site boasts of luxury vacations in resorts with "lofty marble entrance halls" and "luxurious suites on 22 acres of tropical gardens," "award-winning cuisine," "a pampering spa, and almost every land and water-sport imaginable."[24] A BHC can offer all that? Really?

Sure, the American Express subsidiary handles money, but so does everyone else in the country. To explain its decision, the Fed repeated, "Emergency conditions exist that justify expeditious action on this proposal."[25] What, someone had to rush off to Cabo, ASAP? Actually, it was less silly than it seemed, because travel agents had gotten the go-ahead in the Gramm-Leach-Bliley Act to claim status as financial institutions.[26]

Six weeks later, American Express's BHC status paid a nice dividend when it announced it'd be getting a $3.9 billion belated Christmas gift from TARP. The money arrived on January 13, 2009, the same day that forty-two other banks received a total of $11.4 billion.[27]

In general, the Federal Reserve was only too willing to approve BHC requests—and it complied fast, which is the scary part. The normal BHC application process takes about thirty days.[28] In American Express's case, it took four.[29] Simply put, TARP was the best deal in town. All that a firm in trouble had to do was change its status, apply, and cash its billion-dollar checks. The bandwagon quickly evolved into a crowded bus, as everyone wanted to be a BHC. On November 15, 2008, loan servicer Ocwen Financial Corp. applied to the Dallas Federal Reserve to purchase Kent County State Bank and become a BHC.[30] On December 8, 2008, Capmark Financial Group Inc. applied to become a BHC (as well as to TARP). But in February 2009, Capmark withdrew its BHC application, and as of June it had not received any TARP money.[31]

Shortly after Capmark put in its BHC application, Discover Financial Services, the fourth-largest credit card company in America (spun off from its former parent Morgan Stanley in June 2007), got approval to become a BHC. It had been the last stand-alone consumer credit card company in the United States after American Express.[32]

Century-old commercial lender CIT Group became a BHC on December 22, 2008, and bagged $2.33 billion worth of TARP dollars on New Year's Eve.[33] Its stock had lost more than 80 percent of its value in 2008.[34] It came to the government for more in July 2009.

After execs for the big three automakers made an embarrassing plea for TARP bailout funds in front of the U.S. Senate Committee on Banking, Housing, and Urban Affairs on November 18, 2008, and a second plea on December 4, 2008, GM decided to take the easiest route of all.[35]

So it applied for its financing arm, GMAC, to become a BHC. And sure enough, on Christmas Eve 2008, GMAC got Federal Reserve approval to become a BHC.[36] Again, the Federal Reserve granted the application on an emergency basis, because of the "economic crisis." GM had been green-lighted for up to $13.4 billion in emergency loans a week earlier, on December 19, 2008. GM subsidiaries bagged another $6 billion from the TARP Automotive Industry Financing Program (AIFP) on December 29, 2008.[37] Three days later, Chrysler Holding LLC got $4 billion from the AIFP, plus the firm got an additional $1.5 billion to finance new auto loans on January 16, 2009.[38]

But even with taxpayer billions, the auto executives couldn't get their companies on track. President Obama announced in late March 2009 that Chrysler and GM submitted subpar restructuring plans and were not worthy of more government help, while the administration simultaneously ousted GM CEO Rick Wagoner.

"Neither GM nor Chrysler is viable and deeper sacrifices must be made, the White House indicated Sunday, setting the stage for a crisis in Detroit that will dramatically reshape the nation's auto industry," the Associated Press reported on March 30, 2009.[39] As of late April 2009, the Treasury had poured a total of $32.7 billion in total loans to General Motors, GMAC, Chrysler Holding, and Chrysler Financial to help the firms avoid bankruptcy and that old "systemic risk" problem.[40] Still, Chrysler LLC filed for bankruptcy on April 30, 2009, announcing a merger with Fiat, which got 20 percent control of the new company.[41]

And it got worse. On June 1, 2009, GM declared bankruptcy and along with it, received $30 billion more in federal funds. So, all told, GM, GMAC, Chrysler Holding, Chrysler Financial, and New CarCo LLC (the entity the government created to deal with the auto mess) sucked up $92.4 billion in public money by the middle of 2009.[42] And it wasn't over. Just two days after GM went under, GMAC, its financial arm, got to take on $4.25 billion in additional debt! Try going to a bank and asking for a million-dollar loan because you can't pay off your college degree or your health-care bills, and see how long it takes for the loan managers to stop laughing. Then in one of the fastest ever large bankruptcies, GM came back to life on July 10, 2009.[43] It shed thousands of jobs in the process.

What the Fed Created, the FDIC Cleaned Up

All of this quick reposturing and loosening of federal protocol allowed big (and even not-so-big) finance firms a legal avenue to get just about as much capital as they wanted. The government's fast-and-easy money policy demonstrated two things. First, that the government was so scared it might upset the already weakened banking system that instead of slowing down the process by which firms could access its money, it let the Fed—the chief bank regulator—invite more firms to hang out under the federal bailout tent. Second, that the government didn't stop to consider the consequences of all of this nominal reclassification.

Big Finance, as we've seen, won out. It got its much-needed capital, new legal titles that allowed it to access ever more capital, and knowledge that fear was a good way to simultaneously extract money and enact deregulation. It was almost the polar opposite of the government's approach in 1933. The public lost this time around, and it was perfectly legal.

While the Fed was creating new banks that would be backed by the FDIC, and the Treasury was doling out TARP money, the FDIC was, in fact, in the business of contraction, a more sensible reaction to failure. In 2008, the FDIC closed twenty-five banks. Included was Pasadena-based IndyMac, which first ran into trouble in late 2007 when it couldn't find a buyer for a chunk of its Alt-A mortgage loans. Alt-A loans are rated one step up from subprime.[44]

By the end of June 2008, customers were lining up in front of IndyMac, pulling out $1.3 billion in deposits as if it was 1929.[45] Senator Charles Schumer's (D-NY) June 26, 2008, comment that IndyMac was having "serious problems" didn't help.[46] The FDIC took over the bank on July 11, 2008. It enlisted Lehman Brothers to find an acquirer, but considering that Lehman went bankrupt a couple of months later, that didn't work out so well.[47]

After cleaning up and restructuring loans on behalf of homeowners, the FDIC left the new, healthier IndyMac to private equity vultures. In early January 2009, the FDIC agreed to sell IndyMac to IMB HoldCo LLC, a thrift holding company owned by a group of private equity investors, led by former Goldman Sachs partner Steven T. Mnuchin of Dune Capital Management LP, for about $13.9 billion.[48] The deal closed on March 19, 2009, with IMB putting together a federal savings bank called OneWest Bank to officially make the purchase, and the FDIC taking a $10.7 billion loss.[49]

The idea that a bank that dealt primarily with a community of customers could be revamped to be the ward of a private equity firm with no desire to run a bank but every desire to restructure it and make a profit after FDIC interventions, doesn't bode well for the future regulatory oversight of the banks the FDIC seizes. Once the FDIC sells them off with no strings attached the resulting institutions would technically become private entities—until the private equity firms decide to turn them public.

By February 2009, the FDIC itself had to ask for a bigger credit line to stay alive through the onslaught of expected bank failures, which it had initially pegged on October 7, 2008, at a cost of $40 billion through 2013.[50] So, the FDIC's chief operating officer John F. Bovenzi testified at a House hearing on February 3, 2009, that the FDIC needed to triple its line of credit from the Treasury Department from $30 billion to $100 billion.[51] But as bank conditions deteriorated more quickly in early 2009, the FDIC requested an extended credit line of up to $500 billion,[52] which was authorized on May 20, 2009, and good until the end of 2010.[53]

If You Can't Beat Them, Buy Them

The extra credit came none too soon for the FDIC. By mid-July 2009, it was taking over its fifty-third failed bank for 2009. This milestone brought the total number of failed banks during 2008 and 2009 to seventy-nine.[54] The last time the bank landscape saw anywhere near as many bank failures was during the Savings and Loan (S&L) Crisis, which kicked into high gear in 1988.[55] The government established the Resolution Trust Corporation (RTC) to dispose of the toxic assets acquired from the period's failed institutions, all 1,043 of them (although keep in mind that twenty years of industry consolidation meant that the failed institutions of the Second Great Depression were a lot bigger than they were in the 1980s).[56] Estimates on the total loss of the RTC fiasco to taxpayers ranged from $125 billion to $350 billion.[57]

The difference was that the S&L assets were simple while the toxic assets that grew and festered before the Second Great Bank Depression were complex. With the S&L Crisis, you could at least understand which asset related to which property. There weren't the oodles of layers and leverage that their progeny had two decades later.

For the banks that lived through the S&L storm, the Second Great Bank Depression was another test, one for which government assistance would be a lifeline. Outside of the loan-based banks, the investment banks that leveraged the packaged loans, and the supermarket commercial banks that did both, there was another breed of financial institution: the stand-alone insurance company.

By early 2008, they were finding that without adequate capital (read: actual money from actual people) to see them through their rapidly depleting reserves, they were facing extinction, and not all would be as lucky as AIG, which so far has gotten $182 billion in government help.[58] Still, insurance companies had to turn to Uncle Sam for anything they could get. Because they couldn't even bend themselves enough on paper to become BHCs, the other way to qualify for the TARP was by gaining status as savings and loan (S&L) companies. Indeed, even though we all knew AIG as a mammoth insurance company, it has technically been an S&L since 1999, when it bought a little S&L in Newport Beach, California.[59] That's the little loophole through which it bagged all of the public money.

On January 8, 2009, insurance companies Hartford Financial Services Group Inc. and Lincoln National Corp. got approval from the Office of Thrift Supervision (OTS), an office of the U.S. Treasury that regulates and supervises the thrift industry, to acquire *existing* S&Ls and become thrift holding companies.[60]

The 198-year-old Hartford Financial Services Group had needed life support ten weeks earlier, when on October 30, 2008, it posted its worst quarterly loss ever, and its stock lost more than half of its value.[61]

This stunning plummet prompted its chairman and CEO Ramani Ayer to try to calm the market, stating, "Volatile credit and equity markets and the largest catastrophe in the past three years significantly affected our results. . . . The Hartford is financially strong with the liquidity and capital to meet our commitments to our customers."[62]

In early November 2008, despite holding out his hat for TARP money, Ayer again accentuated the positive, "The Hartford is financially strong and well capitalized."[63] By early February, he was still singing the firm's praises in a letter to his shareholders, saying, "We finished 2008 well capitalized and well prepared to meet our commitments to our customers."[64]

In order to apply for TARP money, institutions had to prove they had some assets, and if they didn't, they had to buy other banks that did.[65] So, Hartford applied to acquire the Florida-based Federal Trust Bank for $10 million.[66] Lincoln National also applied to become an S&L holding company with the Office of Thrift Supervision, and it simultaneously agreed to acquire Newton County Loan and Savings Bank and applied to TARP for money.[67]

Buying these thrifts allowed insurers to qualify as S&L holding companies and made them eligible for TARP funds. The payoffs were huge. Hartford's $10 million acquisition of Sanford, Florida–based Federal Trust Corp. entitled it to up to $3.4 billion of TARP capital.[68] Lincoln National's takeover of Newton entitled it to up to $3 billion, even though Newton County Loan and Savings Bank had only three full-time employees and $7.3 million worth of assets.[69]

Hartford and Lincoln had followed the lead of two other insurance firms that had applied for acquisition approval from the OTS: Genworth Financial Inc., which had asked to buy the Inter Savings Bank; and Aegon NV, a Dutch firm that owns U.S. insurer Transamerica, which asked for permission to acquire Suburban Federal Savings Bank.[70] On December 15, 2008, Aegon withdrew its application for participation in the TARP, as well as its application to the Office of Thrift Supervision to get a thrift charter.[71] Suburban Federal failed on January 30, 2009. Its deposits were passed to another buyer, the Bank of Essex of Tappahannock, Virginia.[72] Genworth filed its S&L holding company application on November 16, 2008. Three weeks later, Genworth announced it had reached an agreement with InterBank to help secure its TARP funds.[73] Just as the Fed was giving out BHC status with lightning speed, the Office of Thrift Supervision was doing the same for insurance companies that were buying thrifts in order to become S&L applicants.

It didn't stop there. By early February 2009, the whole life insurance industry was trying to get access to TARP money, including two of the largest U.S. life insurers, MetLife and Prudential Life, which had been big investors in the collateralized debt obligation (CDO) market and needed government help to survive the consequences.[74] MetLife claimed in February 2009 that its CDOs lost only $15 million because of subprime loan losses.[75] Prudential's Fixed Income Management had been an early CDO participant (starting in 1991) and a leading manager in the arena of packaged securities. The firm has managed twenty CDOs since entering the CDO market in 2000, totaling $9 billion in CDO capital, including debt and equity participation. It was selected to take over as manager for eight other CDO deals. According to Standard & Poor's, Prudential was one of the world's biggest CLO (collateralized loan obligation—another version of CDO) managers.[76]

The Stage Is Set for Déja Vu

TARP and the other means by which the federal government poured out our generosity to the banking sector led to quick mergers and more bailout access for an array of financial companies that never should have gotten federal backing, from speculative investment banks to risk-taking life insurance companies that had invested too much in securities that were too good to be true. But the federal response to all of their grief was monetary assistance and a shocking lack of prudence, rather than taking the opportunity afforded by their weakened state to administer real reform. Thus, the stage remains set for a repeat occurrence of the Second Great Bank Depression.

Why? The reason is terribly simple. History, particularly the Great Depression, has taught us that the desire to make money or gain power breeds bad habits. Yet our country is built on the premise that making money is on par with our inalienable right to pursue happiness.

And the recent actions of our government have only strengthened the urge—and the ability—for financial firms and the political leaders who stack the decks in the financial firms' favor to make money and become very, very happy.

The BHC/FHC issue may seem complex, but the takeaway is that when the Gramm-Leach-Bliley Act repealed the Glass-Steagall Act in 1999, which we will discuss in greater detail in chapter 6, it also opened the door for a variety of more complicated financial firms, ones that pursue a range of activities that have nothing to do with consumers or public welfare, to prosper from less government regulation. Again, it's all perfectly legal.

The Federal Reserve and the Office of Thrift Supervision—the regulating agencies that are supposed to safeguard the public by keeping an eye on these BHCs and S&Ls—created an unstable environment in which more players needed to be watched. By not considering the consequences of their approvals, they allowed financial firms to easily become BHCs and insurance companies to become S&Ls when they should have exercised their ability and responsibility to say no. AIG became one of the most extensive and complex S&Ls, and would ultimately conspire with its regulators to extort hundreds of billions of dollars of public money. That's a recipe for future disasters. So the stage is set for more government bailouts because any financial firms left standing, particularly ones that have the government-sponsored stamps "BHC" and "FHC," will be able to engage in every single one of the behaviors that led to the Second Great Bank Depression, even while being floated by government (read: public) money. That's a very precarious position for all of us.

4

Government Sachs

Hence that general is skillful in attack whose opponent does not know what to defend; and he is skillful in defense whose opponent does not know what to attack.

> —*Sun Tzu*,
> The Art of War

If Machiavelli's Prince had worked on Wall Street, he would have been the CEO of Goldman Sachs. In corporate America, money and power are commensurate with the prestige of the firm—and the prestigious firms have the most intense internal politics. Wall Street is built on a culture of corporate warfare, not the stereotype of frat boys challenging one another to beer pong tournaments, but a grueling daily struggle to navigate a limitless sea of competition. In this environment, the successful warriors work tirelessly to position themselves for every opportunity, catapulting over the weak, fending off opponents, and always—always—forming alliances with those who might prove useful later on.

In Wall Street's corporate conquest, no one has been more dominant than the men—and yes, they are, to date, all men—of Goldman Sachs. The list is impressive: Stephen Friedman, Robert Rubin, Jon Corzine, and Henry Paulson. These are just some of the more recognizable names of men who have triumphed at Goldman Sachs, who made enormous sums of money in the process, and who, even more importantly, used their Goldman Sachs alliances to parachute into positions of enormous global political influence. If we are to understand the men behind our current mess, there is no better place to begin than the hallowed halls of the "gilded firm."

It's not as if these men were a group of conspirators actively plotting to take over the world. Instead, they appeared to be instinctive opportunists. As each left for formidable careers outside of Goldman Sachs, the ones left behind had a shot at the top of the firm. They were bound by loyalty laced with a primal drive for power. One former partner called them "pragmatists." The most prominent of these financial-political barons combine to constitute the formidable base of Goldman Sachs prowess.

During the latter part of 2008, former senior Goldmanites were liberally sprinkled across the nation's top financial firms and federal departments. Robert Rubin was a senior adviser at Citigroup (the biggest U.S. bank until October 2008, when it was surpassed by JPMorgan Chase).[1] John Thain was CEO of Merrill Lynch, and just before that, he had run the New York Stock Exchange, after serving as co-president of Goldman Sachs. Under his leadership, Merrill would be merged with Bank of America to create a new behemoth bank. Bob Steel was heading Wachovia, Jon Corzine was running New Jersey, Stephen Friedman was chairing the New York Federal Reserve (and is still on the board of Goldman Sachs), and Hank Paulson was heading the U.S. Treasury. And there was Lloyd Blankfein, who was running Goldman Sachs. These are just the Goldman elite in the United States, and we are not even counting the Goldmanites they employed.

To a large extent, these guys have operated on the borderline of ethics, though it's likely they don't spend a lot of time pondering ethical quandaries. For instance, in December 2008, as Friedman led the New York Fed toward an unprecedented restructuring of the banking industry, which left Goldman in a cushy condition relative to its former competitors, he bought 37,300 shares of Goldman stock, the value of which increased by $1.7 million several months later. Although Friedman resigned on May 7, 2009, he said he had seen "no conflict whatsoever in owning [those] shares."[2] He had merely bought them because they were trading at a low price. Which is savvy investing strategy, to be sure, but borderline unethical when your decisions can influence the price of that stock.

It may be that I have looked for Goldman links to the Second Great Bank Depression because I worked there. But it's hard to deny their predominance. Whether it was created by luck or by design, you can decide. You know where I stand.

Oh, the Status

Unless you've been embraced into the bosom of Goldman Sachs, even for a brief spate of time, it's hard to fully grasp its "culture of excellence."[3] It's like Harvard, the *New York Times*, the Senate, and the New York Yankees all rolled into one. Once you drink the Kool-Aid and manage not to spit it out, you really do begin to think you're better than everyone else—that the entitlement bestowed upon you is somehow your destiny. For some people, life at Goldman Sachs cultivates a subconscious sense of *smug*. This smugness is essential to understanding why so many of the Goldmanites in power feel above explaining their actions to the public or expressing anything that might look like contrition or humility.

I can't deny that when I was first offered a job there I felt that I had arrived on Wall Street. But for a select few, getting into Goldman is much more than a fleeting rush; it's a path to extreme wealth, power, and influence over everyone else.

Goldman prides itself on the pedigree of its people (Ivy League–educated, well-connected, Washington ties not mandatory but a plus, and so on).

It turns out, though, I'm not much for Kool-Aid.

I did not leap from my old position at Goldman Sachs to a plum spot in the U.S. government. Henry Paulson did not call on me to run TARP. And I now make as much in one year as Lloyd Blankfein made in a few hours in 2007. So I'm a little in awe of the power that certain men from Goldman Sachs have garnered through the years. But I also find that power to be incredibly misplaced. The pursuit of power, though integral to many Wall Street firms, was so ingrained at Goldman Sachs that it made me feel disdainful more than anything else.

To give you an example of the mind-set: two days after 9/11, Goldman's then CEO Paulson sent out a corporatewide voice mail. In a deep throaty tone that would five years later be known to all of America, he stressed how "the people of Goldman Sachs" would persevere. As if the company was a country.

It's not that other Wall Street firms don't breed the same propensity for excess among their anointed executives or rung-climbers; it's simply that Goldman Sachs bred it better and spread it wider. How else can one explain why Goldman's former copresident John Thain spent $1.2 million on his new office at Merrill Lynch? On second thought, who doesn't need a $87,000 area rug, a $26,000 pedestal table, or a $68,000 nineteenth-century credenza, not to mention a $1,400 "parchment waste can," when you want to give your new office that "home-like" ambience?[4] Oh wait, Thain bought all that junk while the firm was combusting.

Thain, Paulson's protégé, shot into the top slot at Merrill Lynch in December 2007, the first time in Merrill's history that an outsider nabbed that job.[5] But the firm had just posted a record $8.4 billion of write-downs, plus, it had already laid off 3,300 people that fall.[6] That Thain thought a colossal office renovation would be a fitting first task merely underscores his mental separation from reality.

Six months later, under Thain's tutelage, Merrill Lynch racked up its fourth consecutive quarterly loss, of $4.9 billion. From July 2007 to July 2008, Merrill Lynch lost an average of $52 million a day.[7] You'd think that would concern the man in charge. The only thing Thain forgot to buy was a fiddle to play while Merrill was burning.

Genius or Really Lucky?

Recent events have only solidified Goldman's superior status and comparatively high stock price relative to its competitors. In late 2006, Goldman CFO David Viniar laid down the gauntlet to lessen Goldman's exposure to risk, stressing the need to reduce its mortgage-related securities positions and buy insurance protection against future losses.[8] The firm bought protection in the form of credit default swaps, whose costs increased as demand for them did; in that way, Wall Street sensed a crisis before it became widely known to the rest of the world and the industry's regulators. As it turned out, many were purchased from the notorious AIG.[9]

Viniar's decision was prescient, though, because in two years these securities would ruin several of Goldman's key competitors. Akin to giving the finger to its rivals, Goldman stock hit its stride the day after Merrill's CEO E. Stanley O'Neal got thrown to the corporate curb with a securities and retirement package worth $161.5 million.[10] O'Neal snagged a board director spot less than three months later with Alcoa, the global aluminum producer.[11]

In late 2007, just as many firms became more and more entangled with collateralized debt obligations (CDOs)—those alluring agents of our country's financial meltdown—Goldman took the opposite tack, sort of. Its mortgage department was still churning out CDOs to clients while the trading group was selling similar products to get them off its books. In other words, Goldman was creating with one hand the very securities that the other hand was trying to dump.

Two Goldman traders in the structured-products trading group, Michael Swenson and Josh Birnbaum, backed by their boss, Dan Sparks, had bet that the value of subprime-related securities would drop. They booked $4 billion on that bet, which made up for half of the mortgage-related losses the firm was facing that year.[12]

Also, in 2007, while Citigroup and Merrill Lynch were tossing out their chief executives, Goldman hit record profits and paid Lloyd Blankfein a total compensation worth $70.3 million—the second-highest ever for a Wall Street CEO.[13] (John Thain topped the chart that year, having worked for only one month at the helm of Merrill Lynch. His total compensation, including stock and option awards, was valued at $83 million.)[14] Goldman generated record earnings of $11.6 billion.[15]

Goldman continued to leave its competitors in the dust during 2008, although its profits certainly took a hit as the credit crisis deepened and liquidity in the trading markets dried up. When Bear Stearns collapsed in March 2008, investors kept their faith in Goldman shares.[16] Goldman was like the roadrunner—unstoppable. Even as Goldman's quarterly earnings per share plummeted 53 percent versus the same quarter a year earlier, and the firm wrote off $2 billion in residential mortgages and leveraged loans, it still managed to maintain its competitive sheen.[17]

The media's enthusiasm for the firm certainly didn't hurt. CNBC's *Mad Money* host, Jim Cramer, who began his career on Wall Street in the 1980s at—drum roll, please—Goldman Sachs, held Goldman stock in his charitable trust and promoted the stock on his buy list as late as

March 24, 2008.[18] Of course, Cramer was infamously bullish on Bear Stearns a couple of weeks before its demise. In response to a viewer question about the firm on March 11, 2008, he responded—or rather, in his inimitable style, he yelled—"Don't move your money from Bear! That's just being silly. Don't be silly!"[19]

Five days later, JPMorgan Chase agreed to take over Bear Stearns, for $2 per share.[20] As I explained earlier, this takeover only happened thanks to strong-arming from Paulson's Treasury Department, coupled with the Federal Reserve agreeing to back Bear's worst assets.[21] As Bear Stearns was plunging into a financial abyss, many employees clambered for spots at Goldman Sachs, in a Wall Street version of the movie *Sleeping with the Enemy*. Needless to say very few Bear Stearns alumni made it into the gilded firm—yes, Wall Street gerrymandering is war. Even fewer Bear alums—namely, zero—have become treasury secretary of the United States. Of course, not all of Wall Street's animals are created equal. As the pigs make clear in Orwell's *Animal Farm*, "Some animals are more equal than others."[22]

Mentors and Kings

Goldman's influence during the Second Great Bank Depression spans a number of its former leaders who are still very active in federal politics. Robert Rubin began his career at Goldman in 1966.[23] Stephen Friedman joined the firm the same year and became a partner seven years later. From there, Friedman ascended to the vice chairman and co–chief operating officer spot in 1987 beside Rubin. Friedman then served as cochairman, again alongside Rubin, from 1990 to 1992 and as sole chairman from 1992 to 1994 after Rubin left to become President Clinton's first director of the National Economic Council.[24] Friedman would later occupy the same post under George W. Bush.[25] The parallel paths of the two men, which would take them through the company's ranks and into the top realms of politics, are illustrative of Goldman's fundamental importance to the current crisis.

In January 2008, Friedman became chairman of the board of directors at the New York Fed, the branch of the Federal Reserve Bank that has the closest relationship with Wall Street.[26] As we have seen, these two institutions have been going steady for a while. As I've mentioned, the relationship is so tight, in fact, that while Friedman chaired the New York Fed, he was on the board of directors of Goldman Sachs.[27] For the first year of the Second Great Bank Depression, he was also the boss of soon-to-be treasury secretary Timothy Geithner, who was then president of the New York Fed.[28] Though not in the limelight during the bailout proceedings, Friedman did have a front-row seat, given his position and relationships with the bailout's key players, including his onetime protégé, former treasury secretary Paulson.[29] Friedman was also heavily involved in selecting Geithner's replacement at the New York Fed, William C. Dudley, another Goldman alum. Which makes Friedman one of several Goldmanites in a position to continue to shape the future of Wall Street.

Back in the day, Paulson had challenged Friedman to a wrestling match at a corporate off-site event (business speak for "a boondoggle"). Friedman, a Cornell wrestling team Hall of Famer and Eastern Champion in 1959, pinned Paulson, even though Paulson was bigger and heavier.[30] Perhaps Paulson wisely let his mentor win, especially considering that after Friedman left the helm at Goldman, Paulson ascended to take his old post and the two men remained colleagues during Paulson's Treasury years.

When I was at Goldman Sachs, there was a ritualistic mentee-mentor part of the job. As a managing director, you were assigned someone to mentor. The idea of pulling people up through the ranks and indoctrinating them with your experiences and philosophy is very much a part of Goldman's culture and extends to the greater political arena.

From December 2002 to December 2004, Friedman served as director of the National Economic Council under President Bush.[31] On the other side of the political fence, he retained his position as chairman of the president's Foreign Intelligence Advisory Board and of the Intelligence Oversight Board under President Obama.[32] (One of the joys of our postpartisan era!)

In 1994, Jon Corzine, a protégé of Robert Rubin and, by many internal accounts, one of the "nicer" execs who came from Goldman Sachs, succeeded Friedman as CEO. It was a post that Jon Corzine held comfortably for more than four years, until he started to lose money and talk about taking the firm public. That annoyed the investment bankers, who didn't think they needed public money to put deals together and didn't like the idea of a public anything. So, once Jon Corzine made some more mistakes in 1998, such as extending $300 million toward the bailout of Long Term Capital Management and pushing Goldman Sachs to create a charitable foundation that was more ambitious in size than his partners would have liked, his days were numbered.[33] In a heartbeat, Corzine's friends became his adversaries. As one former Goldman partner put it, "the knives came out."

Corzine's descent was aided by the concurrent rise of the very same investment bankers he had pissed off. During the early and mid-1990s, mergers and acquisitions (M&A) became one of the key moneymaking ventures on Wall Street. The deregulated energy and telecom and banking industries propelled certain M&A specialists on Wall Street to the top of the bonus charts.

Those deals also catapulted a very powerful investment banker, Henry Paulson, to the CEO position at Goldman. Paulson had been the number two man in the firm, reporting to Corzine. He was also a long-time opponent of taking the firm public.[34] Paulson supported Corzine toward the end of his reign only when Corzine agreed to make him a cochairman and co-CEO in June 1998. The two shared ruling honors for a whopping seven months, but things were too crowded for Paulson.[35]

After an ugly power struggle, Paulson pushed Corzine out the door, aided in the hostile takeover by ace dealmaker John Thornton.[36] In January 1999, Paulson assumed the sole CEO slot, propped up by people in the investment banking division who hadn't seen the point of going public. Paulson had agreed with them at first, when it benefited—and solidified—his ascent, but perhaps sensing the need for public money to compete with the growing books of commercial mega-banks, he changed his mind. In exchange for Thornton's assistance, Paulson named him co-president and co–chief operating officer.[37] Thornton took the spots alongside another ambitious young man named John Thain, Corzine's onetime protégé who had defected to join Paulson's coup.[38] (Corzine might have been tempted to be angry about a friendship so shallow that it cost him his job, but it's probably hard to stay mad when the boot came with hundreds of millions of dollars.) Paulson described the management shakeup as an "orderly transition," and by the spring of 1999, Goldman became the Hank, John, and John show.[39]

There was simply no better position in the global banking community than partner at Goldman Sachs as it turned from a private 130-year-old, blue-blood firm to a public company, through a $3.6 billion initial public offering (IPO) on May 4, 1999. On that beautiful, money-scented day, Goldman's shiny new 69 million shares soared from a 53 open to a 70⅜ close.[40] This meant that the top 221 partners owned 264 million shares, netting about $63 million per partner.[41] A little more than a week later, on May 13, Robert Rubin resigned his post as Clinton's treasury secretary.[42] Five months after that, he headed back to the private sector, ultimately landing at Citigroup.[43] Perhaps he was envious of his Goldman friends, now rendered cartoonlike with dollar signs for eyeballs.

The IPO itself was done with an air of superior detachment. No media were invited to the usually public glee-fest when Paulson rang the opening bell at the New York Stock Exchange that morning. The only cameras present were from Goldman, and the shocking profits were kept in-house, too. The partners retained 48.3 percent of the shares. Despite having been booted, Corzine remained the single biggest shareholder; his take was $305 million.[44] That fortune came in handy when he mounted one of most expensive Senate campaigns in the country's history to date, 95 percent of which was self-financed.[45] Corzine served as New Jersey senator from January 2001 to 2005, before he became governor, defeating Republican candidate Douglas R. Forrester to take the seat vacated when James E. McGreevey resigned.[46]

Global Flow, D.C. Dollars

People don't get elected to be CEOs or senior executives on Wall Street. There is no translucent democracy here. They win these positions through stealth, posturing, and ruthless combat. From the view at the top of the world's most powerful global bank, it's logical to want to grab the power and ability to shape the world beyond the firm's confines. To go, as it were, global.

One way to do that is to run the world's central banks. On February 1, 2008, former Goldman managing director Mark Carney became the governor of the Bank of Canada (and ex officio chairman of the bank's board of directors) less than five months after the Canadian dollar traded down to par with (equal to) the U.S. dollar for the first time in three decades.[47]

Another way to go global is to run influential international economic consortiums *and* a central bank. Across the Atlantic, Mario Draghi was appointed to be the governor of the Bank of Italy on December 29, 2005, for a six-year term; Draghi had served as vice chairman and managing director at Goldman Sachs International from 2002 until 2005.[48] Considered a proponent of a more open policy toward international investors, Draghi stepped into the job after his predecessor, Antonio Fazio, resigned amid criticism over his handling of a takeover of a major Italian bank, Banca Antonveneta. Fazio had advocated takeover by another Italian bank over bids from international investors.[49]

Draghi's influence extended across the Atlantic into Paulson's Treasury and the Bush administration. When Timothy Geithner was trying to make his international mark on repairing the economic crisis in his opening days as President Obama's treasury secretary, Draghi would prove to be a key international connection.

Draghi was considered the mastermind of a wider G20 plan to diffuse some of the dominant financial control from the United States. He, along with International Monetary Fund (IMF) chief Dominique Strauss-Kahn, designed this plan to boost the IMF and the Financial Stability Forum (FSF) to a more powerful and prominent status in world government. At the G20 summit dinner at the White House on November 14, 2008, as international financial leaders were gathered to discuss the growing global economic recession, Draghi gave the main address. According to the daily Italian newspaper *Il Giornale*, he was the only central banker featured in the photo-op of the twenty-five participants. A day earlier, Draghi and Strauss-Kahn had sent a joint letter to the G20 ministers and governors to specify how they saw the enhanced "roles of [their] respective bodies" going forward.

Although the FSF, founded in 1999, is supposed to focus on global financial regulation among other things, it requires the support of the U.S. government, as do many other world institutions.[50] The problem is that Draghi is the Robert Rubin of Europe, a big proponent of the same kind of deregulation of the international banking system that enables reckless transactions in the United States; his aim is to copy and bring this "freedom" abroad, which has the potential to do no less than infiltrate and bring down the global economy.

Draghi built his financial chops as the director general of the Italian Treasury between 1991 and 2001.[51] He chaired the committee that deregulated the Italian banking system through the Second Banking Directive of 1992, which became part of the Consolidated Law on Banking of 1993. Similar to the Glass-Steagall Act of 1933, the Italian banking system had required that banks be separated into specialized functions since 1936. The Second Banking Directive was followed by the Consolidated Law on Finance of 1998.[52] Both made it possible to merge risky and nonrisky banking activities; these laws paralleled the Glass-Steagall repeal in the United States in 1999.

Draghi also promoted looser stock market rules that allowed hostile takeovers. That philosophy helped him get the Central Bank of Italy governor slot. In early 2009, he proclaimed that tighter regulations were needed, but given his historical bent, it remains to be seen whether these mere words will be converted to action.[53]

Robert Zoellick is another former Goldman Sachs executive who has an influential global role. On May 30, 2007, President Bush nominated Zoellick to replace the scandal-plagued Paul Wolfowitz as head of the powerful D.C.-based World Bank.[54] Treasury Secretary Hank Paulson was prominent in the nomination ceremony. The World Bank, which acts as a lending bank to developing countries, attaches far stricter conditions for these loans than the U.S. government ever attached to TARP money or Fed loans for Wall Street banks.

Zoellick had the Wall Street–Washington revolving door constantly spinning. He assumed office at the World Bank on July 1, 2007, from his post as managing director and chairman of Goldman Sachs's Board of International Advisors Department, where he served from 2006 to 2007.[55] Prior to that Goldman stint, he was Condoleezza Rice's deputy secretary of state. But the deputy role was not something that fit his ambitions. His friends said he felt marginalized there, because his subordinates were managing more of the major international matters related to Iran, Iraq, and North Korea than he was.[56]

At any rate, that position didn't offer him the autonomy or influence that he had when he was a U.S. trade representative. At one point, D.C. buzz had it that Zoellick had been one of the contenders for the treasury secretary position vacated by John Snow in 2006, but as we well know, another Goldman power player, Henry Paulson, became President Bush's pick for the post. So Zoellick trotted over to Goldman.

You know a company is powerful when between the possibility of remaining somewhere in the State Department or returning to Goldman Sachs, the latter offers more of a spark. Bush rewarded Zoellick's global ambitions when he selected Zoellick to head the World Bank.

But why settle for merely controlling money when you can control money *and* have political power? The third way to run the world, in other words, is to exert political power over money. That's what being treasury secretary is for!

Before Goldman alumni Paulson and Rubin moved from the private sector to head the Treasury, Henry Fowler traveled in the opposite direction. He joined Goldman in 1969, following an illustrious career in the political arena that spanned three presidents: Truman, Kennedy, and Johnson. Fowler went from Washington to Goldman, where he remained until he retired in 1980. He guided the firm in developing its international advisors board, of which he remained a member for a number of years after retiring as general partner and from which a number of global economic and financial policy heavyweights have emerged.[57]

Robert Rubin's Always Up to Something

Sometimes the call of Wall Street dollars is louder than the call of public service. Robert Rubin had a much broader impact on the nation as treasury secretary than he did during his tour at Goldman Sachs as cochairman.[58] But he still got to play a part in something pretty big after he left the Treasury.

In July 1999, Robert Rubin abruptly left the Beltway at the height of his prestige.[59] On the day he resigned, after four years as Bill Clinton's treasury secretary, Rubin's explanation was relatively coy: "This has been a remarkable experience, but I was ready to go, ready to return to New York." He said that he had "only some very vague plans about what to do next."[60] Things came into focus on September 17, 1999, when he told the *New York Times* that he would rejoin the financial world "in some fashion and in some serious way."[61]

He wasn't kidding.

Six weeks later, Rubin's plan really sharpened when he nabbed a plum spot at Citigroup. His appointment there happened to come a few days after Congress and the Clinton administration agreed on the most massive piece of banking and financial deregulation in the country's history, the repeal of Glass-Steagall.[62]

That's totally a coincidence, I'm sure.

Citigroup was the big winner in that legislation, and its CEO, Sanford "Sandy" Weill, was one of its strongest corporate proponents in a sea of formidable supporters. Rubin himself said that he played a role in ironing out the bill's final version. But he claimed that had nothing to do with his joining the company that had pushed to break down the barriers that had kept risk away from regular bank depositors' money for decades.[63]

At Citigroup, Rubin received an annual base salary of $1 million and deferred bonuses for 2000 and 2001 of $14 million annually, plus options grants for 1999 and 2000 of 1.5 million shares of Citigroup stock.[64] So, while those sweeping changes to the financial system were being confirmed by Congress, Rubin may not have been in Washington, but he was well placed to reap the rewards.

Using the theories of free market competition, Citigroup lobbyists stressed that the barriers that kept American banks, investment banks, and insurance companies from merging—as their European counterparts were able to—had to be destroyed. Furthermore, the logic went, too much regulation had kept the U.S. banking system from reaching its full globally competitive potential. It was a refrain that had come up repeatedly during Rubin's tenure as treasury secretary.

Rubin went on to do great things—and to make $126 million in cash and stock—over the next decade.[65] Whenever there was a major scandal or crisis brewing, Rubin was there from his vantage point in the bosom of the largest American bank. When Enron and WorldCom flamed out in bankruptcy and disgrace in December 2, 2001, and July 21, 2002, respectively—they'd held the top-two positions of all-time biggest U.S. bankruptcies before being pushed down by Lehman

Brothers and Washington Mutual in September 2008—Rubin was involved behind the scenes.[66]

During that infamous period, rating agencies were criticized for not moving faster to make corporate downgrades when companies' embellished earnings became suspect. (As we've discussed, these same rating agencies returned to the spotlight during the Second Great Bank Depression because they were paid to rate securities for clients who profited from those very ratings. More AAAs meant more sales for a rating agency's clients, and more fees for the rating agency.) Rubin snapped to attention when Moody's Investors Service said it was going to downgrade Enron, whose stock was in a free fall. Citigroup, after all, was a big Enron creditor. Rubin placed a well-timed phone call on November 8, 2001, a month before Enron's bankruptcy, to one of his pals in Washington, undersecretary Peter Fisher, who had been at the New York Fed while Rubin was the treasury secretary.[67] He asked Fisher to call the ratings agencies on behalf of Enron. Fisher declined. Enron's pending merger with Dynegy disintegrated, Citigroup lost the deal, and Enron filed for bankruptcy a month later—leaving Citigroup with lots of unpaid debts.

A spokeswoman for the Treasury later said that what Rubin had actually asked Fisher was "what he thought of the *idea* of Fisher placing a call to rating agencies to *encourage* them to work with Enron's bankers to see *if there is an alternative* to an immediate downgrade."[68] (Italics mine.) An investigation into these calls was launched soon afterward. Rubin was cleared by the Senate Governmental Affairs Committee. He told the Senate staffers that the phone call to Fisher was "not only proper, but I would do it again."[69]

And in one of those gray-area, revolving-door legalities, it was true. But only because Bill Clinton, as one of his last acts as president, canceled an executive order that had prohibited officials from lobbying their own political stomping grounds on behalf of the private sector for five years after leaving office.[70]

Rubin was also dead set against regulating derivatives during his time in Washington. But once these derivatives became the center of the economic disintegration in late 2008, Rubin demurred that he really wasn't against regulation, it was just that his hands had been tied.[71]

Having Influence Means Actually Influencing

The Enron debacle may seem quaint compared to the subprime mortgage craziness, but rest assured, Robert Rubin was in the thick of that crisis, too. The Fed was a bit slow to gauge the true significance of the mortgage mess, as it has been reminded endlessly in the months since. After its regular monetary policy meeting on August 7, 2007, the Fed issued a statement indicating that the economy would continue to expand over the coming quarters:

> Financial markets have been volatile in recent weeks, credit conditions have become tighter for some households and businesses, and the housing correction is ongoing. Nevertheless, the economy seems likely to continue to expand at a moderate pace over coming quarters, supported by solid growth in employment and incomes and a robust global economy.[72]

And with that, Ben Bernanke left interest rates unchanged. It turned out that wasn't so good for Citigroup, which needed access to cheaper money because its losses were mounting. Enter Rubin. Thanks to the records that University of Pennsylvania's Wharton School lecturer Kenneth H. Thomas obtained through a Freedom of Information Act request, we know that Rubin put in a call to Ben Bernanke the next day. The official explanation of the call was that Rubin wanted to tell Bernanke he was doing a good job and that he had made the right decision about not chopping rates.[73]

But ten days later, on August 17, 2007, Bernanke cut the discount rate—the rate the Fed charges banks to borrow money—by half a percentage point to 5.75 percent.[74] It would be the first of a series of cuts that ultimately hacked the federal funds rate—the rate at which banks lend to one another—down to zero and the discount rate to 0.25 percent by December 2008.[75] We, of course, will never know what compelled Rubin to call Bernanke, but we can guess it wasn't simply an irrepressible need to extend a compliment.

At the time, Rubin's former company Goldman was doing much better than Citigroup as the failing subprime markets continued to decrease confidence and credit, and slowly pile up the losses.[76] Goldman, as we saw earlier, had sold its subprime CDO positions. Citigroup, however, had stuck itself in a nasty situation. Sure, Citigroup scooped up fees when it agreed to underwrite the CDOs, but it made the mistake of agreeing to put up 90 percent of the financing to back the CDOs in the event the credit markets dried up.[77] As a result, Citigroup suffered a triple hit: losses on underlying subprime loans, losses on CDOs that contained the loans, and losses on options that it would buy back CDOs from various investors if these exhibited losses over a certain amount.

The Citigroup board kicked out Charles Prince, and Robert Rubin became interim chairman of Citigroup in November 2007.[78] Rubin held the position for a month, before Vikram Pandit stepped in as CEO in December 2007; Sir Win Bischoff slid over to Pandit's chairman slot. Rubin then moved back to his role as chairman of the executive committee of the board.[79]

Despite Rubin's guidance, there was little Citigroup could do but lose money. During 2008, the firm posted billions of dollars of losses and write-downs.[80] In August 2008, Rubin became a "senior counselor" of the firm, relinquishing his role as head of the board's executive committee.[81] Despite TARP capital injections of $25 billion on October 28, 2008, Citigroup shares had hit a thirteen-year low by mid-November.[82] To attempt to remedy the free fall, on November 23, 2008, the Treasury, the Fed, and the FDIC coordinated a seismic guarantee of $301 billion of toxic assets. That same day, the Treasury pumped another $20 billion of TARP money into the firm.[83]

By early 2009, Citigroup was on the financial equivalent of life support. Its decay calls into question the competitive relevance of a big supermarket bank; Rubin's push to bring about the deregulation allowed Citigroup to become too big to succeed. In the whirlwind of criticism surrounding the inability of Rubin and the other executives to keep Citigroup more solvent, Rubin resigned as the firm's senior counselor on January 9, 2009.[84] Citigroup had leveraged a pile of consumer deposits and had become the very prototype of disaster that the Glass-Steagall Act of 1933 had been designed to prevent.

Rubin wrote of his departure, "My great regret is that I and so many of us who have been involved in this industry for so long did not recognize the serious possibility of the extreme circumstances that the financial system faces today."[85]

Yet More Goldmanites in the Mix

Goldman didn't historically feed the government's prestigious spots. But during the last few decades, as men were rising and needed somewhere to go while those below them nibbled at their feet, it became more crucial to carefully weigh one's step beyond the elite Goldman circle. Washington and the political arena offered the same sort of prestige and power, if not the money. But where else would you go, after you've exhausted tens of millions of dollars or so of annual compensation, if not to the Hill?

There was another man whom Paulson plucked from Goldman Sachs to help him out as the economic crisis was growing in the middle of 2008. On July 21, 2008, Goldman Sachs Financial Institution's chairman Kendrick Wilson got the D.C. nod to advise Paulson, his old boss, on the nation's banking crisis, although all of Wilson's experience was in merging and reorganizing banks, not in helping, say, homeowners facing foreclosures. While at Goldman, Wilson advised Bank of America on its takeover of Countrywide Financial, one of a series of dumb, and ultimately very expensive, moves by Ken Lewis, given the deterioration of Countrywide's loan portfolio.[86] He had also been advising Wachovia on what do with its loan portfolio,[87] paving the way for his former Goldman colleague, Robert Steel, who took over the company in July 2008.[88] Chummy, huh? So Wilson took a temporary leave—he didn't even resign!—from Goldman Sachs to advise Paulson on what to do with the country's banking crisis.[89]

Paulson and Wilson had met while they were students at Dartmouth College. It was Paulson who helped recruit Wilson to Goldman, and the pair had been annual bone-fishing buddies in the Bahamas.[90] But Wilson was tied to even bigger fish than Paulson: he had gone to Harvard Business School with George W. Bush. While Wilson was standing in line at an airport north of New York City, he got the call from the Oval Office. Bush urged, "Kenny, your country needs you."

Wilson was considered *the* banker to the banks. "Anyone who is anybody in financial services knows Ken Wilson," said Citigroup's chief financial officer Gary Crittenden at the time.[91] Wilson also received quite a gift for his help to the Bush administration: he got to advise on major Treasury plans for the burgeoning crisis as a "contractor."

But because Wilson wasn't on the regular government payroll, he didn't have to publicly disclose his financial records, including his total stock holdings in Goldman Sachs. Because his holdings are private, it is likely, but not totally clear, that since his stock had lost a lot of value at the time, he kept it in the hopes it would rebound.[92] Even Hank Paulson didn't get that benefit, although in hindsight, Paulson was forced to sell his Goldman stock and options at a much better comparative level. And because he was exempt from paying capital gains tax on the sale, he did okay.[93]

Another man who moved around between the big banks and Washington was Bob Steel, who had retired as vice chairman from Goldman in February 1, 2004.[94] But that was before his old boss needed his help to save the banking system. See, there might be competition between men during their time in the same firm, but once they're on the outside, they know they can trust one another more than anyone else. It just works that way. So when Paulson called on Steel to take the post of Undersecretary of the Treasury for Domestic Finance, there was one answer. Steel was there. He was sworn in on October 10, 2006.[95]

Once in the Beltway, Steel was known as Paulson's closest confidant and was heavily involved in creating the agreement behind JPMorgan Chase's purchase of Bear Stearns in March 2008. Steel was the man who briefed President Bush on the deal and played a crucial role in constructing the Bush administration's policy regarding the mortgage market crisis in early 2008, which included plans to attend to the mounting problems at government-sponsored entities such as Fannie Mae and Freddie Mac.[96]

As it was for Rubin, though, Washington turned out to be an interim career move between two bank positions. On July 9, 2008, Steel resigned from his position, and on the *same day* he went to run Wachovia Bank, at the time the fourth-largest bank in America.[97] The whole arrangement raised the ire of ethics watchdogs. "It's not technically a conflict of interest as long as he didn't work on issues that impact only Wachovia," said Melanie Sloan, executive director of Citizens for Responsibility and Ethics in Washington. "But it smells bad. If one day you're regulating banks and the next day you're at the bank, one has to wonder if the decisions you made at Treasury were in view of future employment options."[98]

When Steel was hired to run Wachovia, the Goldman investment banker relationship came into play once again. At the time, Wilson was advising Wachovia on the strategy and management of the troubled loans in its portfolio. Not surprisingly, that advisory role would be much easier if a former Goldmanite was in charge over there.[99]

On taking over the bank, Steel had pledged to keep Wachovia an independent entity.[100] A few months later, he vowed to sell the bank's noncore assets to raise $5 billion in capital during 2009.[101] Less than two weeks later, the bank posted close to $9 billion in losses for its second quarter.[102] By the time of Steel's hiring, Wachovia stock had already dropped 62 percent from the beginning of 2008.[103]

By early September 2008, it was down nearly 80 percent, and federal officials were pressuring it to cut a deal or face collapse.[104] But there was a glitch. On September 15, financial stocks were in the toilet, Lehman Brothers went bust, and Bank of America got stuck with Merrill Lynch.[105] Yet, Steel told Jim Cramer on *Mad Money* that Wachovia had a "great future as an independent company. . . . But we're also focused on the very exciting prospects when we get things right going forward." Wachovia shares fell 25 percent that day.[106]

With his company's stock in free fall, Steel swung into action the next day. He held a conference call regarding the possibility of selling a chunk of Wachovia or merging with another company. On September 17, 2008, Steel called Morgan Stanley's CEO John Mack to talk about a potential merger.[107] Mack and Steel had both attended Duke University and were on its board of trustees.[108]

Amid all of the chaos, customers were extracting billions of dollars of deposits from Wachovia.[109] This happened during the period that Steel was in merger talks with Citigroup and Wells Fargo.[110] Then things got tricky. First, Wachovia agreed to sell its banking operations to Citigroup, then on October 2, 2008, Wachovia's board said it would sell the full company to Wells Fargo in a $15.4 billion deal.[111] Wachovia shareholders would get $7 a share for their stock, 35 percent lower than the closing stock price on the day Steel was on Cramer's show.[112] No matter, though. Wachovia was headed by Steel. It was also a client of Goldman Sachs, which pocketed a cool $25 million fee for its services in advising the merger.[113]

In late January 2009, a few months after the Wells Fargo deal, it emerged that the SEC was investigating Steel for his *Mad Money* remarks, though no charges have been filed as of this writing.[114] The investigation continues. But it remains to be seen whether Goldman Sachs will take any responsibility for anything negative, despite the firm's fingers being all over the deal—and whether it will be deemed misleading or merely hopelessly optimistic to tout your company's rosy future right before that future changes dramatically.

The End Game

As with any important historical period, hindsight will provide clarity and be subject to interpretation. Each period has its key characters and events. There are only a few choice slots from which you can dominate domestic and global finance. And as it turns out, Goldman occupied many of them leading up to the Second Great Bank Depression. No doubt its imprint will remain, if not increase, going forward. Even if there are fewer Goldmanites in positions of power, the influence they wielded during their tenures at senior banking and political roles will have an impact that will last for decades.

It is human nature to protect what's yours. In the case of the banking world, whatever may have been going on in the minds of the elite Goldman alums, through their words and their actions they protected their individual pots of gold and philosophies at the expense of the general population and the public good. And that's simply not right.

We should ponder another question. Maybe checks and balances for corporate and political leaders are in order to reduce the risk that a small group with a single philosophy or power base has too much control over our financial world and lives.

5

We Already Have a Bad Bank: It's Called the Federal Reserve

Let me issue and control a nation's money, and I care not who writes the laws.

> —*Mayer Amschel*
> *Rothschild, founder of*
> *the House of Rothschild*

In 1941, the investment banker Cyrus Eaton wrote in the *University of Chicago Law Review*, "The doctrine that finance must be the servant rather than the master has been proclaimed before, although it has been increasingly neglected in practice in the United States."[1] Sixty-eight years later, finance was still the master, and the Federal Reserve, the Treasury, and Congress were the servants and coconspirators.

The Fed was the first agency to flex its muscles and open its books, and ultimately on a substantially grander scale than the Treasury ever did, under the auspice of averting a full-fledged financial crisis. In August 2007 the Fed purchased $19 billion of mortgage-backed securities and $19 billion of repurchase agreements, and added $62 billion of temporary reserves.[2] A month later, the Fed injected another $31 billion into the U.S. money markets in three separate operations, later following it with one more round of $20 billion in December. These are all fairly large amounts, but still within the realm of the Fed's normal responsibility to grease the wheels of credit.[3]

(A note on use of the word *injection*—the word conjures medical or druglike images for a reason. The intent of a cash injection into the markets is to stimulate the flow of money, similar to how an adrenaline shot stimulates the oxygen and blood flow in a person. If the injection is strong enough, one may suffice. In the case of the Second Great Bank Depression, multiple injections of cash were required to resuscitate a system that was a willing participant in its own attempted suicide. Call *that* "a cry for help.")

The last time the Fed had to combat freezing credit was after 9/11. Then, it acted in a more subdued way by lowering discount rates and providing loans to the banks affected by the attacks. The idea was to help the system, not to be its mother.[4]

Before the Fed unleashed Operation Print Money for the Banks, it maintained $770 billion of nonrisky Treasury bonds on its books.[5] As the national lender of last resort, the Fed could give financial institutions cash in the form of short-term loans and, in return, these firms would post secure assets, such as Treasury bonds, as collateral. The reason was simple: the sounder the collateral, the better the loan terms for the borrowing bank. It behooved banks to post these highest-quality bonds, so they did.

The Fed would receive interest payments on those Treasury bonds and hand a portion of them back to the Treasury Department as they came in. It was a symbiotic relationship in which the Fed was effectively paying interest on the Treasury's public debt, so that the Treasury didn't have to do it.

That low-risk practice went out the window during the Second Great Banking Depression. As the great bailout unfolded, the complexity of the Fed's books increased in tandem with its appetite for risky, unquantifiable asset- and mortgage-backed securities. The new trend was coupled with an appreciable move toward secrecy. Banks began to post all sorts of junk to the Fed just to get it off their books, and in return they received low-cost loans.

The consolidation of America's money into fewer and fewer banks over the last three decades made the Fed's trashy asset books even worse.

"In 1977 commercial banks held 56 percent of all financial assets. By 2007 the banking share had fallen to 24 percent. The shrinkage meant the Fed was trying to control credit through a much smaller base of lending institutions. It failed utterly—witness the soaring debt burden and subsequent defaults," William Greider wrote in the *Nation* on March 11, 2009.[6] Yet way before anyone could have fathomed the immense scope of the bailout, the Fed had begun to quietly blow up the loan balloon it hoped would quickly sail off with the subprime crisis.

During the winter of 2007, the Fed transformed itself into a sort of pawnshop for banks that needed quick cash; as long as the banks were in decent condition and could collateralize their loans, they could get money at a discount rate, at auction, through the Term Auction Facility (TAF) program—sort of in the same way you can get a $100 loan from a pawnshop by putting up your grandmother's old jewelry.[7] Competition for the money was fierce. Although there were $119 billion worth of requests from 166 bidders, the Fed only gave out $40 billion in its first two December 2007 auctions.[8] Come the spring of 2008, the Fed was blazing through uncharted territory. It had gone above and beyond its official mandate to keep credit flowing through the economy. Again in a very secretive way, the Fed became not only a bank of last resort for the banks, but the biggest hedge fund manager in the world.

A standard hedge fund takes in money or assets and promises to use them to provide a handsome return for the investor through various bets—on housing, oil, weather, whatever. Hedge fund managers make fees, typically 2 percent management fees, based on these returns and the volume of assets they have under management, plus 20 percent performance fees.[9] Hedge funds borrow money against these assets from commercial and investment banks to make even bigger speculative wagers. The thinking goes: the more you bet right, the more money you make. The operative word here is *more*.

So, during a time when banks couldn't give away their nonperforming (banktalk for "toxic") assets at any price, the Fed inhaled trillions of dollars' worth of them and in return issued them debt at interest rates that no normal American would ever get (really low ones).

Because risky assets were sitting on the Fed's books as collateral for loans, the Fed was put in the passive role of hoping the assets' value would turn around someday or that the banks that pawned them off would be able to retrieve them and pay back their loans. A good hedge fund would never allow itself to operate in such a submissive manner. But the Fed doesn't have to worry about positive returns; its supply of money is endless.

Chase Hunts a Bear with the Fed's Rifle

On March 11, 2008, the Fed created the Term Securities Lending Facility (TSLF). The TSLF allowed the Fed to lend banks as much as $200 billion for up to 28 days, rather than the quick-shot overnight loans that had been the standard in the past. Collateral could come in the form of anything with a AAA rating, even though many AAA securities should have been rated as junk.[10] The Fed's evolution into a quasi–hedge fund manager gained steam when it backed a quasi–hedge fund, Bear Stearns, the former investment bank and my former employer. Stepping outside the normal bounds of its authority, the Fed provided the financial backing that allowed JPMorgan Chase to take over Bear Stearns. This move was part of an almost militaristic coup.[11] The Fed's allies in this operation were the Federal Reserve Bank of New York, run by Timothy Geithner; the Treasury Department, run by Henry Paulson; and the Securities and Exchange Commission (SEC), run by Christopher Cox.

The entire process took about two weeks. Stage one began on the evening of Thursday, March 13, 2008, when, according to Tim Geithner's congressional testimony, he took part in a conference call with "representatives from the Securities and Exchange Commission, the Board of Governors of the Federal Reserve, and the Treasury Department."[12]

On that call the SEC staff informed him that "Bear Stearns' funding resources were inadequate to meet its obligations and the firm had concluded that it would have to file for bankruptcy protection the next morning."[13] In other words, the investors had already headed for shore, and the loan sharks, the firms that had lent Bear money backed by tanking collateral, wanted blood.

This situation unleashed a sleepless night of consideration, culminating in a call at the crack of dawn the next day. Geithner, leading the strike, had spent the night poring over options with the Fed and the Treasury. Ben Bernanke, with insistence from Paulson and Geithner, concluded that the Fed would come up with the money to ensure that the deal went through.

JPM Chase head Jamie Dimon was no idiot. If he was going to take Bear on, he didn't want to take on its potential losses, too. He needed government guarantees, and he got them. But later that day, it dawned on JPM Chase and the Fed just how much junk they were dealing with: among other things, securities stuffed with subprime mortgages, credit default swaps, and loans from and to other banks. There was a regulatory catch, too. The Fed couldn't directly lend to Bear because it was an investment bank and was outside the Fed's jurisdiction.

But this problem, too, had a workaround. The New York Fed would extend an overnight loan to JPM Chase from its discount lending window, and JPM Chase could then lend that money to Bear Stearns. This operation would keep the firm afloat while it was prepped for the hand-off to JPM Chase and would help ensure that the deal went through.

Stage two came two days later, but not without some second thoughts. Early in the morning on Sunday, March 16, JPM Chase rescinded its offer to take Bear Stearns. Bernanke leapt into action, boosted by fear that the Asian markets would catch wind of the percolating catastrophe before they opened that night. So he did the unprecedented. He agreed to back Bear Stearns's dying assets if JPM Chase would take the firm. Treasury Secretary Paulson jumped in and advised JPM Chase to offer $2 per Bear share, rather than the $4 it was prepared to offer. He and Geithner also called Bear Stearns chair Alan Schwartz, telling him he had to accept JPM Chase's offer.[14]

Later that evening, Geithner informed James Dimon that the New York Fed would assist the acquisition with $29 billion in financing, backed by Bear Stearns assets.[15] It would also fast-track the necessary regulatory approvals to move the merger forward.

Stage three unveiled the Primary Dealer Credit Facility (PDCF), which was announced the same day that Geithner agreed to put up the cash to back the Bear Stearns deal.[16] Citing a familiar refrain, the Fed created this facility due to the "unusual and exigent circumstances" that "existed in financial markets, including a severe lack of liquidity."[17] The PDCF allowed investment banks to borrow from the

Fed for the first time.[18] It was meant to be a temporary program to provide quick loans that would mature the day after they settled with an interest rate equal to that of the New York Fed primary credit rate.[19] As of this writing, that interest rate is .5 percent.[20] In conjunction with the opening of this facility, as requested by the SEC, New York Fed examiners were supposedly sent to all the major investment banks to report back to the Federal Reserve on the banks' financial conditions. If this in fact happened, it wasn't very effective, given that by the end of 2008, several major banks were on life-support (make that public-bailout-support).

For the most part, when a company acquires another company, it has to come up with the money and take on any risk that the merger might bring. No such thing with the Bear Stearns deal. The government spotted the money and took on the risk for JPM Chase.

The fourth and final stage came on March 24, 2008, when JPM Chase announced that due to employee shareholder protests, the offer would be upped to $10 a share, bringing the price tag to $1.2 billion.[21] In a sign of just how little that really was to pay for one of the nation's most venerable brokerage firms, which had survived as an independent company for eighty-five years through the Great Depression and twelve recessions, former Bear Stearns CEO James Cayne sold his Bear stock—just two days after the deal was completed—for $61 million.[22] Two years earlier, that stock had been worth $1 billion.[23]

Don't feel too bad, though. Most of that stock had been given to Cayne as part of his compensation package, meaning that he didn't directly pay for the shares.[24]

It didn't take long for the government's dealmakers to spin the Bear Stearns takeover as a tough but successful maneuver. "By reducing the probability of a systemic financial crisis, the actions taken by the Fed on and after March 14 have helped avert substantial damage to the economy, and they have brought a measure of tentative calm to global financial markets," Geithner cooed a week and a half after the deal.[25]

Everyone was happy, although the markets hadn't even begun to enter crisis mode at that point. In an understated portent of things to come, Geithner added, "The Federal Reserve, working closely with other major central banks, will continue to provide liquidity to markets to help facilitate the process of financial repair."[26]

Geithner Wasn't Kidding

During the summer of 2008, despite the whole Bear Stearns maneuver, the home mortgage market was coming apart at its foundation. Foreclosure rates nationwide were up 55 percent in August 2008, compared to July 2007, and for the year there were more than 3 million foreclosure filings, an 81 percent increase from 2007.[27] Existing single-family home sales fell to 4.3 million in 2008 from nearly 5 million in 2007, a 12 percent decrease.[28] New one-family home sales fell from 776,000 to 482,000 over the same period, or a decrease of 38 percent.[29] Credit also stopped flowing, as mortgage lenders realized that their existing loans might not be paid and it would be a bad idea to take on more debtors.

Still, thanks to Geithner's soothing words there was an air of calm before the storm on Capitol Hill and in the media—or at least a sense that things were going to get better sooner rather than later. (That unfounded optimism would resurface in the middle of 2009, after much more financial wreckage had occurred, simply because the stock market bounced back for a spell.) The summer of 2008 was the summer of mixed messages. Some of the media balanced the more prevalent and accurate feeling among most Americans that things weren't actually getting better, even as they reported that the government was trying to deflect a greater housing-led crisis with a veneer of altruism.

"If you're a homeowner teetering on the edge of foreclosure, help is on the way. We'll explain what the Senate did for you today in a rare Saturday session," reported CNN anchor Kyra Phillips on July 26, 2008.[30] She was referring to a $300 billion bill that would allow distressed homeowners to refinance their mortgages. The bill, the Housing and Economic Recovery Act of 2008, was signed with a flourish by President Bush four days after that broadcast.[31]

The general message from Washington was that everything would be okay, we're on top of this mess. "We look forward to putting in place new authorities to improve confidence and stability in markets and to provide better oversight for Fannie Mae and Freddie Mac," White House spokesperson Tony Fratto said on the day the bill was signed.[32]

Then there were the higher-profile Washington insiders who traded premature optimism for downright delusion about the actual state of the economy, going so far as to blame the American people for the financial crisis. "You've heard of mental depression; this is a mental recession,"[33] said Phil Gramm, the former head of the Senate Banking Committee who had led the charge for deregulation of the banking and derivatives industries, in a *Washington Times* interview on July 9, 2008.[34]

With a complete lack of empathy, he concluded, "We have sort of become a nation of whiners. You just hear this constant whining, complaining about a loss of competitiveness, America in decline."[35]

Gramm made those clueless comments while he was cochair of John McCain's presidential campaign. It was Gramm's callous representation of an increasingly fearful American population that led to his ouster from the McCain campaign on July 18, 2008, but the damage had been done. McCain, who ultimately bore responsibility for Gramm's viewpoint, appeared out of touch with the economic plight of the country.[36] That apathetic tone may have been the biggest reason McCain did not get elected president.

Despite the grim numbers, the powers that be in the Treasury were dogmatically confident (outwardly, anyway) that they had met and weathered a horrific storm after the Bear Stearns situation. Indeed, Treasury Secretary Henry Paulson was quite insistent that bailing out institutions would certainly not be a pattern.

"For market discipline to constrain risk effectively, financial institutions must be allowed to fail. Under optimal financial regulatory and financial system infrastructures, such a failure would not threaten the overall system," he stated in a July 2, 2008, speech at the Chatham House in London in front of international policymakers.[37]

Paulson reiterated this point to the House Committee on Financial Services eight days later. "Market participants must not expect that lending from the Fed or any other government support is readily available."[38] (Unless he deemed otherwise.)

Paulson applied the same free-market logic to individual homeowners during a July 8, 2008, hearing before the FDIC's Forum on Mortgage Lending to Low and Moderate Income Households, essentially saying that hundreds of thousands of homeowners should likewise be allowed to fail on their mortgages, although he admitted that the fault for the bad loans really lay with the mortgage companies.

"Due to the lax credit and underwriting standards of the past years, some people took out mortgages they can't possibly afford and they will lose their homes," Paulson said with an assassin's calm on July 8. "There is little public policymakers can or should do to compensate for untenable financial decisions." He further argued against government intervention in the mortgage market because an undefined "some" people might make a quick profit by flipping homes.

"Now that their investments have not turned out as they had hoped, these people may walk away, even though they can afford their mortgage payment," he said. "These borrowers can and should be living up to their mortgage commitment—government intervention here would be inappropriate."[39]

Bernanke, meanwhile, was far more constrained in his rhetoric. His remarks around that time focused on revamping regulatory agencies and leaving the door open for more bailouts—something he'd still be doing a year later. "The enormous losses and write-downs taken at financial institutions around the world since August, as well as the run on Bear Stearns, show that in this episode, neither market discipline nor regulatory oversight succeeded in limiting leverage and risk-taking sufficiently to preserve financial stability," he told the same forum.[40] But all his talk of regulation was just that: talk. The worst was yet to come.

Giving Loans against "Non–Investment Grade Securities"

By the fall of 2008, the notion that integral financial institutions should be allowed to fail outright without injections of government cash had evidently been thrown out the window. The Fed was opening more facilities and was lending money left and right using low-grade assets as collateral. Its stated intent was to enhance market liquidity in the face of a dead credit market. In other words, because lenders were holding their money tight, the Fed had to change the rules and start new programs to help increase the free flow of capital, sort of acting like Drāno for a pipe clogged with bushels of hair.[41]

In September 2008 alone, the Fed injected $904 billion into the financial markets. From September 15 to 18, the Fed pumped $125 billion into the financial markets through open-market regulation. On

September 18, the Federal Open Market Committee expanded its currency swap lines by $180 billion to provide liquidity for the U.S. dollar. Eleven days later, the Fed tripled total short-term lending, expanded its credit swap lines again, and noted they expected to hold two TAF auctions that would total $300 billion.[42]

What had started as a housing problem was turning into a far greater credit problem. Despite all the extra cash flowing to banks and the Fed taking on risky assets that were unmarketable to the private sector, loans were still hard to come by. The TAF program was supposed to increase credit flow, but things weren't happening fast enough, so the Fed upped its loan authorization to $900 billion on October 6, 2008.[43] But by the last quarter of 2008, a Fed survey of banks showed that lending standards on commercial, industrial, and consumer loans were still tight and outstanding consumer credit remained nearly unchanged, at about $2.6 trillion.[44] Furthermore, on the business credit side, an overall lack of commercial paper—an unnecessarily vague term for the short-term loans companies use to meet regular operating expenses, such as payroll—caused the Fed to create the Commercial Paper Funding Facility LLC (CPFF). Under the CPFF, the Fed could finance approximately $1.8 trillion worth of commercial paper. For its part, the Treasury Department made a "special" deposit of $50 billion at the Federal Reserve Bank of New York to support this facility.[45] This extra help, by the way—in true nontransparent form—was not mentioned in the press release that introduced the CPFF (nor on the Treasury Web site).[46]

The Fed continued to create a plethora of new facilities identified by cute little acronyms, which were designed to hold riskier collateral than the Fed had ever taken on in the past. (If you want the real scoop on these facilities as they keep unfolding, you can follow them on my Web site, www.nomiprins.com. Details are in the appendix.) There didn't appear to be any orderly rollout or overall plan for these facilities. They seemed to crop up sporadically to deal with that day's or that week's problems.

On September 14, 2008, the Fed allowed noninvestment grade securities to be pledged as collateral at the PDCF, which had been established on March 16, 2008. In February 2009 the PDCF was extended until October 30, 2009.[47]

On September 19, 2008, the Fed created the Asset Backed Commercial Paper Money Market Mutual Fund Liquidity Facility (AMLF) "which extends loans to banking organizations to purchase asset backed commercial paper from money market mutual funds."[48]

Then, the following month, the Fed instituted the Money Market Investor Funding Facility (MMIFF), which along with the AMLF and the CPFF is "intended to improve liquidity in short-term debt markets and thereby increase the availability of credit," and pledged to lend the MMIFF up to $540 billion.[49]

And so, the Fed, working fast and furious, continued its transformation into a hedge fund of last resort, relaxing its collateral posting rules and lending trillions of dollars to the Street. Where banks once had to pony up secure assets such as Treasury bonds to get loans from the Fed, they could now post far more risky assets in return for very favorable loan conditions, and the Fed would keep a lid on who they were, and how much they got.[50]

Remember: That $700 Billion Is the Smallest Part of the Bailout

Even with all the bailout money flowing by the end of September, the Fed and the Treasury were faltering. They couldn't stop the oncoming financial crisis, as the credit and housing markets continued to decline and big banks continued to fail. But, as noted above, the Fed could and did throw trillions of dollars at the banking epicenter of the crisis, announcing "several initiatives to support financial stability and to maintain a stable flow of credit to the economy during this period of significant strain in global markets."[51]

Some argued that the Fed was doing its job to promote liquidity in the system, as explained in its mission statement: "If a threatening disturbance develops, the Federal Reserve can also cushion the impact on financial markets and the economy by aggressively and visibly providing liquidity through open market operations or discount window lending."[52]

But the scope with which it provided loans for lemons was unprecedented. And as we've seen, even before the Emergency Economic

Stabilization Act of 2008, which included the Troubled Asset Relief Program, was passed on October 3, 2008, the Fed was doing its own bailing.[53] Yet there was no Congressional furor about the trillions of dollars of Fed facility programs as the facilities were spawned, so deft was the body in its motions.

Indeed, cloaking the cost of its part of the bailout in business-as-usual language became part of the Fed's strategy. Press releases were designed to accentuate the positives of some new loan facility or drastic liquidity-providing measure, without even admitting the risk it might incur. For instance, on September 29, 2008, the Fed announced a mammoth $780 billion shot into the markets, including $330 billion worth of currency swaps with foreign central banks, was cushioned with reassuring verbosity: "The Federal Reserve announced today several initiatives to support financial stability and to maintain a stable flow of credit to the economy during this period of significant strain in global markets."[54]

With all of Bernanke's stress on the need for more powerful regulatory oversight of the financial arena, the question of just who was regulating the Fed was largely absent. Indeed, the Fed's actions were far less transparent than the Treasury's, which isn't saying much. The Fed created facilities to dole out—or, in Fed-speak, to "lend"—cash to bleeding banks, in return for securities backed by sinking subprime, auto, and consumer loans.

And Bernanke thought that was quite all right; it was just business as usual for the Fed. "Consistent with the central bank's traditional role as the liquidity provider of last resort, the Federal Reserve has taken a number of extraordinary steps," Ben Bernanke said on December 1, 2008, at the Greater Austin Chamber of Commerce in Austin, Texas. "We narrowed the spread of the primary credit rate . . . extended the term for which banks can borrow from the discount window to up to 90 days . . . and developed a program, called the Term Auction Facility, under which predetermined amounts of credit are auctioned to depository institutions for terms of up to 84 days."[55]

Only it *wasn't* consistent with the Fed's traditional role. In fact, it was new to the Fed's range of powers, as Allan Meltzer, a professor of economics at Carnegie Mellon University and the author of *A History of the Federal Reserve*, told the *New York Times*. "If you go all the way back to 1921, when farms were failing and Congress was leaning on the Fed to bail them out, the Fed always said, 'It's not our business.' It never regarded itself as an all-purpose agency."[56]

To some extent, the New York Fed had dabbled in bailouts with the Long Term Capital Management (LTCM) crisis in 1998, mostly because the hedge fund was on the hook for lots of money to various investment banks, not because ordinary people would really be affected—sound familiar? The New York Fed stepped into the role of super-negotiator and organized for a bunch of banks, including Goldman Sachs, Merrill Lynch, JPMorgan Chase, and UBS, to pony up $3.6 billion to buy LTCM and pay off its debts.[57]

Former Fed chairman Alan Greenspan eased monetary policy in order to loosen up the credit markets that were freezing up, in fear of what a LTCM collapse could mean. The difference between the current situation and the LTCM bailout is that the government orchestrated a private buyout of LTCM and didn't use public funds to save a risk-taking fund. Plus, the size of the LTCM bailout was nothing compared to the Second Great Bank Depression bailout. It only amounted, in fact, to the size of Merrill Lynch execs' 2008 bonuses.

Still, the LTCM bailout showed that the Fed was willing to step in to find a way to pay banks back for choosing bad business partners. That precedent was exploited to the max in 2008 and 2009. The Fed's facilities were created with an utter lack of accountability and transparency. Multiple Freedom of Information Act (FOIA) requests to the Fed, seeking details of who used the lending facilities and to what extent, were rejected.

The Silent Coconspirator

Every successful heist requires a diversion from central command. Whatever the size of the loot, the idea is to keep the victims' focus somewhere else. During the Second Great Bank Depression, while we were focused on a $700 billion Treasury bailout package, the Fed used a sleight of hand it had honed for decades to take on trillions of dollars in useless assets, giving cheap loans in return to the very banks that had created the bad assets.

The chairman of the Federal Reserve is sort of like the CEO of money in America. Some chairmen pursue the influence of the position more than others. Alan Greenspan, chairman of the Board of Governors of the Federal Reserve System from 1987 to 2006, was far more involved in politics (and more famous as a result) than his predecessors were. He had been involved in the political sphere as an adviser for Richard Nixon's presidential campaign in 1968 and had served as chairman for the Council of Economic Advisers during Gerald Ford's presidency. He had a propensity for enacting a strong rate policy. He lowered rates in 1997 in response to the Asian currency crisis and hiked rates in 1999 as the U.S. economy and markets were booming. At the turn of the century, he also publicly warned about "unsustainable" growth rates and "overextended" stock prices.[58]

The Federal Reserve Board's official mandate is to maintain stability in the economy while facilitating growth, by keeping the supply of money and the availability of credit balanced. The Fed operates to achieve maximum employment, stable prices, and moderate long-term interest rates. Its principle tool is "printing" money, a process in which the Fed attempts to expand the economy by making cash for lending available by buying banks' securities.

The Fed also regulates banks by setting and monitoring minimum reserve and capital levels (Title 12, part 208, of the Federal Reserve Act, if you want to check it out, something the Fed failed at miserably leading into the Second Great Bank Depression). In addition, during the past two decades, the Fed has been the main okay-nod behind bank holding company mergers.[59] During the end of 2008, the Fed ramped up this role with a vengeance.

According to the Fed's Web site, "Congress created the Federal Reserve System in 1913 to serve as the central bank of the United States and to provide the nation with a safer, more flexible and more stable monetary and financial system." Over the years, the Fed's role in banking and the economy has expanded, but its focus has remained the same. Today, the Fed's three official functions are to conduct the nation's monetary policy, provide and maintain an effective and efficient payments system and to supervise and regulate banking operations."[60]

That's typically covered in the press and by mainstream economists as setting interest rate targets up or down a tiny percentage, which the Fed does to make sure we have enough unemployed people to keep inflation down. Really.

Thus, there are two tools with which the powers in Washington can calibrate the American economy. Congress and the president focus on fiscal policy, which relates to decisions on spending and taxes, while the Fed enacts monetary policy, influencing the flow or availability of money and credit. "Fine-tuning" the economy is how people typically refer to the Fed's actions in raising or lowering interest rates, although it is equally widely acknowledged that "fine-tuning" is not really possible. The Fed's tools include direct lending to banks, if necessary, and setting reserve requirements.[61] The Fed stealthily and massively stretched its scope during the Second Great Bank Depression.

The Federal Reserve was spawned in secrecy, so it's no wonder the notion stuck through the century. During a clandestine meeting at Jekyll Island, Georgia, in 1910, between the richest financiers in the country and their well-connected government official friends, participants discussed the formation of the Federal Reserve, using only their first names as identifiers.[62] With that kind of foundation, it's apparent that the dangers inherent in the Federal Reserve Board were imbedded even before it was officially established.[63]

Woodrow Wilson was elected president in the fall of 1912 on a Democratic platform that promised to fight the powers of the money trusts. Technically, this platform opposed establishing a central bank that would have, by definition, created another kind of concentration of power. According to the 1912 Democratic Party platform statement:

> We oppose . . . the establishment of a central bank; and we believe our country will be largely freed from panics and consequent unemployment and business depression by such a systematic revision of our banking laws as will render temporary relief in localities where such relief is needed, with protection from control of dominion by what is known as the money trust.
>
> We condemn the present methods of depositing government funds in a few favored banks, largely situated in or controlled by Wall Street, in return for political favors, and we pledge our party to provide by law for their deposit by competitive bidding in the banking institutions of the country, national and State, without discrimination as to locality, upon approved securities and subject to call by the Government.[64]

You'd never sneak that into the Democratic Party platform now, that's for sure. Public and political opinion against the consolidation of the country's wealth provided the backdrop for both the Federal Reserve Act of 1913 and the Clayton Antitrust Act of 1914.[65] Populist opposition extended even further against a central government bank that would establish a partnership between government and private entities, although the Democratic Party's public statements opposing a federal bank would prove to be mere rhetoric.[66]

On December 23, 1913, Wilson signed the Federal Reserve Act, which had been formulated by Congressman Carter Glass (D-VA) and Senator Robert L. Owen (D-OK). Among other things, the act "provided for the establishment of Federal Reserve Banks . . . to establish a more effective supervision of banking in the United States."[67] Wilson regretted the act soon after he signed it, realizing that the nation's wealth concentration would only increase under this central body of power. Despite some concurrent political opposition, the New York Federal Reserve Bank became and has remained the most influential bank in the Federal Reserve system, much to the joy of Wall Street—which could focus its attention more easily with the richest Fed bank in its hometown.[68] Under Geithner's leadership, it would become an equally chummy friend to that Wall Street community a century later.

Controlling the Punch Bowl

William McChesney Martin Jr., the Fed chairman for almost two decades from April 1951 to January 1970, once joked that the Fed's job is "to take away the punch bowl just as the party gets going."[69] It was during his reign that the Bank Holding Company Act of 1956 was passed, a solid piece of regulatory legislation that Martin Jr. favored.[70]

While Martin Jr. was still chairman of the Board of Governors of the Fed, he made a statement on April 18, 1969, before the House Committee on Banking and Currency to advocate for further regulation of one-bank holding companies "in the public interest."

He said, "The Congress took steps years ago, in the Banking Act of 1933, to separate banking from nonbanking businesses, a policy that was reinforced by the Bank Holding Company Act of 1956 as to companies that own two or more banks. Under section 4 of the 1956 Act, such companies are limited to banking and closely related activities. The Board unanimously agrees that there are sound reasons for separating banking and commerce, and that it is essential, if this policy is to continue, to bring one-bank holding companies under the Holding Company Act."[71]

Martin Jr., who died at the age of ninety-one, the year before the Glass-Steagall Act was repealed, was downright clairvoyant about the dangers of blurring the lines between various types of banking activity four decades before the Second Great Bank Depression surfaced. "To my mind, the greatest risk is in concentration of economic power. If a holding company combines a bank with a typical business firm, there is a strong possibility that the bank's credit will be more readily available to the customers of the affiliated business than to customers of other businesses not so affiliated. Since credit has become increasingly essential to merchandising, the business firm that can offer an assured line of credit to finance its sales has a very real competitive advantage over one that cannot. In addition to favoring the business firm's customers, the bank might deny credit to competing firms or grant credit to other borrowers only on condition that they agree to do business with the affiliated firm. This is why I feel so strongly that if we allow the line between banking and commerce to be erased, we run the risk of cartelizing our economy."[72]

But Martin Jr. failed to tighten monetary policy quickly enough. During the mid-1960s, inflation had started to climb, and by the time Martin Jr. retired in 1970, inflation was 6 percent and quickly rising out of control.[73] This pattern became more pronounced in the early 1970s and into the late 1970s, under the Fed chairmanship of Arthur F. Burns for most of the decade and under G. William Miller toward the end. The hyperinflation of the 1970s was exacerbated by the oil shocks of 1973 and 1978.[74]

The Last Banking Crisis

The early years of Alan Greenspan's reign were marked by the Savings and Loan (S&L) Crisis, in which the Fed took an active role but did not dramatically open its discount windows to nonbank entities or change its collateral posting rules.[75]

The S&L Crisis began quietly in 1984 and escalated in 1988—the first year the FDIC suffered an operating loss—and 1989.[76] So, on August 9, 1989, the Financial Institutions Reform, Recovery, and Enforcement Act of 1989 (FIRREA) created the Resolution Trust Corporation (RTC) to dispose of the toxic—mostly real-estate—assets from these *failed* institutions.[77] It was the 1990s version of a "bad bank." (In 2009, a more bank-generous Washington was considering disposing of assets from *existing* institutions.) But the RTC couldn't find buyers for its bad assets—shocking, considering they were bad because no one wanted to buy them in the first place, (just like during the Second Great Bank Depression). So, a year later, Congress got impatient and pressured the RTC to get rid of them anyway. The catch? When you sell stuff quickly, you don't get top dollar for it.

No matter. The RTC had a fire sale, and investors squeezed the government (and the public money that funded the RTC). At the first RTC auction in Dallas in July 1991, assets worth $25 million sold for 20 cents on the dollar. In May 1992, another RTC auction sold assets for only 17 cents on the dollar. By December 1995—the last year of the RTC's existence—prices barely reached 70 cents on the dollar.[78] So eventually the assets did regain some value, but only after enough were sold at exceedingly low prices, which had the effect of rendering the remaining assets more valuable. Still, the assets never achieved the value at which they had been purchased.

During its six-year existence, the RTC and the Federal Savings and Loan Insurance Corporation (FSLIC) sold off $519 billion worth of assets for 1,043 thrift closings.[79] But the RTC never brought the profits to the American people that Washington had promised (sound familiar?). Instead, it left the public on the hook for $124 billion in losses, while the thrift industry lost another $29 billion.[80] In 1997, the government was still paying $2.6 billion in annual interest on the bonds, with $2.3 billion coming from the Treasury, backed by those assets.[81] Tell that to the next person who says a bad bank is a good idea.

The early 1990s brought a recession under President George H. W. Bush that became an insane boom time during the Bill Clinton deregulation years and through the late 1990s. That party was followed by a mini-recession in 2001 and 2002, after which Greenspan's rate cuts ultimately spurred a tremendous debt-led boom and the Second Great Bank Depression.

Advocating the Wrong Policies

There are many causes for the current economic disaster that have nothing to do with the Fed. But one lethal cocktail did—the combination of lowering rates with promoting home ownership, particularly through the funky types of adjustable loans that then Fed chairman Alan Greenspan advocated as the subprime market blossomed from 2003 through 2005.

"American homeowners clearly like the certainty of fixed mortgage payments," Greenspan said in a speech to the Credit Union National Association in Washington on February 23, 2004. "American consumers might benefit if lenders provided greater mortgage-product alternatives to the traditional fixed-rate mortgage"; particularly if they are "willing to manage their own interest-rate risks, the traditional fixed-rate mortgage may be an expensive method of financing a home."[82]

With that kind of cover from the Fed boss, subprime lenders got into high gear. Stan Kurland, president of Countrywide Financial Corporation, didn't hide the firm's intentions in 2004. "Countrywide has a long history of working to meet the needs of borrowers. Our determination to dominate the ARM market builds on that history," he said. "As of March 2004, more than 40 percent of our retail and wholesale nonconforming fundings were for adjustable rate products. The ARM product menu is strong and deep, enabling consumers and business partners to meet their financial goals in ways that are affordable and beneficial, despite the recent rise in interest rates."[83]

Greenspan was a major and vocal proponent of deregulation of basically everything and said that "free markets" were not to be tampered with. He believed, by definition, that orchestrated tampering with the functionality of the markets will always be too late to be effective,[84] or "in essence, prudential regulation is supplied by the market through counterparty evaluation and monitoring rather than by authorities."[85]

In May 5, 2005, ever the free-market advocate—why constrict the poor markets with rules, when they'd have so much more fun without them?—Greenspan sounded like the head of marketing for any Wall Street credit derivatives department. He actually talked down critics of more regulation for the growing credit derivatives market, stating that the entities with less regulation had more incentives to monitor and control risk. He staunchly believed that "private regulation generally has proved far better at constraining excessive risk-taking than has government regulation."[86]

Five months later, he said in a speech to the National Italian American Foundation in Washington, D.C., "Being able to rely on markets to do the heavy lifting of adjustment is an exceptionally valuable policy asset. The impressive performance of the U.S. economy over the past couple of decades, despite shocks that in the past would have surely produced marked economic contraction, offers the clearest evidence of the benefits of increased market flexibility. In contrast, administrative or policy actions that await clear evidence of imbalance are of necessity late."[87]

So the market would take care of everything, and those unregulated entities, well, they'd exercise self-discipline. Yeah, right. Except that four years later, the costs incurred by that realm of thinking hovered at more than a cool $13 trillion, including a $182 billion bailout for AIG, an insurance-company-turned-unregulated-credit-hedge-fund classified as an S&L for a whole bunch of counterparties, none of which were that prudent.[88] But in the end, the Fed under Greenspan's successor, Ben Bernanke, bailed out AIG and Greenspan's ideology.[89]

"Had the Models Been Fitted More Appropriately"

Things finally caught up with Greenspan in late 2008, as the markets crumbled, and the mainstream press caught up with the progressive press in blaming many of his policies.

On October 23, 2008, Greenspan was called before Representative Henry Waxman (D-CA) and the House Committee on Oversight and Government Reform, alongside other powerful men who held posts during the subprime and credit buildup, such as John Snow, the former secretary of the treasury, and Christopher Cox, the chairman of the SEC.[90] The testimony went like this:

> REP. WAXMAN: . . . you had a belief that free, competitive—and this is your statement—"I do have an ideology. My judgment is that free, competitive markets are by far the unrivaled way to organize economies. We've tried regulation. None meaningfully worked." That was your quote. . . . And now our whole economy is paying its price. Do you feel that your ideology pushed you to make decisions that you wish you had not made?

> MR. GREENSPAN: Well, remember that what an ideology is, is a conceptual framework with the way people deal with reality. Everyone has one. You have to—to exist, you need an ideology. The question is whether it is accurate or not. And what I'm saying to you is, yes, I've found a flaw. I don't know how significant or permanent it is. But I've been very distressed by that fact. But if I may, may I just answer the question—

> REP. WAXMAN: You found a flaw in the reality—

> MR. GREENSPAN: Flaw in the model that I perceived as the critical functioning structure that defines how the world works, so to speak.

> REP. WAXMAN: In other words, you found that your view of the world, your ideology was not right. It was not working.

> MR. GREENSPAN: Precisely. That's precisely the reason I was shocked, because I had been going for 40 years or more with very considerable evidence that it was working exceptionally well. But just let me, if I may—

> REP. WAXMAN: Well, the problem is that the time has already expired.[91]

After epic turmoil in world markets led by announcements of bank insolvency and mounting criticisms about the cause of their melt-down, which Greenspan described as "a once-in-a-century credit tsunami," he found "a" flaw. Greenspan claimed, "Those of us who have looked to the self-interest of lending institutions to protect share-holder's equity (myself especially) are in a state of shocked disbelief. Such counterparty surveillance is a central pillar of our financial markets' state of balance. If it fails, as occurred this year, market stability is undermined."[92]

Now, really, it is we who should be in shocked disbelief at Greenspan's philosophical bantering about the need for an ideology—whether dangerous or not, apparently—and at his blaming the economic crisis on the models, not on the plethora of deregulation that allowed the banking industry to pile on such excessive and risky debt with no regard to the possible downside. Why didn't he blame the exceptionally bad judgment of the biggest bank regulator and regulating body in the world? Even if the models were wrong, it was the Fed's responsibility—no, its mandate, in fact—to monitor the capital on hand in the banking industry to back mounting losses.

Greenspan went on to say that the sophisticated asset-pricing models the Fed had effectively relied on collapsed because the data being put "into the risk management models generally covered only the past two decades, a period of euphoria. Had instead the models been fitted more appropriately to historic periods of stress, capital requirements would have been much higher and the financial world would be in far better shape today."[93]

That would be all fine and dandy, and it is partly true. The rosy default rates of prime mortgage borrowers were certainly not an adequate measure of the default rates of subprime ones. But the profound stress was caused far more, as I've explained, by the leverage in the system than by how subprime loans were modeled when they were transformed into an abundance of asset-backed securities.

So, it was the models' fault? That's rather disingenuous. Because, as it turned out, there was plenty of evidence to suggest that a housing downturn and rising foreclosure rates would become a broad financial concern, given the fact that a record amount of securitizations based on loans in the housing sector had been issued. You simply had to pay attention to it, something neither Greenspan nor Bernanke seemed interested in doing.

Fighting the Fed

Over the years, several chairmen of the House Banking Committee, including Wright Patman (D-TX) and Henry B. Gonzalez (D-TX), have criticized the Federal Reserve and questioned its lack of transparency.[94]

Representative Ron Paul (R-TX), a ranking member of the U.S. House Financial Services Subcommittee on Domestic Monetary Policy and Technology, introduced legislation on several occasions to abolish the Fed or make it more transparent.[95]

On February 26, 2009, after Fed Chairman Ben Bernanke had funneled trillions of dollars into the banking system, Paul introduced the Federal Reserve Transparency Act of 2009, or H.R. 1207.[96] On the House floor, he stated, "Serious discussion of proposals to oversee the Federal Reserve is long overdue. I have been a longtime proponent of more effective oversight and auditing of the Fed, but I was far from the first congressman to advocate these types of proposals."

(Note: The Federal Banking Agency Audit Act [P.L. 95-320] was enacted in 1978 specifically to enhance congressional oversight responsibilities. It gave the GAO—once the General Accounting Office, now the Government Accountability Office—the authority to audit the Board of Governors, the Reserve Banks and the branches.[97] Unfortunately, it didn't give the GAO the ability to audit any of the Fed's monetary policy or its Federal Open Market Committee operations, which were central to the secrecy with which it opened its books to banks.)

Paul went on to say, "Since its inception, the Federal Reserve has always operated in the shadows, without sufficient scrutiny or oversight of its operations. While the conventional excuse is that this is intended to reduce the Fed's susceptibility to political pressures, the reality is that the Fed acts as a foil for the government. The Federal Reserve has, on the one hand, many of the privileges of government agencies, while retaining benefits of private organizations, such as being insulated from Freedom of Information Act requests."[98] Unfortunately, there is little additional momentum in Congress toward a full analysis of the Fed's operations and decisions and a serious questioning as to whether its responsibilities should be limited to monetary policy, not bank regulation, at which it has failed miserably. It may require quadrillions, instead of trillions, of dollars in outlay to spawn that kind of questioning or outrage.

Representative Alan Grayson (D-FL) jumped on board to provide necessary bipartisan support for Paul's proposed legislation. On May 21, 2009, in a letter called "Bring Some Accountability to the Federal Reserve," he wrote, "Since March 2008 . . . the Fed has resorted to using its emergency powers to pick winners and losers, and to take massive credit risk onto its books. Since last September, the Fed's balance sheet has expanded from around $800 billion to over $2 trillion, not including off-balance sheet liabilities it has guaranteed for Citigroup, AIG, and Bank of America, among others . . . An audit is the first step in bringing this unaccountable system under the control of the public, whose money it prints and disseminates at will."

Paul's Federal Reserve Transparency Act would enable the GAO to audit the Fed and report its findings to Congress. As of July 14, 2009, it had 261 cosponsors in the House of Representatives.[99]

The GAO already has the right within the Federal Reserve Act to audit the annual statements of the Fed, which makes it all the more ridiculous that the Fed has been reticent about disclosing which banks got which sweetheart loans, for how much, and against which exact collateral during the Second Great Bank Depression. But the Fed has its protections. United States Code 31 USC Sec. 714 prohibits audits of the Federal Reserve Board and Federal Reserve banks over a number of items, including "(1) transactions for or with a foreign central bank, government of a foreign country, or nonprivate international financing organization; (2) deliberations, decisions, or actions on monetary policy matters, including discount window operations, reserves of member banks, securities credit, interest on deposits, and open market operations; (3) transactions made under the direction of the Federal Open Market Committee; or (4) a part of a discussion or communication among or between members of the Board of Governors and officers and employees of the Federal Reserve System."[100]

The intent of the Federal Reserve Transparency Act should be a given, and not require an additional Congressional maneuver. But our tax dollars are hard at work, reinventing the oversight wheel that appears to be in chronic flat tire mode while loopholes that keep the wrong bodies in control abound.

The Q&A section on the Federal Reserve's Web site states: "The Federal Reserve's ultimate accountability is to Congress, which at any time can amend the Federal Reserve Act."[101] But as Grayson's letter explained, the "Federal Reserve is an odd entity, a public-private chimera that controls the US monetary system and supervises the banking system . . . While the Governors are appointed by the President with confirmation by the Senate, the regional Reserve Banks have boards of directors chosen primarily by private banking institutions."[102]

Indeed, the Fed has always had a much closer relationship with private banks than the public. That's because as a condition of membership in the Federal Reserve, member banks—both state- and OCC-chartered (the Office of the Comptroller of the Currency)—are required to subscribe to stock in their district's Federal Reserve Bank. The required subscription is equal to 6 percent of the bank's capital and surplus; 3 percent must be paid in, and the remaining 3 percent is subject to call by the Board of Governors of the Federal Reserve. This means the bigger banks own more of the Fed. Member banks also receive 6 percent dividends on their shares, not too shabby in times of stock market turmoil, when no bank offers that to individual shareholders.[103]

The problem with today's Fed is its out-of-control, unaccountable secrecy. It has opened the spigots of funding to a pack of financial firms that simply don't deserve that kind of largesse. Plus, the Fed blessed bigger mergers and the conversion of investment banks to bank holding companies without blinking an eye. Bernanke talks about the need for better regulation, yet shirks transparency with his own books. The Fed simply operates above any law and beyond reason. That is, always was, and will prove to be a developing disaster. If not repaid, those trillions of dollars' worth of loans—as of mid-July 2009, over $7.6 trillion, to be exact[104]— will fester in the dark pockets of the Fed's books, enabling the banks to go about their old business, with a super-lender there to catch them when they falter again. And the kind of secrecy that Wall Street and its supporters in Washington really like will remain the norm.

The Open-Door Policy Is Now Closed

It didn't matter whether it was the liberal or conservative media asking for disclosure. The Fed's answer was always, "That's none of your business." On November 7, 2008, Bloomberg L.P. filed an official complaint with the Southern District Federal Court in New York against the Fed to try to force it to disclose information about $2 trillion worth of loans to banks.[105] In a FOIA request on January 28, 2009, Bloomberg asked the Treasury for a detailed list of the Citigroup and Bank of America securities it planned to guarantee but hadn't received a response as of this writing.[106]

This FOIA request was in addition to several similar ones Bloomberg had made in May and October 2008, as well as the aforementioned complaint filed in Federal Court.[107] The Fed's response was consistently opaque. It was perfectly fine to withhold internal memos, as well as information about trade secrets and commercial information. "The Board must protect against the substantial, multiple harms that might result from disclosure," Jennifer J. Johnson, the secretary for the Fed's Board of Governors, wrote in an e-mail to Bloomberg News. "It would be a dangerous step to release this otherwise confidential information."[108]

Dangerous? *Really*? Who exactly did the Fed think it was protecting from danger? Oh, yeah, right—the banks. Just in case their outrageous greed, ineptitude, loss, and self-mutilation weren't dangerous enough, disclosing how bad off they *really* were would have been catastrophic. This kind of quasi-regulatory secrecy keeps instability reigning supreme. (The SEC isn't any better; it won't disclose pending investigations, ostensibly to protect firms suspected of fraudulent behavior. Only after the media get wind of foul play does the SEC reluctantly comply with the idea of transparency, which is usually after a lot of hardworking people have lost a lot of money.)

In addition to filing two lawsuits against the Treasury for failing to respond to FOIA requests for details of the bailout funds extended to AIG, the Bank of New York Mellon, and Citigroup, Fox Business Network filed another suit against the Fed in January 2009 for ignoring Fox's November FOIA request for the names of the banks that had received $2 trillion in funds and the collateral they provided in return between August 2007 and November 2008.[109] Fox ultimately won its case against the Treasury but lost its case against the Fed.

Considering that the dissolution of the banking system took place in full public view, the Fed's persistent denials came across as a mix of juvenile playground banter and a blatant disregard for public responsibility.

To add to the FOIA requests, I teamed up with the Investigative Fund of the Nation Institute in December 2008. We forwarded a list of all of the meetings that took place between the Fed, the Treasury, and Wall Street heads during the fall of 2008, along with a pretty straightforward request. We wanted the minutes detailing what took place during those power meetings, to examine the exact conversations that carved up the old Wall Street and spurted out the new financial landscape. We heard back four months later. Yeah, we got a bunch of names of people who attended the meetings—which was basically the information we had provided to them in the first place—but no minutes.

Ben Bernanke didn't comment on any of these FOIAs directly. But during his testimony at a House Financial Services hearing in mid-November 2008 he made it clear there would be no public vetting of the Fed's bailouts. Representative Spencer Bachus (R-AL) pressed him on his rather obvious hypocrisy, "You've always advocated . . . transparency. I know you're refusing to disclose the names of those institutions or the composition of those assets. Is that a short term . . . I'll call it a refusal to disclose or when do you anticipate letting the public know?"

Bernanke replied, "Congressman, I think there's been some confusion about what this involves."

Representative Bachus nodded. "Sure."

"Some have asked us to reveal the names of the banks that are borrowing," Bernanke said. "How much they are borrowing. What [type of] collateral they are posting. We think that's counterproductive."

Really, Ben? It's counterproductive to discuss just what it is you're doing with the toxic assets and the banks at the core of the second-biggest meltdown in our country's history? He explained:

> The success of this depends on banks being willing to come and borrow when they need short-term cash. There is a concern if the name is put in the newspaper that such and such bank came to the Fed to borrow overnight, even for a perfectly good reason, others might begin to worry if this bank is creditworthy, and this

might create a stigma and make banks unwilling to borrow. That will be counterproductive.[110]

It's rather absurd to think that banks in critical condition wouldn't borrow from the Fed to help them lend to their consumer and business bases simply because the Fed might tell on them. These are public institutions. They are getting public money. The Fed was enabling them to maintain the secrecy of their positions during a time when secrecy spurred a greater crisis of confidence than disclosure would have.

Besides, the Fed is not a Swiss bank account. It may not be a fully public agency, but it does have a responsibility to the public. And the uncertainty surrounding the nature of its dealings with the banks made the whole crisis that much worse. In a criminal court, the Fed could be deemed guilty of conspiracy to commit grand larceny, if not the crime itself.

At another hearing on February 10, 2009, Bernanke changed his tactics, this time before the Committee on Financial Services. He acknowledged the public's interest in what the Fed was doing and with whom, and promised two new transparency-oriented initiatives. One was establishing a Web site that would provide "the full range of information that the Federal Reserve already makes available, supplemented by new explanations, discussions, and analyses."[111] This proposal was completely duplicative and useless. Check the site.

Bernanke also said that at his request, board vice chairman Donald Kohn would lead a committee to "review the Fed's publications and disclosure policies with respect to its balance sheet and lending policies."[112] But it was clear where Kohn stood on that. In a hearing a month earlier, Kohn had said, "I would be very, very hesitant to give the names of individual institutions. . . . I'd be very concerned . . . that if we published the individual names of who's borrowing from us, no one would borrow from us."[113]

And just in case anyone got any wrong ideas, Bernanke promised that there would remain certain "nondisclosure of information," but only when it was justified by criteria for confidentiality, as characterized by "factors such as reasonable claims to privacy, the confidentiality of supervisory information, and the effectiveness of policy."[114]

The Tag-Team Bailout Approach

In a lot of ways, the Treasury Department's $700 billion bailout gave cover to everything that was going on at the Fed, and vice versa. The Fed's books became increasingly complex and risky. That's evident if you simply compare the regularly reported Federal Reserve Statistical Release from February 28, 2008,[115] which was four pages long and easy to read before the Bear Stearns situation, to the eleven-page report issued a year later, which contained a plethora of new facilities and entries that seemed to be spawned at random to put out insta-financial fires—with money instead of water, of course.[116]

A little more than six months later, the Fed resembled a bad bank, injecting large chunks of money into the financial system in return for junky collateral and directly taking subprime assets for the first time on November 25, 2008.[117] That same day the Fed created the Term Asset-Backed Securities Loan Facility (TALF), which allowed investors holding mortgage-backed assets to get loans worth less than the actual value of the securities.[118] The measure was meant to protect against losses, but still, if the value dropped below what the Fed paid for the securities, the taxpayers would be on the hook.[119] Plus, if no one wanted the assets, their value was zero at that moment, no matter how the ratings agencies and their models ranked them.

On February 19, 2009, economist Paul Kasriel noted the elasticity of the Fed's programs, "When TALF was first proposed, back in November of last year, its funding allocation was $200 billion. Under the Treasury's new FSP [Financial Stability Program], TALF's funding amount has been increased to $1 trillion."[120] As a veteran of the economic research department of the Federal Reserve Bank of Chicago and the former senior vice president and director of economic research at Northern Trust Corporation, Kasriel knew what he was talking about.

Although the Fed's losses had been minimal during its initial foray into lending against risky assets, given the lack of forthrightness regarding the details behind the assets, it would have been hard to tell what kind of losses were mounting. But, in the words of James Hamilton, professor of economics at the University of California, "if more of the big boys go under, I'm not sure how the Fed would even account for them. It's like they are making this up as they go along. One thing's for sure; those new assets are capable of losing money in a way that we haven't seen before."[121]

These new buckets of risk on the Fed's books make it more likely that the Treasury will have to raise more debt to compensate for the loss of interest or for direct hits from the devalued securities that were posted as collateral. And where does that money come from? Yep—the taxpayers. But the risks of this build-up were never presented to the public. What was apparent, no matter how it was spun, was the extreme favoritism toward the banking sector that the bailout represented. All that was offered in return to the American public was the paper-thin promise of looser credit and the protection of our tax dollars.

Indeed, the Treasury Department, the Fed, and the FDIC promised on October 14, 2008, "These steps will ensure that the U.S. financial system performs its vital role of providing credit to households and businesses. . . . By participating in these programs, these institutions, along with thousands of others to come, will have enhanced capacity to perform their vital function of lending to U.S. consumers and businesses."[122]

But what they didn't disclose was that about a week earlier, as we've discussed, the Fed had announced that it would begin to pay interest on bank reserves. So instead of following its mandate to provide incentives to banks to part with their capital, thereby loosening credit for American citizens, the Fed was encouraging banks to hoard their cash so they could earn interest.[123]

All of the stabs at pushing money into the financial system simply never really made their way to the public as promised. On January 15, 2009, the Group of Thirty, an international nonprofit organization of top economists led by former Fed chair Paul Volcker, put in their two cents' worth in a report about the economic crisis: "The issue posed by the present crisis is crystal clear. How can we restore strong, competitive, innovative financial markets to support global economic growth without once again risking a breakdown in market functioning so severe as to put the world economies at risk?"[124]

The report concluded that central banks should be strengthened but not only during times of crisis. The Fed and other central banks should promote and maintain financial stability even when the economy is at its strongest, because market participants often make their riskiest deals during those periods.

According to a CNN report, the group had cautioned, "Regulators should pay particularly close attention to relatively new and largely unregulated financial instruments such as credit default swaps, collateralized debt obligations, and over-the-counter derivatives."[125]

What the Group of Thirty failed to mention was the unregulated role that the Fed itself was playing in building up an unprecedented book of risky assets for firms that had no business and no historical precedent gaining access to the Fed's money.

But all those billions and trillions in Federal funds were about protecting the American taxpayer, right? Well, that's the line we got, but the trickle-down thing just didn't work out. On January 30, 2009, the Fed once again switched up its own regulations to help certain banks borrow even more money. The first rule change allowed bank holding companies (BHCs), as Goldman Sachs and Morgan Stanley had become, to borrow money even if they are unable to put up enough collateral. The second major rule change allowed BHCs to borrow money from their own affiliates with greater ease. This shift would let companies move money around internally, potentially creating the appearance of more liquidity, and effectively allow them to mislead the public about their true financial health.[126]

The Real Cost and Risk of the Bailout

Even from the beginning of the bailout, as the banking system continued to exhibit a desperate propensity to inhale money, the true cost of keeping it functional seemed almost too big to comprehend—not that anyone wanted to do the math. Big, scary media headlines went from pegging the bailout cost at $2 trillion[127] in late October 2008, to more than $4 trillion by mid November,[128] to $7 trillion by late November 2008.[129]

By the time this book went to press, the full scope of the subsidization of the banking industry encompassed more than $13 trillion, and more than half of that came directly from the Fed.[130] It's all enough to make your head spin. But first, there are some dots to connect. What was the Fed thinking? Shouldn't it have had less, rather than more, unilateral power? How does the Fed relate to the taxpayer?

The answers require examining the individual tentacles of that $13.3 trillion rescue of the banking system, which by early June 2009 was roughly divided into $7.6 trillion from the Fed, $2.3 trillion from the Treasury (not including additional interest payments), and $1.5 trillion of fresh FDIC guarantees, if needed. In addition, there was $1.4 trillion of joint assistance and a $300 billion housing bill.[131] The figures are sobering.

In the meantime, we're on the hook for any money that the Fed isn't transferring to the Treasury, in addition to interest payments on rising national debt to back the continued costs of the bailout. "Taxpayers are taking on more risk than before. If the Fed takes a loss, its profits suffer. If the Fed turns over less to the Treasury, we will see raises in taxes or debt to compensate," Paul Kasriel told me.[132]

And therein lies the dual danger. On the fiscal side, there's the resulting inflation problem that comes from deluging the world with our Treasury debt: the more Treasury bonds that are out there, the less valuable they are and, thus, the higher their rates and the higher our interest payments. In fiscal year 2008, the interest payments for all public debt were $451 billion, with a 2008 national deficit of $455 billion.[133] Official predictions for the 2009 deficit were $1.8 trillion and for 2010, $1.2 trillion, though I believe it will be higher.[134]

This kind of interest "becomes a circle and a noose to the economy because we have to keep printing money to make interest payments at rising rates," Blythe McGarvie, an economist and the founder and CEO of Leadership for International Finance, told me. "If nothing else, this financial collapse has shown that too much borrowing, or leverage, will bring down a company. Similarly, a nation can be hollowed out."

From a macroeconomic standpoint, rising inflation disrupts the ideals of full employment, hard work, and responsibility for risk. McGarvie added, "Banks are reshaping themselves in order to get a handout— that's not embracing capitalism, it's crippling it."[135] The asset drain will cause an increase in U.S. government interest payments and debt, which, as I mentioned, will deflate the value of U.S. Treasury bonds, U.S. goods, and the dollar.

During the economic crisis the Fed presented four gifts to the financial sector that will have long-lasting negative effects on the nation's financial security. The first two were the risk-laden lending facilities and the Fed's refusal to entertain public accountability, but the last two will prove even more dangerous and more expensive. The Fed's quickness to transform anything (except Lehman Brothers) into a bank holding company and its speedy, seemingly thoughtless bank merger blessings will have lasting negative repercussions over the short and long term. Big, convoluted institutions drained trillions of dollars of public capital and wrecked the general economy. Yet they are destined to remain financial mammoths because the Fed wouldn't let them go extinct. That's not what a bank regulator should be doing to promote general economic and financial stability. The Fed did an abysmal job of guarding the nation from Wall Street's excesses as they were building, and rather than admit or correct its errors, the Fed simply printed more money, in the hopes of shoving them under the rug. Yet, both the Bush and the Obama administrations wanted to give the Fed more power as a systemic risk regulator. What does that say about the likelihood that all of this will happen again?

6

Everyone Saw This Coming

Give 'em the old three ring circus. Stun and stagger 'em. When you're
in trouble, go into your dance.

—*Billy Flynn*, Chicago

We might not have gotten into this mess if the state of the general
economy weren't inextricably linked to financial firms that take
unwarranted risks and hoard excessive profits. But that's not the case.
The truth is that Wall Street simply can't buy and sell the underlying
waste of our economic system and expect things to be peachy. The
meltdown was predictable, and various people did in fact predict it.
In 2004, I wrote a whole book about how big mergers and complex
securities were a disaster waiting to happen. Catastrophe is inevitable
when there are no meaningful boundaries guiding companies in an
exceedingly complex financial system.

Why do I say catastrophe is inevitable? Because none of today's disasters are new. We have already seen most of the ingredients of this
financial crisis in one form or another—some readers may have even
lived through the Great Depression. And yet the people in power, both
on Wall Street and in Washington, have worked extremely hard to not
learn the lessons of earlier crises.

The Second Great Bank Depression wasn't some random event. It's not as if every ordinary citizen spontaneously decided to stop paying bills. It's not as if every international government woke up one day to an economic catastrophe and blamed it on a Wall Street gone crazy. It wasn't even the culmination of a string of bad luck. Not quite. This epoch contains the same elements as every other Wall Street–led scheme. The nineteenth-century railroad barons couldn't have succeeded without starry-eyed investors putting up funds for companies that were later shown to be engaging in stock fraud.[1] The Great Crash of 1929 wouldn't have occurred if companies hadn't fabricated earnings and investors hadn't flocked to buy their stocks with oodles of borrowed money.[2]

Back then, many stocks were purchased on margin—another name for our old friend leverage. A small number of stocks could be put up as collateral for large loans that could be used to buy more stocks. As stocks fell in value, the original collateral was not worth as much, so lenders made margin calls, demanding even more collateral. To get money to pay off those margin calls, investors needed to sell their stocks. When investors sold more, stock values fell further. So began the vicious downward spiral that led to the 1929 crash.

This exact cycle occurred again during the Second Great Bank Depression. Investors and banks had borrowed large sums of money backed by small amounts of securities, or assets that were backed by subprime mortgages.

All of that borrowed money was floated on an ever-shrinking and devalued pot of loans and assets. Investors and banks that had borrowed against them were stuck owing a lot of money to make up for the assets' decline in value. The problem was, banks had no way to make up the difference because no one was buying their structured assets. That's the real reason credit seized up. All of the actual money in the system was sucked out to back the aforementioned $140 trillion worth of borrowing. The underlying collateral of structured assets, which were re-dubbed "toxic," had no buyers and, therefore, no value.

During the Great Crash, investors who were forced to liquidate their holdings exacerbated the plunge in stock prices. U.S. stock prices dropped 33 percent from their then historic peak in September 1929 to their low in November.[3] By July 8, 1932, after three painful years, the Dow Jones reached a low of 41.22 points, an 89 percent drop from its pre-crash high. It took twenty-five years to regain its high of 382, with a lot of ups and downs in between.[4]

A Law That Really Worked

The Great Depression was an economic and emotional blight on American history. During the early 1930s, a quarter of the nation was unemployed.[5] Home foreclosures were at record highs. In 1933, at the peak of the four-year depression, around 1,000 homes were foreclosed every day,[6] and 10 percent of American homes were bank-owned.[7] One out of five banks shut down.[8] Between 1929 and 1933, 9,000 banks had to suspend their operations because of financial problems.[9] (By comparison, 10,000 homes were foreclosed daily by early 2009, and a total of 2.3 million properties had undergone foreclosure actions during 2008.[10] For the first three months of 2009, foreclosure action was brought against more than 800,000 properties, up 24 percent from the first quarter of 2008.)[11]

Jolted by the Crash of 1929 and its economic fallout, Americans in the 1930s were fearful of the present and desperately hoped for a better future. But it took three years of pain and denial before FDR was elected president by a landslide, receiving 57 percent of the popular vote and winning forty-two states on November 8, 1932.[12]

FDR's famous inauguration address on March 4, 1933, in which he said "the only thing we have to fear is fear itself," brought the country together amid disdain for the bankers who had wrecked so many lives.[13] Roosevelt christened his presidency the next day with two proclamations: one called Congress back to the Capitol Building for a special session, and the other declared a bank holiday under the dormant provisions of the wartime Trading with the Enemy Act.[14] (Although sometimes, the enemy lies within.)

Not surprisingly, Secretary of the Treasury William H. Woodin was crucial to FDR's efforts. Like so many treasury secretaries before and after him, Woodin came from the private sector. A close personal friend of FDR's and a Republican to boot, he had gone to Columbia University but left to make it as a businessman before completing his degree.[15]

In 1922, Woodin became president of the American Car and Foundry Company and also served as chairman of the board of several leading locomotive companies. In shades of Tim Geithner decades later, Woodin was appointed to be a director of the Federal Reserve Bank of New York, before being appointed treasury secretary in 1933. He was forced to resign roughly ten months later.[16] The Senate Banking Committee discovered that Woodin was on J.P. Morgan's preferred customer list, and he had retained some preferred stock options as a result.[17] It was tough to break Wall Street ties, even then. Woodin died soon afterward.[18]

But before that, he did the nation a lot of good. Geithner should have taken note. After consulting with Woodin, the president declared the bank holiday, which lasted four days and was meant to "prevent further runs on the banks and allow Woodin time to draft the necessary legislation." Which Woodin did.

The night of March 5, 1933, FDR met with a group of congressional leaders at the White House, including Senator Carter Glass (D-VA) and Representative Henry Steagall (D-AL), chairmen of the committees that would create the legislation that restructured the banking landscape. The banks did stabilize after they reopened, and that paved the way for the Glass-Steagall Act of 1933, which passed in Congress on June 15, 1933.[19] FDR signed it into law the very next day.

Glass and Steagall insisted that a single bank entity should not control financial products that had widely varying levels of risk that could cause damage to the American public.[20] The Glass-Steagall Act prohibited commercial banks (banks that take customers' deposits or give them loans) from engaging in reckless speculation by creating, borrowing excessively against, or trading risky assets. These tasks were left to the investment banks.

The Pecora Commission of 1932 was instrumental in helping legislators understand the problems stemming from the industry and in creating lasting solutions to protect the public. Named for assistant district attorney from New York Ferdinand Pecora, who served as chief counsel, it investigated the irresponsible practices of Wall Street and helped galvanize public support for measures like the Glass-Steagall Act, which changed the very structure of Wall Street.[21]

The commission's hearings were held from April 11, 1932, to May 4, 1934, before the Senate Committee on Banking and Currency

Investigation of Wall Street.[22] The hearings revealed a range of shady practices by banks and their affiliates.[23] Conflicts of interest, such as banks underwriting unstable securities in order to pay off bad loans, were central to the committee's findings. So was the havoc that investment trusts, or off-book entities, had wreaked on the economy by allowing banks to hide their true conditions.[24] These findings were a revelation for many regular Americans and inspired a widespread cry for change.[25] Unfortunately, the lure of money seems to aid forgetfulness. These shady practices would return in the 1990s under other names to cause further mayhem.

The commission's work led to two major regulatory acts besides Glass-Steagall: the Securities Act of 1933 and the Securities Exchange Act of 1934, which created the Securities and Exchange Commission (SEC) to enforce the rules of that act.[26] These acts obligated institutions that raised public debt to provide better disclosure of their books, and regulators to make sure that happened.[27]

Unfortunately, the SEC didn't quite offer the public the security it was supposed to provide.[28] The idea behind the creation of the SEC was that it would "protect and make more effective the national banking system and Federal Reserve System" and "insure the maintenance of fair and honest markets."[29] But the SEC did not grow alongside the increasingly complex financial firms and transactions it was supposed to be regulating and the structures those firms created to make money. Wall Street, as we shall see in the next section, took full advantage of the loopholes.

When Pecora published his memoirs in 1939, *Wall Street under Oath: The Story of Our Modern Money Changers*, he wrote, "Bitterly hostile was Wall Street to the enactment of the regulatory legislation. Legal chicanery and pitch darkness were the banker's stoutest allies."[30] You gotta love a guy who's not afraid to tell it like it is and pursue real change, despite the might of the mighty.

FDR and the sitting Congress had the spine to combat this lack of transparency and Wall Street aggression with deep, not cosmetic, changes—which is why the banking industry fought them for years. Eventually, to the multitrillion-dollar detriment of the nation, the bankers won. The Second Great Bank Depression that began in 2008 was the result. Then, as now, there were certain firms at the center of the storm.

Goldman, Sachs and Company was one of the firms hauled in front of the Pecora Commission.[31] By the turn of the twentieth century, Goldman was raising the most short-term debt, called commercial paper, in the United States.[32] The firm was also the leading industrial-sector banker in the country. Partners under the Goldman umbrella invested in and established the Goldman Sachs Trading Group in the 1920s. Through it, Goldman sponsored a set of investment trusts, or mini-trading corporations (the Goldman Sachs Trading Corp., Shenandoah Corp., and Blue Ridge Corp.). Their closest modern-day equivalent is the hedge, and private equity, fund. They took in investor money, made speculative bets on shady securities, and borrowed substantially against the securities to make more.

These trusts posted enormous profits before collapsing to nearly nothing in 1929, causing director and Goldman Sachs partner Waddill Catchings (coauthor of the New-Era apologist book *The Road to Plenty*) to resign in June 1930.[33]

In 1932, comedian Eddie Cantor, the Jay Leno of the time, was one of forty-two thousand investors who lost a fortune in the Goldman Sachs Trading Corporation. He sued Goldman for $100 million and made Goldman Sachs a national joke to ease the pain: "They told me to buy the stock for my old age . . . and it worked *perfectly*. Within six months, I felt like a *very* old man!"[34]

There were other eerie similarities between then and now: the Ponzi scheme–like companies that Goldman and others sponsored in the 1920s made lots of money on empty promises of perpetual asset appreciation; they were quickly overvalued, perversely reflecting the promise of future growth of American industry. In reality, they did not demonstrate solid growth of any kind but rather growth on paper from buzz.[35] Similarly, the misplaced enthusiasm about home ownership demonstrated by Greenspan, Bush, and others helped stoke the Wall Street fires full of loans to burn and profit from.

One of the longest-lasting positive aspects of the Glass-Steagall Act was that it established the Federal Deposit Insurance Corporation (FDIC) to permanently protect the people's cold, hard-earned cash— despite FDR's understandable reservations about insuring commercial banks.[36] After the slew of bank runs and bank failures during the Great Depression, FDR didn't want banks to get too comfortable knowing that their deposits were backed by the U.S. government.[37] He astutely feared that the same money-hungry banks would be more likely to abuse the dollars entrusted to their care. In a 1932 letter written before Election Day and printed in the *New York Sun*, Roosevelt gave the following opinion on deposit insurance: "It would lead to laxity in bank management and carelessness on the part of both banker and depositor. I believe that it would be an impossible drain on the Federal Treasury to make good any such guarantee."[38] That lesson would be entirely forgotten during the Second Great Bank Depression.

In spite of these concerns, FDR signed the Glass-Steagall Act that created the FDIC on June 16, 1933, and its insurance went into effect on January 1, 1934.[39] The FDIC became a permanent government agency with the Banking Act of 1935. Initially, all consumer accounts were guaranteed up to the amount of $2,500, but the same year that the insurance went into effect, in July 1934, the cap was raised to $5,000.[40] That meant 45 percent of all deposits in the banking system were covered.[41]

The only reason that the FDIC made sense, then, was that it coincided with the Glass-Steagall Act, which separated the more stable consumer-oriented commercial banks from the riskier speculative investment banks. The FDIC was only supposed to provide backing for the less risky ones. Sure, certain consumer-oriented commercial banks knew the government had their backs, but equally important was that speculative banks, which created and traded risky securities—and which, by virtue of the fees they took in for their services, were prone to advise on corporate mergers and acquisitions whether they were for the public good or not—knew that they did not have the backing of the U.S. government. (Investment banks would, however, have FDIC backing during the Second Great Bank Depression.)

Over the years, the FDIC raised the level of insurance on consumer deposits to adjust for inflation. The Depository Institutions Deregulation and Monetary Control Act of 1980 raised it to $100,000.[42] The Federal Deposit Insurance Reform Act of 2005 increased the FDIC's insurance of certain consumer retirement deposits to $250,000.[43] As panic was setting into the U.S. economy in late 2008, Congress passed the Emergency Economic Stabilization Act of 2008 that until December 31, 2009, would raise the insurance limit on any other consumer deposits from $100,000 up to $250,000. On May 19, 2009, it was extended by Congress through December 31, 2013.[44] Raising the cap was one of the only smart responses to the economic crisis.

Who Killed Glass-Steagall?

The Great Depression fallout that brought Wall Street's leveraged bets to bear onto the general economy replayed itself during the election of 2008, but with one major difference: Barack Obama did not have a decisive plan to dissect the banking industry into manageable parts. That didn't change once he got into office, either.

The Glass-Steagall Act of 1933 was one of the main legislative pillars of the New Deal. The other four were the Emergency Banking Act of 1933, which legalized the bank holiday and allowed federal regulators to inspect banks to make sure they were financially sound before reopening (in contrast to the early 2009 bank stress tests, which allowed banks to provide their own results regarding their health); an executive order that made it illegal to hoard gold, gold bullion, or gold certificates; the Home Owners Loan Act of 1933, which established the Home Owners' Loan Corporation to provide mortgage money to people at risk of foreclosure; and the Social Security Act, which established the Social Security Board.[45]

As I've mentioned, Glass-Steagall separated financial institutions into two categories: commercial banks, which dealt with public deposits and loans; and investment banks, which dealt with speculative trading activities and corporate mergers and acquisitions. It was the perfect solution: beautiful in its simplicity and powerful in its effectiveness. Under the terms of the act, commercial banks would receive more government backing, which was only fair after years of nationwide economic depression. Investment banks would not, which was also only fair after the speculation by investment banks that had *caused* years of economic depression.

You may get tired of my beating this dead horse, but you have to believe me: the horse totally deserves it. I cannot overstate the value of Glass-Steagall. If it had not been repealed a decade ago, our current banking system meltdown would not have occurred. Deposits and loans would not have been used as collateral for an upside-down pyramid of risky securities. The competitive corporate drive to become bigger combined with unconstrained financial players wouldn't have spawned a tornado of toxic assets and mega-leverage. And bank execs wouldn't have scooped up immense rewards before the economy became a total mess.

Senator Byron Dorgan Predicts We'll Rue the Day

Glass-Steagall's demise is not surprising when we see the array of forces lined up against it. One of the men heading the charge, with a private-sector mentality from the pulpit of public office, was none other than Robert Rubin, a former Goldman Sachs cochairman and President Bill Clinton's treasury secretary.[46]

He began to lobby for the repeal of Glass-Steagall in May 1995 when he testified before the House Committee on Banking and Financial Services. "The banking industry is fundamentally different from what it was two decades ago, let alone in 1933," Rubin said. He stressed how *global* banking had become, arguing that raising capital on the back of diverse new products had become an international game. He stoked an already illusory fear that if the U.S. banking industry didn't have the same opportunities and structure as existed abroad, banks would move their most profitable businesses across the ocean.

Rubin was downright hostile to the core concepts of Glass-Steagall, which he considered a cost-and-efficiency roadblock to bank profits. He declared that the act could "conceivably impede safety and soundness by limiting revenue diversification."[47] And who'd ever want to be an impediment to safety?

Hell-bent on removing barriers to banking activities, Rubin testified again on February 24, 1999, imploring that the United States was missing an important boat that had already set sail, while implying that without the repeal of Glass-Steagall, the industry and its customers would suffer. And the world as we know it would cease to exist. (Okay, he didn't exactly say that, but his point was pretty clear.) This time, Rubin made his case before the Senate Banking Committee:

> Financial modernization is occurring already in the marketplace through innovation and technological advances. With the lessening of regulatory barriers, financial services firms are offering customers a wide range of financial products. Banks and securities firms have been merging; banks are selling insurance products; and insurance companies are offering products that serve many of the same purposes as banking products—all of which increases competition and thus benefits consumers.[48]

To be sure, there were critics of repeal back then. Notably, Senator Byron Dorgan (D-ND) warned in 1999 that a "financial swamp" would result from the casino-like prospect of merging banking with the speculative activity of real estate and securities.[49]

Another critic was the late Paul Wellstone (D-MN), who stressed, "We seem determined to unlearn the lessons of history. Scores of banks failed in the Great Depression as a result of unsound banking practices, and their failure only deepened the crisis. Glass-Steagall was intended to protect our financial system by insulating commercial banking from other forms of risk. It was designed to prevent a handful of powerful financial conglomerates from holding the rest of the economy hostage. Glass-Steagall was one of several stabilizers designed to keep that from ever happening again, and until very recently it was very successful."[50]

Nonetheless, President Bill Clinton signed the Gramm-Leach-Bliley Act (also called the Financial Modernization Act) into law on November 12, 1999.[51] During the signing ceremony at the Eisenhower Executive Office Building, there was no show of partisanship. The Democrats and the GOP were in sync. Republican Senate Banking Committee leader Phil Gramm said, "We are here today to repeal Glass-Steagall because we have learned that government is not the answer. We have learned that freedom and competition are the answers. We have learned that we promote economic growth and we promote stability by having competition and freedom."[52]

Rubin's protégé Lawrence H. Summers, who had taken over as Clinton's treasury secretary while Rubin took a plum job at Citigroup and carried his mentor's deregulation mantle, remarked, "Today Congress voted to update the rules that have governed financial services since the Great Depression and replace them with a system for the twenty-first century. This historic legislation will better enable American companies to compete in the new economy."[53]

A decade later, Clinton renounced any blame for the Second Great Bank Depression. He claimed that killing off Glass-Steagall had nothing to do with the crisis. "There are some people who believe that that bill enabled them to somehow participate in some of the riskier housing investments," Clinton said. "I disagree with that. That bill primarily enabled them to, like the Bank of America, to buy Merrill Lynch here without a hitch. And I think that helped to stabilize the situation."[54] Now, as you can imagine, I strongly disagree with Clinton on this issue. And I would hope you do, too. Buying Merrill Lynch, with its $70 billion worth of collateralized debt obligation positions, was risky. The government pumping Bank of America with almost $220 billion of capital injections and guarantees to keep it alive following its merger with Merrill Lynch did *not* go off without a hitch.[55] Earth to Clinton. Repealing Glass-Steagall was financially destructive to the general economy. Big mergers create big problems.

Far from being on the defensive, Clinton was brimming with money-making glee when he signed Gramm-Leach-Bliley: "Financial services firms will be authorized to conduct a wide range of financial activities, allowing them freedom to innovate in the new economy. The Act repeals provisions of the Glass-Steagall Act that, since the Great Depression, have restricted affiliations between banks and securities firms. It also amends the Bank Holding Company Act to remove restrictions on affiliations between banks and insurance companies. It grants banks significant new authority to conduct most newly authorized activities through financial subsidiaries."[56] Bank holding companies, previously regulated by the Bank Holding Company Act, were allowed to mutate into the giants that trashed the world economy.

The repeal of Glass-Steagall was not accompanied by legislation to strengthen regulatory oversight for newly consolidated supermarket financial firms amalgamated from broker-dealers, commercial banks, and insurance companies. Yet that didn't seem to matter as Clinton promised, "This historic legislation will modernize our financial services laws, stimulating greater innovation and competition in the financial services industry. America's consumers, our communities, and the economy will reap the benefits of this Act."[57]

The scene was set for disaster. History had already shown that if commercial banks speculate or borrow too heavily against their customers' assets, the system self-destructs. It was only a matter of time after the Glass-Steagall repeal that history would repeat itself. Without a reinstatement of Glass-Steagall, which is not even near the table in Congress, it will again.

When Congress approved the bill on November 5, 1999, Dorgan said, "I think we will look back in ten years' time and say we should not have done this but we did because we forgot the lessons of the past, and that that which is true in the 1930s is true in 2010. We have now decided in the name of modernization to forget the lessons of the past, of safety and of soundness."[58] Sadly, he was right.

But levelheadedness was lost in the blur of a reckless desire to deregulate, or destroy legislation that had already taken its share of knocks but had still proved effective for nearly seven decades in preventing a widespread banking meltdown. The act was repealed without any serious public consideration of the potential consequences. It was a one-sided hatchet job that led to spectacular financial devastation, and a completely unlevel playing field controlled by the bigger banks.

To this day, none of the architects or the advocates of Glass-Steagall's destruction have taken their rightful blame for their role in destabilizing the system. Yet, bringing back Glass-Steagall would be the single most effective way to reconstruct the financial industry in a way that wouldn't require public support for the losses caused by the unbridled risk-taking of the banks that hold our money.

"An Awfully Big Mess"

As part of the rush to deregulate, Congress watered down the SEC rules that were put in place to protect the public from reckless corporate behavior. As we'll see, after Glass-Steagall was repealed, many banks went shopping to buy investment banks and insurance companies. Some investment banks, however, preferred to remain insulated from commercial banks. But the problem was that investment banks couldn't compete with the money and leverage of the "supermarket" commercial banks, which had access to their customers' deposits as collateral. The solution for the investment-only banks was to raise their own leverage limits, so they could borrow more money for speculative activities, without having to post as much collateral or capital. To raise leverage limits, investment banks had to pick apart the net capital rule that the SEC had set in 1975. It had required broker-dealers to cap their debt-to-net capital ratio at twelve to one.[59] In other words, they couldn't borrow more than twelve dollars' worth of debt for every one dollar of real capital, or equity, that they held. Changing the net capital rule was referred to in the business as "low hanging fruit," or something easy to deal with. It was just a matter of time and tactical influence.

Shortly after the Glass-Steagall repeal, there was one firm that sprinted out of the box to raise leverage in order to maintain its edge. On February 29, 2000, Goldman Sachs CEO Henry Paulson testified at the Senate Banking Committee hearing on the "Financial Marketplace of the Future." He pressured for lifting the seemingly innocuous 1975 net capital rule. In his testimony, he stated, "We and other global firms have, for many years, urged the SEC to reform its net capital rule to allow for more efficient use of capital. This is the single most important factor in driving significant parts of our business offshore; so that our firms can remain competitive with our foreign competitors, risk-based capital standards must become the norm."[60]

In short, Paulson was pushing for investment banks to take on more risk in order to stay competitive with the new supermarket banks and their larger balance sheets. In late April 2004, the five members of the SEC met in a basement hearing room to consider lifting the net capital rule. There were few dissenting voices out there at the time. One, from a risk-management consultant from Indiana, warned that the decision was a "grave mistake," as paraphrased in the *New York Times*. Another, Harvey J. Goldschmid, then an SEC commissioner, expressed a prophetic truth about the ramifications of tripling leverage for the most powerful investment banks: "If anything goes wrong, it's going to be an awfully big mess." Regardless, after less than an hour of discussion—fifty-five minutes to be exact—a vote was taken.[61] It took four years from the time of Paulson's Senate plea, but on April 28, 2004, the biggest investment banks—those with more than $5 billion in assets, such as Lehman Brothers, Bear Stearns, Merrill Lynch, and Goldman Sachs—got approval from the SEC to increase their official leverage from twelve to one to thirty to one.

The damage potential was even greater than it initially seemed after the SEC hearing. According to the *New York Sun*, "Using computerized models, the SEC . . . allowed the broker dealers to increase their debt-to-net-capital ratios, sometimes, as in the case of Merrill Lynch, to as high as 40-to-1."[62]

Leverage gluttony had prevailed with the SEC's blessing. Before crashing on September 21, 2008, Lehman had a thirty-to-one leverage ratio, or thirty borrowed dollars per one dollar of real capital. Morgan Stanley had thirty to one and Goldman Sachs was at twenty-two to one. Of the major supermarket banks, Bank of America had a leverage ratio of about eleven to one, JPMorgan Chase had about thirteen to one, and Citigroup had fifteen to one—but that only counts the leverage we knew about.[63] Most likely, if the supermarket banks' off-balance sheet deals—which included leverage of items in structured investment vehicles (SIVs)—had been included, their ratios would have been even wider.[64]

Lee Pickard, who headed the SEC's trading and markets division from 1973 to 1976, and helped write the original net capital rule in 1975,[65] later said, "The SEC modification in 2004 is the primary reason for all of the losses that have occurred."[66] It was a decision that helped spur the Second Great Bank Depression and that altered the credit landscape for big-time investment banks in this way: Assume that an investment bank holding more than $5 billion in total assets owns $100 million' worth of toxic assets. Under the old rule, it could have borrowed $1.2 billion against those assets. If the assets lost all of their value, the investment bank would have been out collateral for $1.2 billion. That's a lot but still perhaps manageable. Instead, under the 2004 rule change, the bank was allowed to borrow $3 billion, increasing its potential loss almost threefold.

Investment banks such as Bear Stearns and Lehman Brothers went bust because they didn't have enough substitute collateral behind the money they had borrowed. At the same time, their creditors wanted to be paid back. The credit problem that engulfed the overall economy would have been nearly two-thirds the size if leverage had remained at twelve times, instead of being upped to thirty times. As we know, the federal government, otherwise known as *our tax dollars*, saved Merrill Lynch.

The Bank Holding Company Bonanza

Another important problem that the pre-1933 banking system exposed was that when banks consolidated themselves as bank holding companies, they could buy all sorts of nonbanking companies. Some of the companies under the bank holding company umbrella were less stable than simple consumer-oriented banks that only took deposits and provided loans. This precise problem was remedied by the Glass-Steagall Act, which prohibited bank holding companies from owning other types of financial service firms.[67] Glass-Steagall contained overall systemic risk by limiting the risk-taking investment banks to a smaller, isolated category that could not merge and corrode the commercial banks. Today, Treasury Secretary Geithner is talking about having a single regulator, such as the Fed, contain systemic risk; instead he should resurrect Glass-Steagall, which successfully did just that. "From the 1940s to the 1970s, only a handful of banks failed each year, usually as a result of insider abuse or fraud," Bernard Shull and Gerald A. Hanweck wrote in their 2001 book on the history of the U.S. banking system, *Bank Mergers in a Deregulated Environment.*[68]

The Bank Holding Company Act of 1956 strengthened the intent of the Glass-Steagall Act by legislating that bank holding companies, defined at the time as companies that owned two or more banks, could not acquire banks outside the state where they were headquartered and would be severely limited in their ownership of nonbanking firms. The Bank Holding Company Act also gave the Federal Reserve Board the power—and the responsibility—to approve or deny bank holding company applications. Today, a bank holding company is defined as a company that owns or controls one or more banks, or that holds 25 percent or more of a bank's voting shares. Fed approval is also needed if a bank holding company wants to buy 5 percent or more of another bank or bank holding company, effectively, merging with that company.[69]

The Fed's power to deny a bank holding company the right to form still stands, but it was not used in the years leading up to the Second Great Bank Depression.[70] In fact, the Fed did not reject a single merger or acquisition application since October 2005.[71] So much for using your power for good.

The Fed's ability to decide the fate of a bank holding company is vital. When banks buy other businesses, their focus may be diverted to more speculative, easy-money opportunities, to the detriment of the boring, yet stable, consumer deposit and loan business. Before the Bank Holding Company Act, bank holding companies—Transamerica, for instance—were involved in other financial services, such as insurance and real estate, and had even invested in commodities, such as fish packing.[72] Banks throughout the country were similarly able to use customer deposits as capital or collateral to take on nonbanking investments. If those tertiary investments grew too risky, consumer deposits were imperiled.

Like Glass-Steagall, the idea behind the Bank Holding Company Act was simple. Risk is mitigated if banks aren't allowed to buy anything and everything; clarity is fostered over the books of that bank, which makes regulation easier; and too much financial concentration (the "too big to fail" thing) is prevented from destabilizing the system.

You might say that the Bank Holding Company Act was too simple—and perhaps too smart—for its own good. Much of its intent was decimated less than three decades later by an increase in bank mergers in the mid-1980s, spurred by government intervention under Ronald "Government Is Not the Answer" Reagan.[73]

"Given the willingness of the U.S. government to underwrite takeovers, [the large number] of bank and thrift failures in the 1980s created choice acquisition targets for merging banks interested in new markets," University of California economics professor Gary Dymski wrote in his 2002 paper *The Global Bank Merger Wave*.[74] Similar (but bigger) government-backed mergers occurred in late 2008 in a nominal attempt to stabilize the economy.

The restrictions put forth in the Bank Holding Company Act were substantially deregulated by the Riegle-Neal Interstate Banking and Branching Efficiency Act of 1994 (IBBEA). The act allowed interstate bank mergers and led to even greater concentration among fewer power players in the banking industry. Five years later, of course, the Gramm-Leach-Bliley Act, in addition to decimating Glass-Steagall, negated the rest of the intent of the Bank Holding Company Act by allowing bank holding companies to again buy nonbank companies like insurance firms and just about anything else.

The Fed and the SEC, meanwhile, remained ill-equipped to monitor the spate of bank mergers and the increasingly complex web of financial and other services and activities that banks pursued. Their authority and staffing levels remained on par with the much simpler and clearer banking functions that had existed for most of the middle part of the twentieth century. That's assuming that with appropriate staff levels, they would have had the courage to contain Wall Street's prowess and truly protect the public. And that, sadly, is a huge leap. Indeed, the Fed's philosophy throughout the Second Great Bank Depression reeked of its pre–Great Depression negligence—only on an even larger scale. Therefore, it is becoming even more crucial for us to reinstate Glass-Steagall, now more than ever, before the banking world can run the American economy through the ringer again and expect to be bailed out for the risk its structure, practices, and rules incur.

7

Bonus Bonanza

Let Wall Street have a nightmare and the whole country has to help get them back in bed again.

—*Will Rogers,*
August 12, 1929[1]

People take pay very seriously on Wall Street. I know this because I worked for investment banks for more than ten years. I didn't start out making a lot of money—and I didn't end with the multimillion-dollar paychecks of those that stayed "in the game," as they call it—but I quickly learned that what you make and how well you argue your worth to your bosses will determine your entire career in the industry. If you don't act like you care deeply about what you make, you're not going to be successful.

To be fair, there are whiffs of meritocracy. But Wall Street mostly measures its actors by propulsion, and money equals validation in a hyper-competitive world. Money confirms your worth in the general pecking order of your firm and to the rest of the Street. To be super-successful (which I wasn't), you have to convince yourself that you are not only better than everyone else, but that you are *entitled*. Your status, which includes the internal politics of your rise, how the higher-ups view you, and how the CEO views them, is tied to your total compensation, your Number.

You are always aware of your Number.

Around the time that bonuses are unveiled in late December or early in the New Year, depending on the firm, you're told—well, not so much told as made aware—not to disclose your Number to anyone. This way, senior managers can control dissent among the ranks and avoid annoying conversations in which employees compare their pay. The Number is part of the strategy. The people who make the most money tend to be the best negotiators and are the ones in the right line of ascent. Your line of ascent shows up in your compensation. To make a fortune on Wall Street, it's not enough to produce revenue for your firm. You have to be in bed with the right manager, and he (or she) in turn has to be in bed with the right manager in his (or her) line of ascent. Hitch your money shuttle to the right rocket at the right firm, and you, too, can touch super-wealth and power.

But the value of money is fleeting. The financial world does not create anything beyond the temporary value that it extracts, which makes bonuses on Wall Street as ephemeral as they are extreme. A trader is as good as his or her last trade, the firm's stock as good as its last quarter's earnings and whether they beat or missed analyst expectations. On Wall Street, pay is based on the deals that closed that year, never mind whether the long-term effects of those deals are ruinous. The money is already in your pocket; if not in cash, then in other forms of compensation. The bonus system is gluttonous in the short term and careless in the long term.

Life is a lot harder to stomach when you've lost your job and your retirement fund, and the IRS is auditing you, and then you hear that one or ten or twenty or a hundred people on Wall Street each bagged $10 million or more during what had been a horrific year for most everyone else. You can't help but wonder just what the hell made these people God's gift or why your tax dollars are subsidizing them, either directly, through federal bailouts, or indirectly, through the transfer of wealth they created. No one in Washington asked you or me whether we wanted to contribute to executives' bonuses.

Beyond that, and I say this as a former bonus recipient, Wall Street doesn't produce anything of lasting value. Transactions are fleeting and revenues are booked up front, regardless of how transactions turn out down the line. If a merger fails, so what? Investment banks collect fees when mergers are initiated, and they keep their millions even if the mergers turn out to be a terrible idea. The goal is very simple: make money. The goal is not to promote growth and economic welfare throughout the land.

People get paid for creating an illusion of value that is based on some ill-defined notion or demand for a particular product, on assumptions, on internal evaluations, and on sheer spin. The more competitive and complex the financial industry became, the more firms had to find ways to extract money by creating increasingly complex securities and transactions. Plain-vanilla securities, as they're called, didn't return as much to investors or make as much for Wall Street bankers at year's end. It's the same with any new consumer technology. When iPhones came out in June 2007, they sold at $499 a pop. Less than two years later, the original model went for $199. Apple needed something to get that $500-per-item price back, so it came out with the iPhone 3G. In the same way, Wall Street always needs to create something new or to leverage or package something to the hilt to keep the money flowing.

My brother works as a trader for one of the largest pension funds in the country. He makes slightly more than the national median wage. But the Wall Street firms that supply him with financial services pay people up to ten times more than the median, even though his fund is their client. As the market and pension funds were melting in late 2008 through 2009, he was incensed to see that brokers from the bigger firms kept pulling up in Lincoln Town Cars. "Why can't they take a cab or rent a car like anybody else from the airport?" he wondered. It was as if they were living in a tomb: a tomb with no newspapers or CNN. Of course, the brokers weren't paying for the Town Cars—the pensioners were picking up the tab, without even getting so much as a "thank you."

Few people begrudge Bill Gates or Steve Jobs or Michael Dell their wealth because it was generated on tangible achievements, on products and services that a vast number of people actually use and have a need for. An actor or an actress might get paid millions for a film, but at least the film has lasting life and entertainment value. The same goes for an obscenely paid football player. At least, he might produce a great moment that becomes part of the national culture. On a less public but equally important level, people all over the country build cars, teach kids, put out fires, and design homes. What they do has a lasting and necessary impact. Only a banker would say that about another banker.

From my own experience, I get far more fulfillment from writing an article than I did from convincing a client to do a trade, even if I believed the trade would benefit the client. But for the most part, transactions on Wall Street simply don't provide any immediate benefit to most of the country. Pushing money around and extracting huge profits are not activities that make Americans better, safer, or even more entertained.

CEOs Dodge the Blame

Congress tends to mimic public outrage in the wake of financial scandals—although it doesn't always find time for follow-through. No congressperson in recent years has more vehemently denounced the gluttony of once-exulted executives than Congressman Henry Waxman (D-CA), the former chairman of the House Committee on Oversight and Government Reform.

On March 7, 2008—a few weeks before the fall of Bear Stearns and six months before subprime loan problems would seem like a mole on an elephant compared to the effects of a full-blown banking and economic crisis—Waxman summoned to Washington a trio of men who'd made a ton of money during the trippy times of the housing boom.

The motley three financial kings were Angelo Mozilo, founder and CEO of Countrywide Financial Corporation, and former chairmen and CEOs E. Stanley O'Neal of Merrill Lynch and Charles Prince of Citigroup.[2] They had collectively sucked up more than $460 million in compensation from 2002 to 2006.[3] The topic of the hearing was *CEO Pay and the Mortgage Crisis*.[4] (It might have been more useful to call it *Why Will All Three Companies Implode a Few Months from Now?*)

Even as financial companies showed signs of impending failure—or, as in the case of Countrywide Financial, sat accused of committing outright fraud—their execs, from lenders to developers to bankers, were reaping extravagant compensation.[5] (Waxman was pulling down somewhere between $150,000 and $165,000 annually for his public office, still better than the median American salary but hardly enough to cover the private drivers for the men who sat before him, whose dollars kept many a congressperson in office.)[6]

"The CEOs of the five hundred largest American companies received an average of $15 million each in the year 2006, and that was a 38 percent increase in just one year," Waxman said, infuriated. The year 2006 was the pinnacle for bonuses, after which the subprime and credit balloons began to leak.

It wasn't only the CEOs raking it in, of course. There were traders at some Wall Street firms who made as much as CEOs at others did. But in general, CEOs set their own standard, particularly when the economy goes south. Those financial titans who can't even claim to have produced anything tangible are the biggest pillage culprits.

The anger at the hearings was almost palpable. Mozilo had already sealed a $4 billion deal on January 11, 2008, for Bank of America to acquire his flailing company.[7] But during the years when he and the other two head execs sitting before Waxman had compiled their stash, stock in their companies had been buzzing. Mozilo effused to the committee, "From 1982 to April 2007, our stock price appreciated over 23,000 percent. As a result, earlier in this decade I received performance-based bonuses earned under a formula based on earnings per share."

It was as if to say, "So, why am I here?" The man had balls. Even with full knowledge of the true condition of the loans on his books, Mozilo felt compelled to give a shout-out to capitalism. "You know," he said, "the capitalistic system when not abused is a wonderful system, but when abused it is terrible."[8] Mozilo, like so many other moguls, cried abuse only when constraints were put on *his* money. He had whined about his downsized 2006 compensation package in an e-mail that Elijah E. Cummings (D-MD) read to the committee.

"Boards have been placed under enormous pressure by the left wing, anti-business press and the envious leaders of unions and other so-called CEO comp watchers," Mozilo wrote. "I strongly believe that, a decade from now, there will be a recognition that entrepreneurship has been driven out of the public sector."[9] We now realize that any entrepreneurship driven out of the financial markets has left town on a stagecoach driven by someone like Mozilo, horsewhip in hand.

Mozilo shouldn't have been concerned that the long-term prospects for CEOs would wane. Historically, the "pressure" that made him feel uncomfortable tends to give way to continued excess. One step back. Two steps forward. This is particularly true when no meaningful systemic changes or restraints are put on the routine practice of getting paid up front for transactions that have long-term impact.

Mozilo danced around the more important questions at the hearing, the ones regarding the plethora of abuses that were standard fare at his firm and that implicated Countrywide as a central player in the subprime component of the larger economic crisis. Back in November 2007, Senator Chuck Schumer (D-NY) wrote a letter to the Federal Housing Finance Board warning its chairman, Ronald A. Rosenfeld, about the Federal Home Loan Bank's $51 billion in cash advances to Countrywide that were collateralized by $64 billion in bad mortgages.

"I find these numbers alarming as reports continue to emerge about how Countrywide's reckless and predatory lending practices were a leading contributor to today's foreclosure crisis," Schumer wrote to Rosenfeld.[10]

Waxman's committee questioned Harley Snyder, chair of the Countrywide Compensation Committee, and Mozilo on protecting shareholder interests and the convenient timing of their stock buybacks. Waxman pointed out to Snyder that it wasn't only Mozilo selling shares during Countrywide's stock-buyback period. So was the board.

"How were those sales in the best interests of the shareholders?" Waxman asked. Snyder dodged the question. "The shareholders had the same opportunity to sell their stock as we had," he said. "Our stocks were sold . . . under a prearranged selling order . . . when stock reaches a certain price which is prearranged, pre-set, that is when the stock is sold."[11] What Snyder didn't say was that those shareholders, like Enron's, didn't exactly have access to the same information on the firm's condition that the insiders did.

Waxman pressed further. "Both [of] you in your roles as CEO and board member have an obligation to act in the best interests of your shareholders. But I am having a difficult time reconciling that issue with Mr. Mozilo's compensation." Mozilo, you see, had been a busy man. When the mortgage crisis started in October 2006, he filed a stock trading plan to sell 350,000 shares per month. He revised the plan twice, first in December, so he could sell 465,000 shares per month, then on February 2, 2007, to sell 580,000 shares per month.

"That was the same day that Countrywide's stock hit a record high of $45 a share," Waxman said. "In total, I believe Mr. Mozilo sold 5.8 million shares for $150 million between November 2006 and the end of 2007." Mozilo pleaded ignorance on the number and said he was selling stocks because of a prearranged retirement schedule.

Waxman wasn't having it. "We don't have exact figures, but it looks like Countrywide shareholders lost all of the $2.5 billion the company spent on repurchasing shares while you were selling stock," he said.

Waxman then turned to Richard Parsons, who chaired Citigroup's board of directors' Personnel and Compensation Committee (and became Citigroup's chairman on January 21, 2009). "If the CEO of Citigroup proposed to sell $150 million worth of stock at the same time Citigroup was engaged in a massive stock buyback, would this raise any red flags for you?" he asked.

Parsons demurred completely and rambled a bunch of corporate mumbo jumbo:

> Well . . . we have procedures in place that would first flag it, second, cause counsel to opine on it, and perhaps more importantly to your question . . . we have a stock ownership requirement that would probably preclude the CEO, such as Mr. Prince, from doing just what your question implied. . . .
>
> But beyond that answer, what we would do, I am sure, is we would consult with counsel, we would consult to understand the reasons, and we would make a judgment based on the facts as we found them then.[12]

In other words, trust us: before we loot the firm, we dot each "i" and cross each "t."

There were other nagging questions besides Mozilo's questionable stock sales. Congressman Paul E. Kanjorski (D-PA) couldn't get his head around the high 18 percent mortgage payment failure rate that appeared as early as 2006:

> Don't you put all those [numbers] together in statistics and say, "These packages we are selling now are failing at such a horrific rate that they'll never last and there will be total decimation of our business and of these mortgages?"[13]

Apparently, total decimation didn't concern Mozilo. The mortgages were sold off his books long before they started to fail. How would he know about their problems? "These mortgages are put in very complex securities and have a lot of charges to them," he responded. "So it's very different to see a loan or series of loans, are they in that particular security or another security? The only one who would know that would be the security holder."[14]

In other words, his company's failures weren't related to the actual mortgages it sold. Note Mozilo's use of the word *complex*. Complexity comes up as one of the most overused excuses for executives' rise and the economy's subsequent fall.

Mozilo's e-mailed response in May 2008 to a mortgage holder who wrote to Countrywide asking for a loan modification was a bit blunter. Mozilo was annoyed that his customers were questioning his firm's methods. "This is unbelievable. Most of these letters now have the same wording. Obviously, they are being counseled by some other person or by the Internet. Disgusting," Mozilo wrote and then accidentally hit "reply" instead of "forward."[15]

Bank of America Acquires a Countrywide Can of Worms

Condemnation for the little guy aside, it's hard to guess what Mozilo knew about Countrywide's subprime loans before he signed the company over to Bank of America. Did Mozilo recognize the mess he was creating and hide it? Or did he stay insulated from that, collecting his fat checks with ignorance? Four months after facing Waxman, Mozilo would walk away from his failed thrift a very rich man. The timing for dumping Countrywide into Bank of America's lap was fortuitous for him and for Goldman Sachs and Sandler O'Neill Partners LLP, which each banked more than $12 million in advisory and contingency fees on the deal.[16]

It would prove a disaster for Bank of America CEO Ken Lewis. When the deal was struck in mid-January 2008, Countrywide was valued at $4 billion, and Bank of America's share price was $38.50.[17] Two weeks later, Countrywide posted a loss of $422 million for the fourth quarter of 2007.[18] By the time the acquisition was completed on

July 1, 2008, tumbling stock prices drove the deal's value down to $2.5 billion.[19] After eight months, $46 billion of TARP money, $118 billion in government-backed asset guarantees, and a lousy merger with Merrill Lynch, Bank of America's stock would bottom out at $3.14, in March 2009.[20] But what happened after Mozilo got his takeout wasn't something he considered to be his problem. It is possible that Mozilo believed that the impending litigation that was handed over to Bank of America and the congealing losses on Countrywide's books had nothing to do with any abuse he imparted, but that seems a stretch.

The deal went through, as most of the big ones do, despite Countrywide shareholder lawsuits alleging everything from insider trading and inflated loan fees to "collusion between the two companies."[21] The suits had been mounting across the country from municipal employee pension funds and from homeowners—the very people who relied most on ethical investing practices from the big banks for their financial security. The Arkansas Teacher Retirement System brought a consolidated complaint, filed October 24, 2007, which alleged insider trading among Countrywide executives.[22] In late February 2008, a class-action lawsuit filed in a Delaware court accused Countrywide of unjustly profiting from inflated fees charged to homeowners with delinquent or foreclosed homes.[23]

The lawsuits also included one filed by New York State comptroller Thomas P. DiNapoli and New York City comptroller William C. Thompson, on behalf of state and city pension funds. It claimed that "unlawful actions and omissions by Countrywide deprived investors of the information needed to make prudent decisions."[24] In other words, the suit charged that Countrywide had committed mortgage fraud.

A similar suit was brought by California attorney general Edmund Brown against Mozilo and Countrywide president David Sambol on June 25, 2008, for using deceptive advertising to lure clients into risky subprime home mortgages, then reselling those mortgages as securities and reaping huge profits. "Countrywide was, in essence, a mass-production loan factory, producing ever-increasing streams of debt without regard for borrowers," Brown said.[25]

Countrywide settled predatory lending claims filed by eleven state attorneys general, led by Illinois and California, on October 6, 2008, and agreed to modify principal and interest rates worth $8.4 billion on nearly 400,000 loans it had initiated.[26] It neither admitted nor denied any wrongdoing, and no fines were levied.[27]

The settlement might have been helpful for borrowers, but it led to a class-action lawsuit from angry investors, brought in December 2008 by Greenwich Financial Services, a Westchester, New York, hedge fund. Greenwich Financial claimed that Bank of America didn't have the right to modify Countrywide's agreements because the loans had been bought at a discount.[28] In short, no one was happy with the deal that turned into an albatross around Bank of America's neck.

As of this writing, Mozilo appeared to be partway to getting his just desserts. In early June 2009 the SEC charged him with fraud and insider trading. Of particular note were his internal e-mails, in which Mozilo referred to a subprime product as "toxic" and said the company was "flying blind." The SEC reported he had cashed in nearly $140 million on his alleged insider stock sales. In addition, it charged that Countrywide made repeated exceptions to its already lax underwriting standards for mortgages without telling investors. Former president of Countrywide, David Sambol, and former Countrywide chief financial officer, Eric Sieracki, were also charged with fraud.[29]

Big Bonuses and Big Layoffs

Waxman's committee also probed several other high-ranking executives at Countrywide, Merrill Lynch, and Citigroup. Representative John A. Yarmuth (D-KY) questioned the panel of executives on whether it thought that excessive compensation in general was tearing at the very fabric of society. The executives thought no such thing. To them, excessive compensation *was* the fabric. Parsons, chair of the Citigroup Compensation Committee, scoffed:

> You have to be competitive. You have to be in the marketplace. And my own impression is that with all its flaws, the market economy still works best out of all the models we have out there to look at and to choose from.[30]

Competitiveness in 2007, when the economy began to tank, apparently meant king-size pay packages for loser executives. Chuck Prince left Citigroup with a $38 million package, plus perks like a car, a driver, an office, and an administrative assistant, all for up to five years.[31] A year later, Citigroup announced that it was firing 50,000 employees worldwide.[32] The firm started to make good on that promise by the fourth quarter of 2008, announcing that it had cut nearly 30,000 workers from the previous quarter.[33] By March 6, 2009, the firm was on government-administered life-support, trading at a buck.[34]

Citigroup employees did not exactly receive the same kind of exit package that CEO Chuck Prince did. They got a more typical and modest arrangement of two weeks' pay for each year of service, with a maximum of a year's worth of severance pay.[35] By the end of the first quarter of 2009, Citigroup exceeded its own downsizing expectations, chopping 65,000 heads from peak levels, to 309,000.[36]

Over at Countrywide, Mozilo had raked in more than $470 million in compensation and stock sales from July 2003 to June 30, 2008—the day before he resigned and the day before the Bank of America deal officially closed—the third-highest compensation of any financial or home-building executive during that time.

(First place went to Charles R. Schwab, CEO of the investment bank Charles Schwab, who got more than $816 million in cash and stock sales during that time. Second was Dwight C. Schar, then CEO of NVR, Inc., a Virginia-based company that builds and sells single-family detached homes, townhouses, and condos, who got more than $626 million over the same period.)[37]

Employees again got the short shrift when Countrywide announced in September 2007 that it was laying off up to 12,000 workers.[38] They weren't given the same sort of perks Mozilo got in his lucrative, though downsized, retirement package.[39]

Stanley O'Neal golden-parachuted out of Merrill Lynch in October 2007[40] with a $160 million compensation package, which included $131 million in stocks and options, $24.7 million in retirement benefits, and $5.4 million in deferred compensation.[41] Days before O'Neal's resignation, the company had announced a staggering $2.3 billion third-quarter loss.[42] That would later be dwarfed by a nearly $5 billion loss announced in the summer of 2008 and a total net loss of $27.6 billion for 2008.[43]

Despite the staggering numbers and the executives' brazenness, all of this wealth transfer and congressional conversation brought no legislative changes. The familiar refrain of shock and awe, followed by an uneasy legislative silence, was heard every time another piece of news on egregious compensation hit the headlines.

What's a Few Million in Bonuses When Your Losses Are in the Billions?

Seven months after Mozilo and the others had been called, Henry Waxman's Committee on Oversight and Government Reform held another hearing on October 7, 2008. This time, in the midst of a full-blown economic crisis, the committee gathered to examine the reasons behind the $85 billion taxpayer bailout for AIG.[44]

Once again, executive pay was a hot topic. It was disclosed during the hearing that in 2005 and 2006, while AIG was still thriving, then CEO Richard Sullivan pulled down $8.4 million in cash bonuses.[45] It was a modest sum compared to the bonuses collected by some of his Wall Street brethren, but an astonishing thing happened after AIG posted a $5 billion fourth-quarter 2007 net loss.

In March 2008, while the AIG board of directors' Compensation Committee mulled over how much to reward Sullivan and other executives for their hard work in 2007, Sullivan urged them to exclude the $5 billion in losses, which were mostly from AIG's Financial Products Division. You know, just ignore them. The board agreed and rewarded Sullivan with a cool $5 million in cash.[46] Pay for performance no longer applied. Pay for hiding losses had kicked in.

Waxman's October 2008 hearing also revealed that AIG executives took a $443,000 corporate retreat at the opulent St. Regis in Monarch Beach, California, a week after AIG got its $85 billion from the American taxpayers. "Check this out," Elijah Cummings (D-MD) said, "AIG spent $200,000 for hotel rooms. Almost $150,000 for catered banquets. AIG spent—listen to this one—$23,000 at the hotel spa and another $1,400 at the salon. They were getting their manicures, their facials, their pedicures, and their massages while American people were footing the bill. And they spent another $10,000 for—I don't know what this is—leisure dining. At bars?"

Cummings then asked Eric Dinallo, the superintendent of the New York State Insurance Department, for his expert opinion on the rather excessive charges. Mind you, this is the man whose job it is to "ensure

the continued sound and prudent conduct of insurers' financial operations" and to "eliminate fraud, other criminal abuse and unethical conduct in the industry."

"Let me ask you, not as insurance commissioner [*sic*], but as a taxpayer, does this look right to you?"

Astoundingly, Dinallo kind of thought it did. "I do agree there is
some profligate spending there—but the concept of bringing all of the
major employees together to ensure that the $85 billion could be as
greatly as possible paid back, would have been not a crazy corporate
decision."

"Well, I would tend to disagree with you," Cummings shouted,
"when it comes to pedicures, facials, manicures—the American people
are paying for that."

"I agree."

"And they are very upset!"

"I said, there are regrettable and wrong headlines in that, but the
idea of making sure you can get the game plan back on track, so you
can pay off the loan, is not an irrational one," Dinallo concluded.[47]

Again, let me remind you that this is the guy who was in charge of
watching over the industry.[48] So you can imagine what was going on
inside the executive offices. At any rate, the game plan apparently never
did get back on track. AIG lost an incredible $61 billion in the fourth
quarter of 2008 alone, even after sucking in all that bailout money.

AIG tried hard to pad its executives' personal checking accounts in
the same spirit of excess. Sullivan's successor, Robert Willumstad,
was the CEO of AIG for only three months, from mid-June 2008 to
mid-September 2008, before he was forced out by then treasury secretary Henry Paulson as part of the original bailout deal.[49] (Paulson
installed his buddy and Goldman Sachs board member Edward Liddy
as CEO at an annual salary of $1. Not that the compensation would
hurt Liddy, who got $63 million from 2001 to 2005 as CEO of fellow
insurance giant Allstate.[50] Liddy would appear for a separate hearing
about AIG bonus payouts before the House Committee on Financial
Services on March 18, 2009.)[51]

Still, Willumstad was contractually entitled to a $22 million
severance package. With sensibility uncharacteristic of the industry,
Willumstad declined.[52] "I prefer not to receive severance payments

while shareholders and employees have lost considerable value in their AIG shares," he wrote to Liddy. Willumstad and AIG also agreed in December 2008 that he would rescind one million AIG shares that were part of his deal to become CEO in the first place.[53] Willumstad was one of few big-name CEOs to eschew entitlement during the crisis.

They Kept the Money

In the end, all of the points Waxman made were valid and reminiscent of those he had made in other hearings. Still, most of the execs made up what they lost in embarrassment points by keeping their money. Shame alone won't propel them to give back more. They had worked through their shame issues way before they made all of their money, and they had the government's help.

Consider the Countrywide VIP scandal, also known as the "Friends of Angelo" program, in which favorable loan conditions were given to high-ranking government officials, including Chris Dodd (D-CT) and Kent Conrad (D-ND), plus a slew of former Fannie Mae CEOs.[54] The story of that cozy friendship ring broke on June 12, 2008, just two weeks before Brown filed suit against Countrywide. In September 2008, the *Wall Street Journal* reported that a Los Angeles grand jury was investigating the loans.[55]

Remarkably, or perhaps unremarkably as these things go, Dodd is still the chairman of the Senate Committee on Banking, Housing, and Urban Affairs, and Conrad is still the chairman of the Senate Budget Committee. It wasn't them but the combination of public wrath and lawsuits that made Mozilo "forgo" his official $37.5 million severance pay, although he didn't give up a supplemental retirement plan (worth $23.8 million in December 2006) and $20.6 million in deferred compensation.[56]

Even with all of the hearings, investigations, subpoenas, and lawsuits, there weren't any corporate paybacks. After all, when CEOs and executives siphon a lot of money from our system, they usually keep it, and the system stays intact.

There was some chatter from nonprofit groups and from Waxman about legislating a recovery, or "claw back," of the estimated $500 million paid to execs at AIG, Bear Stearns, Citigroup, Countrywide,

Lehman, Merrill Lynch, and Washington Mutual. But it remained talk, for the most part. "I think you can count on two hands the number of voluntary or involuntary returns of compensation by executives," said Paul Hodgson, a senior research associate at the research firm Corporate Library, which tracks corporate governance. "More companies are introducing claw-back provisions, but instituting the provisions and actually clawing back the pay are two different things."[57]

It's doubtful that claw backs for bonuses paid for overly risky behavior will become law, although two legislators came close to including a claw-back provision in the economic stimulus package. Senators Olympia Snowe (R-ME) and Ron Wyden (D-OR) sponsored an amendment that passed by voice vote on February 9, 2009, that would have given companies that received TARP money 120 days to pay back—with preferred stock—all bonus money exceeding $100,000 or face a tax of 35 percent on whatever money remained unpaid.[58] But the amendment never made it to the bill that was signed into law on February 17, 2009.[59]

"Somehow it got stripped out behind closed doors," a Wyden spokeswoman told the Associated Press.[60]

But, really, claw backs shouldn't be necessary. If the legislative landscape that encourages risky behavior was sufficiently altered to ensure both less risky practices and compensation tied to long-term growth, rather than to short-term gain, the overall systemic risk would be reduced—as would the profit from that excessive risk. There would be no need for an after-the-fact compensation adjustment.

Yet even after these guys pump up their books, churn unscrupulous deals, cash out big, and let it all collapse, most of them walk away with the money. Many remain at their posts or reappear in hedge funds or on their friends' boards.

The claw-back concept made another comeback in March 2009 when AIG caused public uproar and political overreaction after it announced it had to pay $165 million in bonuses.[61] The sum was relative chump change, but after more than $182 billion in bailout money had already been given to the insurance company, the public wasn't happy.[62]

Although Treasury Secretary Timothy Geithner and the rest of the Obama administration claimed they hadn't known much about the bonuses until it came time for AIG to pay up—when in doubt, claim ignorance—the bonuses were first revealed in SEC filings in

September 2008. So they had been public information for a long time, and numerous news outlets had reported on them.[63]

On March 18, 2009, the culprit came forward. Chris Dodd admitted that he had added the language to the federal stimulus package that allowed existing bonus contracts to stand—of course, he did so only at the insistence of the administration, he said.

"The administration had expressed reservations," Dodd told CNN. "They asked for modifications."[64]

After cable news started hammering day and night on the AIG bonuses, President Obama tried to get Geithner to use the legal system to block them, and an Obama insider said that the bonus money would be taken out of a pending $30 billion bailout gift to AIG, which Geithner confirmed.[65]

Ultimately, it was the House that responded most publicly to the outcry over the bonuses, by passing a 90 percent tax on bonuses greater than $250,000 for TARP recipients.[66] It was a controversial measure that passed overwhelmingly, although some who voted for the bill expressed reservations. It also led certain banks, like Goldman Sachs, Morgan Stanley and JPMorgan Chase, to apply to pay back their TARP money as soon as possible, but they would retain ample federal backing from other avenues besides TARP. The banks knew that, even if Congress didn't bother to question it. While Congress was debating TARP recipient restrictions, the idea of attaching restrictions to other forms of federal assistance never came up. Still hasn't.

"It is an extreme use of the tax code to correct an extreme and excessive wrong done to the American taxpayer," Dave Camp (R-MI), who voted for the measure, admitted on the House floor. Camp is right, but not quite for the reasons he mentioned. Using the tax code and restructuring the financial arena to produce less risk and bonus excess would be more beneficial to the stability of the overall economy. At any rate, the Senate knocked down the bill and claw backs have kind of faded away.[67]

Conflict of Interest

On October 6, 2008—the same day Countrywide agreed to refinance 400,000 home mortgages—Dick Fuld, the former CEO of Lehman Brothers, was in Waxman's hot seat.

Fuld is a self-proclaimed "Lehman lifer." He was first employed at the company as an intern in 1966 while attending the University of Colorado and started to work full time in 1969 while earning his business degree at New York University.[68] He was named vice chairman of Shearson Lehman Brothers in 1984, after American Express bought Lehman and merged with Shearson.[69] From 1990 to 1993, Fuld was president and co-CEO of Shearson Lehman Brothers before being named CEO of Lehman Brothers Holdings, Inc., in 1994, after Lehman went public. Along the way, he gained posts in prominent New York City financial and investment institutions, such as the Federal Reserve Bank of New York and the Partnership for New York City, Inc.[70] And as Fuld moved up the ranks, Lehman's stock price puffed up, from $5 per share when it went public in 1994 to $86 per share by 2007.[71] Just a year later, on September 15, 2008, Lehman declared bankruptcy.[72]

Before that, Fuld cashed out. When asked, he declared that he only made "somewhere near" $350 million, not $500 million, which Fuld told Henry Waxman was "inaccurate."

"Not that anyone on this committee cares about this, but I wake up every single night wondering what I could have done differently," Fuld said shamelessly.[73]

But when asked why he thought that Lehman was allowed to fail while the Federal Reserve saved other companies such as Bear Stearns, mortgage giants Fannie Mae and Freddie Mac, and insurance giant AIG, Fuld was more contrite. "Until the day they put me in the ground, I will wonder," he said.[74]

Representative Dennis Kucinich (D-OH) wondered the same thing. He also pondered why Goldman Sachs was still standing so tall. So he asked Luigi Zingales, a finance expert, a professor at the University of Chicago Graduate School of Business, and the author of the 2003 book *Saving Capitalism from Capitalists,* who responded with the following:

> When you hear about that, you know, a decision was made to let Lehman go down. Goldman Sachs is still standing for sure. Are you concerned, given these facts, that there is an apparent conflict of interest by the treasury secretary in permitting a principal of a firm that he was a CEO with to be involved in these discussions about the survival of Lehman?[75]

Zingales began a long-winded, though insightful, answer about Goldman's involvement with AIG, a major player in the credit default swap market. He noted that another big name, JPMorgan Chase, had $7 trillion in the credit default market and would be out that amount if AIG went under.[76] His implication was that Lehman's entanglements weren't as important, and in this, he revealed one of the true reasons for the continued AIG bailouts. But he didn't directly answer the question until pressed.

"Let me ask you this," Kucinich interrupted him. "You throw Lehman Brothers overboard. Does that help what competitive position may remain with respect to Goldman Sachs?"

"I think it is clear that Goldman Sachs benefits from Lehman Brothers going under, yes," Zingales said.

Therein lies the checkmate against Fuld. After his forty-year-career with Lehman, the ultimate punishment may have been the cold reality that his ties to the powerful deciders in D.C. were simply not strong enough.

Still, Fuld managed to save a small fortune, $100 million according to the *New York Times*, and $350 million according to his statements to Waxman. Sure, he took a hit. At one time his company stock was valued at $800 million, but I'm thinking whatever he kept in the end is still a pretty livable nest egg.

Lehman's ordinary employees, like Enron's and Countrywide's, didn't get out quite so well. Days before Lehman declared bankruptcy, Lehman Holdings, the bankrupt entity, laid off about a thousand workers via letters saying that their promised severance payments and health benefits would cease immediately.[77]

Please Don't Call It a Bonus

From 2000 to 2008, Wall Street paid more than $185 billion in bonuses to its employees, including $130 billion in the latter four years, according to a report issued on January 28, 2009, by New York State comptroller Thomas P. DiNapoli.[78]

While most Americans were focused on keeping their jobs in early 2009, public wrath over Wall Street bonuses was strong. The outrage led President Obama to acknowledge the "shameful" excess, striking a populist pose on February 4, 2009, by announcing a $500,000 cap on the cash part of executive compensation for those firms that going forward wanted to float on a bed of TARP dollars.[79]

Six days later, on February 10, 2009, Treasury Secretary Geithner's first public speech was full of harsh admonishment. "Investors and banks took risks they did not understand," He said. "Individuals, businesses, and governments borrowed beyond their means. The rewards that went to financial executives departed from any realistic appreciation of risk."[80]

There were more tame compensation restrictions to come. Dodd inserted a bonus limit for executives from firms receiving federal financial aid to one-third of their yearly salary until the money gets repaid into the stimulus package Obama signed in February 2009.[81] But the thing is, despite the astonishing $18.4 billion that Wall Street paid itself for an abysmal 2008, the remaining firms will still find a way to pay their execs sick sums of money in the future.[82] The big financial companies are raising base salaries to make up for the bonus cap. In late May 2009, Morgan Stanley chief financial officer Colm Kelleher saw his base yearly salary more than double to $750,000 from $323,000.[83] It's even easier to structure noncash compensation methods than it is subprime collateralized debt obligations (CDOs) or to rename bonuses "retention awards," as one senior Morgan Stanley executive told his employees to call them.

"There will be a retention award. Please do not call it a bonus. It is not a bonus. It is an award. And it recognizes the importance of keeping our team in place as we go through this integration," James Gorman, co-president of Morgan Stanley, told his advisers during a recorded conference call obtained by the *Huffington Post* on February 11, 2009. Gorman said the awards would be linked to 2008 performance and added, "I think I can hear you clapping from here in New York. You should be clapping because frankly that is a very generous and thoughtful decision that we have made."[84]

The argument over entitlement and talent versus stability and restraint reigns supreme on Wall Street, with many media outlets and pundits chiming in to lament the loss of "talent" in the industry as a result of bonus or other compensation restrictions, bailout or no bailout.

"In placing limits on executive pay, the administration faces a few potential pratfalls. First, if the plan is too restrictive, it could drive away talent from the companies that perhaps need a bailout the most. After all, why take a job at a place that's in need of a turnaround if there's little reward at the end of the day?" Brian Wingfield and Josh Zumbrun wrote on Forbes.com on February 4, 2009.[85]

But that's a bunch of bull. It doesn't take talent to win when your firm makes the rules, holds the cards, and *is* the house. And it's extreme negligence when you lose. At any rate, if the industry and the transactions in which it engages were less risky, and therefore less dangerous to the greater population, and more regulated, and therefore not spilling extra profits to the house by extorting them from the public, even the most "talented" of the "talent" wouldn't need to get paid $25 million for three months just to show up. (Yes, that means you, Peter Kraus, for your nonstint at Merrill Lynch before it merged with Bank of America).

Outside of normal-perspective land, cash composes a disproportionately low percentage of an executive's compensation package. That's why the seemingly magnanimous Wall Street execs can forgo a year or two of cash bonuses to get the government off their backs and out of their capital pool.[86]

Just ask former treasury secretary Henry Paulson. For 2005, he received only $600,000 in cash but $38.2 million in other forms of compensation, including $30.1 million in restricted shares (which had a five-year vesting period had he not become treasury secretary) and 220,000 stock options.[87]

At the start of the TARP capital injections in October 2008, Paulson had to work to convince Goldman Sachs CEO Lloyd Blankfein and JPMorgan Chase CEO Jamie Dimon to take TARP money. Blankfein and Dimon didn't want to seem weak by being clustered among all of the other loser banks. At least that's what they conveyed. But they pocketed the money anyway—who wouldn't? Especially without any stringent restrictions on how they could use it?

After much congressional debate, language was added to the stimulus that merely took into account golden parachutes and did away with favorable tax treatment for compensation payments greater than $500,000.

Bonuses Always Bounce Back

But in the end, none of this political posturing over compensation legislation language really matters. Wall Street anticipated a weak bonus year for 2009 for two reasons. First, because anyone who could evaluate a decaying asset at all—I'm excluding Washington from this skill—knew that the banking system would only deteriorate further in the near future, even if Washington backed private investors to buy toxic assets. Second, banks still owed money they had borrowed using their inferior assets as collateral. The payback clock didn't stop simply because banks wouldn't disclose exactly what they owned or owed, which really should have been part of Obama's conditions.

But bonuses always bounce back. During the last twenty-five years, there have been four periods of decreased bonuses. Each was followed by increases that made up for those dents within a year or two. Yes, this time the meltdown is more pronounced, but I'm taking that into account. Someone will get paid to put the pieces of broken banks back together again and repackage and resell the toxic assets.

Recall that during the Savings and Loan Crisis, 747 savings and loan banks were shut, the Federal Savings and Loan Insurance Corporation went bust, and the Resolution Trust Corporation swooped in to collect bad (mostly real-estate) assets. Ultimately, this exercise cost the American public half a trillion dollars.[88]

Wall Street bonuses were down in 1988 and 1989 by 21.3 percent and 5.5 percent, respectively.[89] Guess what? By 1991, they had doubled.

In 1994, during the Mexican Peso Crisis, Wall Street bonuses were cut 15.7 percent, only to rebound 26.7 percent the following year. Similarly, recall that in 1998, the Fed, spurred by a bunch of personally invested CEOs, bailed out Long Term Capital for a paltry $3.65 billion during the Russian debt crisis. Wall Street pared back, and cut bonuses by 18.8 percent. They jumped by 48.5 percent the next year.

Then there was the triple whammy of the Enron and WorldCom scandals in late 2001 and 2002, compounded by the recession that was caused by a spate of scandalous corporate bankruptcies and a nervous post-9/11 stock market. Bonuses were down 33.5 percent and 25 percent during those two years. By 2004, they zoomed back to pre-recession levels.

Bonuses nearly doubled over the next two (subprime, CDO, and credit derivatives growth) years, reaching all-time highs in 2006, a record year for two since-deceased investment banks, Bear Stearns and Lehman Brothers. Bonuses remained in the clouds through 2007.

For 2008, bonuses were down just 44 percent, to 2004 levels despite a complete Wall Street hemorrhaging; the near-fatal condition of the country's largest bank, Citigroup; the closing of two major investment banks; and the immensely stubborn and reckless merger of another, Merrill Lynch, into Bank of America, for which Merrill CEO John Thain bagged a $15 million sign-on bonus and $68 million in stock options.[90]

Even if bonuses slide another 30 percent in 2009, which, given the positive projections at the beginning of the year, is likely, they would still return to 2007 levels by 2010. Besides, there are many ways to get around the $500,000 cash cap: giving out restricted shares and stock options, creating an offshore company, whose exercisable shares are directly related to the shares of the main company, or repaying TARP out of drastically reduced tax payments (that is, pay back Uncle Sam with Uncle Sam's money). Goldman's 2008 taxes, for instance, dropped to $14 million from $6 billion in 2007.[91]

In late June 2009, Citigroup had the gall to announce that it would get around its bonus caps by increasing some employees' base salaries by as much as 50 percent.[92] Around the same time, the *Guardian* reported that Goldman would pay its biggest bonuses ever, after posting a $3.4 billion profit less than eight months after it took its first government (read: public) cent.[93]

But, in the end, Wall Street bankers won't even have to wait that long. Change a few category titles here and reported losses there, and bonuses have a way of perking right back up.

It's the Complexity, Stupid!

On February 11, 2009, yet *another* congressional hearing was held, this time by the House Committee on Financial Services, to attempt to understand the gap between executive pay and the dissolving banking industry.

Congressman Paul E. Kanjorski framed the situation. "As executives of large companies, you once lived behind a one-way mirror, unaccountable to the public at-large and often sheltered from shareholder scrutiny. But when you took taxpayer money, you moved into a fish bowl. Millions are watching you today, and they would like some degree of explanation and responsibility. I do, too."[94]

The concept that companies took the money from the public didn't sit well with the CEOs. It was a point of professional pride to set the record straight. Like Mozilo, Lloyd Blankfein of Goldman Sachs blamed "complexity" for the failure of the financial system, in an op-ed attached to his prepared statement: "*Complexity* got the better of us. The industry let the growth in new instruments outstrip the operational capacity to manage them. As a result, operational risk increased dramatically and this had a direct effect on the overall stability of the financial system."[95]

This was really rich, coming from a man whose firm boasts the ability to "anticipate the rapidly changing needs of our clients" and stresses "creativity and imagination in everything we do."[96]

"We understand that the old model no longer works and the old rules no longer apply," Vikram Pandit, the CEO of Citigroup, stated in his prepared statement. Don't count on Pandit and his friends to make a new model and new rules that in any way benefit you, however.

Still, my favorite comment came from JPMorgan CEO Jamie Dimon, a firm that, as I mentioned, took government money only for the good of the country.

"As this committee is aware, JPMorgan Chase did not seek the government's investment," Dimon said. "But we agreed to support the government's goal of obtaining the participation of all major banks."[97] Taking one for the team was apparently part of the TARP deal in the first place. Even Ken Lewis tried to go there early on when his bank was part of the first nine TARP recipients.

"Now explain, why was it so important to the government that everybody agreed, that the nine largest banks are *all* in this?" Leslie Stahl of *60 Minutes* asked Ken Lewis in an October 2008 interview. Lewis has made $165 million in total compensation during the last five years.

"If you have a bank in that group that really, really needed the capital, you don't want to expose that bank," Lewis said.

"In other words, stigmatize it," Stahl said.

"Right, exactly."

"So everybody knows that they're not as good as somebody else."

"Exactly."[98]

So basically, Lewis, like the rest of his compatriots, would opt for secrecy over restraint every time. And that secrecy let him keep his money, even as his bank flirted with low single-digit stock prices on the back of nearly a quarter of a trillion dollars' worth of government money six months after that interview.

Take V

And the hearings kept going. On March 25, 2009, Geithner told the House Financial Services Committee that the administration had proposed legislation to allow the government to regulate nonbank financial activity as stringently as it regulates banks.[99] He also pointed out limits already in place on executive pay for TARP-recipient banks going forward, but so far there has been no mention of a system ensuring that executives are appropriately paid for performance.

That sounds uplifting, except the black cloud that remains is that at the same hearing, Fed Chairman Ben Bernanke basically advocated keeping the compensation system the way it is, with the public impotent to do anything legal about it. "We have pressed AIG to ensure that all compensation decisions are covered by robust corporate governance, including internal review, review by the Compensation Committee of the Board of Directors, and consultations with outside experts," Bernanke said. "Operating under this framework, AIG has voluntarily limited the salary, bonuses, and other types of compensation for 2008 and 2009 of the CEO and other senior managers."[100]

This whole notion of voluntary regulation is abhorrent. There should be no voluntary regulation when public funds are involved. I don't have the voluntary right not to disclose my income to the IRS. I accept that, even though I don't respect the general inequities in the tax code for mere mortals against intensively staffed companies.

Basically, Bernanke, the man who regulates the biggest financial firms in the country, said that even under intense public and political scrutiny, the existing compensation system for the top AIG executives should be kept as is. This for a company that after all the ruckus over $165 million in executive bonuses, turned out to have really paid a total of $454 million to six thousand workers.[101]

But what bugs me and should bug you even more than the money these guys pocketed is this acceptance of the status quo. Assuming that the economy eventually recovers—or at least that its favorite outside indicators, such as stock market levels, say it has—without significant restructuring of the tax code for all elements of compensation, be they in cash, stock, options, or anything else under any name, we don't have a snowball's chance in hell of preventing the kind of risky excess that feeds personal and systemic greed.

Plus, even though we just went through a whole chapter together about all the personal takeouts of financial leaders and their closest management circles, we should keep in mind that the egregious bailout amounts bestowed upon the industry overshadowed compensation figures by trillions of dollars.

That's why, in the end, the only true way to contain the risk that accompanies the most blatant excess is to focus on restructuring the financial system. And Wall Street will fight any revision, tooth and nail. Game on.

8

Big Banks Mean Big Trouble

It is easier to rob by setting up a bank than by holding up a bank clerk.
—*Bertolt Brecht*[1]

The phrase "too big to fail" came up a lot during the Second Great Banking Crisis. It irritated me more than most expressions because it implied that banks were like these biological organisms with powers of reproduction that couldn't be stopped. It makes them sound so ominous. Yet the expression raises a larger question: why would anyone, particularly an entity responsible for monitoring and regulating the banking system—like, um, the Federal Reserve—let any company in the system *get* too big to fail?

If it were your personal checking account backing a financial institution, wouldn't you try to stop it from getting "too big to fail"? You know, try to keep Humpty Dumpty from teetering on the edge of the wall, about to splat onto the pavement? It wouldn't have been that hard.

Here's how it could have gone down:

Commercial Bank says to Investment Bank, "Let's merge and become Super Bank."

> Investment Bank says to Commercial Bank, "Great, we can use your deposits as collateral to back my bets."

> Commercial Bank says, "Cool, let's ask the Fed if it's okay and go get us some leverage and market share."

And the Fed could have said, "No way, you guys are too big and scary already for us to keep up with. Frankly, we have no idea what it is you do every day."

Only, as we've discussed, the Fed has a hard time with no. So, time and time again, it said, "Yes. Yes, you can."[2]

Or Congress could have stepped in and said, "You know, it's not a very good idea, in general, for a consumer-oriented commercial bank to merge with a speculative investment bank. That's the sort of combination that led to the Great Depression in the 1930s and was the reason we passed laws against that kind of thing."

Only, as we've discussed Congress didn't. As we've seen, it repealed those laws in 1999.

So Commercial Bank acquired Investment Bank, piled on risk and debt, and wound up taking trillions of dollars from taxpayers to clean up the resulting mess.

You might be wondering why that happened. After all, banks *could* have been stopped from getting too big to fail and sucking up mountains of public money, because, despite all the deregulation, leaders and regulators in Washington still had the ability to put on the big bank brakes. Instead, Washington chose to go in the opposite direction. Legislators *made* these banks too big to fail by not questioning all the shotgun financial marriages. In fact, they *encouraged* them. In the process, banks gained more control over the market and made massive profits before they tanked. The CEOs who pushed the most mergers made the most money, and you paid for their hubris.

The consolidated banking system runs counter to the free market competition that so many bank-friendly politicians, CNBC hosts, and public leaders talk about. Cornering the market is not only anticompetitive, it's economically dangerous. Unfortunately, all of the safeguards to keep banks from getting too big to fail were methodically shattered.

The History of Small Is Better

Let's go back one hundred and fifty years and talk railroads—it'll help clarify the idea of small and stable versus big and dangerous. The first transcontinental railroad was completed in 1869, the same year that began a period of manic investment floated on extensive borrowing from and between banks. Railroads in 1869 were the new hot thing. That is, until someone got hurt. Unexpected cost overruns by the Northern Pacific Railway bankrupted its main investor, Jay Cooke and Company, leading several other major banks to fail. Suddenly, the banks found that no one wanted to buy bonds in railroad companies anymore. Nearly 90 railroad bankruptcies followed, and 101 national banks failed in September 1873.[3] The recession that killed public confidence in the market following the Panic of 1873 lasted four years.[4]

The overgrowth of the railroad industry was made possible by banks' eagerness to profit from, and extend huge amounts of credit into, a speculative new market. This financial-zeal-gone-wild contributed to the rise of the trust system and, ultimately, to the Sherman Antitrust Act of 1890. Understand, though, it wasn't the failure of railroads that brought down the banks or created the market panic. It was the leverage, or borrowing, that screwed everything up. In the same way, it wasn't the subprime market collapse that wrecked the banks and the greater economy; it was all of the gluttonous borrowing on top of the subprime loans that did the deed.

The Standard Oil Trust that sprouted in 1882 was the brainchild of industrialist John D. Rockefeller.[5] The concept was that any oil company could join the trust and get a share of its profits or stand alone and die. Bigger was sold as safer. Trusts in cotton oil, linseed oil, sugar refineries, and whiskey copied the idea.[6] Senator John Sherman (R-OH), however, realized that one company dominating an entire industry was the antithesis of free market capitalist ideology—which it still is—and in 1890 he authored the Sherman Antitrust Act. Not only would the Sherman Act prohibit concentration and control in the hands of a few players, but it would prevent the possibility that the failure of a few big players could lead to another economic downfall. The Sherman Act passed overwhelmingly in both houses of Congress.[7]

So, I ask you, does any of this sound familiar? Companies too big to fail bringing down the economy? Congress got the joke more than a century ago. It just doesn't today.

Alas—sometimes you need a good "alas"—the Sherman Act did not apply to banking. The Supreme Court had ruled decades earlier, in *Nathan v. Louisiana* in 1850 and *Paul v. Virginia* in 1868, that Congress had no authority over banks because bank transactions were not considered interstate commerce. Congress can legislate commercial transactions between states but must stay out of transactions within a state.[8]

Of course, companies found ways to weasel around the law. In 1914, amid public outcry, Representative Henry de Lamar Clayton (D-AL) proposed an amendment to the Sherman Act that became known as the Clayton Antitrust Act.[9] Banking again remained nearly untouched, as the Clayton Act's restrictions applied only to commodities traders, not to financial firms. In one of the first steps in the evolution of the Federal Reserve Board's power, the Clayton Act did give the Fed regulatory power over banks.

Although banks remained unencumbered by antitrust restrictions, in 1944 the Supreme Court ruled in *U.S. v. South-Eastern Underwriters Association* that the federal government and the Sherman Act could regulate insurance firms.[10] Still, the Bank Holding Company Act of 1956, which I talked about earlier, was enacted to prevent banks from buying up other banks across state lines, thereby keeping them smaller and more manageable.

Too Big to Do Anything but Fail

Half a century later, those state boundaries blocking bank expansions were proving to be really annoying. Big bankers just had to find a willing politician to fix this cumbersome regulation.

One of the main champions of interstate banking was then Bank of America head Hugh McColl.[11] In July 1992, presidential nominee Bill Clinton and McColl met at a Holiday Inn in Valdosta, Georgia. Southern comfort food —"rice and butter beans and tomato and okra," McColl later recalled—was the backdrop, as the two men met to talk about some serious banking deregulation and horse trading.

In exchange for McColl's promise to support inner-city banks, Clinton agreed to support interstate banking.[12] Sure enough, two years later, on September 29, 1994, President Bill Clinton signed the Riegle-Neal Interstate Banking and Branching Efficiency Act of 1994 for his banker buddy. The act, which went into effect in 1997, repealed the interstate restrictions of the Bank Holding Company Act. It unleashed a wave of 4,657 bank mergers from 1994 to June 1999.[13]

The 1999 Gramm-Leach-Bliley Financial Modernization Act— recall, that's the act that allowed commercial banks to buy investment banks and insurance companies—made mergers even more attractive.[14] The merger mania in the late 1990s was further spurred by the subsequent hyper-competition that arose between key industry players. Bigger wasn't just about getting so big the government would have to support you in case of failure. It was mostly about getting deposits that could be used as collateral for juicier transactions. Banks simply couldn't post competitive quarterly earnings if they couldn't borrow against a big pool of capital, which deposits handily provided.

Mergers and acquisitions between banks became an increasingly high-stakes game of one-upmanship. Chemical and Chase merged in 1995 in a deal worth 1.4 times book value.[15] Just two years later, in 1997, McColl's NationsBank acquired Barnett for 4 times book value.[16] Megadeals were a license to print money.

Then came the last of McColl's conquests, a $62 billion merger between Bank of America and NationsBank that went through in late September 1998. At the time, it was the biggest financial merger in the United States.[17] But the real poster child for supermarket bank mergers came about a week later when the $70 billion Citicorp– Travelers Group merger was completed in October 1998.[18] That deal was followed by several other impressive deals, including the Norwest Corporation acquisition of Wells Fargo in November 1998 for $34 billion; the Chase acquisition of J.P. Morgan in December 2000, also worth $34 billion; the Bank of America acquisition of Fleet Boston in April 2004, worth $49 billion; and, on July 1, 2004, the JPMorgan Chase acquisition of Bank One Corporation, worth $59 billion. The banking landscape was fast becoming a competitive game between a handful of very large banks. Among the teams in the financial big leagues were Citigroup, JPMorgan Chase, Bank of America, Washington Mutual, and Wachovia, which in October 2006 acquired Golden West Financial Corporation for $26 billion.[19]

These banks would turn out to have the biggest problems during the latter third of this decade. They overleveraged their subprime loan books, got too involved with collateralized debt obligations and credit derivatives, and came running to the federal government for bailout billions. They would be at the center of the Second Great Bank Depression and would never admit it was their burgeoning debt and risky financial creations that did them in (they blamed the decline of subprime mortgage payments and housing prices).

And yet the Federal Reserve kept approving mergers in the midst of the Second Great Bank Depression. The first was JPMorgan Chase's acquisition of Bear Stearns in March 2008 for $1.2 billion, followed by Bank of America's September 2008 acquisition of Merrill Lynch initially valued at $50 billion, the September 2008 JPMorgan Chase acquisition of WaMu for $1.9 billion, and rounded out by Wells Fargo getting Wachovia in a $12.7 billion deal announced in October 2008. Way to go, Fed, render the industry even more concentrated, with even bigger players. Really destabilize our future.

The new big bank merger wave at the end of 2008 didn't face any pushback on Capitol Hill, either. The few remaining regulations were ignored, such as the cap in the Riegle-Neal Act that limited banks to less than 10 percent ownership of total U.S. deposits. As always, banks found legislative loopholes: the limit only applies to bank holding company mergers. Because JPMorgan Chase, for instance, acquired WaMu, a thrift, the limit didn't apply. The deal got around the law because WaMu's primary business, as a thrift, was to originate home mortgages, which it did using existing deposits.[20] Never mind that the U.S. government considered WaMu's holdings to be bank deposits. WaMu had $182 billion of customer deposits, and after the acquisition JPMorgan Chase had $900 billion in total deposits, the most of any bank in the country.[21] Total deposits at savings and commercial banks during the summer of 2008 were about $7 trillion for the country, giving JPMorgan Chase roughly 13 percent of all deposits at the time.[22]

Citigroup Buys Up Everything

Financial titan Sandy Weill was one of the merger kings of the 1980s and the 1990s. After navigating a succession of top spots in firms from

American Express to Travelers Insurance, he set his gaze on a choicer prize, Citicorp, and created the biggest supermarket bank in America. The new bank, Citigroup, would provide it all: insurance coverage and commercial and investment banking. All that Weill needed to do was repeal a major piece of Great Depression regulatory legislation: that Glass-Steagall Act of 1933. So that's what he set about doing.

With incredible brazenness and the help of influential friends, on April 4, 1998, the boards of Travelers and Citigroup agreed to a $70 billion merger, a then illegal proposition under Glass-Steagall.[23] To push the deregulatory envelope and legalize the marriage, Weill held a news conference suggesting that Congress repeal Glass-Steagall.[24]

He had a powerful ally. Then Fed chairman Alan Greenspan proved receptive during a secret meeting with Citicorp and Travelers representatives, and he essentially cleared the deal.[25] Trusting nothing to chance, Weill still needed to officially kill Glass-Steagall, and lobbyists for Travelers and Citicorp fought hard to get it repealed.[26] Their expenditures in 1998 reached $9 million, with seventeen lobbying reports filed under "banking" and eleven filed under "taxes."[27] The Citicorp-Travelers merger was completed October 8, 1998.[28] Before that, in November 1997, Travelers bought Salomon Brothers and merged it with Smith Barney, already a Travelers affiliate.

"Merging Smith Barney and Salomon Brothers accomplishes in a short time what it would have taken either of us a considerable time to build," Smith Barney CEO and Weill protégé James Dimon said at the time of the Salomon pickup.[29] A decade later, Dimon would be a financial titan in his own right and would pop up as a defiant character in today's crisis.

Citigroup became the world's largest corporate-combo financial services company. It could do just about everything: sell you a mortgage, insure your life, and consolidate your ever-increasing debt.[30] Citigroup would also become the most valuable financial company, with a market capitalization of about $135 billion and $698 billion in total assets at the time of the merger.[31]

Mergers don't always result in good corporate governance, however. Sandy Weill stepped down as CEO at the end of 2003.[32] The same year, Citigroup agreed to pony up $400 million to settle charges that it had manipulated research to land clients.[33] The Citigroup board was also distinguished as the worst in the nation by the Corporate Library in 2003.[34] Weill would stay on that board as chairman until 2006 and, as of 2009, still holds the title of chairman emeritus.[35] Also in 2009, in light of the billions in bailout money going to Citigroup, Weill gave up a consulting gig that had allowed him to use a company jet, a car and a driver, and an office and earn as much as $173,000 yearly.[36]

Big mistakes were made under Weill, and they continued after his resignation as CEO. Citigroup's financial supermarket invested in subprime mortgages, which were considered a sure bet until suddenly they weren't. The subprime mess effectively ended Citigroup's supermarket model. In January 2009, Morgan Stanley acquired 51 percent of Citibank's Smith Barney brokerage unit and paid $2.7 billion in cash up front.[37] Vikram Pandit, Citigroup's current CEO, announced plans to sell CitiFinancial, its consumer finance division, and Primerica insurance units in January 2009, dismantling a chunk of the supermarket Weill built.[38]

Bank of America Works to Keep Up

Ken Lewis spent most of his career rising through the ranks of Bank of America's regional commercial bank divisions. He joined North Carolina National Bank (NCNB, the predecessor to NationsBank and Bank of America) in 1969 as a credit analyst in Charlotte and worked himself up to chairman, CEO, and president of Bank of America in April 2001.

Lewis learned much from his forerunner, Hugh McColl, and reestablished Bank of America as an active political player and a merger maniac.[39] McColl had Bank of America spend $4.6 million on lobbying efforts in 1998—the same year that talk of repealing Glass-Steagall was heating up.[40] In 1999, lobbying expenditures plummeted to $340,000.[41] Under Lewis, lobbying expenditures from 2006 to 2008 were again ramped up, reaching $4.1 million in 2008.[42]

Lewis and McColl suffered equally from merger fever, and advisers were paid handsomely to keep the fever boiling. As mentioned, Bank of America acquired FleetBoston Financial Corp for $49 billion on April 1, 2004. Goldman Sachs got $25 million as Bank of America's advisers on the deal, while Morgan Stanley advised FleetBoston for the same amount. On January 3, 2006, Bank of America acquired MBNA Corp for $36 billion. Keefe Bruyette & Woods Inc. was paid $31 million in fees by Bank of America, and MBNA paid $40 million in fees to UBS Investment Bank and another $8 million to Perella Weinberg Partners. The next year,

Bank of America acquired ABN AMRO North America Holding for $21 billion on October 1, 2007. Goldman Sachs, Morgan Stanley, and UBS Investment Bank each bagged $2 million for advising ABN.[43]

Then, Bank of America had to go and buy Countrywide Financial. Fortunately for the firm, Countrywide was a comparatively cheap deal, announced on January 11, 2008, at $4 billion. Otherwise it could have really ripped the firm's capital apart. On April 27, 2009, to distance its acquisition from the bad memories of 2008 and impending SEC indictments for its former leaders, Bank of America renamed its Countrywide arm "Bank of America Home Loans," a move called "rebranding" in corporate land.

For his merger efforts, Lewis netted $110 million in salary, stocks, and bonuses from 2001 to 2007.[44] As we have seen, 2008 and 2009 did not treat him as kindly. Case in point, on September 15, 2008, Bank of America announced its biggest and dumbest acquisition of all, the purchase of Merrill Lynch in a $50 billion all-stock deal.[45] When the deal went through on January 1, 2009, Bank of America was trading at $33.74. Three weeks later, its stock price had lost 80 percent of its value, falling to $6.68.[46] The only people to make money on the deal were Bank of America's advisers, Fox-Pitt Kelton and JC Flowers and Co., which each got $10 million.[47]

It wasn't only Lewis's merger instincts that were under scrutiny; it was his decision to pay the bonuses of his marquee (for all the wrong reasons) acquisition, Merrill Lynch, even while Bank of America was getting bailouts left and right from the government.

On March 17, 2009, the House Committee on Oversight and Government Reform requested Merrill Lynch's records regarding those $3.6 billion in bonuses, which were agreed to before Bank of America bought Merrill.[48]

Finger Interests, Ltd., a longtime Bank of America shareholder, led the charge to change Bank of America's leadership at the bank's April 29, 2009, annual shareholders meeting. Managing partner Jerry Finger said in a press release:

> We believe the board allowed management to pursue acquisitions that have permanently reduced shareholder value through dilution, particularly with the acquisition of Merrill Lynch approved by shareholders without access to full disclosure on December 5,

2008. The board—including its leadership—and management knew, or should have known, of massive fourth quarter losses at Merrill during October and November prior to the shareholder vote, but did not communicate those losses or amend the proxy that shareholders used to vote on the merger. Since the announcement of the merger, the market capitalization of Bank of America has fallen by over 80%.[49]

Jerry Finger sort of got his wish for a leadership change: on April 30, 2009, it was announced that shareholders had voted to relieve Ken Lewis of his chairman duties, although he would keep his key CEO slot.[50] It was Amy Wood Brinkley who took the bigger fall. On June 4, 2009, Bank of America announced that she was being forced out after eight years as chief risk officer and a thirty-one-year tenure with the company.[51] Brinkley had given up her bonus in 2008 but she still took home $37.2 million over the course of her term as chief risk officer. She was replaced by Greg Curl who, ironically, was the lead negotiator for the Merrill acquisition.[52] So now Merrill's guy is running risk at Bank of America. That's comforting.

JPMorgan Chase Wisely Waits for the Government's Merger Assistance

Under William B. Harrison's leadership, commercial bank Chase acquired investment bank J.P. Morgan for $33.5 billion on December 31, 2000, a year after Glass-Steagall was repealed.[53] (Not to shy away from making a buck on its own deal, J.P. Morgan paid itself $58 million in fees, and Chase paid itself $50.5 million in fees.) With Harrison out of the picture, JPMorgan Chase CEO Jamie Dimon consistently stayed above the fray during the Second Great Bank Depression, as his firm avoided the thrashing that his main competitors, Citigroup and Bank of America, took.

Before picking up the pieces of WaMu, which had been the nation's biggest savings and loan bank until it disintegrated in September 2008, Dimon had been Sandy Weill's right-hand man for many years, having gotten his start as a gofer in the budget department at Shearson Hayden Stone under Weill.[54] Dimon's early career was defined by an undying loyalty to Weill. When Weill's unkempt, cigar-chomping style didn't jibe with the crisply dressed, conventional executive culture at

American Express in 1985, Dimon followed his mentor out the door.[55] A little more than a year later, Dimon stood by Weill's side to help rejuvenate Commercial Credit Company, a failing consumer loan outfit.[56] But big egos can only coexist for so long. The inevitable falling out between Weill and Dimon was spawned in part when Dimon passed over Weill's daughter, Jessica Bibliowicz, for a promotion at Travelers. The friction reached fruition when Dimon was asked to resign as Citigroup president in 1998.[57]

Dimon rebounded nicely two years later, taking the chairman and CEO position at Bank One in March 2000. On July 1, 2004, JPMorgan Chase acquired Bank One for $59 billion. Bank One paid Lazard $20 million in fees, and JPMorgan Chase paid itself $40 million in fees.[58] With the deal came Dimon, who took Harrison's slot and became CEO and president on December 31, 2005.[59] Between 2002 and 2007, Dimon netted $95 million in stocks, salary, and bonuses.[60]

Under Dimon, JPMorgan Chase was a busy shopper in 2008, but the government had its back, so why not? It acquired Bear Stearns in an all-stock deal valued at $236 million, announced on March 16, 2008, and completed on March 31, 2008, with the previously mentioned guarantee from the Fed to back up to $29 billion of Bear's illiquid assets.[61] JPMorgan Chase acquired WaMu for $1.9 billion— announced and effective on September 25, 2008, in a transaction facilitated by the FDIC.[62]

In addition to the merger financing from WaMu, JPMorgan Chase received $25 billion in TARP money, used the FDIC's Temporary Liquidity Guarantee Program to raise $40 billion of cheap debt, and got a half a billion dollars from the AIG bailout to cover its credit default swap exposure to AIG.[63] No wonder it was able to reap $5.6 billion in net income in 2008.[64] With all of that subsidization, Dimon was defensive about executive bonuses. When Obama called them "shameful," Dimon responded, "I wish the president didn't blanket everyone with the same brush," during the Crain's Future of New York City conference on February 4, 2009.[65] That was a bit cheeky of Dimon, considering that the JPMorgan Chase stock price had fallen from $52.54 in May 2007 to $24.04 on February 4, 2009, before rebounding steadily on that public dime.

Wells Fargo

John Gerard Stumpf, CEO of Wells Fargo, kept the lowest profile of the big bank bunch. But he was still invited on March 29, 2009, along with other bankers, to speak with President Obama at the White House about the ongoing economic crisis and specifically about the problem of securities backed by toxic mortgages. Results of the meeting were vague, but Stumpf summed up the response from other executives while talking to reporters after the meeting. "The basic message is we're all in this together," Stumpf said. "We're trying to do the right thing for America."[66]

Like Ken Lewis, Stumpf spent his career in mostly regional banks, working in Arizona and Texas before landing at San Francisco–based Wells Fargo, where he became the CEO in 2007. Once there, though, he got into the groove of big acquisitions.

Under his tutelage, Wells Fargo acquired Wachovia in a $15.1 billion deal that was announced on October 3, 2008.[67] Wachovia had endured a $5 billion run on its deposits a day after the WaMu failure.[68] In just a year, Wachovia went from being the fourth-placed bank in market value to near total collapse before Stumpf stepped in and upended a Citigroup agreement, facilitated by the FDIC, to take over Wachovia.[69] Not as used to the big bucks as his compatriots are—from 2000 to 2007 he made between $1.4 and $5.3 million per year (though he was not named CEO until 2007)—Stumpf agreed to forgo his 2008 bonus.[70]

It was only fitting, given his firm's stock price. From a five-year high of $39.79 on September 19, 2008, Wells Fargo stock prices dropped to $17.22 on March 18, 2009. In March 2009, Wells Fargo cut its dividend 85 percent, and like JPMorgan Chase, Wells Fargo stocks rebounded. Wells was able to survive the crisis because it had focused on traditional commercial banking business and hadn't gotten involved in as many risky endeavors and toxic assets.[71]

AIG's Outrageous Acts

Then there was AIG. As we know, the American International Group, Inc., a ninety-year-old insurance behemoth that in 2007 had $1 trillion in assets and $110 billion in revenues, succeeded in sucking up taxpayer money where Lehman Brothers had failed. On September 16, 2008, the day after Lehman declared bankruptcy, AIG received $85 billion in taxpayer money. In exchange, the U.S. government took an 80 percent ownership stake and brought in a new CEO, former Allstate head Edward M. Liddy.[72] AIG was an insurance company to the outside world, but it was a mammoth betting machine at its core. As I've mentioned, the legal reason the firm could get federal aid was that it was classified as a savings and loan company, and those little name changes can be really expensive for the public and really useful for a corporation.

The external reasoning for the AIG bailout was that as the nation's largest insurer, it was more important to the economic system's overall viability than Lehman was.

It didn't hurt that AIG had some pretty tight relationships—of the credit default swap variety—with some powerful Wall Street players. Namely, Goldman Sachs and JPMorgan Chase.[73] See, AIG owed these and other companies lots of money. Bank of America's Merrill Lynch had $6.2 billion in exposure as an AIG counterparty.[74] Goldman, an AIG counterparty since the mid-1990s, was exposed to the tune of $10 billion in mid-September 2008. Even though it said that it had hedged this money with cash collateral and credit default swaps, Goldman still ended up getting $13 billion of the bailout money that went to AIG, while AIG stockholders saw their investments wiped out.[75] This pumped up the money that Goldman got from the government directly through TARP. In fact, Goldman managed to scrounge up more than its exposure required, considering by that time the firm had been hedged and pretty well protected. Nice looting job.

"The ultimate taxpayer protection will be the stability this troubled asset relief program provides to our financial system, even as it will involve a significant investment of taxpayer dollars. I am convinced that this bold approach will cost American families far less than the alternative—a continuing series of financial institution failures and frozen credit markets unable to fund economic expansion," Hank Paulson said on September 19, 2008, apparently deciding that he'd underestimated the severity of the financial crisis in July.[76]

Yes, even to the man who only a few months earlier had been quite insistent that it wasn't the government's role to bail out Lehman Brothers, it became clear that on the surface anyway, the Treasury and the Fed had to do something.

But why did the AIG bailout even happen? Well, the argument the Fed used was that if AIG went bankrupt, the whole banking industry would crumble, because global investment banks were on the hook for $50 billion worth of credit exposure to AIG. In reality, the Treasury and the Fed went on to dole out far more than $50 billion to keep AIG alive, so that math doesn't exactly compute.

Of course, other problems in the United States caused by AIG's risky investments were just as bad. Local and state governments had invested $10 billion in AIG and 401(k) plans and in total had bought $40 billion worth of insurance from AIG. But these players ultimately mattered less.

"In light of the prevailing market conditions and the size and composition of AIG's obligations, a disorderly failure of AIG would have severely threatened global financial stability and, consequently, the performance of the U.S. economy," Fed chairman Ben Bernanke said on September 23, 2008, in front of the Senate Committee on Banking, Housing, and Urban Affairs.[77]

The first big piece of the AIG bailout was an $85 billion loan extended on September 16, 2008. The move diluted AIG shares, because the government took an 80 percent equity interest.[78] AIG had to issue more shares for that to happen, significantly increasing the pool of AIG shares in the process.[79] Cranky investors were left wondering why they weren't allowed to vote on the loan.[80] The Federal Reserve Bank of New York extended another round of money to AIG on October 8, 2008, by buying up $37.8 billion worth of AIG shares owned by third parties.[81] A few weeks later, AIG announced that it was quickly taking advantage of taxpayers' unwilling generosity, gobbling $90.3 billion of government credit by October 23, 2008.[82]

Even more taxpayer money was on its way. On November 10, 2008, the Treasury used $40 billion of the TARP fund to buy AIG shares and reduce AIG's original $85 billion loan cap to $60 billion.[83] Meanwhile, the interest rate on the original loan was dropped to as low as 5 percent, and the payback time was upped from two to five years. If similar loan extensions were given to borrowers on their mortgages, their payments and struggles would be reduced. That restructuring of the AIG bailout included a Fed purchase of $52.5 billion worth of AIG's toxic mortgage-backed assets that replaced the $37.8 billion loan granted on October 6, 2008.[84]

Finally, another $30 billion worth of credit was extended after AIG announced a $61.7 billion loss for the fourth quarter of 2008, bringing the AIG bailout to nearly $182 billion.[85] That credit line was good for five years. AIG could draw on it "as needed and [it] will serve as a backdrop for our restructuring activities," said Edward Liddy, AIG CEO and chairman, during a conference call on March 3, 2009.[86] Liddy decided he was done doing the government a big favor by running AIG and, on May 21, 2009, he announced that he would step down from his post as soon as replacements were found for the CEO and chairman positions, which he recommended be made distinct.[87]

After the Fed put itself in the hole for roughly $182 billion for AIG alone, Bernanke concluded on March 24, 2009, before a House Committee on Financial Services hearing that the government had failed in its role as market regulator.[88] This epiphany did not stop him from positioning for more Federal Reserve authority under Treasury Secretary Tim Geithner's plan for an "über-regulator" or "systemic risk regulator" that would oversee all of the various types of financial firms in the system, not only the commercial banks—although the Fed's bailouts transcended this group anyway.[89]

"AIG built up its concentrated exposure to the subprime mortgage market largely out of the sight of its functional regulators. More-effective supervision might have identified and blocked the extraordinarily reckless risk-taking at AIG Financial Products Division," Bernanke said during the March 24 hearing.[90]

He didn't mention that AIG had an admitted obligation to responsibly invest its shareholders' and investors' money. "We will create unmatched value for our customers, colleagues, business partners and shareholders as we contribute to the growth of sustainable, prosperous communities," the code of conduct for AIG employees reads.[91]

As far as AIG was concerned, its securities investment models designed by finance professor Gary Gorton were working, even though AIG was aware that those models did not take into account external market risk factors.[92] AIG leaders had been downright giddy a year earlier. "It is hard for us with, and without being flippant, to even see a scenario within any kind of realm of reason that would see us losing $1 in any of those transactions," then chief financial officer Joseph Cassano said on a conference call on August 9, 2007.

"No, I agree with you, I tend to think that this market is overreacting," Tom Cholnoky, a Goldman Sachs analyst, replied.[93] (Cassano would walk off with an eight-year accumulation of $315 million in his pocket in cash and bonuses after being fired in March 2008. He also kept pulling in $1 million each month as a consultant until the end of September 2008, even after taxpayers had bailed out AIG.)[94]

Of course, AIG wasn't the only one receiving bailouts about a year after Cassano's ebullience; so were its big-name backers, including Goldman, which were getting cash from all sides—from the government directly through TARP and indirectly by way of AIG. Transactions between AIG and third parties included a total of $12.9 billion that went to Goldman (the largest single recipient), $11.9 billion to Société Générale, $8.5 billion to Barclays, and $6.8 billion to Merrill Lynch.[95]

It was all so shameless, yet the architects of this money transfer, namely, Geithner, Bernanke, and Paulson, remained silent about it, preferring to let the public and Congress focus on $165 million of bonuses that AIG paid out, ostensibly from bailout money.

"The AIG bailout has been a way to hide an enormous second round of cash to the same group that had received TARP money already," former New York governor Eliot Spitzer wrote on Slate.com on March 17, 2009. He added, "The appearance that this was all an inside job is overwhelming. AIG was nothing more than a conduit for huge capital flows to the same old suspects, with no reason or explanation."[96]

The question raised by Spitzer warrants further inspection. If all signs pointed to Goldman being financially solvent, why was it allowed to recoup its AIG losses via public funds? Furthermore, Goldman appeared to have known that AIG's financials were on a downward trend in 2006 and 2007, when it demanded more collateral from AIG to cover risks to its investments.[97] Did an AIG derivatives insider warn Goldman, or did Goldman figure out the situation itself? Either way, why didn't anyone else seem to know about AIG's declining position a year before the rest of the world did? And why did the Washington crowd allow itself to believe that without backing AIG, the world as we know it would cease to exist?

More to the point of too-big-to-fail-is-too-big-period—why not bust up AIG into an insurance component and a trading component, pull a Glass-Steagall on this insurance company cloaked in a savings and loan wrap, and then after that's done, why not do the very same thing to every other mega-bank to create a more manageable financial system for the sake of our collective future economic stability?

9

Change, Really?

The era that defined Wall Street is finally, officially over.
—*December 2008,*
Condé Nast, Portfolio
magazine[1]

We must not forget that we finance our own government.

We are a nation of taxpayers, and nearly 80 percent of the tax revenue our government takes in each year comes directly from We the People.[2] Our country is founded on the principle that in return for paying taxes, we get a say in how things are run. Taxation with representation. So here is what we must find out: How do we ensure that the banking system doesn't collapse and, moreover, remains stable in the future? In other words, how do we ensure that we don't keep getting screwed?

Despite documented reports on the lack of transparency in the TARP process, there was no demand for comprehensive evaluations of junky assets. It turned out that promises for greater transparency from the Obama administration amounted to a Web site overhaul and a name change, which added more columns to a TARP activity report, none of which clearly answered the simple question "So, how are we doing?" In a stunning lack of departure from business as usual, President Obama (along with Tim Geithner) asked former Fannie Mae CEO Herbert Allison to replace Neel Kashkari as head of the TARP program.

On June 19, 2009, Allison made his case to do just that, in front of the Senate Committee on Banking, Housing, and Urban Affairs.[3]

Allison had all of the checks necessary for the role. Bipartisan political ties? Check. President Bush's treasury secretary Henry Paulson handpicked him to run Fannie Mae in September 2008, offering him the job while Allison was on a Caribbean vacation.[4] And Allison served as finance adviser to John McCain's 2000 presidential campaign. Ties to Geithner? Check. Allison served on an advisory committee to the Federal Reserve Bank of New York when Geithner was president there.[5] Ties to Wall Street? Check. Allison rose through the ranks of Merrill Lynch to become its president and chief operating officer, before resigning over internal politics in 1999 after three decades at the firm.[6] Ties to the investment community that buys and sells structured securities? Check. From Merrill Lynch, Allison became CEO of TIAA-CREF, a ninety-year-old pension and financial services firm with nearly $400 billion under management.[7] Allison's first major act at the firm was firing five hundred employees, a deed that became known as the "Herbicides."[8] That was the same year the firm launched its collateralized debt obligation business.

Allison also managed to raise some eyebrows over his generous compensation during his years at TIAA-CREF, even though salaries on the "buy side," or asset-management side, of the financial world are generally not as good as those on the "sell side," or investment-banking side. Still, Allison had enough money in 2006 to purchase the $25 million Westport, Connecticut, home of Phil Donahue and Marlo Thomas.[9] None of this necessarily makes him a bad pick for running TARP, or a bad person. He certainly has good taste in real estate. But it does show that ties to Big Finance retain a solid place in the Obama administration and in running the biggest bailout in U.S. history.

Until Washington gets a grip on that one, no meaningful solution to this crisis will result. Wall Street legal teams will continue to exploit loopholes in everything from how stocks are traded to how executives are compensated. The House's swooning to pass a 90 percent tax on bailout-firm bonuses on March 19, 2009, was a knee-jerk, theatrical reaction to public uproar over the news that AIG was going to pay $165 million worth of bonuses while existing by the grace of the public's dime.[10] Unfortunately, the act dealt with the symptoms, not with the source, of the structural problems in the foundation of the financial sector. The act stalled in the Senate. But true change requires more than campaign vows and dramatic congressional gestures; it requires courage the likes of which haven't reigned on Capitol Hill since the 1930s and briefly in the mid-1950s. It requires not only a reregulation, but also a complete restructuring of the financial arena, of all banks, insurance companies, and hedge funds. Not just the illusion of transparency, but the real thing. Not merely promises of accountability, but true, legally binding responsibility.

We have an astounding capacity to forget, to patch over the holes and paint the walls and pretend the house is sound. To keep on living our lives, making believe that everything is back to normal. Although it may be hard to imagine right now, there will come a time when everything will seem fine—or the news at least will focus on the rallying stock market, which will be accepted to mean that everything is fine. We won't want to deal with the messy (and boring) difficulties of financial regulation. We will become enamored of, even as we resent, the glitz of Wall Street once again. We will start obsessing about how much our portfolios are up. When all of these things happen without any structural change, that's when we're in real trouble. Because when we forget, that's when the pillage will begin again.

Washington is masterful at conducting lengthy, painful debates over minutiae, which sap the country's hope—not to mention the federal budget—and also distract us from undertaking more essential action on the profound structural problems. Expensive piecemeal remedies aimed at solving the financial system's total failure have continued through the Bush and Obama administrations. We are suffering from a bipartisan disconnect.

How many times have we heard statements like, "If we don't fix the banks, the public will suffer," from both Democrats and Republicans? And how many times have our elected officials decided that the solution is to "stock up" in failing behemoths such as Citigroup to help them over their capital hump? The government seems intent at plastering the (many) cracks in the walls of finance, rather than rebuilding its foundation. But we need an overhaul, not a tune-up.

Rather than take the opportunity to engineer drastic responses to the Second Great Bank Depression, the Obama administration and the current treasury secretary, Tim Geithner, opted to massage the hand-me-down plans of the Bush administration and former treasury secretary Hank Paulson. These plans, as we have seen, simply followed the "we must stay competitive" deregulation craze of the Clinton administration and Treasury Secretary Robert Rubin, which took its tone from the "government is not the solution" rhetoric of Ronald Reagan. Certainly bad government is not the solution, but we can hope for better than that.

Instead of instituting actual sweeping reform, Obama and Co. merely call their ideas reform. As Obama took office on January 20, 2009, the first half of the TARP package—some $350 billion of tax-payer money—had already been dispersed.[11] As of March 31, 2009, that investment had lost 45 percent of its value, and that wasn't including the $78 billion overpayment to begin with![12] But did the incoming administration take the time to consider how it might use the second half of the TARP funds *differently*? No. Obama's team was determined to continue the same pattern of disbursement that had already failed so miserably and had actually sparked a sort of childish petulance in the banking community, with a twist or two.

America elected Obama because he presented himself as a thought-ful and visionary thinker—because he seemed to approach the country's problems in exactly the opposite way that his fly-by-the-seat-of-his-pants predecessor had. So, what has happened to the enlightened perspective of our new president? Why has he not brought the same intellect to bear on the financial morass? He does not seem to be asking the essen-tial questions: Why are we capitalizing banks when we don't know what they hold on their books or how much borrowing they did using those assets as collateral? Why aren't we questioning the Fed's stealthy and expensive cash injections? Why are we backing the purchase of toxic assets by private investors with federal money? Why not just say, "No!" to the crazy federal bailout expenditures? Why meet with scripted, self-interested bankers about ways to save the economy, instead of with independent minds such as Robert Kuttner, Naomi Klein, Dean Baker, Bob Johnson, Thomas Ferguson, Michael Hudson, Bill Greider, and others who have pointed out real problems and solutions? Come on!

No, it's not simple, but it's doable. In the case of the banking world, it means pulling an FDR: shut it down, evaluate its loss, and dissect it into manageable, backable parts. As I've explained, we must separate the risky banks from the nonrisky ones, take away government backing from any firm that lobbied against government regulations, and dramatically roll back the amount of risk that the market is legally able to take on.

None of these potential stability-creating measures has been addressed, however. Instead, Geithner took a stab at making broad-brush promises during his first week on the job, saying, "We will unveil a series of reforms to help stabilize the nation's financial system and get credit flowing again to families and businesses. Included in those reforms will be a commitment to increase transparency and oversight."[13]

Geithner, like so many on the Hill, talks big about transparency but demonstrates no understanding about the connection between the creation of certain securities that were then used to build a cloud of pure profit for Wall Street and how this harmed everyone else on the planet. That's why he had to ask *them*, the bankers, to tell *him* what they've been doing, as if that will lead to an objective evaluation. It would be more helpful if Geithner put rules in place to control what bankers can do to begin with. It would save on the question-answer portion of this period.

On February 10, 2009, in the official televised unveiling of his much-anticipated "new plan," Geithner actually commended the efforts of the prior administration and Congress in dealing with the crisis. And why not? —he played ball for that team, too.

"Last fall, as the global crisis intensified," he said, "Congress acted quickly and courageously to provide emergency authority to help contain the damage. The government used that authority to pull the financial system back from the edge of catastrophic failure."[14]

As Geithner spoke, however, the financial system was in a worse, less capitalized state than it had been in the fall of 2008. Nearly every major banking stock price was lower, meaning that its net worth, or market capitalization, was lower. The FDIC's report of that quarter showed that reserves held against loan losses had increased substantially by the end of 2008 versus the end of 2007. Worse, these reserves still weren't keeping pace with the losses. The problems were not in the entire banking sector; in fact, two-thirds of the nation's banks had posted profits. It was the "big banks" that were the troublemakers.[15]

But Geithner didn't go there; sometimes the truth is too painful to deal with. He did, however, open up the opportunity to outperform his predecessor (which won't be difficult, because my five-year-old nephew could pose more probing questions about the first round of bailouts than Paulson seems to have considered).

Instead, Geithner threw a bone to Paulson by praising his tactics before stressing how he, Geithner, would do better. "The actions your government took were absolutely essential," he said, "but they were inadequate. The force of government support was not comprehensive or quick enough to withstand the deepening pressure brought on by the weakening economy. The spectacle of huge amounts of taxpayer assistance being provided to the same institutions that help caused the crisis, with limited transparency and oversight, added to public distrust. This distrust turned to anger as boards of directors at some institutions continued to award rich compensation packages and lavish perks to their senior executives."[16]

Geithner's statement reminded me of a tried-and-true corporate ascension tactic. When you get someone else's spot, talk down everything that person did. If you fail, you blame it on his or her mistakes. If you succeed, you get the corner office and a larger bonus.

In addition, promising transparency is a perennial vow of rotating Washington leaders. During the Second Great Bank Depression, it was the buzz-promise of choice, just as stressing the need for "corporate governance" was common during post-Enron 2002. Under Geithner, the Treasury Department's idea of transparency was to add more columns to its spreadsheets, but it did not add a column presenting an evaluation of what each TARP investment is actually worth, or what is lost. That's not transparency. That's not change. That's deflection and illusion.

There are certain things you're expected to say when you take office, particularly during a crisis. With the prevalent public disdain of Wall Street and distrust of all things financial, what you promise is oversight, transparency, and reform. How you act, though, tells the real story.

On January 27, 2009, Geithner laid out some new rules to keep Wall Street lobbyists out of the Emergency Economic Stablization process, make information about the bailout more transparent by putting it on the Internet, and constrain executive compensation.[17] On the same day, however, he appointed Mark Patterson, a former Goldman Sachs lobbyist, as chief of staff at the Treasury. Goldman Sachs had already received $10 billion in TARP money and a $12.9 billion "cut" from the money the government lavished on AIG.[18]

Patterson got the prime spot in the Treasury through a glaring loophole in the executive order on lobbyists that President Obama had issued a week earlier. The order contained a "revolving door ban" that prohibited government appointees from lobbying or creating regulations or contracts related to their former employer for a period of two years from their appointment. But it neglected to cover the other side of the door, which still allows lobbyists—and CEOs such as Henry Paulson and Robert Rubin—to hop directly *to* a government area, *after* servicing or lobbying for a company directly related to their Washington post.[19]

That's like letting the fox into the henhouse, and then locking the door so it can't get out.

Ethics aside, Geithner went on to more practical matters in late April 2009. He outlined several steps of his master plan to fix the financial mess. The first was to make banks clean up and strengthen their balance sheets.[20] This he would do by administering a "stress" test to nineteen banks.[21] The test would entail asking the banks to tell the Fed—whose job it had been to monitor adequate bank capital all along—how many losses they'd incur if, say, the unemployment rate rose to 8.4 percent by 2009 and to 8.8 percent by 2010. Unfortunately, by the time the test results came back, the actual unemployment rate had surpassed Geithner's pessimistic projection; it hit 8.9 percent on May 7, 2009. The next month it jumped even higher, to 9.4 percent on June 5, 2009.[22] That the most adverse unemployment scenario for 2009 was reached as test results were coming in didn't bode well for the way in which the Fed came up with its hypothetical situations. Furthermore, the banks had a lot of input into the construction of the stress tests and were in charge of providing their own pricing, with no external objective evaluation under the various scenarios. That's like asking a high school student who wants to get into a good college to design his or her own SAT test. Sure, there's a chance he or she will design it to be impossibly difficult, but it's highly unlikely. During FDR's time, once the banks were shut, external regulators came in to assess the health of the ones that would reopen; the banks themselves weren't considered trustworthy enough. But that's another forgotten lesson.

In the second step of Geithner's plan, he promised to bring together the various government agencies that deal with banks to determine an appropriate risk level. And the last main pillar of his plan was for the Treasury Department to team up with the Federal Reserve to commit up to $1 trillion to help get credit flowing again.[23] The Federal Reserve would continue to scoop up lousy assets from bank books in return for lending them money; as I mentioned earlier, the Fed had already been (stealthily) doing a lot of this scooping, to the tune of several trillion dollars. As we have seen, the Federal Reserve hides behind its status as an independent entity, with both public and private aspects—although, of course, the private ones give cover to the banks. Further details revealed that this $1 trillion would be part of a "public-private partnership" that would lend money at a six-to-one ratio to private investors—they put up $100, the government gives them $600—to buy the assets they didn't want before, but with much more government help to do so. In practice, this meant that the government would capitalize hedge funds that used to borrow money from firms such as Bear Stearns to buy complex securities.

In mid-June 2009 the Obama administration released details of its new "rules of the road" financial regulations in an eighty-eight-page white paper. It was billed as the most sweeping overhaul of the financial system since the Great Depression. But it was, for the most part, a deck chair rearrangement. The plan consolidated certain regulatory agencies, notably getting rid of the Office of Thrift Supervision, and created a new Financial Services Oversight Council chaired by the Treasury Department, which seemed utterly redundant; slapping a new layer of regulatory bureaucracy on an increasingly complex banking system seemed more an exercise in appearances than action. Though Obama blamed the financial crisis on a "culture of irresponsibility," the absolute worst part of his new proposals expanded the authority of the Fed. It's like rewarding the king of this irresponsible culture with a larger kingdom. The most positive part of the plan was the suggested creation of the Consumer Financial Protection Agency. Which is why it had bank lobbyists immediately up in arms.

Tight Credit, Loose Talk

Washington promised us that if we bailed out the banks, we would be rewarded with looser credit and perhaps a more stable economy. But that was a myth, one that deflected deeper inspection of the nature of the bailouts. Perhaps that's why the focus of congressional and media ire consistently returned to the credit myth, and everyone bemoaned, Why, oh why, isn't the Treasury money being used to loosen credit, as promised? Instead, people should have questioned the root cause of the supposed necessity for a bailout to begin with.

Unfortunately, the notion of loosening credit, because capital was being soaked on impact, was itself a lie. In addition, the first phase of TARP didn't go toward shoring up mortgage loans for homeowners facing foreclosure, despite the frenzy of debate on this topic in Congress before the Emergency Economic Stabilization Act was passed. A move to slow foreclosures might have stopped the toxic assets from being so toxic, because it would have meant more money flowing into them and would have helped homeowners simultaneously. But, no, banks didn't want to do that—not if they could push Washington to take their junk. Banks used TARP to plump up their own competitive infrastructures, period. Their main priority was survival. Following that, they wanted to sidestep any future tightening of regulations. Somewhere as an afterthought came the notion of helping the little people.

Plus, first of all, the people getting the money never promised to do anything useful with it. And, second, recall that the guy who was giving out the initial money, Paulson, overpaid $78 billion for preferred shares and racked up approximately $157 (rounded) billion in additional losses in the first six months of the Treasury part of the bailout.[25] Third, the entity giving out the most money, the Fed, was doing so without accountability or line-item transparency. Fourth, Congress was either neglecting or badly performing its duty to protect the public by having numerous hearings on bonuses and no hearings at all about just what the hell firms were doing that gave them the ability to bestow such grand bonuses.

I really wish they'd have a hearing titled, "What should we do to make sure this doesn't happen again?" Or, "What should we do to rein in the Fed's and the Treasury's dispensing of bailout money and cheap loans to the banking systems under the guise of helping the public?"

Or, "Why do we keep talking to Wall Street leaders about how to fix the economy they wrecked?" I wish we could have millions of people march in front of Congress with signs saying, "Stop the Madness! Stop the Bailout! Stop the Bank Supremacy!" and have it spur intelligent debate and legislation, as citizens did earlier in our country's history.

Bigger Isn't Better: Bring Back Glass-Steagall

Neither the Fed nor the Treasury Department (under Paulson and Geithner), nor Congress questions the logic of not only allowing but promoting the merger of weak and nontransparent financial firms during a crisis period.

But let me ask you, suppose you were making coffee in the morning— something I've been doing a lot while trying to wrap my head around this mess—and in your fridge sat two cartons of milk. One was stamped a day past fresh and smelled kind of bad, and the other was two days past and smelled worse. Would it occur to you to mix the two, to get a better chance of filling your mug with nonspoiled milk? Of course not.

The idea of mixing poorly functioning banks is not quite as simple as mixing spoiled milk, but logic tells us it is not the best plan. And not only was gut instinct ignored again and again, but so were all the signs that merging certain banks would end in disaster. The Bank of America and Merrill Lynch merger was a train wreck, driving the stock of an already weakened mega-bank into the ground. The December 31, 2008, merger of Wachovia and Wells Fargo wasn't a much better idea.[26] A month after the marriage, Wells posted a $2.55 billion fourth-quarter loss, and Wachovia lost $11.2 billion during the same period. (Which Wells chose not to include in its bottom line. Why? Because it didn't have to.)[27]

The JPMorgan Chase–Washington Mutual–Bear Stearns government-backed bargain merger, negotiated by Jamie Dimon, did a bit better because Dimon had the government shoulder most of the risk for losses.[28] But still, on October 15, 2008, JPMorgan Chase posted a net loss, including $95 million related to the Bear Stearns merger, despite the government's $29 billion backing of Bear Stearns's bad assets (on which the government took a $1.2 billion charge, or "hit" against loan reserves).[29] To be fair, JPMorgan Chase also booked an after-tax $581 million gain on Washington Mutual's operations related to this acquisition, which closed on September 25, 2008, but much of that was due to a lucrative tax loophole tied to deferred losses.[30] A similar loophole was used by Wells Fargo when it acquired Wachovia—one that also made the acquiring bank's books look a lot healthier than they actually were.

It is illogical to spend money to save institutions that are individually weak and thus will be weaker together. It doesn't make sense to merge risk- and debt-laden companies with each other and hope that the outcome will somehow be stronger, leaner, more stable, and transparent.

And yet even with all of the recent Washington talk about "real reform," there has been no serious discussion of how we have "reformed" our way into this mess. With the passing of the Gramm-Leach-Bliley Act in 1999, Washington sealed our collective fate. As we have seen, a gleeful bipartisan effort repealed the Glass-Steagall Act of 1933—a piece of legislation that had effectively prevented such mergers (particularly of the investment bank–commercial bank variety) and saved the country a lot of grief (and money) for more than six decades.

The rush to mergers is part of the reason the banking system is collapsing under the weight of its own incestuous impulse to combine risky overleveraged entities into bigger ones, backed by government and taxpayer money. This insanity has not only continued; it was promoted by the very same agencies that are supposed to be regulating it, namely, the Federal Reserve and, to a much lesser extent, the Office of Thrift Supervision.[31] It was these entities, in charge of regulating their respective corners of the financial world, that approved mergers that created those too-big-to-fail institutions. Worse, in the fallout from the Second Great Bank Depression, instead of slamming on the merger brakes, they sped things up and gave the green light to new mergers—you know, the ones that are failing. It's not surprising that we can't have an honest debate about the problems of mergers if nearly all of the enablers don't think there are any problems with mergers!

This nonsensical overconcentration of the industry has to stop. At least, this one aspect of Glass-Steagall must be resurrected. Legally, too much concentration in the banking sector violates the intent, if not the necessary formalized legislation, of antitrust law. Financially, it's a damn expensive mess to clean up.

Self-Regulation Is Not the Answer
It should be apparent, but it isn't to Washington, that Wall Street firms should be treated with suspicion or at least cynicism when they offer

to regulate their enormous personal bonuses or their firms' excessive leverage.

With artfully articulated disdain, President Obama told a roomful of reporters gathered at the Oval Office that he was incensed that the Street would pay out $18.4 billion in 2008 bonuses, even though no bank ended the year in better shape than it had started it.

> And when I saw an article today indicating that Wall Street bankers had given themselves $20 billion worth of bonuses—the same amount of bonuses as they gave themselves in 2004—at a time when most of these institutions were teetering on collapse and they are asking for taxpayers to help sustain them—that is the height of irresponsibility. It is shameful.

But he also said that as a solution, he'd have a "conversation" with "these folks on Wall Street to underscore that they have to start acting in a more responsible fashion."[32]

Why? You can't simply have a chat with them. You can't merely wrist slap the very people who wrote the rules and paid themselves before the catastrophic fallout and expect them to change their collective mind-set. The most you can expect is the kind of scripted faux remorse that Wall Street CEOs provided to Congress after this news. These executives are very gifted at saying just what they need to, when they need to. It doesn't mean anything. Believe me. I lived and worked and breathed with Wall Street executives for years. I've seen them lie with nary a facial muscle moving. I've been at meetings that centered on strategizing about lying.

Wrist slaps don't work with Wall Street. In my first book, *Other People's Money*, I wrote about the shallowness of the Eliot Spitzer–led Wall Street settlement that sought to shake up the Street and temper its imbedded conflicts of interest, because it didn't address the structure of Wall Street, either. Fines only wind up somewhere else on the bank books, as expenses to be tax deducted.

Spitzer's personal ethics aside, his investigation annoyed Wall Street about as much as a mosquito bite would. By April 2003, the SEC had taken over his investigation that had examined, among other things, analysts who touted the stellar health of a firm's clients, despite obvious decay, fraud, and brazen scandals. The investigation was sparked by the Enron and WorldCom scandals and wound up costing the industry $1.4 billion in fines.[33]

As part of the settlement, these fines did not come with any admission of guilt. They did come with promises that more disclaimers would accompany the analysts' public statements. Basically, analysts could still tout the stocks of their firm's clients; they merely had to mention that those companies were clients (which was obvious anyway and meant that the settlement settled nothing).

In particular, Citigroup, Merrill Lynch, and Credit Suisse were accused of fraud. The same firms that paid fines related to their deceptive practices are the ones—such as Lehman Brothers and Bear Stearns and Merrill Lynch, particularly—that died while burning through trillions of dollars in market value, that posted billions of dollars of write-downs (as did Citigroup, Bank of America, UBS, Credit Suisse, and Goldman Sachs), and that inhaled our public bailout money and loans.

Then the media, of course, condemned all of the practices that led to the fines. Congress talked about them. And life went on as usual—except Wall Street also went on to use high-risk loans to fuel record growth, profits, and compensation from 2004 to 2006, instead of relying on the telecom and energy industries to extract fees and profits.

Clearly, the firms did not take very seriously statements by then SEC head William Donaldson (and former CEO of investment bank Donaldson, Lufkin & Jenrette, DLJ). Back then, Donaldson declared, "The cases also represent an important new chapter in our ongoing efforts to restore investors' faith and confidence in the fairness and integrity of our markets."[34]

The main difference was that Wall Street, the banks, and the Fed and Treasury vaporized more money in 2008 and 2009 than during the scandals of the early part of the millennium. Six years and a massive full-scale global economic implosion later, Obama SEC head appointee Mary Shapiro echoed Donaldson's vows almost to the letter, except for a few Mad-Lib adjustments, promising "commitment to investor protection, transparency, accountability, and disclosure" and emphasizing that the SEC "must play a critical role in reviving our markets, bolstering investor confidence, and rejuvenating our economy."[35]

The SEC is supposed to regulate all public companies and ensure the integrity of their books. That's its *job*. The problem is that ensuring integrity in a den of iniquity is a tall order. When the market is good, it makes regulatory bodies complacent, and when the market is bad, they suddenly have to scramble to take care of the inevitable jump in cases. Either way, life is never easy for the SEC, which is why it needs to step up to regulate better, not step aside in complacency or make postcrisis promises.

In 2001, the SEC had a spending authority of $423 million dollars. The figure was bumped up to $716 million in 2003, following the Enron and WorldCom scandals, and it reached a high of $913 million in 2005, where it remained, more or less, through the financial crisis of 2008–2009.[36] Despite slight budget increases, the number of staff members fell substantially between 2005 and 2007, in the middle of the housing boom, record Wall Street profits, and the buildup of leveraged debt.[37] Indeed, just as the SEC had done pre-Enron, it lagged behind the ball and lost staff during a period when things "looked" good.

By the time it was necessary to study what the leveraged subprime securities market had done to the banking industry, there weren't enough people working at the SEC to deal with it. Shapiro's first request in 2009 was for resources and support, "to investigate and go after those who cut corners, cheat investors, and break the law."[38] The SEC's philosophy continues to be, better late than never.

That's how you fall prey to Wall Street deflection tactics. Take Goldman CEO Lloyd Blankfein saying on September 21, 2008, "When Goldman Sachs was a private partnership, we made the decision to become a public company, recognizing the need for permanent capital to meet the demands of scale. While accelerated by market sentiment, our decision to be regulated by the Federal Reserve is based on the recognition that such regulation provides its members with full prudential supervision and access to permanent liquidity and funding."

He was talking as if Goldman Sachs wanted regulation. What the firm happened to need was money, and it was scared stiff of suffering the fate of Lehman Brothers, so it decided to simply become a regular bank for a short while: "We believe that Goldman Sachs, under Federal Reserve supervision, will be regarded as an even more secure institution with an exceptionally clean balance sheet and a greater diversity of funding sources."[39]

Four and a half months later, the firm took it back. "Operating our business without the government capital would be an easier thing to do," Goldman CFO David Viniar told a Credit Suisse Group conference in Naples, Florida. "We'd be under less scrutiny and under less pressure."[40]

On April 13, 2009, having passed the government stress tests—as if it had any chance of not passing—Goldman Sachs was proud to announce "[an] offering of $5 billion of its common stock for sale to the public. . . . After the completion of the stress assessment, if permitted by our supervisors and if supported by the results of the stress assessment, Goldman Sachs would like to use the capital raised plus additional resources to redeem all of the TARP capital."[41]

Okay, go ahead and laugh. So, they want to pay back $10 billion in TARP to be under less scrutiny, yet they are going to sit on the $12.9 billion they got from the AIG bailout, the almost $30 billion of cheap debt they raised under the Temporary Liquidity Guarantee Program (TLGP), and the approximately $11 billion they still have available under the Fed's Commercial Paper Funding Facility LLC (CPFF).[42]

See? For every flip, there is always a flop. Whenever an advantage presents itself, a Wall Street exec will grab it—even if it means contradicting what he just did yesterday. Success on Wall Street is defined by figuring out how to creatively bend the rules in order to squeeze more money from clients, investors, and the world. So, why would you trust Wall Street to create the rules in the first place? Even the bonus payouts that caused such duress to Congress were cloaked in new disguises to avoid detection.

For instance, American Express CEO Ken Chenault received $26 million in compensation in 2007, including $1.24 million in salary, $6 million in bonus cash, $6.5 million in stock awards, $8.3 million in options, and approximately $4 million in other forms of compensation. For 2008, he certainly toed the public line and received zero in cash bonuses, but he still made more than in 2007—ready for this?—$27.3 million, including $1.25 million in salary, $10.13 million in stock awards, $8 million in option awards, and $6.1 million in nonequity incentive plan compensations, plus $1.8 million in other forms of compensation.[43] On January 9, 2009, American Express received $3.39 billion in TARP money.[44]

It's Obvious We Need Better Regulation

Identifying the villains makes us feel better. And when they are imprisoned or fined or fired, many of us take comfort: there is justice in the world after all, we think, and maybe this time things will change. But let's be honest: 2008 is the new 2001, just as in 2001 Enron was the new savings and loan (S&L) scandal. When the underlying conditions remain, and those underlying conditions encourage excess, then the same basic problem will keep coming back with a new face.

Every period of scandal has its villains. This time around, Bernie Madoff heads a whole new pack of them. But their prison terms don't change the system in which they operate. Besides, as much as federal prosecutors want their public pound of flesh, many of these executives were merely operating along gray lines—legality, ethics, and morality aside—and keeping up with the Joneses. Self-entitled excess can't be simply chalked up to greed. In the dog-eat-dog world of Wall Street and Corporate America, excess symbolizes competitive advantage and pedigree within a select pecking order. But rather than pointing fingers, we need to do the harder work of reconstructing a better, more stable financial system. On top of that, several important reforms are needed that must work simultaneously.

We need to put *all* derivatives, $684 trillion of them in whatever their forms, on regulated platforms.[45] We should not do it in the way that Wall Street has suggested and Treasury Secretary Geithner has echoed, which is to regulate only the ones that are already easiest to understand and have the least built-in profits. No, we need to outlaw all over-the-counter manifestations of these products as well. It is always suspect when Wall Street agrees to do something, because it's usually to avoid a harsher and more necessary regulation later. And to find a more secretive ploy to making money.

On October 31, 2008, even before the ink on their TARP checks was dry, sixteen major banks, including major TARP recipients Bank of America, Merrill Lynch, JPMorgan Chase, Morgan Stanley, Citigroup, Goldman Sachs, and Wachovia, wrote a letter to Tim Geithner, then president of the Federal Reserve Bank of New York.[46] In it, the group committed to use a warehouse for credit derivatives, which would basically act as a clearinghouse that would process payments, the terms of derivatives, and credit events (a company or a package of loans default-ing). In other words, it would provide the red tape.

Those major dealers committed to having a central cash settling of contracts by November 30, 2009, such that a full "96% of settlement volume on electronically matched transactions across market participants [will be] settled via TIW [Trade Information Warehouse] and CLS."[47]

On the surface, this seems like a good thing. Regulators and members of the futures industry convened before the House Agriculture Committee to debate the regulation of credit default swaps (CDSs) and other derivatives in early February 2009.[48] They reviewed a related draft bill, the Derivatives Markets Transparency and Accountability Act of 2009.[49]

The proposed act suggested that over-the-counter, or OTC (that is, privately traded), derivatives be subject to reporting rules set by the Commodity Futures Trading Commission. The commission would also determine which OTC agreements could "disrupt the market," and therefore open up a wide interpretative gap as to which ones counted.[50] So, the lobbyists prevailed. The act did not make every OTC agreement subject to mandatory transparency or regulation, meaning that Wall Street will figure out a way to make money and keep certain agreements hidden.

Lobbyists were also against provisions that would make it illegal for market participants to use naked CDSs (CDSs for which they had no exposure to the underlying security), for fear that this would keep banks and other investors out of the market. They were dead set on this.

"This provision would cripple the CDS market by making investment capital illegal and removing liquidity providers," warned Stuart J. Kaswell, the executive vice president and general counsel of the Managed Funds Association (MFA), in his testimony.[51]

Proponents of CDS regulation included various smaller corporate entities and their lobbyists, such as the National Cotton Council of America of Cordova, Tennessee, represented by Gary Taylor, CEO of Cargill Cotton Inc. He argued that speculative investment funds and OTC transactions "disrupted the futures and markets of energy and agriculture commodities." He called for setting limits on hedge fund traders.[52] The cotton industry could claim legitimate need for derivatives to hedge its risk of certain crops not paying off, because it is subject to the weather and other external factors. It might make those markets a little less fluid, but that also means they'll be less volatile. And you know that if the members of a market want regulation, it's entirely necessary.

But it's unfair that certain financial firms can trade the same derivatives without constraints and have no responsibility to provide cotton, no matter what external conditions are like. The problem is that when you have various interests gaming the markets for their own reasons, you create too many ways for certain groups to profit and others to be impaired. The solution is that anyone trading a derivative should do so because it's attached to a legitimate business purpose, beyond simply making money, or there should be a clearer line between investment banks that do so on behalf of their clients as opposed to only for their trading books.

Some Solutions

1. Don't Let Risk Lurk Off the Books

We need to remove any off-book means of hiding debt, something that we were all so horrified about during the Enron days. This means getting rid of structured investment vehicles (SIVs) and all of their manifestations.

These SIVs are a way to hide debt legally and have no other legitimate purpose, yet there is no discussion about eliminating them. Whatever future name Wall Street may concoct for places to hide debt or losses off book, regulators should simply have a blanket retort: "You can't do that." Done.

2. Don't Let Investment Banks Be Bank Holding Companies

There is a big structural problem in letting any firm become a bank holding company (BHC). When firms such as Goldman Sachs and Morgan Stanley were approved by the Federal Reserve Board to become BHCs on September 21, 2008, they exposed the federal government's true gullibility and desperation.[53] The change in designation instantly enabled these companies to draw on a wider government and taxpayer safety net, and all they had to do was "volunteer" for more regulation from the government.

But it is naive to think that this means they will be subject to stricter regulatory oversight. As I mentioned earlier, the Gramm-Leach-Bliley Act stealthily inserted an all-encompassing definition for what a financial holding company (FHC) is, broadening the one in the 1956 Bank Holding Company Act to include any firm that is "financial in nature" or "incidental to such financial activity" or "complementary to a financial activity and does not pose a substantial risk to the safety or soundness of depository institutions or the financial system generally."[54]

This designation includes almost any financial firm. As FHCs, financial firms will get to do everything they were already doing before they attained that status. Furthermore, as BHCs, they also have access to more federal support. And given that the firms converting to BHCs had a minimum of two years to comply with BHC rules (meaning two years to crush these rules), those firms brought under the protective umbrella of the federal government will continue to reap bailout money and loans, propelling an inherently risky system.

Meanwhile, remember that Goldman Sachs announced on April 13, 2009, that it was going to raise its own money to pay back the $10 billion that it took from TARP. CEO Lloyd Blankfein even went on National Public Radio's popular show *All Things Considered* to discuss his intent, telling NPR's Robert Siegel, "I will tell you precisely when Goldman Sachs gives its money back: as soon as we are able to, while still being able to perform our functions in the capital markets systems subject to the approval of our regulators."[55] How damn mercenary of him. But he conveniently mentioned nothing about the other $54 billion in government assistance.[56] And, sadly, he wasn't asked to. He did acknowledge public anger over Wall Street bonuses. "I'll accept the premise that the numbers, in the benefit of hindsight, of course, look much too high, because today they'd never be those numbers," Blankfein said. "Because today, people aren't creating that kind of value. So it's almost a foreign thought that we ever could have been in that world.

"But let me transport you back to 2005, 2006. In those years, Goldman Sachs actually had issues retaining our talent," he said defensively.[57]

3. Don't Nationalize Risky Banks, Break Them Up
The debate over nationalizing banks by having the government take them over until stability is achieved, or creating bad banks as a kind of

holding pattern for toxic assets to be separated from the rest of a bank's books, got a lot of play during the Second Great Bank Depression. But the government had already poured trillions of dollars into the backing of, or lending against, bad assets from these banks. And it had purchased substantial stakes through preferred or common shares in them. Some people believe that the next logical step is for the government to simply run the banks. Not only do I think this idea of nationalizing the banks (if they remain structured as they are) is dangerous, the underlying decision to capitalize the banks' bad assets (the crux of all of the federal bailout plans) was terrible.

Most of the discussions avoid the fundamental problem: banks should not be constructed as they currently are. They should be separated into commercial and speculative entities. Otherwise, nationalization attempts would entail taking on huge risk and potential losses, rather than simply backing consumer-oriented or public good–oriented banking functions. Therefore, to nationalize effectively would require breaking up the banks first. To contemplate the idea without this consideration is asking for the government to take on a possible bottomless pit of loss.

As for creating a "bad bank," we should resist taking on the toxic assets of the entire banking industry at all costs. Not only because there is no clear way to evaluate these assets, which are merely estimates from a host of self-interested parties—those selling them and others who might buy them on the cheap—but because the toxic assets are tied to substantial amounts of borrowing or leverage. If you take on the asset, you take on that leverage, and that could be an incredibly costly exercise. Again, it would be better for all of those former free-market advocates in the industry and the government to separate the banks into consumer and speculative companies. Then the government could back the consumer ones. Let the toxic assets stay on the books of the speculative firms; some will implode, some will survive. That's the thing about free-market capitalism. Let it happen. Plus, why would you nationalize—that is, have a government take over and run—something you can't quantify? These institutions aren't simple deposit-and-loan banks, as Glass-Steagall's survival would have rendered them. They are convoluted cesspools of seething risk. If we do nationalize, it should be limited to the consumer-related parts.

On January 26, 2009, David E. Sanger of the *New York Times* noted that "privately, most members of the Obama economic team concede that the rapid deterioration of the country's biggest banks, notably Bank of America and Citigroup, is bound to require far larger investments of taxpayer money."[58] When he wrote the piece, those two banks had already sucked in $509 billion from us taxpayers.[59]

Sanger didn't comment on how dangerous it is to fund the destruction of "too big to fail" entities. Besides, the idea of "investment" keeps getting mixed up in the press and in D.C. with the word *nationalize*. The terms *nationalization* or *partial nationalization* had been batted around by members of Congress, such as House speaker Nancy Pelosi (D-CA), who disclaimed it almost as soon as she mentioned it in an interview on ABC's *This Week* in late January 2009. "Well, whatever you want to call it," said Ms. Pelosi, "if we are strengthening them, then the American people should get some of the upside of that strengthening. Some people call that nationalization. I'm not talking about total ownership," she abruptly added.[60]

As if capitalizing banks, which is what the government is doing, and running them are somehow equivalent. On the back of that debate, *Newsweek* ran a cover on the February 16, 2009, issue stating, "We Are All Socialists Now."[61] The idea was that banks want help from the government when they screw up and no oversight when they're raking it in. And the government merely runs in and complies.

If Wall Street wants a "bad bank," then we can be pretty sure of one thing: for the rest of us, it's a bad idea. On January 28, 2009, Reuters reported that the Obama administration was considering creating a "bad bank," which "cheered Wall Street and helped drive financial shares higher."[62] Of course, Wall Street was strongly in favor of a "bad bank" to buy its junk. Who wouldn't want the chance to dump the old, to go about creating the new? That's why spring cleaning was invented.

"Wall Street likes the 'bad bank' stuff," said Joseph Saluzzi, the cohead of equity trading at Themis Trading. "It's still just a rumor, but a lot of people are betting on it being true, and they like the idea of it."[63]

A week later, Senator Chuck Schumer told Bloomberg News that "the Obama administration should provide guarantees for the toxic assets clogging lenders' balance sheets, rather than set up a 'bad bank' to purchase them." He cited two problems with the notion of a "bad bank." "It would probably be very expensive, costing as much as $4 trillion," he reasoned, and, "second, it'd be hard to value those assets."[64]

This is true. The idea of a "bad bank" lends credence to the idea that if only TARP had stayed on former treasury secretary Henry Paulson's original course of buying up junk, things would have been better. The fact remains that whatever evaluation model you use for them, rounding up and dumping arbitrary amounts of toxic assets somewhere will not do more than calm the financial markets for the amount of time it takes people to realize there's more where that comes from.

Plus, guessing the value of toxic assets is a dangerous pursuit, which might seem obvious by now but the government has chosen not to acknowledge it in any meaningful way. "Meaningful" as in an objective evaluation of all of the toxic assets on all of the banks' books: a complete show-and-tell and an external evaluation. That never happened. The government should not own or run what it does not understand and can't therefore adequately manage or regulate.

4. Fix the Entire Banking Foundation
In this convoluted crisis, perhaps the most disturbing discussion is the one that we're not having: a debate that clearly examines the very structure of the banking industry. Indeed, you can keep patching holes in walls forever, but if you don't do something about a decaying foundation, sooner or later, you'll be sitting in a pile of rubble (again), wondering what happened (again).

This crisis, like the one that led to the Great Depression, was a perfect storm but not a random one. After all, it had happened before. Too much leverage. Too risky assets. Too few banks. Too little oversight. Each of these contributory factors was man-made and avoidable.

The solution in the 1930s was the New Deal, which didn't simply fund problems; it found solutions. In fact, the only stability during the current crisis has come from the elements of the New Deal that haven't been deregulated. FDR's creation of the FDIC to insure customer deposits staved off a national bank run, even though for years banks have lobbied to reduce insurance payments to the FDIC.

The New Deal meshed government rescue with economic restructuring and accountability. We deeply need that today. Sadly, it is as

needed as it is unlikely. A more plausible outcome is that no meaningful regulation will be enacted to keep securitization technology
from being used to create more complex assets or to place the most
convoluted credit derivatives on exchanges, and, thus, corresponding
capital requirements will not be increased. In a couple of years, after
Goldman Sachs and others have sufficiently recapitalized themselves
at the expense of government protection structures that were never
meant for investment banks, these firms may even decide to go private, and the binge-and-bonus cycle will begin again. As Paulson rides
off into the sunset, bags a book deal, or eventually heads to some new
influential position elsewhere, the real cost of the financial system's
bailout will dog the Obama administration, particularly if it remains
unwilling to dig into the structural legislation on which our current
banking system resides.

And Wall Street will regroup and revive. Even by the winter of
2008, echoes of "time to buy" had peeked through the darker com-
mentary. Jim O'Shaughnessy, the chairman of O'Shaughnessy Asset
Management, told a Reuters Investment Conference in December
2008 that none of today's conditions are as bad as those that marked
the 1930s Depression. "Much of the damage is out of the way," he said.
"Price alone would lead us to conclude that now is a fantastic time for
investors with cash to move that cash into the stock market."[65] Bringing
confidence into the economy by buying stocks does not change the core
problems of the banking industry's structure.

While the second half of the bailout plan was being debated by
Treasury Secretary Tim Geithner and Federal Reserve chairman Ben
Bernanke, they expertly dodged multiple bullets of culpability for
their roles in allowing such a catastrophically dumb and risky merger
as Bank of America with Merrill Lynch. (Yes, Thain and Lewis deserve
blame, but really, how could anyone not know that Merrill Lynch was
having massive problems?)

Again, it is convenient—and, let's face it, satisfying—to crucify the
leaders of the institutions that continue to blow up, like Thain and
his $35,000 office commode, and not fix the structure that fosters the
behavior of the heads of those firms.[66]

But let's not forget the legislative and regulatory environment that
made it all possible. Because if we do, then just like after the Great

Depression, the Savings and Loan Crisis, the Long Term Capital Management bailout, and the Enron and WorldCom scandals, we will encounter another crisis after we get through this one.[67] How many trillions of taxpayer dollars does it take before we act to prevent the same disaster from happening again?

As economist Dean Baker aptly told me, "There needs to be a limit to the size of the industry and its key players. If you have an economically powerful industry, you'll have a politically powerful one. How do you get around a 'too big to fail' company, if at the end of the day these firms control regulators by controlling the regulatory legislation that gets passed? Even if you could argue that you have the best rules, if you don't have the political structure to enforce them, they will not work."[68]

True, the proximity of Wall Street to Washington is not simply helping Wall Street titans get big bonuses through risky practices. If that were the case and it could be confined to the lives of the privileged, it would be one thing. But the consequences of their piracies have seeped into the greater economy, and that is not acceptable.

Rather than allowing the creation of larger, riskier monsters, like Bank of America–Merrill Lynch or whatever combinations Goldman Sachs and Morgan Stanley become, we need a Glass-Steagall–like reclassification of Wall Street, going in the direction of smaller, more regulated, less risky entities.

Wall Street needs a total dissection, a purge, and a 100 percent disclosure of the risk on its current books, period. It also needs to bring in nonregulated entities like hedge funds, private equity funds, and off-book gimmicks into open purview and tax policies.

True, there are some things that can't be changed. You can't do much about greed. Even Stanley Weiser, the cowriter on Oliver Stone's 1980s tale-of-the-times hit *Wall Street*, said, "If director Oliver Stone and I had a nickel for every time someone uttered the words 'greed is good,' we could have bought up the remains of Lehman Brothers."[69]

Everyone comes to Wall Street for the money. The ones at the top are there for the money and the power. No one comes for the ability to help humanity. If that were the case, they'd all be working for nonprofits. To them, this period represents a setback. It's Darwinian—this crisis is a winnowing of the herd. Some will never return. Others will reemerge from our current quagmire and thrive again.

Weiser went on to say, "I wish I could go back and rewrite the greed line to this: 'Greed is good. But I've never seen a Brinks truck pull up to a cemetery.'"[70]

He is quite literally dead on. Greed kills. Greed is literally choking the life out of our country. So let's adopt that same Darwinian attitude. Let's acknowledge that our lives have been forever changed as a result of the financial crisis. And let us learn from this madness, so that we may thrive once again—thrive not because of unchecked greed and the false hope of endless profits, but rather let us thrive with a reliable, regulated system of checks and balances that ensures the possibility of growth for all.

5. Don't Capitalize Banks You Can't Understand

Between these punts at an explanation lies the true problem. It's the same one that has been at the core of this crisis and that stemmed from the complete deregulation of the industry in 1999. As we have seen, the problem is that no one has a clue about the true nature of Citigroup's books or the health of AIG's. Or of Bank of America's, Wells Fargo's, or, for that matter, JPMorgan Chase's, although its CEO Jamie Dimon maintains the best poker face. And why are we so in the dark? Because the banks were allowed to grow to be too big to regulate and too complex to decipher.

The very idea that the government should capitalize these convoluted institutions, rather than separating out and concentrating on the specific divisions that are fully understandable and whose risks are quantifiable, defies logic. It has also proved to be tremendously inefficient and costly.

No amount of equity injections or Geithner's stress tests or private- or public-government-backed investment plans will change that. No one should think of nationalizing, as in taking over and running, anything he or she can't quantify. Ever.

You might buy a used car from a friend, but would you buy a bunch of them without finding out how many there are and what condition they're in? If you end up with ten cars that won't run, you're in trouble. But what if it's ten thousand?

The fact remains that whatever evaluation model you use for these toxic assets, however you capitalize them, and whatever "bad bank" construct you go with, sequestering these assets somewhere will only pacify the financial markets for as long as it takes people to realize that "out of sight, out of mind" doesn't solve the problem.

Why? Because we're still not even discussing the borrowing that Wall Street did on the back of those securities. Remember, Wall Street of the last ten years has been defined by an insane fixation on borrowing money whenever possible, even borrowing against wealth that doesn't really exist. So, let's just say that all of the banks borrowed up to ten times the amount those securities were once worth—a very conservative estimate, considering how hard banks worked to overturn the net capital rule in 2004, which enabled some banks to borrow up to thirty times what they had in their (already illiquid) wallets. Yet, as I've mentioned, even with that conservative estimate, we're looking at a possible systemwide loss of $140 trillion. By that token, the $13 trillion of federal bailouts and loans, including the measly $700 billion in TARP money that the media likes to focus on, is a drop in a big scary bucket.

As so many of the Americans forced into foreclosure already know, these "toxic assets" don't live in isolation. They are like weeds overrunning a lawn. We can't simply remove a section and assume that the lawn will automatically convert to pure grass. These assets have separate lives as collateral for other things: borrowing, credit derivatives, and so on. We must determine what they connect to, in order to decipher how much loss they represent. And that entails analyzing and reconstructing the whole system, as well as the assets within it.

Before pouring more money into the banks and taking on more of their toxic assets in return for loans, we need to stop, take a breath, and evaluate the banks' books. Even now, well after the TARP checks have been signed, it is important for taxpayers and economic experts to know what the banks' books look like. And we still really don't.

Next, we need to dissect all banks into manageable, backable parts. We must take apart the supermarket banks and distinguish between consumer-oriented and speculative banking. How? By bringing back a modern version of the bipartisan Glass-Steagall Act of 1933. Wall Street screwed up then, and banks were given a choice. They could deal with citizens' daily financial activities and be backed by the government, or they could go their own way and speculate to their greed's content.

By separating the banking landscape into less risky commercial banks that dealt directly with consumers (and their deposits and loans), and risky investment banks (that packaged, leveraged, speculated, and traded these loans and other complicated securities), the government capped its (and the public's) potential losses. FDIC insurance only had to cover banks whose functions were finite. It made sense. Compared to the madness we're in today, it makes almost too much sense.

The same should apply for our current situation. The government should back only commercial banking activities. It should start, for example, by injecting capital directly into the loan principals of ordinary Americans. The government should not provide funding for speculation on the back of other people's money or homes or to fix the problems that speculation creates. That's a new bubble waiting to burst.

And the government should definitely *not* be backing insurance companies, such as AIG, that overspeculated in credit derivatives on behalf of those banks. Plus, it should demand transparency, in regard not only to where our bailout money goes, but to what banks were doing with our deposit money to begin with.

Sure, no bank wants to disclose all of its ugly information; no one wants to come face-to-face with the breadth and depth of potential losses. But neither is anyone in Washington asking for it. It must happen.

6. Stop the Fed!

We should start with the biggest, most secretive bank in the country, the Fed. Already, its informational stalemate has amounted to grand larceny. Its lack of transparency and cooperation will continue to ooze taxpayer money until there is a complete show-and-tell of every book in the banking system. Only then will we know what the Fed has taken on its books, who it's helping and by how much. To that end, please visit http://action.firedoglake.com/page/s/Fed1207 and join me in supporting H.R.1207 to audit the Fed.

As German chancellor Angela Merkel said during a June 2, 2009, speech at a conference of the Initiative for a New Social Market Economy, "I view with great skepticism the powers of the Fed . . . and also how, within Europe, the Bank of England has carved out its own small line. . . . We must return together to an independent central-bank policy and to a policy of reason, otherwise we will be in exactly the same situation in ten years' time."[71]

amazon.com

Returns Are Easy!
Visit http://www.amazon.com/returns to return any item - including gifts - in unopened or original condition
within 30 days for a full refund (other restrictions apply). Please have your order ID ready.

Your order of September 22, 2011 (Order ID
103-4397844-5385055)

Qty.	Item	Item Price	Total
1	It Takes a Pillage: An Epic Tale of Power, Deceit, and Untold Trillions Prins, Nomi --- Hardcover (** **P-1-F37E325** **) X0008KN569 MM-M06-9V187 (Sold by Televista Inc.)	$10.96	$10.96

Subtotal		$10.96
Shipping & Handling		$1.99
Promotional Certificate		$-1.99
Shipment Total		$10.96
Paid via credit/debit		$10.96
Balance due		$0.00

V3

**We've sent this part of your order to ensure quicker service.
The other items will ship separately at no additional
shipping cost.**

Have feedback on how we packaged your order? Tell us at
www.amazon.com/packaging.

977/DhMKn9kcR/-1 of 1-//1S/sss-us/4016267/0926-20:30/0926-15:53/rtfelici

The Fed's secretive, far-reaching power has destroyed any trust that once existed among banks and, as a result, has frozen credit. Why? Because with the Fed acting as mega-money-supplier, banks don't need to worry about the state of each others' books. The Fed will take care of things. Transparency and trust are unnecessary.

But we must move past the fear of the unknown. The losses sitting on the books of banks are enormous. Denying that fact doesn't change it; all of the secrecy only enflames the crisis. But exposing the details, fixing the loans, and reconstructing the banking system will ultimately heal the crisis.

Sadly, the rush to bigness that was blessed by the Fed and the prevailing idea that you have to save, and even grow, giant firms imply that no real lessons were learned. The way to avert a credit crisis is to regulate its source, to take away the ability for the financial system to leverage and trade itself beyond its capacity to absorb the risk that it will incur—and that will harm the entire economy. We cannot continue to let any financial institution become too big and complicated for the government to understand, particularly when the government is expected to save it from demise.

Without regulatory mechanisms to curtail a credit monster borne of lax lending, packaging, leveraging, and trading, there will be no stabilization of our economy and the banking system and no end to the ongoing public fallout. How low must we go? Again, it's time to learn from FDR already. Divide the banking system into regulatable, backable parts: the less risky commercial banks get government support; the risky investment banks and hedge and private equity funds don't. Financial functionality becomes transparent and useful, not merely speculative. People at the top could still get rich, just not as rich—and not at the cost of ravaging the general population and generations to come.

Wall Street has operated in an environment with virtually no restrictions on the number of securities it could create—as long as it could drum up demand for them, no matter how spurious they were. Wall Street firms obliterated past rules to pile on extreme amounts of leverage, on and off their main books. They created a credit derivatives market in which contracts could be bought and paid for without any legitimate tie to underlying collateral. (It would be like buying and selling car insurance for the sheer hell of it, without owning a car or even being able to drive.) They operated on a highway with no speed limit. No wonder a great pile-on crash occurred as soon as one car broke down.

We need to set speed limits. We need a safer system. We need a complete reconstruction of the banking landscape along the lines of the Glass-Steagall Act of 1933. FDR signed it to bring stability, transparency, and accountability to the financial sector, as well as to contain the expenses that the government would have to incur in order to rescue the financial sector from itself.

Pour Some Sugar on It

Unfortunately, these conversations are not being carried out in depth. Instead, the discussion is focused on cosmetic regulatory fixes that may help a little but won't fix the system. It happens every time. And with every major uptick of the Dow, calls for more stringent rules, bonus caps, and the like become dim background noise.

Nothing sweeps problems under the carpet like spin. By April 2009, the media were predicting the possible end of the economic crisis because the Dow and bank stocks had rallied. Was it because there were any signs at all of job growth? Or of foreclosures stalling? Or small businesses opening? No, not all. The markets rose because the country's second-biggest home-lending bank, Wells Fargo, announced that it would have better-than-expected (by none other than bank analysts') earnings estimates. A record first-quarter profit, no less. So everything was going to be better, just like that. And the choir rose in song as Bloomberg reported the following:

"The worst is behind us. We're working our way through the credit crisis and that's why the market is cheering," enthused Alan Gayle, senior investment strategist at RidgeWorth Capital Management in Richmond, Virginia, which oversees $60 billion.

"Government stress tests of U.S. banks' ability to withstand a deeper recession are likely to indicate that most don't need more taxpayer money," said Federal Reserve Bank of Kansas City president Thomas Hoenig.

Even Lawrence Summers, White House chief economic adviser, was confident that what he called the economic "free-fall" would end soon.[72]

Of course, the financial sector was thrilled; it went on to get more federal assistance at our expense and got to keep the lax structure in which it existed. If someone gave you a whole bunch of money, people would have confidence in your ability to pay them whatever you might owe them, too. It doesn't mean you discovered a safer way to operate. Thus, on April 9, 2009, Wells Fargo, after an abysmal year, preannounced (so strategic) good earnings, "exceptionally strong mortgage banking results for the first quarter of 2009, $100 billion in mortgage originations and a 41% increase in mortgage applications, and strong indication for the second quarter of 2009."[73] This kind of sleight of hand is what begins a new pillage cycle. Wells Fargo didn't distinguish whether these were new mortgages or refinanced old ones. Refinanced old ones mean that people are taking advantage of lower rates to lower their payments, which might or might not be good for staving off foreclosures, but the lack of explanation reeks of Wall Street as usual.

Meanwhile, in a speech at Peking University on May 31, 2009, Tim Geithner, aka Pollyanna, swung into sugarcoating mode: "We are starting to see some initial signs of improvement. The global recession seems to be losing force. In the United States, the pace of decline in economic activity has slowed."

Now, how many of you readers feel better about your personal finances right now given that the "pace of decline" has slowed?

Geithner continued on about his true constituents, "The financial system is starting to heal. The clarity and disclosure provided by our capital assessment of major U.S. banks has helped improve market confidence in them, making it possible for banks that needed capital to raise it from private investors and to borrow without guarantees."[74]

Nice that the treasury secretary, who is a public servant, feels that things are getting better—for the banks. But has he tried to get a job in the real world recently? Naturally, Wall Street is doing better than Main Street. Thirteen trillion dollars of government assistance will do a lot for your industry. So it's not surprising that on May 5, 2009, the *Wall Street Journal* wrote: "Merrill Lynch has gone on a hiring spree.

The firm is offering one of the highest-paying recruiting deals in the industry for top-producing advisers who join the firm."[75]

There was more sugar from the media. On June 3, 2009, Evan Newmark of the *Wall Street Journal* even called for Paulson to be named a national hero. He wrote, "The TARP bailout worked. The Wall Street crisis is over."[76] Six days later, the Treasury Department announced that ten banks could pay back $68 billion of their TARP money. Tim Ryan, CEO of the Securities Industry and Financial Markets Association (SIFMA), wrote an op-ed in the *Financial Times* on behalf of the banks, stating: "The industry accepts its share of responsibility for its role in the economic crisis and its duty to be part of the recovery. We intend to partner with governments to overhaul the regulatory system to help prevent such a crisis again. . . . Financial market participants know the time for change and reform in financial services has come."[77]

These banks actually owed $229.7 billion between the TARP, TGLP, AIG money, and other avenues, but gee, it's swell that the Treasury Department was going to "allow" them to pay back a whole $68 billion, to escape government restrictions without imposing any new ones for the rest of the money.[78]

Geithner should have taken a moment to look at that real world. He seemed oblivious to the *New York Times* warning that came out about a week before that speech. With job losses rising, "growing numbers of American homeowners with once solid credit are falling behind on their mortgages, amplifying a wave of foreclosures." The article also stated that "Economy.com expects that 60 percent of the mortgage defaults this year will be set off primarily by unemployment, up from 29 percent last year."[79]

Adding more pain to the mix, housing values plummeted, according to the S&P/Case-Schiller Home Price Indices, to a seven-year low of 128.81 by the first quarter of 2009.[80] That's not improvement, Tim. But don't worry, you've got someone else on your side: none other than Jim Cramer.

In a *New York* magazine article with the headline "Thank Bernanke," Cramer concluded that "Ben Bernanke will go down as the greatest Federal Reserve chairman in history." According to Cramer, "The moment of crisis has passed, the parallels to the Great Depression are gone, all because Bernanke learned the lessons of history and refused to let it repeat itself. Bernanke once seemed Lilliputian compared to Greenspan. Now their statures have been reversed."[81]

Okay, I do agree with Cramer on one thing. Bernanke is bigger than Greenspan. Greenspan never conspired to subsidize the banking industry with $13 trillion.

Free Markets Aren't Free

This kind of shallow analysis means that in a year or two, there will be collective government and media sighs of relief, accompanied by enthusiasm that America's financial tree has shaken off its bad apples, and those spunky free markets have once again corrected themselves.

But we have to remember that the "free" markets aren't actually free—they cost trillions of dollars in Fed and Treasury secrets and bailouts, billions of dollars in bonuses, and millions of jobs. And because the remaining financial titans can afford to wait out a year or two of turmoil—as long as they retain control of the rules, which they will—we'll soon experience another round of convoluted off-book, nontransparent transactions engineered by teams of Ivy League PhDs, abetted by practices paid for by the finance industry.

A few years after the death of Bear Stearns and Lehman Brothers and the acquisition of Merrill Lynch by Bank of America, of Washington Mutual by JPMorgan Chase, and of Wachovia by Wells Fargo, some smoking-hot product will emerge to replace subprime CDOs, just as something replaced Enronian derivatives wizardry, WorldCom broadband bonds, Long Term Capital Management magic, dot-com IPOs, and junk bonds.

The new Wall Street landscape will be divided into a bunch of risk-laden mega-banks, headed by ex-Goldmanites or other members of the political-banking elite squad. Pieces of the investment banks that have supposedly changed their spots through acquisition or altering their status to BHCs to extract more government support will spin off into private companies—streamlined and focused, they will call them—to ward off any possibility of enduring forced regulation, which will be a nonevent anyway. Bonuses will boom, and the cycle will begin again. Then we will wonder why, yet again, so much money has transferred pockets, and no lessons were learned. Why is it that the more Wall Street changes, the more it remains the same?

We have got to be louder in our demands for real change. No Fed secrecy. No Treasury backing for toxic assets. No merging of banks that misbehave or that take our money to finance the deed. No banks that mingle consumer deposits with risky bets. No securities packaged with so many layers that they are impossible to understand, let alone regulate or value. No acceptance of the idea that free markets mean no constraints. No public dime supporting private losses. No status quo. We can achieve this, just as U.S citizens did in the past. A flood of visible public outrage provoked necessary and stabilizing changes in the 1930s, and the president, the treasury secretary, and Congress combined their strengths to reform the banking system.

We may not be in the middle of an exact duplicate of the Great Depression today, with high unemployment rates and bread lines, but in terms of wealth loss and federal subsidies extended to the banking system, we have surpassed those times. We need to flood Congress with our opinions again. We need better than equal treatment for people over banks. Our representatives need to know beyond a shadow of any doubt that we will not give them our votes if they take from us our future. E-mail them, march before their offices, vote against the ones who don't represent you and tell them why, start petitions, Twitter them. Flood their Facebook inboxes. Silence is too costly and unfair. Revolutionize regulation. The government has shown us the money is available.

We must ask ourselves: Do we have what it takes to stop the financial insanity this time? Or will we be lulled into complacency once again, so eager for a return to "normal" that we fail to stop the same systemic cascade of reckless and shady practices and greed from devastating us all over again? And the answer must be: No, we won't! It's past time to flex our will and end the next pillage before it starts.

THE REAL NUMBERS: BAILOUT, TARP, AND CEO COMPENSATION

In the course of considering all the tentacles of the government-sponsored bailout of the financial industry, there were a lot of numbers to process. In order to establish as comprehensive a set of reports as possible, Krisztina Ugrin and I scoured primary sources including Federal Reserve press releases and reports, Securities and Exchange Commission annual reports and proxy statements, Treasury Department press releases, U.S. Department of State reports, AIG's counterparty report, Citigroup's loss sharing program release, Congressional Research Service (CRS) reports, the SIGTARP (Special Inspector General for the Troubled Asset Relief Program) report, Federal Deposit Insurance Corporation (FDIC) press releases and reports, the Reuters and Dealogic Temporary Liquidity Guarantee Program reports, and corporate press releases. Where necessary, we questioned people at the Fed, Treasury Department, and FDIC for clarifications. John Olagues, owner and principal consultant of Truth in Options, stock options consultants, also provided assistance in determining the true value of executive options, in order to determine their total compensation. Each of our reports contains first-source links. To access the reports, please visit http://www.nomiprins.com/bailout.html.

1. Nomi Prins and Krisztina Ugrin, "Bailout Tally," June 2009: This report breaks down the $13 trillion by government area (Treasury Department, Fed, FDIC, etc.) and by company to illustrate exactly how much assistance came from what federal entity. Each of the various lending facilities are delineated as well. We will update this report monthly.

2. Nomi Prins and Krisztina Ugrin, "CEO Compensation and Bonuses": This report provides information on total executive compensation for the top TARP capital purchase program recipients, comparing their compensations in 2007 (before the bailout) with those in 2008 (after the bailout) and also the losses/profits of each firm for those years. We will release the information for 2009, as it becomes available. The report depicts the various reclassifications of compensation that firms have used to pay their executives, outside of any possible government restrictions, as well as an evaluation of the stock and option awards by John Olagues for Citigroup, JPMorgan Chase, and Goldman Sachs.

3. Nomi Prins and Krisztina Ugrin, "TARP Evaluation," June 2009: Because there is certain information missing from the 250-page quarterly SIGTARP report released on April 21, 2009, we compiled a report to augment it. We evaluate TARP investments and provide a point of comparison with other reports that have been released on TARP. We will update the report as new SIGTARP reports are released.

NOTES

Introduction. The More Wall Street Changes, the More It Stays the Same

1. Eric Dash, "Bankers Pledge Cooperation with Obama," *New York Times*, March 27, 2009, http://www.nytimes.com/2009/03/28/business/economy/28bank.html.
2. U.S. Department of the Treasury, *Biography of Secretary Henry M. Paulson*, n. d., http://www.ustreas.gov/education/history/secretaries/hmpaulson.shtml; Associated Press, "Henry Paulson: 'Major Decisions Were Right,'" MSNBC, March 26, 2009, http://www.msnbc.msn.com/id/29896951.
3. U.S. Department of the Treasury, "Secretary Geithner Introduces Financial Stability Plan," press release: TG-18, February 10, 2009, http://treas.gov/press/releases/tg18. htm; U.S. Department of the Treasury, "Treasury Department Releases Details on Public Private Partnership Investment Program," press release: TG-65, March 23, 2009, http://www.treas.gov/press/releases/tg65.htm.
4. Narcotics Anonymous, *"NA White Booklet,"* Narcotics Anonymous World Services, Inc., p. 2, http://www.na.org/admin/include/spaw2/uploads/pdf/litfiles/us_english/Booklet/NA%20White%20Booklet.pdf.
5. U.S. Securities and Exchange Commission, "Statement Regarding Recent Market Events and Lehman Brothers" (Updated), press release 2008–198, September 15, 2008, http://sec.gov/news/press/2008/2008–198.htm.
6. Reuters, "SEC Probes BofA Over Merrill Bonuses," CNNMoney.com, April 14, 2009, http://money.cnn.com/2009/04/14/news/companies/sec_boa.reut/; *U.S. Department of the Treasury, Capital Purchase Program—Transaction Report*, Financial-Stability.gov, December 22, 2008, p. 1, http://www.financialstability.gov/docs/12–29–08.pdf.

7. Nomi Prins and Krisztina Ugrin, "Bailout Tally," June 2009, http://www.nomiprins .com/bailout.html.

8. CNNMoney.com, "Annual Ranking of America's Largest Corporations, *Fortune 500*," April 30, 2007, 1–100, http://money.cnn.com/magazines/fortune/fortune500/2007/ full_list; CNNMoney.com, "Annual Ranking of America's Largest Corporations," *Fortune 500*, April 30, 2007, http://money.cnn.com/magazines/fortune/fortune500/2007/ snapshots/1341.html.

9. Nomi Prins and Krisztina Ugrin, "Bailout Tally," June 2009, http://www.nomiprins .com/bailout.html.

10. GPO, *Economic Report of the President*, U.S. Government Printing Office, Washington, 2003, p. 51, http://www.gpoaccess.gov/usbudget/fy04/pdf/2003_erp.pdf.

11. Nomi Prins, "Subprime Lending's Smartest Guys in the Room," *Mother Jones*, March– April 2008, http://www.motherjones.com/politics/2008/03/subprime-lendings-smartest- guys-room.

12. Office of Federal Housing Enterprise Oversight, *House Price Appreciation Continues at Robust Pace*, March 1, 2006, http://www.fhfa.gov/webfiles/2260/4q05hpi.pdf.

13. Office of Federal Housing Enterprise Oversight, *U.S. House Price Appreciation Rate Steadies*, March 1, 2007, http://www.fhfa.gov/webfiles/2192/4q06hpi.pdf.

14. Federal Reserve Bank of San Francisco, "Oil Prices and the U.S. Trade Deficit," press release: 2006–24, September 22, 2006, http://www.frbsf.org/publications/ economics/letter/2006/el2006–24.html.

15. Standard & Poor's, "S&P/Case-Shiller U.S. National Home Price Values," May 26, 2009, http://www2.standardandpoors.com/portal/site/sp/en/us/page.article/ 2,3,4,0,1148433018483.html.

16. Alexandra Twin, "Dow, S&P Break Records," CNNMoney.com, October 9, 2007, http://money.cnn.com/2007/10/09/markets/markets_0500/index.htm?postversion= 2007100917.

17. Office of the New York State Comptroller: Thomas P. DiNapoli, "New York City Securities Industry Bonuses," press release, January 17, 2008, http://www.osc.state .ny.us/press/releases/jan08/bonus.pdf.

18. Board of Governors of the Federal Reserve System, *Federal Funds Effective Rate*, http://www.federalreserve.gov/releases/h15/data/Monthly/H15_FF_O.txt.

19. Peter A. McKay, "Dow Is Off 7,401.24 Points from Its Record High in '07," *Wall Street Journal*, March 3, 2009, http://online.wsj.com/article/SB123599406229708501.html.

20. Alan Katz and Ian Katz, "Greenspan Slept as Off-Books Debt Escaped Scrutiny (Update 1)," Bloomberg, October 30, 2008, http://www.bloomberg.com/apps/news ?pid=20601087&sid=aYJZOB_gZi0I&refer=home.

21. Alan Sloan, "Why on Earth, *Fortune*'s Allan Sloan Asks, Should We Protect Banks from Their Mistakes?" CNNMoney.com, November 12, 2007, http://money.cnn .com/2007/10/26/magazines/fortune/citishelter.fortune/index.htm.

22. U.S. Department of the Treasury, *Programs: What Is EESA?* May 7, 2009, http:// www.financialstability.gov/roadtostability/programs.htm.

23. Federal Deposit Insurance Corporation, *About FDIC*, n.d., http://www.fdic.gov/ about/index.html.

24. Federal Deposit Insurance Corporation, *Supervisory Insights—Enhancing Transparency in the Structured Finance Market*, December 7, 2007, http://www.fdic.gov/ regulations/examinations/supervisory/insights/sisum08/article01_transparency.html.

25. Satyajit Das, *Credit Derivatives: CDOs and Structured Credit Products* (Singapore: John Wiley & Sons, 2005), quoted in Richard Tomlinson, David Evans, and Christine Richard, "The Ratings Charade," Bloomberg Markets, July 2007, http://www .bloomberg.com/news/marketsmag/ratings.html.

26. Jody Shenn, "CDO Market Is Almost Frozen, JPMorgan, Merrill Say (Update 2)," Bloomberg, February 5, 2008, http://www.bloomberg.com/apps/news?pid=20601087 &refer=home&sid=aCk0Qr1f2Eew.

27. Kathy Krawczyk and Lorraine Wright, "Dividends and Capital Gains Planning after the 2003 Tax Act," *The CPA Journal Online*, October 2004, http://www.nysscpa.org/ cpajournal/2004/1004/essentials/p36.htm.

28. Niall Ferguson, "Wall Street Lays Another Egg," *Vanity Fair*, December 2008, http://www.vanityfair.com/politics/features/2008/12/banks200812.

29. Hedge Fund Research, Inc., *Hedge Fund Inflows Set Another Record in 2007*, January 15, 2008, http://www.hedgefundresearch.com/pdf/pr_20080115.pdf.

30. Alistair Barr, "Hedge Fund Launches Decline in 2006, HFR Says," MarketWatch, March 29, 2007, http://www.marketwatch.com/news/story/hedge-fund-launches-liquidations-drop/story.aspx?guid={00FA3A7D-F81C-40D4-855A-B0F9745D005B}.

31. Nomi Prins and Krisztina Ugrin, "Bailout Tally," June 2009, http://www.nomiprins. com/bailout.html.

32. Fred Lucas, "Value of 2008 Bailouts Exceeds Combined Costs of All Major U.S. Wars," CNSNews, December 18, 2008, http://www.cnsnews.com/public/content/ article.aspx?RsrcID=40964.

33. The White House, *Press Office: Remarks of Lawrence H. Summers, Director of the National Economic Council, at Brookings Institution, Washington, D.C., March 13, 2009*, http://www.whitehouse.gov/the_press_office/Remarks-of-Lawrence-Summers-Director-of-the-National-Economic-Council-at-the-Brook/.

34. Nancy Trejos and Brenna Maloney, "401(k)s, Retirement Savings and the Financial Crisis," *Washington Post*, December 6, 2008, http://www.washingtonpost.com/ wp-dyn/content/graphic/2008/12/06/GR2008120600089.html.

35. United States Department of Labor, Bureau of Labor Statistics, "Employment Situation News Release," June 2, 2009, http://www.bls.gov/news.release/empsit.nr0.htm.

36. Bill Dedman, "U.S. Banks Suffer 149 Percent Rise in Bad Loans," MSNBC, March 17, 2009, http://www.msnbc.msn.com/id/29619163.

Chapter 1. Where'd the Bailout Money Go, Exactly?

1. About the White House: Presidents, "Biography of George W. Bush," The White House, http://www.whitehouse.gov/about/presidents/georgewbush.

2. United States Department of the Treasury, *History of the Treasury: Secretaries of the Treasury*, "Paul H. O'Neill (2001–2002)," http://www.ustreas.gov/education/history/ secretaries/poneill.shtml.

3. United States Department of the Treasury, *History of the Treasury: Secretaries of the Treasury*, "John Snow," http://www.ustreas.gov/education/history/secretaries/jsnow .shtml.

4. United States Department of the Treasury, "Testimony of Treasury Secretary Paul O'Neill before the Senate Finance Committee," press release, February 5, 2002, http://www.treas.gov/press/releases/po981.htm.

5. United States Department of the Treasury, *History of the Treasury: Secretaries of the Treasury*, "John Snow," http://www.ustreas.gov/education/history/secretaries/jsnow .shtml.

6. United States Department of the Treasury, "The Honorable John W. Snow Prepared Remarks: The Financial Services Roundtable Scottsdale, Arizona," press release, April 2, 2004, http://www.treas.gov/press/releases/js1289.htm.

7. United States Department of the Treasury, "Remarks by Treasury Secretary John Snow to the American Tort Reform Association's Annual Membership Meeting," press release, March 16, 2004, http://www.treas.gov/press/releases/js1237.htm.

8. United States Senate Committee on Finance, *Opening Statement of Henry M. Paulson before the Senate Finance Committee*, 109th Cong., 2nd sess., 2006.

9. "Presidential Cabinet Nominations," United States Senate, December 2, 2008, http://www.senate.gov/reference/resources/pdf/cabinettable.pdf.

10. William L. Watts, "Senate Confirms Paulson as Treasury Secretary," Market-watch, June 28, 2006, http://www.marketwatch.com/news/story/senate-confirms-paulson-treasury-secretary/story.aspx?guid=%7B5801D6FE-295A-4326-894B-ACB0454619C5%7D.

11. United States Department of the Treasury, *History of the Treasury: Secretaries of the Treasury*, "Henry M. Paulson, Jr.," http://www.ustreas.gov/education/history/ secretaries/hmpaulson.shtml.

12. "FACTBOX—Goldman Sachs Alumni in the News," Reuters, November 15, 2007, http://www.reuters.com/article/bondsNews/idUSN1555573420071115.

13. News Room: Leadership, "Henry M. Paulson, Jr.," The Nature Conservancy, http:// www.nature.org/pressroom/leadership/art11950.html; Paul Krugman, comment on "Nixonland," The Conscience of a Liberal, comment posted October 15, 2008, http://krugman.blogs.nytimes.com/2008/10/15/nixonland.

14. James Doran, "The Secret Hammer of Wall Street," *The Observer* (UK), August 16, 2007.

15. Landon Thomas Jr., "Paulson Comes Full Circle," *New York Times*, May 31, 2006.

16. United States Department of the Treasury, *History of the Treasury: Secretaries of the Treasury*, "Henry M. Paulson, Jr.," www.ustreas.gov/education/history/secretaries/ hmpaulson.shtml.

17. Jim Rutenberg and Edmund L. Andrews, "Bush Selects Goldman Chief to Take Over Treasury Dept.," *New York Times*, May 30, 2006.

18. United States Department of the Treasury, "United States Treasury Secretary John W. Snow Remarks to the Detroit Economic Club," press release, February 13, 2003, http://www.treas.gov/press/releases/js31.html.

19. "Tax-Cut Bill Wins Final Passage," CNN Politics, May 12, 2006, http://www.cnn .com/2006/POLITICS/05/11/tax.cuts/index.html.

20. Mark A. Stein, "Openers: Suits; True Believer," *New York Times*, June 4, 2006.

21. *United States Internal Revenue Code*, § 1043.

22. Jessica Holzer, "A Loophole for Poor Mr. Paulson," *Forbes*, June 2, 2006, http://www .forbes.com/2006/06/01/paulson-tax-loophole-cx_jh_0602paultax.html.

23. "Goldman Sachs (GS) Registers to Sell 3.23 Million Shares for Shareholder Henry Paulson," Streetinsider.com, June 29, 2006. http://www.streetinsider.com/ Equity+Offerings/Goldman+Sachs+(GS)+Registers+to+Sell+3.23+Million+ Shares+for+Shareholder+Henry+Paulson+--+DJ/1000819.html; Rebecca Christie and

Matthew Benjamin, "Paulson Risks Goldman Standard as Fannie, Freddie Shares Erode," Bloomberg, August 21, 2008, http://www.bloomberg.com/apps/news?pid=20601109&refer=home&sid=a8w9MI4Btco4.

24. Holzer, "A Loophole for Poor Mr. Paulson."

25. Nomi Prins, *Jacked: How "Conservatives" Are Picking Your Pocket* (Sausalito, CA: PoliPointPress, 2006).

26. United States Department of the Treasury, "Remarks by Secretary Henry M. Paulson at Roundtable Discussion on State of U.S. Economy," press release, January 29, 2007, http://www.treas.gov/press/releases/hp240.htm.

27. "Press Release," Board of Governors of the Federal Reserve System press release, August 17, 2007, http://www.federalreserve.gov/newscvents/press/monetary/20070817a.htm.

28. Henry Paulson, interviewed by Steve Liesman, Squawk on the Street, CNBC, August 21, 2007.

29. Damian Paletta, Susanne Craig, and Deborah Solomon, "New York Fed Holds Emergency Meeting on Lehman's Future," *Wall Street Journal*, September 13, 2008.

30. William Cohan, "Paulson Tells Lehman Where to Go," CNN Money, December 15, 2008, http://money.cnn.com/2008/12/12/magazines/fortune/3days_8.fortune/index.htm.

31. Barclays, "Barclays Announces Agreement to Acquire Lehman Brothers North American Investment Banking and Capital Markets Businesses," press release, September 17, 2008, http://www.newsroom.barclays.com/content/Detail.aspx?ReleaseID=1435&NewsAreaID=2.

32. David Teather, Andrew Clark, and Jill Treanon, "Barclays Agrees $1.75bn Deal for Core Lehman Brothers Business," *The Guardian*, September 17, 2008, http://www.guardian.co.uk/business/2008/sep/17/barclay.lehmanbrothers1.

33. Greg Farrell and Henny Sender, "The Shaming of John Thain," *Financial Times*, March 13, 2009.

34. Greg Farrell and Henny Sender, "Lynched at Merrill," *Financial Times*, January 26, 2009.

35. Matthew Karnitschnig, Carrick Mollenkamp, and Dan Fitzpatrick, "Bank of America to Buy Merrill," *Wall Street Journal*, September 15, 2008.

36. Andrew M. Cuomo letter to Christopher J. Dodd, Barney Frank, Mary L. Schapiro, and Elizabeth Warren, "Re: Bank of America–Merrill Lynch Merger Investigation," April 23, 2009.

37. State of New York Office of the Attorney General, "Executive Compensation Investigation: Bank of America–Merrill Lynch," February 26, 2009.

38. Kenneth D. Lewis, e-mail to Bank of America Board of Directors, December 22, 2008.

39. Scott Garret et al., Letter to President Obama, July 10, 2009.

40. U.S. Department of the Treasury, *Capital Purchase Program Transaction Report*, October 29, 2008, 4:30 P.M.

41. "Mugging Bank of America," *Wall Street Journal*, January 17, 2009, http://online.wsj.com/article/SB123215299934192217.html.

42. Andrew M. Cuomo letter to Christopher J. Dodd, Barney Frank, Mary L. Schapiro, and Elizabeth Warren, "Re: Bank of America–Merrill Lynch Merger Investigation," April 23, 2009.

43. United States Department of the Treasury, "Treasury, Federal Reserve and the FDIC Provide Assistance to Bank of America," press release, January 16, 2009, http://www.ustreas.gov/press/releases/hp1356.htm.

44. Bank of America, "Chairman's Letter," *Bank of America: 2008 Annual Report*, March 2009.

45. Bank of America, "Bank of America Announces Results from Annual Meeting," press release, April 29, 2009, http://newsroom.bankofamerica.com/index.php?s=43&item=8443.

46. Dan Fitzpatrick and Marshall Eckblad, "Lewis Ousted as BofA Chairman," *Wall Street Journal*, April 30, 2009.

47. Pallavi Gogoi, "Thain Resigns from Bank of America after News of Bonuses," *USA Today*, January 22, 2009, http://www.usatoday.com/money/industries/banking/2009-01-22-thain-leaving_N.htm.

48. Susanne Craig, "Thain Spars with Board Over Bonus at Merrill," *Wall Street Journal*, December 8, 2008.

49. Grant McCool, "NYAG Cuomo Warns Nine Banks about Bonus Payments," Reuters, October 29, 2008, http://www.reuters.com/article/ousiv/idU.S.TRE49S85720081029.

50. Merrill Lynch, "Merrill Lynch Statement on 2008 Executive Compensation," press release, December 8, 2008, http://www.ml.com/index.asp?id=7695_7696_8149_88278_113419_113455.

51. Andrew M. Cuomo, Letter to Barney Frank, "Re: Merrill Lynch 2008 Bonuses," February 10, 2009.

52. Karen Freifeld and David Mildenberg, "Cuomo Subpoenas Thain and Alphin Over Merrill Bonuses," Bloomberg, January 27, 2009, http://www.bloomberg.com/apps/news?pid=newsarchive&sid=aOcAC1TFziWo.

53. Andrew M. Cuomo letter to Barney Frank, "Re: Merrill Lynch 2008 Bonuses," February 10, 2009; Pallavi Gogoi, "Thain Resigns from Bank of America after News of Bonuses," *USA Today*, January 22, 2009.

54. Andrew M. Cuomo letter to Barney Frank, "Re: Merrill Lynch 2008 Bonuses."

55. Gretchen Morgenson, "Behind Insurer's Crisis, Blind Eye to a Web of Risk," *New York Times*, September 27, 2008, http://www.nytimes.com/2008/09/28/business/28melt.html.

56. Nomi Prins and Krisztina Ugrin, "Bailout Tally," June 2009, http://www.nomiprins.com/bailout.html.

57. John Crudele, "Who's the Fed Chairman Talking with Now?" *New York Post*, October 25, 2007.

58. United States Department of the Treasury, "Statement by Secretary Henry M. Paulson, Jr. on Comprehensive Approach to Market Developments," press release, September 19, 2008, http://www.treasury.gov/press/releases/hp1149.htm.

59. "Paulson Wants a Speedy Debt Deal," BBC News, September 21, 2008, http://news.bbc.co.uk/2/hi/business/7628144.stm.

60. "Treasury's Financial-Bailout Proposal to Congress," *Wall Street Journal Blogs*, September 20, 2008, http://blogs.wsj.com/economics/2008/09/20/treasurys-financial-bailout-proposal-to-congress.

61. Frank Ahrens, "'08: Our Date with Disaster," *Washington Post*, January 1, 2009.

62. United States Department of the Treasury, "Testimony by Secretary Henry M. Paulson, Jr. before the House Committee on Financial Services Hearing on Turmoil in the U.S. Credit Markets: Recent Actions Regarding Government Sponsored Entities, Investment Banks and other Financial Institutions," press release, September 24, 2008, http://www.treas.gov/press/releases/hp1154.htm.

63. United States Senate Committee on Banking, Housing, and Urban Affairs, *Turmoil in U.S. Credit Markets: Recent Actions Regarding Government-Sponsored Entities, Investment Banks, and Other Financial Institutions*, 110th Cong., 2nd sess., 2008, 112–113.

64. United States Department of the Treasury, "FACT SHEET: Proposed Treasury Authority to Purchase Troubled Assets," press release, September 20, 2008, http://www.treas.gov/press/releases/hp1150.htm.

65. Elinor Stebbins, "Pallas Athena, Goddess of Wisdom," *Images of Women in the Ancient World: Issues of Interpretation and Identity* (Spring 1998), http://www.arthistory.sbc.edu/imageswomen/papers/stebbinsathena/athena2.html.

66. Naomi Klein, e-mail message to the author, March 1, 2009.

67. Carl Hulse and David M. Herszenhorn, "House Rejects Bailout Package, 228–205; Stocks Plunge," *New York Times*, September 29, 2008; Vikas Bajaj and Michael M. Grynbaum, "For Stocks, Worst Single-Day Drop in Two Decades," *New York Times*, September 29, 2008.

68. Carl Hulse, "Pressure Builds on House after Senate Backs Bailout," *New York Times*, October 1, 2008.

69. Lori Montgomery and Shailagh Murray, "Senate Approves Bailout," *Washington Post*, October 2, 2008.

70. Center for Responsive Politics, "Mortgage Bankers and Brokers: Top Recipients, 2008," Opensecrets.org, http://www.opensecrets.org/industries/recips.php?cycle=2008&ind=F4600.

71. David M. Herszenhorn, "Bailout Plan Wins Approval; Democrats Vow Tighter Rules," *New York Times*, October 3, 2008.

72. Jeanne Sahadi, "Bailout Is Law," CNN Money, October 4, 2008, http://money.cnn.com/2008/10/03/news/economy/house_friday_bailout/index.htm?postversion=2008100309.

73. United States Department of the Treasury, "Paulson Statement on Emergency Economic Stabilization Act," press release, October 3, 2008, http://www.ustreas.gov/press/releases/hp1175.htm.

74. United States Department of the Treasury, "Kashkari Appointed Interim Assistant Secretary for Financial Stability," press release, October 6, 2008, http://www.ustreas.gov/press/releases/hp1184.htm.

75. Edmund L. Andrews and Mark Lander, "White House Overhauling Rescue Plan," *New York Times*, October 12, 2008.

76. Investopedia, "Preferred Stock," Forbes Digital, http://www.investopedia.com/terms/p/preferredstock.asp.

77. United States Department of the Treasury, "Treasury Announces TARP Capital Purchase Program Description," press release, October 14, 2008, http://www.treas.gov/press/releases/hp1207.htm.

78. Patrick J. Kennedy, "Amends the Financial Services Regulatory Relief Act of 2006," March 9, 2007, Library of Congress, http://thomas.loc.gov/cgi-bin/bdquery/z?d110:HR01424:@@@D&summ2=m&.

79. Greg Ip, comment on "Fed Paying Interest on Reserves: An Old Idea with a New Urgency," *Wall Street Journal Blogs*, comment posted April 29, 2008, http://blogs.wsj.com/economics/2008/04/29/fed-paying-interest-on-reserves-an-old-idea-with-a-new-urgency.

80. Board of Governors of the Federal Reserve System, press release, October 6, 2008, http://www.federalreserve.gov/newsevents/press/monetary/20081006a.htm. Also see Financial Services Regulatory Relief Act of 2006, § 201.

81. Matthew Quinn, "Bernanke Admits Fed Struggling to Revive Private Lending," *Financial Week*, January 13, 2009.

82. Federal Reserve, *Federal Reserve Statistical Release H3*, April 30, 2009.

83. Julie Haviv, "U.S. Mortgage Applications Jump; Rates at Record Low," Reuters, March 25, 2009, http://www.reuters.com/article/marketsNews/idUSNYS00494520090325.

84. "Progress amid the Ruins," *Wall Street Journal*, October 9, 2008.

85. United States Department of the Treasury, "Statement by Secretary Henry M. Paulson, Jr. Following Meeting of the G7 Finance Ministers and Central Bank Governors," press release, October 10, 2008, http://www.ustreas.gov/press/releases/hp1194.htm.

86. David Enrich, "Lending Drops at Big U.S. Banks," *Wall Street Journal*, January 26, 2009.

87. Joseph N. Distefano, comment on "JPMorgan's Dimon: 'We're Not Relying' on U.S. Bank Bailouts," PhillyDeals, comment posted September 26, 2008, http://www.philly.com/philly/blogs/inq-phillydeals/JPMorgans_Dimon_Were_not_relying_on_.html.

88. Andrew Ross Sorkin, ed., comment on "Dimon on the Government's Bailout Moves," Dealbook, comment posted October 15, 2008, http://dealbook.blogs.nytimes.com/2008/10/15/dimon-on-the-governments-bailout-moves.

89. Joe Nocera, "So When Will Banks Give Loans?" *New York Times*, October 24, 2008.

90. United States Senate Committee on Banking, Housing and Urban Affairs, *Pulling Back the TARP: Oversight of the Financial Rescue Program*, 111th Cong., 1st sess., 2009.

91. *February Oversight Report*, Congressional Oversight Panel, February 6, 2009, p. 4.

92. Nomi Prins and Krisztina Ugrin, "TARP Evaluation," June 2009, http://www.nomiprins.com/bailout.html.

93. *February Oversight Report*, Congressional Oversight Panel, February 6, 2009, p. 8.

94. U.S. Office of SIGTARP, "Testimony Before the House Committee on Financial Services Subcommittee on Oversight and Investigations," February 24, 2009, p. 1, http://sigtarp.gov/reports/testimony/2009/Testimony_Before_the_House_Committee_on_Financial_Services_Subcommittee_on_Oversight_and_Investigations.pdf.

95. Nomi Prins and Krisztina Ugrin, "Bailout Tally," June 2009, http://www.nomiprins.com/bailout.html.

96. Sue Kirchhoff, "Paulson Defends Bailout, Lawmakers Seek Foreclosure Aid," *USA Today*, November 19, 2008.

97. United States Department of the Treasury, "Statement by Secretary Henry M. Paulson, Jr. at the Development Committee Meeting," press release, October 12, 2008, http://www.treasury.gov/press/releases/hp1198.htm.

98. Henry M. Paulson interview by Maria Bartiromo, *The Call*, CNBC, January 12, 2009.

99. Jacki Calmes, "Senate Confirms Geithner for Treasury," *New York Times*, January 26, 2009.

100. Federal Reserve Bank of New York, About the Fed, "Organization," http://www.newyorkfed.org/aboutthefed/org_chart.html; Federal Reserve Bank of New York,

Organization, "Stephen Friedman," January 2008, http://www.newyorkfed.org/aboutthefed/orgchart/board/friedman.html.

101. Goldman Sachs, "Managing Directors," January 1, 2009; "An Economic War Council," *Portfolio*, May 12, 2008, http://www.portfolio.com/graphics/2008/05/An-Economic-War-Council.

102. Gary Weiss, "The Man Who Got Saved (or Got Suckered by) Wall Street," Condé Nast, *Portfolio*, June 2008.

103. Federal Reserve Bank of New York, "New York Fed Names Timothy F. Geithner President," press release, October 15, 2003, http://www.newyorkfed.org/newsevents/news_archive/aboutthefed/2003/oa031015.html.

104. Kevin Dowd, "Too Big to Fail? Long-Term Capital Management and the Federal Reserve," *The Cato Institute Briefing Papers* 52, September 23, 1999.

105. Weiss, "The Man Who Got Saved (or Got Suckered by) Wall Street."

106. National Economic Council, *Lawrence H. Summers*, The White House, http://www.whitehouse.gov/administration/eop/nec/chair.

107. Times Topics, "Timothy F. Geithner," *New York Times*, March 24, 2009, http://topics.nytimes.com/topics/reference/timestopics/people/g/timothy_f_geithner/index.html.

108. Sheryl Gay Stolberg, "In a World Not Wholly Cooperative, Obama's Top Economist Makes Do," *New York Times*, February 16, 2009.

109. Andrew Ross Sorkin, ed., comment on "Hearing Over, Geithner's Confirmation Is Expected," DealBook, comment posted January 21, 2009, http://dealbook.blogs.nytimes.com/2009/01/21/hearing-over-geithners-confirmation-is-expected.

110. Politics, "Transcript: Timothy Geithner Confirmation Hearing," *Washington Post*, January 21, 2009, http://www.washingtonpost.com/wp-srv/politics/documents/transcript_geithner_012109.html.

111. Yalman Onaran and Michael McKee, "In Geithner We Trust Eludes Treasury as Market Fails to Recover," Bloomberg, February 25, 2009, http://www.bloomberg.com/apps/news?pid=20601109&refer=home&sid=aLhs5Byln00k.

112. Structured Investment Vehicle: "A pool of investment assets that attempts to profit from credit spreads between short-term debt and long-term structured finance products such as asset-backed securities." Investopedia, "Structured Investment Vehicle," Forbes Digital, http://www.investopedia.com/terms/s/structured-investment-vehicle.asp.

113. Citigroup, "Robert E. Rubin Announces His Retirement from Citi," press release, January 9, 2009, http://www.citigroup.com/citi/press/2009/090109d.htm.

114. Onaran and McKee, "In Geithner We Trust Eludes Treasury as Market Fails to Recover."

115. Christine Harper and Jeff Kearns, "Citigroup Falls Below $1 as Investor Faith Erodes (Update 2)," Bloomberg, March 5, 2009, http://www.bloomberg.com/apps/news?pid=20601087&sid=aKLJO8S5nFaU&refer=home.

116. United States Securities and Exchange Commission, "SEC Halts Short Selling of Financial Stocks to Protect Investors and Markets," press release, September 19, 2008, http://www.sec.gov/news/press/2008/2008-211.htm.

117. United States Department of the Treasury, "Treasury Secretary Tim Geithner Remarks before the Council on Foreign Relations," press release, March 25, 2009, http://www.ustreas.gov/press/releases/tg68.htm.

Chapter 2. This Was Never about the Little Guy

1. Justin Fox, "18 Tough Questions (and Answers) about the Bailout," *Time*, September 30, 2008, http://www.time.com/time/business/article/0,8599,1845816,00.html.

2. E. D. Hirsch Jr., Joseph F. Kett, and James Trefil, *The New Dictionary of Cultural Literacy* (Boston: Houghton Mifflin, 2002), p. 51.

3. Tracy McVeigh, "The Party's Over for Iceland, the Island That Tried to Buy the World," *The Observer*, October 5, 2008, http://www.guardian.co.uk/world/2008/oct/05/iceland.creditcrunch; Lee Christie, "Las Vegas Tops Foreclosure List," CNN Money, February 5, 2008, http://money.cnn.com/2008/02/05/real_estate/zip_code_foreclosures/index.htm.

4. Subprime borrowers: "A classification of borrowers with a tarnished or limited credit history . . . subprime loans carry more credit risk, and as such, will carry higher interest rates as well," Investopedia, "Subprime," Forbes Digital, http://www.investopedia.com/terms/s/subprime.asp; Eric Petroff, "How Will the Subprime Mess Impact You?" Investopedia, http://www.investopedia.com/articles/pf/07/subprime-impact.asp.

5. Data from Realtytrac, http://www.realtytrac.com "Foreclosure Activity Decreases 6 Percent in May," press release, June 11, 2009.

6. Nomi Prins and Krisztina Ugrin, "Bailout Tally," June 2009, http://www.nomiprins.com/bailout.html; United States Department of the Treasury, "Remarks by Secretary Henry M. Paulson, Jr. at the Ronald Reagan Presidential Library," press release, November 20, 2008, https://treas.gov/press/releases/hp1285.htm.

7. Data from the United States Federal Reserve Board of Governors, http://www.federalreserve.gov/econresdata/releases/mortoutstand/mortoutstand20090331.htm.

8. Andrew Ross Sorkin, ed., comment on "As Goldman and Morgan Shift, a Wall St. Era Ends," Dealbook, comment posted September 21, 2008, http://dealbook.blogs.nytimes.com/2008/09/21/goldman-morgan-to-become-bank-holding-companies.

9. 2002–2007 data from Thomson Reuters Financial, http://www.thomsonreuters.com/business_units/financial.

10. Sarah Butcher, "Sector View: Securitization Is Backed by Demand," Risk, October 12, 2004, http://news.risk.efinancialcareers.com/ITEM_FR/newsItemId-3542.

11. Gregory Cresci, "Merrill, Citigroup Record CDO Fees Earned in Top Growth Market," Bloomberg, August 30, 2005, http://www.bloomberg.com/apps/news?pid=10000103&sid=a.FcDwf1.ZG4&refer=us.

12. Jody Shenn, "CDO Market Is Almost Frozen, JPMorgan, Merrill Say," Bloomberg.com, February 5, 2008, http://www.bloomberg.com/apps/news?pid=20601087&refer=home&sid=aCk0Qr1f2Eew.

13. "EU Wants Banks to Come Clean on Toxic Assets," EU Business, February 26, 2009, http://www.eubusiness.com/news-eu/1235566921.44.

14. Lawrence J. White, "Mortgage-Backed Securities: Another Way to Finance Housing" (draft of paper prepared for the Joint Congress of UN-HABITAT and the European Federation of Building Societies Berlin, September 22–24, 2004), Stern School of Business, New York University, August 11, 2004, http://www.stern.nyu.edu/eco/wkpapers/mortgagebacked.pdf, p. 18.

15. Ibid.

16. Data from the Federal Housing Finance Board, Monthly Interest Rate Survey, http://www.fhfb.gov/webfiles/6005/MIRS_table13_2005.xls.

17. Financial Wisdom Online Resource Library, "Does Your Adjustable Rate Mortgage Still Make Sense?" United Services Credit Union, http://www.financialwisdom.com/ResourceLibrary/1stUSCU/CS/ARMMortgage.shtml.

18. Board of Governors of the Federal Reserve System, *Chairman Ben S. Bernanke at the Federal Reserve Bank of Kansas City's Economic Symposium, Jackson Hole, Wyoming*, speech transcript, August 31, 2007, http://www.federalreserve.gov/newsevents/speech/bernanke20070831a.htm.

19. Data from the Federal Housing Finance Board, Monthly Interest Rate Survey, http://www.fhfb.gov/webfiles/6521/MIRS_table36_2006.xls; Nomi Prins, "Subprime Lending's Smartest Guys in the Room," *Mother Jones*, March–April 2008.

20. Associated Press, "Inquiry Is Begun on Home Builder," *New York Times*, March 28, 2007, http://query.nytimes.com/gst/fullpage.html?res=9A02E5DB1330F93BA15750C0A9619C8B63&fta=y.

21. Binyamin Appelbaum, "Beazer: Exec Tried to Destroy Records," *Charlotte Observer*, June 28, 2007.

22. Executive Profile, "Ian McCarthy," *Businessweek*, http://investing.businessweek.com/businessweek/research/stocks/people/person.asp?personId=332734&ric=BZH&previousCapId=332730&previousTitle=Beazer%20Homes%20USA%20Inc.

23. Edgar Online, "New Century Financial Corp—Current Report Filing (8-K) Section 1 Business and Operations," United States Securities and Exchange Commission, filed on April 6, 2007, http://sec.edgar-online.com/new-century-financial-corp/8-k-current-report-filing/2007/04/06/ Section4.aspx.

24. Tim McLaughlin, Jonathan Stempel, and Joe Giannone, "American Home Mortgage Files for Bankruptcy," Reuters/*USA TODAY*, August 7, 2007, http://www.usatoday.com/money/economy/housing/2007-08-06-american-home-mortgage-bankruptcy_N.htm.

25. "Criminal Probe Said to Focus on Collapsed Lender," *Los Angeles Times*, October 3, 2007.

26. Bradley Keoun, "Countrywide Taps $11.5 Billion Credit Line from Banks (Update 7)," Bloomberg, August 16, 2007, http://www.bloomberg.com/apps/news?pid=20601087&sid=aEA8xNnecDiw&refer=home.

27. Associated Press, "Countrywide CEO's Stock Sales Scrutinized," CBS News, October 18, 2007, http://www.cbsnews.com/stories/2007/10/18/business/main3379814.shtml.

28. Prins, "Subprime Lending's Smartest Guys in the Room."

29. Edgar Online, "New Century Financial Corp—Current Report (8-K)," United States Securities and Exchange Commission, March 12, 2007, http://www.sec.gov/Archives/edgar/data/1287286/000129993307001553/htm_18857.htm.

30. William Heisel, "Edward Gotschall Dies at 53; Helped Found Subprime Giant New Century Financial," *Los Angeles Times*, January 13, 2009.

31. Annys Shin, Ylan Q. Mui, and Nancy Trejos, comment on "Ameriquest Settlement," The Checkout, comment posted January 23, 2006, http://voices.washingtonpost.com/thecheckout/2006/01/ameriquest_settlement.html.

32. "Ameriquest Watch," Inner City Press/Fair Finance Watch, last updated December 1, 2008, http://www.innercitypress.org/ameriquest.html.

33. Washington State Department of Financial Institutions, "12,000 Washington Consumers Eligible for State's $21M Settlement with Mortgage Company," press release, August 14, 2003, http://www.dfi.wa.gov/cs/householdsettle_nr.htm.

34. Jason Ryan, "Fraud 'Directly Related' to Financial Crisis Probed," ABC News, February 11, 2009, http://abcnews.go.com/TheLaw/Economy/Story?id=6855179&page=1.

35. Mortgage Fraud, "Just the Facts: The Latest Mortgage Fraud Statistics," United States Federal Bureau of Investigation, http://www.fbi.gov/hq/mortgage_fraud.htm.

36. United States Federal Bureau of Investigation, "More than 400 Defendants Charged for Roles in Mortgage Fraud Schemes as Part of Operation 'Malicious Mortgage,'" press release, June 19, 2008, http://www.fbi.gov/pressrel/pressrel08/mortgagefraud061908.htm.

37. Facts for Consumers, "High-Rate, High-Fee Loans (HOEPA/Section 32 Mortgages)," United States Federal Trade Commission, February 2009, http://www.ftc.gov/bcp/edu/pubs/consumer/homes/rea19.shtm.

38. "Final Lending Plan Clears Senate Panel," *New York Times*, September 22, 1993.

39. "Mortgage-Fraud Bill in Works," *The American Banker*, February 18, 1993.

40. GPO, Introduction of the Predatory Lending Consumer Protection Act of 2000, H. R. 4250, Congressional Record Volume 146, Number 46, April 12, 2000.

41. Mark Jickling, "The Enron Loophole," Congressional Research Service, July 7, 2008.

42. "Where Credit Is Due: A Timeline of the Mortgage Crisis," *Mother Jones*, July–August 2008.

43. Eric Lipton and Stephen Labaton, "A Deregulator Looks Back, Unswayed," *New York Times*, November 16, 2008.

44. United States Senate Committee on Banking, Housing, and Urban Affairs, "Sarbanes Announces Introduction of Legislation to Combat Predatory Lending Practices," press release, May 1, 2002, http://banking.senate.gov/prel02/0501pred.htm.

45. Legislation, "S.1928: Predatory Lending Consumer Protection Act of 2003," Govtrack.us, http://www.govtrack.us/congress/bill.xpd?bill=s108-1928.

46. Holden Lewis, "Study: Flood of Foreclosures Coming," Bankrate.com, April 18, 2007, http://www.bankrate.com/bosre/news/mortgages/20070418_subprime_mortgage_foreclosure_a1.asp?caret=1d.

47. Data from the Federal Housing Finance Board, Monthly Interest Rate Survey, http://www.fhfb.gov/webfiles/6001/MIRS_table09_2005.xls.

48. Bank of America, "Bank of America Agrees to Purchase Countrywide Financial Corp.," press release, January 11, 2008, http://newsroom.bankofamerica.com/index.php?s=43&item=7956.

49. Ari Weinberg, "Countrywide Branches Out beyond Mortgages," *Forbes*, April 16, 2004, http://www.forbes.com/2004/04/16/cx_aw_0416cfc.html.

50. Washington Mutual, "WaMu Closes $7 Billion Equity Issuance, Strengthening Capital Position," press release, April 15, 2008, http://newsroom.wamu.com/phoenix.zhtml?c=189529&p=irol-newsArticle&ID=1129868&highlight=; Washington Mutual, "WaMu Reports Significant Build-Up of Reserves Contributing to Second Quarter Net Loss of $3.3 Billion," press release, July 22, 2008, http://newsroom.wamu.com/phoenix.zhtml?c=189529&p=irol-newsArticle&ID=1177849&highlight=; Christopher Palmeri, "JPMorgan Chase to Buy Washington Mutual," *Businessweek*, September 26, 2008, http://www.businessweek.com/bwdaily/dnflash/content/sep2008/db20080925_760466.htm.

51. Sara Lepro, Associated Press, "Wells Fargo Buys Wachovia for $15.1 Billion," ABC News, October 3, 2008, http://abcnews.go.com/Business/SmartHome/story?id=5946486&page=1.

52. Souphala Chomsisengphet and Anthony Pennington-Cross, "The Evolution of the Subprime Mortgage Market," *Federal Reserve Bank of St. Louis Review*

(January–February 2006): 31–56, http://research.stlouisfed.org/publications/review/06/01/ChomPennCross.pdf.

53. Joint Center for Housing Studies of Harvard University, "The State of the Nation's Housing 2007," 2007, pp. 15–19, http://www.jchs.harvard.edu/publications/markets/son2007/son2007_homeownership.pdf.

54. Jody Shenn, "Subprime Loan Defaults Pass 2001 Peak, Friedman Says (Update 4)," Bloomberg, February 2, 2007, http://www.bloomberg.com/apps/news?pid=newsarchive&sid=aFGf71vlQkWM; *Little Shop of Horrors*, Internet Movie Database, www.imdb.com/title/tt0091419.

55. Office of the Comptroller of the Currency, Administrator of National Banks, United States Department of the Treasury, "Summary of the Highlights of 'The Bankruptcy Abuse Prevention and Consumer Protection Act of 2005,'" Office of the Comptroller of the Currency, Administrator of National Banks, United States Department of the Treasury, October 17, 2005, http://www.occ.treas.gov/law/SummaryoftheHighlightsofBankruptcyLaw109-8.pdf.

56. Office of Federal Housing Enterprise Oversight, "Largest U.S. House Price Increases in More Than 25 Years," Office of Federal Housing Enterprise Oversight press release, September 1, 2005, http://www.fhfa.gov/webfiles/1183/2q05hpi.pdf.

57. Rick Brooks and Constance Mitchell Ford, "The United States of Subprime," *Wall Street Journal*, October 11, 2007.

58. Mark Furletti, "An Overview of Credit Card Asset-Backed Securities," Federal Reserve Bank of Philadelphia, December 2002, http://www.philadelphiafed.org/payment-cards-center/events/workshops/2002/CreditCardSecuritization_012002.pdf.

59. Bond Basics, "Bond Basics: Evolution of Asset-Backed Securities in Europe," Pimco, January 2007, http://europe.pimco.com/LeftNav/Bond+Basics/2007/Bond+Basics+-+Evolution+of+ABS+in+Europe+-+Jan+07.htm.

60. Cohen & Company, "Cohen Brothers, LLC Hires New Chief Executive Officer," press release, February 27, 2006, http://www.cohenandcompany.com/press/PressRelease20060227.asp.

61. Felix Salmon, "Recipe for Disaster: The Formula That Killed Wall Street," *Wired*, February 23, 2009, http://www.wired.com/techbiz/it/magazine/17-03/wp_quant?currentPage=all.

62. Carol D. Leonnig, "How HUD Mortgage Policy Fed the Crisis," *Washington Post*, June 10, 2008.

63. Steven A. Holmes, "Fannie Mae Eases Credit to Aid Mortgage Lending," *New York Times*, September 30, 1999.

64. Leonnig, "How HUD Mortgage Policy Fed the Crisis."

65. Associated Press, "Report: Fannie Mae Manipulated Accounting," MSNBC, May 23, 2006, http://www.msnbc.msn.com/id/12923225; Alt-A: "A classification of mortgages where the risk profile falls between prime and subprime. The borrowers behind these mortgages will typically have clean credit histories, but the mortgage itself will generally have some issues that increase its risk profile." Investopedia, "Alt-A," Forbes Digital, http://www.investopedia.com/terms/a/alt-a.asp.

66. Leonnig, "How HUD Mortgage Policy Fed the Crisis."

67. Charles W. Calomiris and Peter J. Wallison, "Blame Fannie Mae and Congress for the Credit Mess," *Wall Street Journal*, September 23, 2008, http://online.wsj.com/article/SB122212948811465427.html.

68. Federal Reserve Bank of Kansas City, *Subprime Loan Report*, July 2008, http://www .kansascityfed.org/comaffrs/subprime/Omaha.07.02.08.pdf.

69. Ashley Reed and Peter Gibson, "Things That Matter: The Australian Commercial Real Estate–Backed Securities Market," RatingsDirect, March 20, 2003, http:// www2.standardandpoors.com/spf/pdf/fixedincome/20030320_ThingsMatterAust CMBS.pdf.

70. United States Senate Committee on Banking, Housing and Urban Affairs, *Testimony of Professor John C. Coffee, Jr.: Hearings on Enhancing Investor Protection and the Regulation of Securities Markets*, 111th Cong., 1st sess., 2009.

71. *Source*: data from Thomson Reuters Financial, http://thomsonreuters.com/business_ units/financial.

72. Randall Dodd and Paul Mills, "Outbreak: U.S. Subprime Contagion," *Finance & Development* (June 2008): 14–18.

73. "FACTBOX-CDOs: ABS and Other Sundry Collateral," Reuters, June 28, 2007, http://www.reuters.com/article/bondsNews/idUSN2834578820070628.

74. Data from Thomson Reuters Financial, http://thomsonreuters.com/business_units/ financial.

75. Coughlin, Stoia, Geller, Rudman, & Robbins, LLP, "Coughlin Stoia Geller Rudman & Robbins LLP Files Class Action Suit against the Bear Stearns Companies, Inc.," press release, March 17, 2008, http://www.csgrr.com/csgrr-cgi-bin/mil?case=bearste arns&templ=cases/case-pr.html.

76. Thomas S. Mulligan and Tom Petruno, "Lawsuit Accuses Bear Stearns of Fraud," *Los Angeles Times*, April 12, 2008.

77. KBC, "KBC Takes Decisive Measures to Reduce Volatility of Future Results and Pro-actively Publishes Third-Quarter Result Highlights," press release, October 15, 2008, https://multimediafiles.kbcgroup.eu/ng/published/KBCCOM/ PDF/COM_RVG_ pdf_persbericht_15_10_08_EN.pdf.

78. David Evans, "The Poison in Your Pension," Bloomberg Markets, July 26, 2007, http://www.bloomberg.com/news/marketsmag/pension.html.

79. Tim McLaughlin, "Ratings Downgrades Slam Fidelity's Subprime CDO," *Boston Business Journal*, April 18, 2008, http://www.bizjournals.com/boston/stories/2008/04/21/ story9.html.

80. Walden Siew, "Shrinking CDO Market Hits Citi, Deutsche, TCW," Reuters, October 1, 2007, http://www.reuters.com/article/pressReleasesMolt/idUSN2627921220071001.

81. Jody Shenn, "CDO Market Is Almost Frozen, JPMorgan, Merrill Say," Bloomberg, February 5, 2008, http://www.bloomberg.com/apps/news?pid=20601087&sid=aCk0 Qr1f2Eew.

82. Marcy Gordon, Associated Press News, "SEC Adopts New Rules for Credit-Rating Agencies," Talking Points Memo, December 3, 2008, http://www.talking pointsmemo.com/news/2008/12/sec_adopts_new_rules_for_credi.php.

83. Liz Peek, "The Last Word on What Went Wrong," *New York Sun*, September 18, 2007, http://www.nysun.com/business/last-word-on-what-went-wrong/62836.

84. Roben Farzad, "Let the Blame Begin," *Businessweek*, August 6, 2007, http://www .businessweek.com/magazine/content/07_32/b4045048.htm.

85. United States Security and Exchange Commission, "SEC Proposes Comprehensive Reforms to Bring Increased Transparency to Credit Rating Process," press release, June 11, 2008, http://www.sec.gov/news/press/2008/2008-110.htm.

86. United States House of Representatives Committee on Oversight and Government Reform, *Chairman Waxman's Opening Statement: Committee Holds Hearing on the Credit Rating Agencies and the Financial Crisis*, 110th Cong., 2nd sess., 2008.

87. David Teather, "The Woman Who Built Financial 'Weapon of Mass Destruction,'" *The Guardian*, September 29, 2008, http://www.guardian.co.uk/business/2008/sep/20/wallstreet.banking?gusrc=rss&feed=business.

88. Gretchen Morgenson, "Arcane Market Is Next to Face Big Credit Test," *New York Times*, February 17, 2008, http://www.nytimes.com/2008/02/17/business/17swap.html?_r=1&hp&oref=login.

89. Investopedia Staff, "Dissecting the Bear Stearns Hedge Fund Collapse," Investopedia, http://www.investopedia.com/articles/07/bear-stearns-collapse.asp.

90. Naohiko Baba and Paola Gallardo, "OTC Derivatives Market Activity in the Second Half of 2007," Bank of International Settlements, May 2008, http://www.bis.org/publ/otc_hy0805.pdf?noframes=1.

91. Deepak Moorjani, phone conversation with the author, April 29, 2009.

92. Adam Davidson, "How AIG Fell Apart," The Big Money, September 18, 2008, http://www.thebigmoney.com/articles/explainer/2008/09/18/how-aig-fell-apart.

93. Janet Tavakoli, "Buyer Beware," *International Financing Review*, October 25, 2003 (Super-senior tranche: Typically the largest slice of a synthetic CDO, with the lowest risk, "though there is no market standard definition of super senior risk." Sometimes referred to as having a quadruple-A rating, rating agencies in fact do not recognize super-senior tranches. Their risk is defined solely by the market), http://www.tavakolistructuredfinance.com/ifr2.html; "Collateral Postings Under AIGFP," September 16, 2008 to December 31, 2008, http://www.aig.com/aigweb/internet/en/files/CounterpartyAttachments031809_tcm385-155645.pdf.

94. Deepak Moorjani, phone conversation with the author, April 29, 2009.

95. Charles Krauthammer, "Catharsis, Then Common Sense," *Washington Post*, September 26, 2008.

96. Black Coffee Briefings on the War in Iraq, "Iraq: What Lies Ahead," American Enterprise Institute for Public Policy Research, http://www.aei.org/events/filter.,eventID.274/transcript.asp.

97. Senate Committee on Banking, Housing and Urban Affairs, *Testimony of the Honorable Marc H. Morial*, 110th Cong., 2nd sess., 2008; Eric Boehlert and Jamison Foser, comment on "Cavuto Suggests Congress Should Have Warned That 'Loaning to Minorities and Risky Folks Is a Disaster,'" County Fair, comment posted September 19, 2008, http://mediamatters.org/items/200809190021.

98. Frank Ahrens, "'Moral Hazard': Why Risk Is Good," *Washington Post*, March 19, 2008; Jason Ryan, "Fraud 'Directly Related' to Financial Crisis Probed"; Randall Mikkelsen, "FBI Home Mortgage Probe Now Targets 19 Firms," Reuters, April 16, 2008, http://www.reuters.com/article/governmentFilingsNews/idUSN1648358920080416.

Chapter 3. Everybody Wants to Be a Bank

1. Board of Governors of the Federal Reserve System, *Federal Reserve Act*, Section 13, August 13, 2008, http://www.federalreserve.gov/aboutthefed/section13.htm; Joshua Brockman, "Death of the Brokerage: The Future of Wall Street," NPR, September 22, 2008, http://www.npr.org/templates/story/story.php?storyId=94894707.

2. Deloitte LLP, "The Implications of Goldman Sachs and Morgan Stanley Becoming Bank Holding Companies," *Credit Crisis Advisory*, Volume II, November 7, 2008, http://www.deloitte.com/dtt/newsletter/0,1012,sid %253D2212%2526cid%253D233 238,00.html.

3. U.S. Federal Reserve System, *Bank Holding Companies and Financial Holding Companies*, n.d., http://www.fedpartnership.gov/bank-life-cycle/grow-shareholder-value/bank-holding-companies.cfm.

4. Board of Governors of the Federal Reserve System, "Board Announces That Goldman Sachs and Morgan Stanley Transactions May Be Consummated Immediately," press release, September 22, 2008, http://www.federalreserve.gov/ newsevents/press/orders/20080922a.htm.

5. United States Federal Deposit Insurance Corporation, "FDIC Announces Plan to Free Up Bank Liquidity," press release, October 14, 2008, http://www.fdic.gov/news/news/press/2008/pr08100.html.

6. Andrew Bary, "How Do You Spell Sweet Deal? For Banks, It's TLGP," *Barron's*, April 20, 2009, http://online.barrons.com/article/SB124001886675331247.html?page=1; Reuters, "Morgan Stanley Taps TLGP Again with $475 Mln Deal-IFR," Forbes, December 4, 2008, http://www.forbes.com/feeds/afx/2008/12/04/afx5779779.html.

7. Associated Press, "Leveraged-Loan Accounting Gives Banks Edge," *Wall Street Journal*, February 28, 2008, http://accounting.smartpros.com/x60907.xml.

8. Kristin Jones, "Why Is Everyone Becoming a Bank Holding Company? It's All about the Benjamins," ProPublica, November 12, 2008, http://www.propublica.org/article/why-is-everyone-becoming-a-bank-holdingcompany-1112.

9. Dean Baker, phone conversation with the author, January 30, 2009.

10. Jon Hilsenrath, Damian Paletta, and Aaron Lucchetti, "Goldman, Morgan Scrap Wall Street Model, Become Banks in Bid to Ride Out Crisis," *Wall Street Journal*, September 22, 2008, http://online.wsj.com/article/SB122202739111460721.html.

11. The Goldman Sachs Group, Inc., Commission File Number No. 001-14965, Form 8-K, September 21, 2008.

12. Morgan Stanley, "Morgan Stanley Granted Federal Bank Holding Company Status by U.S. Federal Reserve Board of Governors," press release, September 21, 2008, http://www.morganstanley.com/about/press/articles/6933.html.

13. Hilsenrath, Paletta, and Lucchetti, "Goldman, Morgan Scrap Wall Street Model, Become Banks in Bid to Ride Out Crisis."

14. Jones, "Why Is Everyone Becoming a Bank Holding Company?"

15. FT Reporters, "Roubini: Anglo-Saxon Model Has Failed," *Financial Times*, February 9, 2009, http://www.ft.com/ cms/s/0/7dce3c14-f6ba-11dd-8a1f-0000779fd2ac .html?nclick_check=1.

16. Christine Harper, "Goldman Sachs Would Like to Repay Treasury, CFO Says (Update1)," Bloomberg, February 4, 2009, http://www.bloomberg.com/apps/news?pid=20601087&sid=a3xTcf52kEZM&refer=home.

17. Kate Kelly and Robin Sidel, "Goldman, Others Getting Aid Are Eager to Pay It All Back," *Wall Street Journal*, February 4, 2009, http://online.wsj.com/article_email/SB123379690541950257-lMyQjAxMDI5MzAzNjcwOTY2Wj.html.

18. Lloyd Blankfein, "Do Not Destroy the Essential Catalyst of Risk," *Financial Times*, February 8, 2009, http://www.ft.com/cms/s/0/0a0f1132-f600-11dd-a9ed-0000779fd2ac.html.

19. American Express, "American Express Granted Bank Holding Company Status," press release, November 10, 2008, http://home3.americanexpress.com/corp/pc/2008/bhc.asp.

20. Ibid.

21. American Express, "American Express Third Quarter Revenues Rise Earnings Decline on Increased Credit Provisions," press release, October 20, 2008, http://home3.americanexpress.com/corp/pc/2008/3q08.asp; American Express, "American Express Announces Reengineering Plan to Generate $1.8 Billion Cost Benefit in 2009," press release, October 30, 2008, http://home3.americanexpress.com/corp/pc/2008/reeng.asp.

22. American Express, "American Express Reports Fourth Quarter Earnings from Continuing Operations," press release, January 26, 2009, http://home3.americanexpress.com/corp/pc/2009/4q08.asp.

23. Phil Wahba, "Amex Shares Down 12 Percent as Investors Stay Nervous," Reuters, November 13, 2008, http://www.reuters.com/article/hotStocksNews/id USTRE4AC6EY20081113.

24. American Express, "Grand Lido, Jamaica Vacation Packages by American Express Vacations," http://www.americanexpressvacations.com/offers/superclubs grandlidopbx.htm.

25. Andrew Ross Sorkin, ed., "American Express to Become Bank Holding Company," New York Times, November 10, 2008, http://dealbook.blogs.nytimes.com/2008/11/10/american-express-to-become-bank-holding-company.

26. Federal Deposit Insurance Corporation, Gramm-Leach-Bliley Act, Compliance Handbook, June 2006, http://www.fdic.gov/regulations/compliance/handbook/manual%20411.pdf.

27. U.S. Department of the Treasury, "Treasury Provides TARP Funds to Local Banks," press release: HP-1352, January 13, 2009, http://treas.gov/press/releases/hp1352.htm.

28. Kenneth R. Binning, "Bank Holding Companies," WIB/Carpenter & Company, n.d., http://www.wib.org/conferences__education/past_programs/2007_de_novo_bank_forum/handouts/binning_tues_pres.pdf.

29. E-mail response to the author from Banking Supervision and Regulation Board of Governors of the Federal Reserve System, February 28, 2009.

30. MortgageOrb.com, "Ocwen Applies to Become Bank Holding Company," South Florida Business Journal, December 1, 2008, http://www.mortgageorb.com/e107_plugins/content/content.php?content.2625.

31. Business Wire, "Capmark Financial Group Inc. Reports Preliminary Fourth Quarter 2008 Results; Withdraws Bank Holding Company Application," Reuters, February 25, 2009, http://www.reuters.com/article/pressRelease/idUS20059+26-Feb-2009+BW20090226; Eye on the Bailout, "Bailout Recipients," ProPublica, June 5, 2009, http://bailout.propublica.org/main/list/index.

32. Ari Levy and David Mildenberg, "Discover Wins Federal Reserve Approval to Become Bank (Update 2)," Bloomberg, December 19, 2008, http://www.bloomberg.com/apps/news?pid=20601103&sid=aHi4BUux3q6M&.

33. David Goldman, "AmEx: We're Getting TARP, Too," CNNMoney.com, December 23, 2008, http://money.cnn.com/2008/12/23/news/companies/american_express_tarp.

34. Bloomberg News, "CIT Is Approved to Convert into Bank," *New York Times*, December 22, 2008, http://www.nytimes.com/2008/12/23/business/economy/23cit .html.

35. United States Senate Committee on Banking, Housing and Urban Affairs, Examining the State of the Domestic Automobile Industry, Hearings, November 18, 2008, http://banking. senate.gov/public/index.cfm?FuseAction=Hearings.Hearing&Hearing_ID=0b8c3c92-b599-46f4-90b3-7f4e37583268; United States Senate Committee on Banking, Housing and Urban Affairs, The State of the Domestic Automobile Industry: Part II, Hearings, December 4, 2008, http://banking.senate.gov/public/index.cfm?FuseAction=Hearings .Hearing&Hearing_ID=299be20f-5e40-4c5f-89ee-2ade064d4226.

36. Board of Governors of the Federal Reserve System, "Approval of Proposal by GMAC and IB Finance to Become Bank Holding Companies," press release, December 24, 2008, http://www.federalreserve.gov/newsevents/press/orders/20081224a.htm.

37. U.S. Department of the Treasury, "Indicative Summary of Loans for Secured Term Loan Facility," press release, December 19, 2008, p. 15.

38. U.S. Department of the Treasury, "Treasury Announces TARP Investments in Chrysler Financial," press release: IIP 1362, January 16, 2009, http://www.treasury.gov/ press/releases/hp1362.htm.

39. Associated Press, "Obama to Set New GM Timeline," Crain's New York Business.com, March 30, 2009, www.crainsnewyork.com/article/20090330/FREE/903309997.

40. Nomi Prins and Krisztina Ugrin, "Bailout Tally," June 2009, http://www.nomiprins .com/bailout.html.

41. Poornima Gupta and John Crawley, "Chrysler Files for Bankruptcy; Inks Fiat Deal," Reuters, April 30, 2009, http://www.reuters.com/article/topNews/idUSTRE53S8F6 20090430?feedType=RSS&feedName=topNews& pageNumber=1&virtualBrand Channel=0.

42. Nomi Prins and Krisztina Ugrin, "Bailout Tally," June 2009, http://www.nomiprins .com/bailout.html.

43. Kevin Krolicki and David Bailey, "GM Exits Bankruptcy," Reuters, July 10, 2009.

44. Associated Press, "FDIC: Cost of Bank Failures to Exceed $40B," MSNBC.com, February 3, 2009, http://www. msnbc.msn.com/id/29002925.

45. Louise Story, "Regulators Seize Mortgage Lender," *New York Times*, July 12, 2008, http://www.nytimes.com/2008/07/12/business/12indymac.html?_r=1&scp=3&sq= Pasadena-based%20IndyMac&st=cse.

46. Kathy M. Kristof and Andrea Chang, "IndyMac Bank Seized by Federal Regulators," *Los Angeles Times*, July 12, 2008, http://articles.latimes.com/2008/jul/12/business/ fi-indymac12.

47. Richard Clough, "IndyMac Looks Like a Tough Sell: Billions in Deposits Already Have Been Withdrawn," *Los Angeles Business Journal*, July 21, 2008, http://www.allbusiness .com/banking-finance/banking-lending-credit-services-cash/11477757-1.html.

48. Thrift Holding Company: "A unitary thrift holding company can engage in any business, including commercial or industrial activities; open branch offices anywhere in the United States; and put up to 20% of assets in commercial loans. As thrift institutions, unitary savings and loan companies must hold at least 65% of assets in residential mortgages or mortgage securities." AllBusiness.com, Holding Company Definition, Business Glossary, n.d., http://www.allbusiness.com/glossaries/holding-company/4948587-1.html.

49. Greg Morcroft, "FDIC Sells IndyMac at $10.7 Bln Loss," FoxBusiness, March 20, 2009, http://www.foxbusiness.com/story/markets/industries/finance/fdic-sells-indymac—bln-loss/.

50. *Federal Register, Rules and Regulations*, vol. 73, no. 246, p. 78155-78162, FR Doc. E8-30222, December 22, 2008, http://edocket.access.gpo.gov/2008/E8-30222.htm.

51. Federal Deposit Insurance Corporation, *Statement of John F. Bovenzi on Promoting Bank Liquidity and Lending through Deposit Insurance, Hope for Homeowners, and Other Enhancements before the Committee on Financial Services*, U.S. House of Representatives, February 3, 2009, http://www.fdic.gov/news/news/speeches/chairman/spfeb0309.html.

52. Ronald D. Orol, "FDIC Head Says New Borrowing Authority Will Be a Big Help," MarketWatch, April 1, 2009, http://www.marketwatch.com/news/story/fdic-head-says-new-borrowing/story.aspx?guid={C61F6804-F9D6-4BE0-BF6F-16C6E3EA6FC0}&siteid=rss.

53. GovTrack, S. 896—111th Congress (2009): Helping Families Save Their Homes Act of 2009, GovTrack.us, http://www.govtrack.us/congress/bill.xpd?bill=s111-896; House Committee on Financial Services, "Summary of S. 896, the Helping Families Save Their Homes Act of 2009," press release, May 19, 2009, http://www.house.gov/apps/list/press/financialsvcs_dem/press051909.shtml.

54. Federal Deposit Insurance Corporation, Failed Bank List, July 10, 2009, http://www.fdic.gov/news/news/press/2009/index.html.

55. Federal Deposit Insurance Corporation, Managing the Crisis: The FDIC and RTC Experience, January 5, 2005, http://www.fdic.gov/bank/historical/managing/Chron/1980/index.html.

56. Federal Deposit Insurance Corporation, *Resolutions Handbook*, "Glossary," http://www.fdic.gov/bank/historical/reshandbook/glossary.pdf.

57. Jonathan R. Laing, "How Taxpayers Can Profit on the Bailout," SmartMoney, September 29, 2008, p. 2, http://www.smartmoney.com/investing/economy/how-taxpayers-can-profit-on-the-bailout.

58. Nomi Prins and Krisztina Ugrin, "Bailout Tally," June 2009, http://www.nomiprins.com/bailout.html.

59. Bob Eisenbeis, "An Interesting Hearing: AIG—Part Two of Three," Cumberland Advisors, March 18, 2009, http://www.cumber.com/commentary.aspx?file=031809p2.asp&n=1_mc.

60. Office of Thrift Supervision, *Approval of Holding Company Application and Acceptance of a Rebuttal of Control*, Order No.: 2009-02, January 8, 2009, http://files.ots.treas.gov/690002.pdf; Associated Press, "The Hartford Will Buy Thrift to Tap into Rescue Program," *Boston Globe*, January 10, 2009, http://www.boston.com/business/articles/2009/01/10/the_hartford_will_buy_thrift_to_tap_into_rescue_program?mode=PF.

61. Carl Gutierrez, "Hard Times for Hartford," *Forbes*, October 20, 2008, http://www.forbes.com/2008/10/30/ hartford-financial-services-markets-equity-cx_cg_1030markets42.html.

62. The Hartford, "The Hartford Announces Third Quarter Results," press releases, October 29, 2008, http://ir.thehartford.com/releasedetail.cfm?releaseid=343924.

63. The Hartford, "The Hartford Comments on Capital Position," press releases, November 3, 2008, http://ir.thehartford.com/releasedetail.cfm?releaseid=344688.

64. The Hartford, "Stakeholder Letter Q408," February 6, 2009.

65. 110th Congress of the United States of America, *Emergency Economic Stabilization Act of 2008*, January 3, 2008, http://frwebgate.access.gpo.gov/cgi-bin/getdoc .cgi?dbname=110_cong_bills&docid=f:h1424enr.txt.pdf.

66. The Hartford, "The Hartford Announces Agreement to Acquire Federal Trust Bank and Application to U.S. Treasury Capital Purchase Program," press release, November 14, 2008, http://ir.thehartford.com/releasedetail.cfm ?ReleaseID=347832.

67. Lincoln Financial Group, "Lincoln Financial Group Applies to Become Savings and Loan Holding Company," press release, November 17, 2008, http://www.lfg.com/ LincolnPageServer?KPage_PageID=LFG_Page&LFGPage=%2Flfg%2Flfgclient %2Fabt%2Fnews%2F2008%2Findex.html&KURL=%2Flfg%2Flfgclient%2Fabt% 2Fnews% 2F2008%2F20081117%2Fcontent.xml.

68. Jonathan Stempel, "Hartford Financial Soars on Plan to Join TARP," Reuters, November 14, 2008, http://www. reuters.com/article/governmentFilingdNews/ idUSN1444721320081114.

69. Andrew Frye and Linda Shen, "Lincoln, Aegon May Buy S&Ls with 'Unsafe' Practices (Update 1)," Bloomberg, November 17, 2008, http://www.bloomberg.com/ apps/news?pid=20601087&sid=aGac4GCwT6ck&refer=home.

70. Catherine Clifford, "4 Insurers Seek Thrift Status, Gaining Bailout Access," CNNMoney.com, November 14, 2008, http://money.cnn.com/2008/11/14/news/ companies/hartford_financial/index.htm.

71. Aegon, "AEGON Withdraws TARP Application," press release, December 15, 2008, http://www.aegon.com/base/Templates/Standard.aspx?id=207&epslanguage=en&n pid=9061&srcid=182.

72. Federal Deposit Insurance Corporation, "Bank of Essex, Tappahannock, Virginia, Acquires All the Deposits of Suburban Federal Savings Bank, Crofton, Maryland," press release, January 30, 2009, http://www.fdic.gov/news/news/press/2009/pr09013.html.

73. Genworth Financial, "Genworth Announces Filing for Savings and Loan Holding Company Status," press release, November 16, 2008, http://phx.corporate-ir.net/ phoenix.zhtml?c=175970&p=irol-newsArticle_Print&ID=1226911 &highlight=.

74. Collateralized Debt Obligation: "An investment-grade security backed by a pool of bonds, loans and other assets. CDOs do not specialize in one type of debt but are often nonmortgage loans or bonds." Investopedia, "Collateralized Debt Obligation," Dictionary, n.d., http://www.investopedia.com/terms/c/cdo.asp; Prudential Investment Management, Fixed Income CDO Group, n.d., http://www.drydencdo.com/cdo/pru/us _home.html.

75. Joseph A. Giannone, "MetLife Says Portfolio Unharmed by Mortgage Crisis," Reuters, February 7, 2008, http://www.reuters.com/article/bankingFinancial/ idUSN0737191520080207.

76. Prudential, "Prudential Fixed Income Management Names Sara Bonesteel to Lead Efforts in Structured Asset Management Opportunities and Financing," October 2, 2008, http://www.news.prudential.com/article_display.cfm ?article_id=5355.

Chapter 4. Government Sachs

1. Jonathan Stempel, "JPMorgan Passes Citigroup as Largest U.S. Bank," Reuters, October 16, 2008, http://www.reuters.com/article/businessNews/idUSTRE49F45Q20081016.

2. Kate Kelly and Jon Hilsenrath, "New York Fed Chairman's Ties to Goldman Raise Questions," *Wall Street Journal*, May 4, 2009.

3. Goldman Sachs, *The Goldman Sachs Approach, Annual Report 2005*, February 7, 2006, http://www2.goldmansachs.com/our-firm/investors/financials/archived/annual-reports/attachments/annual-report.pdf.

4. Andrew Ross Sorkin, ed., "Thain's Office Overhaul Said to Cost $1.2 Million," *New York Times*, January 22, 2009, http://dealbook.blogs.nytimes.com/2009/01/22/thains-office-overhaul-said-to-cost-12-million.

5. Steve Rosenbush, "Merrill: Thain to the Rescue," *BusinessWeek*, November 15, 2007, http://www.businessweek.com/bwdaily/dnflash/content/nov2007/db20071114_876305.htm.

6. Write-down example: Say I lend you $100 and you pay me 5 percent interest for a year. I expect to get back a total of $105 for the end of the year, so I keep that number on my "book." Now it turns out you can't pay me any interest, for whatever reason. So I reduce that number on my book to $100, or take a write-down of $5. Say you can't pay me back the principal either because you thought you'd be able to sell something worth $100, and now it's worth only $50—or, worse, zero. Now I have to take a write-down of the whole $105. Also see Christine Harper, "A $45 Billion Writedown Won't Stop Wall Street Profit (Update 1)," Bloomberg, November 12, 2007, http://www.bloomberg.com/apps/news?pid=20601109&refer=exclusive&sid=aDDoERW5M.NA; CNN, "Bank of America Will Slash 35,000 Jobs as It Absorbs Merrill Lynch and Fights Recession," *New York Daily News*, December 12, 2008, http://www.nydailynews.com/money/2008/12/12/2008-12-12_bank_of_america_will_slash_35000_jobs_as.html.

7. Louise Story, "Chief Struggles to Revive Merrill Lynch," *New York Times*, July 18, 2008, http://www.nytimes.com/2008/07/18/business/18merrill.html?_r=2&scp=23&sq=merrill%20lynch&st=cse.

8. Jenny Anderson and Landon Thomas Jr., "Goldman Sachs Rakes in Profit in Credit Crisis," *New York Times*, November 19, 2007, http://www.nytimes.com/2007/11/19/business/19goldman.html.

9. Julie Creswell and Ben White, "Wall Street, R.I.P.: The End of an Era, Even at Goldman," *New York Times*, September 27, 2008, http://www.nytimes.com/2008/09/28/business/28lloyd.html.

10. Nancy Moran and Rodney Yap, "O'Neal Ranks No. 5 on Payout List, Group Says: Table (Update 1)," Bloomberg, November 2, 2007, http://www.bloomberg.com/apps/news?pid=20601109&refer=home&sid=aPxzn5U8zNBo.

11. Alcoa, "Alcoa Appoints Two New Directors; Stan O'Neal and Michael G. Morris to Join Company Board of Directors," news release, January 18, 2008, http://www.alcoa.com/global/en/news/news_detail.asp?newsYear=2008&pageID=20080118005598en.

12. Kate Kelly, "How Goldman Won Big on Mortgage Meltdown," *Wall Street Journal*, December 14, 2007, http://online.wsj.com/article/SB119759714037228585.html.

13. Creswell and White, "Wall Street, R.I.P.: The End of an Era, Even at Goldman;" Nomi Prins and Krisztina Ugrin, "CEO Compensation and Bonuses," June 2009, http://www.nomiprins.com/bailout.html.

14. *USA Today*, "Executive Compensation 2007, Interactive Chart," n.d., www.usatoday.com/money/graphics/ceo-comp/flash.htm.

15. The Goldman Sachs Group, "Goldman Sachs Reports Record Earnings per Common Share of $24.73 for 2007," press release, December 18, 2007, http://www2.goldmansachs.com/our-firm/press/press-releases/archived/2007/2007-12-18-pdf.

16. Creswell and White, "Wall Street, R.I.P.: The End of an Era, Even at Goldman."
17. Jenny Anderson, "Swinging between Optimism and Dread on Wall Street," *New York Times*, March 19, 2008, http://www.nytimes.com/2008/03/19/business/19street.html.
18. CNBC.com, "CNBC TV Profiles: Jim Cramer," n.d., http://www.cnbc.com/id/15838187/; Jim Cramer's Mad Money.com, "Jim Cramer's *Mad Money* Stock Picks for Thursday March 20 2008," http://www.cramers-mad-money.com/jim-cramers-mad-money-stock-picks-for-monday-march-24–2008.
19. Alice Gomstyn, "Should You Stay Away from Jim Cramer?" ABC News Business Unit, March 26, 2008, http://abcnews.go.com/Business/PersonalFinance/Story?id=4524010.
20. J.P. Morgan, "JPMorgan Chase to Acquire Bear Stearns," press release, March 16, 2008, www.jpmorgan.com/cm/cs?pagename=JPM_redesign/JPM_Content_C/Generic_Detail_Page_Template&cid=1159338798994&c=JPM_Content_C.
21. Andrew Ross Sorkin, ed., "JP Morgan Pays $2 a Share for Bear Stearns," *New York Times*, March 17, 2008, www.nytimes.com/2008/03/17/business/17bear.html.
22. George Orwell, *Animal Farm: A Fairy Story* (London: Secker & Warburg, 1945).
23. *New York Times*, "People: Robert E. Rubin," n.d., http://topics.nytimes.com/top/reference/timestopics/people/r/robert_e_rubin/index.html; Goldman Sachs, "Board of Directors: Stephen Friedman," http://www2.goldmansachs.com/our-firm/about-us/leadership/board-of-directors.html#StephenFriedman.
24. Kate Kelly and Susanne Craig, "Friedman's 43-Year Storied Career Has Taken Many Twists and Turns," *Wall Street Journal*, May 8, 2009, http://online.wsj.com/article/SB124174050575198775.html; U.S. Department of Treasury, Biography of Secretary Robert E. Rubin, n.d. http://www.treas.gov/education/history/secretaries/rerubin.shtml.
25. Federal Reserve Bank of New York, *Stephen Friedman*, January 2008, http://www.newyorkfed.org/aboutthefed/orgchart/board/friedman.html.
26. Kristina Cooke, "Fed Reappoints Stephen Friedman as NY Fed Board Chair," Reuters, January 27, 2009, http://www.reuters.com/article/companyNewsAndPR/idUSN2746284920090127.
27. Goldman Sachs, "Board of Directors: Stephen Friedman."
28. Federal Reserve Bank of New York, *About the Fed: Organization*, n.d., http://www.ny.frb.org/aboutthefed/org_chart.html.
29. Cityfile, "Stephen Friedman," Cityfile New York, n.d., http://cityfile.com/profiles/stephen-friedman.
30. Ibid.
31. Council on Foreign Relations, *About: Stephen Friedman*, n.d., http://www.cfr.org/bios/13504/stephen_friedman.html.
32. AllGov.com, "Officials: Stephen Friedman," n.d., http://www.allgov.com/Official/Friedman_Stephen.
33. David Plotz, "Jon Corzine," *Slate*, June 2, 2000, http://www.slate.com/id/83533.
34. Leah Nathans Spiro, Gary Silverman, and Stanley Reed, "The Coup at Goldman," *BusinessWeek*, January 25, 1999, http://www.businessweek.com/1999/99_04/b3613001.htm.
35. *BusinessWeek*, "Goldman Sachs Concentrated Emerging Equity Fund: EXECUTIVE PROFILE: Henry Paulson Jr.," http://investing.businessweek.com/businessweek/

research/stocks/private/person.asp?personId=398627&privcapId=841038&previous
CapId=364040&previousTitle=Arcelor%20Mittal.

36. Stanley Reed and Joyce Barnathan, "Goldman's 'Dealmaker Supreme,'" *Business-Week*, January 25, 1999.

37. Goldman Sachs, "John Thornton Retiring as President and Co-COO of Goldman Sachs," press release, March 24, 2003, http://www2.goldmansachs.com/our-firm/press/press-releases/archived/2003/2003–03–24.html.

38. Spiro, Silverman, and Reed, "The Coup at Goldman."

39. Ibid.

40. Leah Nathans Spiro, "Goldman Sachs: How Public Is This IPO?" *BusinessWeek*, May 17, 1999, http://www.businessweek.com/1999/99_20/b3629102.htm.

41. CNNfn, "End of an Era for Goldman," CNNMoney, May 3, 1999, http://www.mutual-funds.biz/1999/05/03/markets/goldman.

42. John M. Broder and David E. Sanger, "A New Economic Team: The Resignation; Rubin Resigning as Treasury Secretary," *New York Times*, May 13, 1999, p. 1, http://www.nytimes.com/1999/05/13/business/a-new-economic-team-the-resignation-rubin-resigning-as-treasury-secretary.html.

43. WSJ.com, "'No Line Responsibilities'" *Wall Street Journal*, December 3, 2008, http://online.wsj.com/article/SB122826632081174473.html.

44. Spiro, "Goldman Sachs: How Public Is This IPO?"

45. Center for Responsive Politics, "Congressional Elections: New Jersey Senate Race—2000 Cycle: Total Raised and Spent," OpenSecrets.org, n.d., http://www.opensecrets.org/races/summary.php?cycle=2000&id=NJS1.

46. *New York Times*, "People: John S. Corzine," March 10, 2009, http://topics.nytimes.com/top/reference/timestopics/people/c/jon_s_corzine/index.html.

47. Bank of Canada, "About the Bank—Biographical note: Mark J. Carney," n.d., http://www.bankofcanada.ca/en/bios/carney.html; Harris Anwar and Theophilos Argitis, "Canadian Dollar Trades Equal to U.S. for First Time since 1976," Bloomberg, September 20, 2007, http://www.bloomberg.com/apps/news?pid=20601083&refer=currency&sid=aDBegmV7h0cU.

48. Group of Thirty, "Members: Mario Draghi," n.d., http://www.group30.org/bios/members33.htm; BBC News, "Italy Chooses Successor to Fazio," BBC, December 29, 2005, http://news.bbc.co.uk/2/hi/business/4566744.stm.

49. BBC News, "Italy Chooses Successor to Fazio."

50. Financial Stability Forum, "About the FSF: Mandate," n.d., http://www.fsforum.org/about/mandate.htm.

51. Banca D'Italia, "Members of the Governing Board: Mario Draghi," n.d., http://www.bancaditalia.it/bancaditalia/direttorio/governatore

52. Banca D'Italia, "Bank of Italy—History—In Europe," http://www.bancaditalia.it/bancaditalia/storia/europa;internal&action=_setlanguage.action?LANGUAGE=en.

53. Banca D'Italia, "Mario Draghi Remarks at Turner Review Rollout, March 27, 2009," http://www.bancaditalia.it/interventi/integov/2009/draghi_270409/draghi_270409.pdf.

54. Steven R. Weisman, "Bush's Nominee Has New Agenda for Bank," *New York Times*, May 31, 2007, http://query.nytimes.com/gst/fullpage.html?res=9C02E3DE1530F932A05756C0A9619C8B63&sec=&spon=&pagewanted=all.

55. The World Bank, *Office of the President—Biography: Robert B. Zoellick*, n.d., http://go.worldbank.org/IHDUWCAI20.

56. Christine Hauser, "Rice's Deputy to Join Goldman Sachs," *New York Times*, June 19, 2006, http://www.nytimes.com/2006/06/19/washington/19cnd-zoellick.html.

57. Harry S. Truman Library, "Oral History Interview with Henry H. Fowler," June 20, 1989, http://www.trumanlibrary.org/oralhist/fowlerh.htm.

58. U.S. Department of the Treasury, *Biography: Robert E. Rubin*, n.d., http://www.treas.gov/education/history/secretaries/rerubin.shtml.

59. Kenneth Klee, "The Return of Robert Rubin," *Newsweek*, November 8, 1999, http://www.newsweek.com/id/90121.

60. John M. Broder and David E. Sanger, "A New Economic Team: The Resignation; Rubin Resigning as Treasury Secretary," *New York Times*, May 13, 1999, http://www.nytimes.com/1999/05/13/business/a-new-economic-team-the-resignation-rubin-resigning-as-treasury-secretary.html.

61. "Rubin Is Planning to Return to Wall Street," *New York Times*, September 17, 1999, http://www.nytimes.com/1999/09/17/business/rubin-is-planning-to-return-to-wall-street.html.

62. Joseph Kahn, "Former Treasury Secretary Joins Leadership Triangle at Citigroup," *New York Times*, October 27, 1999, http://www.nytimes.com/1999/10/27/business/former-treasury-secretary-joins-leadership-triangle-at-citigroup.html.

63. Joseph Kahn, "Consumer Groups Seek Ethics Inquiry on Rubin's New Job," *New York Times*, November 18, 1999, http://www.nytimes.com/1999/11/18/business/consumer-groups-seek-ethics-inquiry-on-rubin-s-new-job.html.

64. Barnaby J. Feder, "Rubin's Pay Is $15 Million, Says Citigroup Proxy Filing," *New York Times*, March 7, 2000, http://www.nytimes.com/2000/03/07/business/rubin-s-pay-is-15-million-says-citigroup-proxy-filing.html.

65. Eric Dash and Louise Story, "Rubin Leaving Citigroup; Smith Barney for Sale," *New York Times*, January 9, 2009, http://www.nytimes.com/2009/01/10/business/10rubin.html.

66. New Generation Research, "20 Largest Public Company Bankruptcy Filings 1980–Present," BankruptcyData.com, http://www.bankruptcydata.com/Research/Largest_Overall_All-Time.pdf.

67. David Teather, "Rubin Cleared of Enron Impropriety," *The Guardian*, January 4, 2003, http://www.guardian.co.uk/business/2003/jan/04/corporatefraud.enron; Landon Thomas Jr., "Cold Call," *New York*, February 11, 2002, http://nymag.com/nymetro/news/bizfinance/columns/businessclass/5693.

68. Rex Nutting and Matt Andrejczak, "Citi's Rubin Made a Call for Enron," MarketWatch, January 11, 2002, http://www.marketwatch.com/story/ex-treasury-chief-rubin-made-a-call-on-behalf-of-enron?siteid=mktw.

69. Richard A. Oppel Jr., "Senate Report Says Rubin Acted Legally in Enron Matter," *New York Times*, January 3, 2003, http://www.nytimes.com/2003/01/03/business/senate-report-says-rubin-acted-legally-in-enron-matter.html.

70. Mark Lewis, "Rubin Red-Faced Over Enron?" *Forbes*, February 11, 2002, http://www.forbes.com/2002/02/11/0211rubin.html.

71. Michael Hirsch, "'Government Sachs' Is Back," *Newsweek*, March 5, 2009, http://www.newsweek.com/id/187705; Peter S. Goodman, "The Reckoning," *New York Times*, October 8, 2008, p. 3, http://www.nytimes.com/2008/10/09/business/economy/09greenspan.html.

72. Board of Governors of the Federal Reserve System, "FOMC Statement," press release, August 7, 2007, http://www.federalreserve.gov/newsevents/press/monetary/20070807a.htm.

73. Craig Torres, "Bernanke Spoke with Rubin as Credit Crisis Worsened (Update 1)," Bloomberg, October 3, 2007, http://www.bloomberg.com/apps/news?pid=20601087 &refer=home&sid=ae21h4HAD6Ag.

74. Board of Governors of the Federal Reserve System, "Federal Reserve Board Discount Rate Action," press release, August 17, 2007, http://www.federalreserve.gov/ newsevents/press/monetary/20070817a.htm.

75. Federal Reserve Bank of New York, *Historical Changes of the Target Federal Funds and Discount Rates, 1971 to Present, December 22, 2008*, http://www.newyorkfed .org/markets/statistics/dlyrates/fedrate.html.

76. Tom Bawden and Susan Thompson, "Goldman Sachs Makes $4bn Profit on Daring Sub-Prime Bet," *The Times*, December 15, 2007, http://business.timesonline.co.uk/ tol/business/industry_sectors/banking_and_finance/article3054952.ece.

77. "Citi May Have a New Mess on Its Hands," *BusinessWeek*, November 12, 2007, http://www.businessweek.com/magazine/content/07_46/b4058049.htm.

78. "Statement from Citigroup on the Resignation of C.E.O. Charles O. Prince III," *New York Times*, November 5, 2007, http://www.nytimes.com/2007/11/05/business/ 05citi-text.html.

79. Citigroup, "Citi Board Names Vikram Pandit Chief Executive Officer and Sir Win Bischoff Chairman," press release, December 11, 2007, http://www.citigroup.com/ citi/press/2007/071211a.htm.

80. Citigroup, "Citi Reports Fourth Quarter Net Loss of $8.29 Billion, Loss Per Share of $1.72," press release, January 16, 2009, http://www.citigroup.com/citi/press/2009/ 090116a.htm.

81. Marshall Eckblad, "Citi's Rubin Is Now a 'Senior Counselor,'" *Wall Street Journal*, August 26, 2008, http://online.wsj.com/article/SB121969810713370413.html.

82. Jonathan Stempel, "Citigroup Stock Drops to 13-year Low, Fear Grows," Reuters, November 19, 2008, http://www.reuters.com/article/newsOne/idUSTRE4AI91420081119.

83. Nomi Prins and Krisztina Ugrin, "Bailout Tally," June 2009, http://www.nomiprins .com/bailout.html.

84. Citigroup, "Robert E. Rubin Announces His Retirement from Citi," press release, January 9, 2009, http://www.citigroup.com/citi/press/2009/090109d.htm.

85. Ibid.

86. Heidi N. Moore, "Ken Wilson: The Goldman Sachs Man Behind Your Bailouts," *Wall Street Journal*, July 21, 2008, http://blogs.wsj.com/deals/2008/07/21/ken-wilson-the-goldman-sachs-man-behind-your-bailouts.

87. Ibid.

88. Eric Dash, "Wachovia Hires a Treasury Insider to Lift It Out of Its Banking Woes," *New York Times*, July 10, 2008, http://query.nytimes.com/gst/fullpage.html?res= 9D02E1D61E3BF933A25754C0A96E9C8B63; Wachovia Corporation, Officers & Directors: Robert K. Steel, https://sites.wachovia.com/inside/page/0,,132_155_ 13180,00.html.

89. Joseph A. Giannone, "Goldman Banker to Advise Paulson on Banks," Reuters, July 21, 2008, http://www.reuters.com/article/gc06/idUSBNG24956720080721.

90. Susanne Craig, "In Ken Wilson, Paulson Gets Direction from the Go-to Banker of Wall Street," *Wall Street Journal*, July 22, 2008, http://online.wsj.com/article/ SB121668792760272225.html.

91. Craig, "In Ken Wilson, Paulson Gets Direction from the Go-to Banker of Wall Street."

92. Heidi N. Moore, "Goldman Banker Wilson Starts First Day at Treasury to Fix the Markets," *Wall Street Journal*, August 7, 2008, http://blogs.wsj.com/deals/2008/08/07/kenny-your-country-has-you-goldman-banker-wilson-starts-first-day-at-treasury.

93. Steve Gelsi, "Paulson Files to Sell $500 mln of Goldman Stock," MarketWatch, June 30, 2006, http://www.marketwatch.com/News/Story/43xRFhd1RRlnqg1H1BkmTP4?siteid=google&dist=TNMostMailed.

94. The Aspen Institute, "Snapshot: Robert K. Steel," n.d., http://www.aspeninstitute.org/people/robert-steel.

95. U.S. Department of the Treasury, "Statement by Treasury Secretary Henry M. Paulson, Jr. on Staff Changes in the Office of Domestic Finance," press release: HP-1073, July 9, 2008, http://www.treas.gov/press/releases/hp1073.htm.

96. Dash, "Wachovia Hires a Treasury Insider to Lift It Out of Its Banking Woes"; Robert Schroeder, "Fannie Mae, Freddie Mac Bill Clears Committee," March 29, 2007, MarketWatch, http://www.marketwatch.com/news/story/fannie-mae-freddie-mac-regulation/story.aspx?guid={CDAF5B87–2C23–423C-B45B-1A38D1F3902F}.

97. Neil Irwin, "Steel Steps Down from Treasury Post to Take Over at Struggling Wachovia," *Washington Post*, July 10, 2008, http://www.washingtonpost.com/wp-dyn/content/article/2008/07/09/AR2008070901938.html.

98. Ibid.

99. Dash, "Wachovia Hires a Treasury Insider to Lift It Out of Its Banking Woes."

100. David Mildenberg and Ari Levy, "Wachovia Hires Steel to Mend Investor Relationships (Update 2)," Bloomberg, July 10, 2008, http://www.bloomberg.com/apps/news?pid=20601087&sid=apkYD10LUGtY&refer=home.

101. Ben White and Eric Dash, "Wachovia, Looking for Help, Turns to Citigroup," *New York Times*, September 26, 2008, http://www.nytimes.com/2008/09/27/business/27bank.html.

102. Wachovia Corporation, "Wachovia Details 2nd Quarter Loss; Outlines Initiatives to Preserve and Generate Capital, Protect Strong Liquidity and Reduce Risk," press release, July 22, 2008, https://www.wachovia.com/foundation/v/index.jsp?vgnextoid=c9956c772350f110VgnVCM200000627d6fa2RCRD&vgnextfmt=default&key _guid=69817798ebbdc110VgnVCM100000127d6fa2RCRD.

103. Mildenberg and Levy, "Wachovia Hires Steel to Mend Investor Relationships (Update 2)."

104. *New York Times*, "Companies: Wachovia Corporation News," *New York Times*, n.d., http://topics.nytimes.com/top/news/business/companies/wachovia_corporation/index.html.

105. Andrew Ross Sorkin, "Lehman Files for Bankruptcy; Merrill Is Sold," *New York Times*, September 14, 2008, http://www.nytimes.com/2008/09/15/business/15lehman.html.

106. Kara Scannell, David Enrich, and Dan Fitzpatrick, "Steel's TV Remarks on Wachovia Probed," *Wall Street Journal*, January 24, 2009, http://online.wsj.com/article/SB123275454114111651.html.

107. Ibid.

108. Aaron Lucchetti, Randall Smith, and Jenny Strasburg, "Morgan Stanley in Talks with Wachovia, Others," *Wall Street Journal*, September 18, 2008, http://online.wsj.com/article/SB122168156315148901.html.

109. Chad Bray, "Wachovia Lost Deposits as Citi Fought Wells Bid," MarketWatch, October 11, 2008, http://www.marketwatch.com/news/story/wachovia-lost-deposits-citi-fought/story.aspx?guid={F4CC7E6D-94CA-4BF8-8447-5D4F2C2B2AD9}.

110. Andrew Ross Sorkin, ed., "Citi Blasts Wachovia–Wells Fargo Merger Plan," *New York Times*, October 3, 2008, http://dealbook.blogs.nytimes.com/2008/10/03/citi-blasts-wachovia-wells-fargo-merger-plan.

111. Wachovia Corporation, "Wachovia Statement: Wachovia's Board Approves Wells Fargo Merger Proposal," press release, October 3, 2008, https://sites.wachovia.com/inside/page/0,,134_307^1806,00.html.

112. Rob Curran, "Citigroup Leads Stocks Down Despite the Bailout," *Wall Street Journal*, October 4, 2008, http://online.wsj.com/article/SB122304344267402263.html.

113. Wachovia Corporation, *Proposed Merger, Proxy Statement—Prospectus*, November 21, 2008, p. 8, https://www.wachovia.com/file/WB_WF_Proxy_Statement_Prospectus.pdf.

114. Scannell, Enrich, and Fitzpatrick, "Steel's TV Remarks on Wachovia Probed."

Chapter 5. We Already Have a Bad Bank: It's Called the Federal Reserve

1. Cyrus S. Eaton, "Financial Democracy," *The University of Chicago Law Review* 8, no. 2 (February 1941): 196.

2. Nomi Prins and Krisztina Ugrin, "Bailout Tally," June 2009, http://www.nomiprins.com/bailout.html.

3. Board of Governors of the Federal Reserve System, "Federal Reserve Will Offer $20 Billion in 35-Day Credit through Its Term Auction Facility on December 20, 2007," press release, December 19, 2007, http://www.federalreserve.gov/newsevents/press/monetary/20071219b.htm.

4. William Poole, "The Role of Federal Reserve Banks in the Federal Reserve System," Federal Reserve Bank of St. Louis, March 30, 2006, p. 2, http://stlouisfed.us/news/speeches/2006/PDF/03_30.pdf.

5. Board of Governors of the Federal Reserve System, *H.4.1 Factors Affecting Reserve Balances*, Federal Reserve Statistical Release, December 20, 2007, http://www.federalreserve.gov/releases/h41/20071220.

6. William Greider, "Fixing the Fed," *The Nation*, March 11, 2009, p. 2, http://www.thenation.com/doc/20090330/greider/2.

7. Board of Governors of the Federal Reserve System, "Federal Reserve and Other Central Banks Announce Measures Designed to Address Elevated Pressures in Short-Term Funding Markets," press release, December 12, 2007, http://federalreserve.gov/newsevents/press/monetary/20071212a.htm.

8. Board of Governors of the Federal Reserve System, "Federal Reserve Announces Results of Auction of $20 Billion in 28-day Credit Held on December 17, 2007," press release, December 19, 2007, http://federalreserve.gov/newsevents/press/monetary/20071219c.htm; Board of Governors of the Federal Reserve System, "Federal Reserve Announces Results of Auction of $20 Billion in 35-day Credit Held on December 20, 2007," press release, December 21, 2007, http://federalreserve.gov/newsevents/press/monetary/20071221a.htm.

9. Alternative Investment Management Association, "AIMA's Roadmap to Hedge Funds," November 2008, pp. 29, 117.

10. Board of Governors of the Federal Reserve System, "Federal Reserve and Other Central Banks Announce Specific Measures Designed to Address Liquidity Pressures in Funding Markets," press release, March 11, 2008, http://federalreserve.gov/newsevents/press/monetary/20080311a.htm.

11. Federal Reserve Bank of New York, "Summary of Terms and Conditions Regarding the JPMorgan Chase Facility," press release, March 24, 2008, http://www.ny.frb.org/newsevents/news/markets/2008/rp080324b.html.

12. Federal Reserve Bank of New York, *Actions by the New York Fed in Response to Liquidity Pressures in Financial Markets, Testimony, April 3, 2008*, http://www.newyorkfed.org/newsevents/speeches/2008/gei080403.html.

13. Ibid.

14. *Frontline*, "Timeline: Inside the Meltdown," PBS, February 17, 2009, http://www.pbs.org/wgbh/pages/frontline/meltdown/cron.

15. Federal Reserve Bank of New York, "Statement on Financing Arangement of the JPMorgan Chase Facility," press release March 24, 2008, http://www.newyorkfed.org/newsevents/news/markets/2008/rp080324b.html; Federal Reserve Bank of New York, *Actions by the New York Fed in Response to Liquidity Pressures in Financial Markets, Testimony, April 3, 2008*.

16. Federal Reserve Bank of New York, "Federal Reserve Announces Establishment of Primary Dealer Credit Facility," press release, March 16, 2008, http://www.newyorkfed.org/newsevents/news/markets/2008/rp080316.html.

17. Federal Reserve Bank of New York, *Understanding the Recent Changes to Federal Reserve Liquidity Provision*, May 2008, http://www.newyorkfed.org/markets/Understanding_Fed_Lending.html.

18. Board of Governors of the Federal Reserve System, "Federal Reserve Announces Two Initiatives Designed to Bolster Market Liquidity and Promote Orderly Market Functioning," press release, March 16, 2008, http://www.federalreserve.gov/newsevents/press/monetary/20080316a.htm; Zubin Jelveh, "Odd Numbers," *Portfolio*, May 28, 2008, http://www.portfolio.com/views/blogs/odd-numbers/2008/05/28/should-the-fed-lend-to-investment-banks.

19. Federal Reserve Bank of New York, *Primary Dealer Credit Facility: Frequently Asked Questions, February 3, 2009*, http://www.newyorkfed.org/markets/pdcf_faq.html.

20. The Federal Reserve Bank Discount Window and Payment System Website, http://www.frbdiscountwindow.org.

21. "JP Morgan Quintuples Bid to Seal Bear Deal," *Wall Street Journal*, March 25, 2008.

22. Kush Media, "History of US Economic Recessions," n.d, http://recession.org/history.

23. "Cayne Pockets $61.3 Million for Bear Stock," *Wall Street Journal*, March 28, 2008.

24. Ibid.

25. Federal Reserve Bank of New York, *Actions by the New York Fed in Response to Liquidity Pressures in Financial Markets, Testimony, April 3, 2008*.

26. Ibid.

27. RealtyTrac, "Foreclosure Activity Increases 81 Percent in 2008," press release, January 15, 2009, http://www.realtytrac.com/ContentManagement/pressrelease.aspx?ChannelID=9&ItemID=5681.

28. National Association of Realtors, *Statistical Data, 2009*, http://www.realtor.org/wps/wcm/connect/b56fe8804d277ee29517f526a9949436/REL0901SF.pdf?MOD=AJPERES&CACHEID=b56fe8804d277ee29517f526a9949436.

29. U.S. Census Bureau, "New Residential Sales in December 2008," joint press release, January 29, 2009, p. 1, http://www.census.gov/const/newressales_200812.pdf.

30. "Moving Forward Helps Those in Foreclosure . . . ," CNN Newsroom, July 26, 2008, http://transcripts.cnn.com/TRANSCRIPTS/0807/26/cnr.06.html.

31. GovTrack, H.R. 3221: Housing and Economic Recovery Act of 2008, n.d., http://www.govtrack.us/congress/bill.xpd?bill=h110-3221.

32. Roger Runningen, "Bush Signs Measure for Homeowners, Fannie, Freddie (Update 2)," Bloomberg, July 30, 2009, http://www.bloomberg.com/apps/news?pid=2060110 3&sid=am2yQYThqmxQ&refer=us.

33. Patrice Hill, "McCain Adviser Talks of 'Mental Recession,'" *Washington Times*, July 9, 2008, http://www.washingtontimes.com/news/2008/jul/09/mccain-adviser-addresses-mental-recession/.

34. "Phil Gramm," *New York Times*, n.d., http://topics.nytimes.com/top/reference/timestopics/people/g/phil_gramm/index.html.

35. Hill, "McCain Adviser Talks of 'Mental Recession.'"

36. "Phil Gramm Steps Down after 'Whiners' Comment," CNN, July 18, 2008, http://www.cnn.com/2008/POLITICS/07/18/gramm.resignation/index.html.

37. U.S. Department of the Treasury, "Remarks by U.S. Treasury Secretary Henry M. Paulson, Jr. on the U.S., the World Economy and Markets before the Chatham House," press release: HP-1064, July 2, 2008, http://www.ustreas.gov/press/releases/hp1064.htm.

38. U.S. Department of the Treasury, "Oral Statement by Secretary Henry M. Paulson, Jr. on Regulatory Reform before House Committee on Financial Services," press release: HP-1074, July 10, 2008, http://www.treas.gov/press/releases/hp1074.htm.

39. U.S. Department of the Treasury, "Remarks by Secretary Henry M. Paulson, Jr. on U.S. Housing Market before FDIC's Forum on Mortgage Lending to Low and Moderate Income Households," press release: HP-1070, July 8, 2008, http://www.treas.gov/press/releases/hp1070.htm.

40. Board of Governors of the Federal Reserve System, *Chairman Ben S. Bernanke at the Federal Deposit Insurance Corporation's Forum on Mortgage Lending for Low and Moderate Income Households, Arlington, Virginia, Speech, July 8, 2008*, http://www.federalreserve.gov/newsevents/speech/bernanke20080708a.htm.

41. Board of Governors of the Federal Reserve System, *Chairman Ben S. Bernanke at the Greater Austin Chamber of Commerce, Austin, Texas, Speech, December 1, 2008*, http://www.federalreserve.gov/newsevents/speech/bernanke20081201a.htm.

42. Board of Governors of the Federal Reserve System, "Federal Reserve and Other Central Banks Announce Further Measures to Address Elevated Pressures in Funding Markets," press release, September 18, 2008, http://federalreserve.gov/newsevents/press/monetary/20080918a.htm; Joint Economic Committee, *Financial Meltdown and Policy Response*, Research Report #110-25, September 2008, p. 6–7; Board of Governors of the Federal Reserve System, "Federal Reserve and Other Central Banks Announce Further Coordinated Actions to Expand Significantly the Capacity to Provide U.S. Dollar Liquidity," press release, September 29, 2008, http://federalreserve.gov/newsevents/press/monetary/20080929a.htm.

43. Board of Governors of the Federal Reserve System, "Board Announces That It Will Begin to Pay Interest on Depository Institutions' Required and Excess Reserve Balances," press release, October 6, 2008.

44. Board of Governors of the Federal Reserve System, *The October 2008 Senior Loan Officer Opinion Survey on Bank Lending Practices, November 3, 2008,* http://www.federalreserve.gov/boarddocs/SnLoanSurvey/200811/fullreport.pdf.

45. Board of Governors of the Federal Reserve System, *Report Pursuant to Section 129 of the Emergency Economic Stabilization Act of 2008: Commercial Paper Funding Facility,* pp. 2–6, http://www.federalreserve.gov/monetarypolicy/files/129cpff.pdf.

46. Board of Governors of the Federal Reserve System, *Report Pursuant to Section 129 of the Emergency Economic Stabilization Act of 2008: Commercial Paper Funding Facility,* p. 2.

47. Board of Governors of the Federal Reserve System, "Federal Reserve Announces Extension through October 30, 2009, of Its Existing Liquidity Programs That Were Scheduled to Expire on April 30, 2009," press release, February 3, 2009, http://www.federalreserve.gov/newsevents/press/monetary/20090203a.htm.

48. Board of Governors of the Federal Reserve System, "Federal Reserve Board Announces Two Enhancements to Its Programs to Provide Liquidity to Markets," press release, September 19, 2008, http://www.federalreserve.gov/newsevents/press/monetary/20081021a.htm; Nomi Prins and Krisztina Ugrin, "Bailout Tally," June 2009, http://www.nomiprins.combailout.htm.

49. Board of Governors of the Federal Reserve System, "Federal Reserve Announces the Creation of the Money Market Investor Funding Facility (MMIFF)," press release, October 21, 2008, http://www.federalreserve.gov/newsevents/press/monetary/20081021a.htm; Nomi Prins and Krisztina Ugrin, "Bailout Tally," June 2009, http://www.nomiprins.combailout.html.

50. Board of Governors of the Federal Reserve System, "Federal Reserve Board Announces Several Initiatives to Provide Additional Support to Financial Markets, Including Enhancements to Its Existing Liquidity Facilities," press release, September 14, 2008, http://www.federalreserve.gov/newsevents/press/monetary/20080914a.htm.

51. Board of Governors of the Federal Reserve System, "Federal Reserve and Other Central Banks Announce Further Coordinated Actions to Expand Significantly the Capacity to Provide U.S. Dollar Liquidity.

52. Board of Governors of the Federal Reserve System, *The Federal Reserve System: Purposes and Functions, 2005,* p. 16, http://www.federalreserve.gov/pf/pdf/pf_2.pdf.

53. GovTrack, *H.R. 1424: Emergency Economic Stabilization Act of 2008,* n.d., http://www.govtrack.us/congress/bill.xpd?bill=h110-1424.

54. Board of Governors of the Federal Reserve System, "Federal Reserve and Other Central Banks Announce Further Coordinated Actions to Expand Significantly the Capacity to Provide U.S. Dollar Liquidity."

55. Board of Governors of the Federal Reserve System, *Chairman Ben S. Bernanke at the Greater Austin Chamber of Commerce, Austin, Texas, Speech, December 1, 2008.*

56. Edmund L. Andrews, "A New Role for the Fed—Investor of Last Resort," *New York Times,* September 18, 2008.

57. Michael Siconolfi, Anita Raghavan, and Mitchell Pacelle, "How Salesmanship and Brainpower Failed to Save Long-Term Capital," *Wall Street Journal,* November 16, 2008, http://home.gwu.edu/~alexbapt/ltcm111698.htm.

58. A&E Television Networks, "Alan Greenspan Biography," n.d., http://www.biography.com/search/article.do?id=9319769.

59. Board of Governors of the Federal Reserve System, *All Regulations,* March 12, 2009, http://www.federalreserve.gov/bankinforeg/reglisting.htm.

60. Federal Reserve Bank of Dallas, *Understanding the Fed*, n.d., http://www.dallasfed .org/fed/understand.cfm.

61. Board of Governors of the Federal Reserve System, *Appendix: Federal Reserve Regulations*, n.d., pp. 117, 119, http://www.federalreserve.gov/pf/pdf/pf_appendixes.pdf.

62. G. Edward Griffin, *The Creature from Jekyll Island* (Westlake Village, CA: American Media, 2002), pp. 3–24.

63. Board of Governors of the Federal Reserve System, *FAQs: Federal Reserve System*, March 7, 2007, http://www.federalreserve.gov/generalinfo/faq/faqfrs.htm.

64. John T. Woolley and Gerhard Peters, The American Presidency Project (online), Santa Barbara, California, hosted by the University of California, Gerhard Peters (database), http://www.presidency.ucsb.edu/ws/index.php?pid=29590.

65. Federal Reserve Bank of New York, *The Founding of the Fed*, n.d., www.newyork fed.org/aboutthefed/history_article.html; FRASER, *Federal Reserve Archival System for Economic Research, Money Trust Investigation, Investigation of Financial and Monetary Conditions in the United States under House Resolutions Nos. 429 and 504*, n.d., http://fraser.stlouisfed.org/publications/montru.

66. William Greider, *Secrets of the Temple: How the Federal Reserve Runs the Country* (New York: Simon & Schuster, 1989), pp. 277–78.

67. The Federal Reserve Bank of New York, *The Founding of the Fed*, n.d., http://www .newyorkfed.org/aboutthefed/history_article.html.

68. Ibid.; Board of Governors of the Federal Reserve System, *H.4.1 Factors Affecting Reserve Balances, Federal Reserve Statistical Release*, May 7, 2009, http://www .federalreserve.gov/releases/h41/Current.

69. The Federal Reserve Board, *Membership of the Board of Governors of the Federal Reserve System, 1914–Present, January 29, 2009*, www.federalreserve.gov/BIOS/ boardmembership.htm#chairmen; N. Gregory Mankiw, "How to Avoid Recession? Let the Fed Work," *New York Times*, December 23, 2007, http.//www.nytimes .com/2007/12/23/business/23view.html?ex=1356066000&en=3337604c8708710a& ei=5090&partner=rssuserland&emc=rss.

70. FRASER, *Federal Reserve Archival System for Economic Research, Events in the Life of William McChesney Martin Jr.*, n.d., http://fraser.stlouisfed.org/martin/ timeline/board.html.

71. Ninety-first Congress of the United States of America, Bank Holding Act Amendments, April 18, 1969, p. 196.

72. Ibid.

73. Roger Lowenstein, "Reserved," *New York Times*, November 6, 2005, www.nytimes. com/2005/11/06/magazine/06wwln_essay.html; *Federal Reserve Bank of San Francisco, Economic Letter: Exploring the Causes of the Great Inflation, 2000–21*, July 7, 2000, www.frbsf.org/econrsrch/wklyltr/2000/el2000-21.html.

74. "Paul A. Volcker News," *New York Times*, n.d., http://topics.nytimes.com/topics/ reference/timestopics/people/v/paul_a_volcker/index.html.

75. Federal Deposit Insurance Corporation, *An Examination of the Banking Crises of the 1980s and Early 1990s, Volume I*, n.d., http://www.fdic.gov/bank/historical/ history/3_85.pdf.

76. Associated Press, "F.D.I.C. Faces First Loss Ever," *New York Times*, March 29, 1988, www.nytimes.com/1988/03/29/business/fdic-faces-first-loss-ever.html; Federal Deposit Insurance Corporation, *The S&L Crisis: A Chrono-Bibliography*, December 20, 2002, http://www.fdic.gov/bank/historical/s&l.

77. Federal Deposit Insurance Corporation, *Resolutions Handbook*, "Glossary," April 2, 2003, p. 97, http://www.fdic.gov/bank/historical/reshandbook/glossary.pdf.

78. U.S. Department of the Treasury, "Keynote Remarks to the Harvard Law School Symposium on Building the Financial System for the 21st Century, U.S. Deputy Treasury Secretary Kenneth W. Dam," press release: PO-848, December 7, 2001, http://www.treas.gov/press/releases/po848.htm.

79. Timothy Curry and Lynn Shibut, *The Cost of the Savings and Loan Crisis: Truth and Consequences*, FDIC, December 2000, p. 1, http://www.fdic.gov/bank/analytical/banking/2000dec/brv13n2_2.pdf.

80. Ibid., p. 33.

81. U.S. House of Representatives, *Treasury Under Secretary for Domestic Finance John D. Hawke, Statement, September 9, 1997*, https://www.treas.gov/press/releases/rr1909.

82. Greg Ip, "Fed Chief Questions Loan Choices," *Wall Street Journal*, February 23, 2004, http://www.themandersgroup.com/GreenspanArticle.pdf.

83. Countrywide Home Loans, Inc., "Countrywide Dominates Adjustable Rate Mortgage Market," press release, June 2, 2004, http://prnwire.com/cgi-bin/stories .pl?ACCT=104&STORY=/www/story/06-02-2004/0002185601&EDATE=.

84. The Federal Reserve Board, *Remarks by Chairman Alan Greenspan—Economic Flexibility, Speech, October 12, 2005*, http://www.federalreserve.gov/boarddocs/ speeches/2005/20051012/default.htm.

85. The Federal Reserve Board, *Remarks by Chairman Alan Greenspan, Speech, May 8, 2003*, http://www.federalreserve.gov/boarddocs/speeches/2003/20030508/default.htm.

86. The Federal Reserve Board, *Remarks by Chairman Alan Greenspan—Risk Transfer and Financial Stability, Speech, May 5, 2005*, http://www.federalreserve.gov/Boarddocs/ Speeches/2005/20050505/default.htm.

87. The Federal Reserve Board, *Remarks by Chairman Alan Greenspan—Economic Flexibility, Speech, October 12, 2005*.

88. Nomi Prins and Krisztina Ugrin, "Bailout Tally," June 2009, http://www.nomiprins .com/bailout.html.

89. Edmund L. Andrews, "Exit Greenspan, amid Questions on Economy," *New York Times*, February 1, 2006, http://www.nytimes.com/2006/02/01/business/01fed.html.

90. House of Representatives, Committee on Oversight and Government Reform, *Committee Holds Hearing on the Role of Federal Regulators in the Financial Crisis, October 23, 2008*, http://oversight.house.gov/story.asp?ID=2256.

91. Jon Ward, "He Found the Flaw?" *Washington Times*, October 24, 2008, http:// washingtontimes.com/weblogs/potus-notes/2008/Oct/24/he-found-flaw.

92. House of Representatives, *Committee of Government Oversight and Reform, Testimony of Dr. Alan Greenspan, October 23, 2008*, http://oversight.house.gov/ documents/20081023100438.pdf.

93. Ibid.

94. U.S. House of Representatives, *Statement of Congressman Ron Paul—Introducing the Federal Reserve Transparency Act, Ron Paul's Speeches and Statements, February 26, 2009*, http://www.house.gov/apps/list/speech/tx14_paul/AudittheFedBill.shtml.

95. House Committee on Financial Services, Subcommittee Assignments for the 111th Congress, http://financialservices.house.gov/subassignments.html; U.S. House of Representatives, *Statement of Congressman Ron Paul—Abolish the Federal Reserve, Ron Paul's Speeches and Statements, September 10, 2002*, http://www.house.gov/

paul/congrec/congrec2002/cr091002b.htm; GovTrack, *H.R. 2755—110th Congress (2007): Federal Reserve Board Abolition Act*, GovTrack.us, http://www.govtrack .us/congress/bill.xpd?bill=h110-2755; U.S. House of Representatives, *Statement of Congressman Ron Paul—Introducing the Federal Reserve Transparency Act, Ron Paul's Speeches and Statements, February 26, 2009.*

96. GovTrack.us., *H.R. 1207—111th Congress (2009): Federal Reserve Transparency Act of 2009*, GovTrack.us, http://www.govtrack.us/congress/bill.xpd?bill=h111-1207.

97. Pauline Smale, "Structure and Functions of the Federal Reserve System," *CRS Report for Congress*, June 15, 2005, http://fas.org/sgp/crs/misc/RS20826.pdf.

98. U.S. House of Representatives, *Statement of Congressman Ron Paul —Introducing the Federal Reserve Transparency Act, Ron Paul's Speeches and Statements, February 26, 2009.*

99. GovTrack.us, *H.R. 1207—111th Congress (2009): Federal Reserve Transparency Act of 2009*, GovTrack.us, http://www.govtrack.us/congress/bill.xpd?bill=h111-1207.

100. See 31 USC §714.

101. The Federal Reserve Board, *FAQs: The Federal Reserve System*, March 7, 2007, http://www.federalreserve.gov/generalinfo/faq/faqfrs.htm.

102. Alan Grayson, "Grayson Letter: Bring Some Accountability to the Federal Reserve," FDL, May 21, 2009, http://action.firedoglake.com/page/content/graysonletter.

103. Board of Governors of the Federal Reserve System, "De Novo Bank Application Process," Partnership for Progress, n.d., http://www.fedpartnership.gov/bank-life-cycle/start-a-bank/de-novo-bank-application-process.cfm.

104. Nomi Prins and Krisztina Ugrin, "Bailout Tally," June 2009, http://www.nomiprins .com/bailout.html.

105. Justia Docs, *Bloomberg L.P. v. Board of Governors of the Federal Reserve System*, Case No. 08-cv-9595 (LAP), November 7, 2008, http://docs.justia.com/cases/federal/district-courts/new-york/nysdce/1:2008cv09595/335178/1.

106. Mark Pittman and Bob Ivry, "U.S. Taxpayers Risk $9.7 Trillion on Bailout Programs (Update 1)," Bloomberg, February 9, 2009, http://www.bloomberg.com/apps/news? pid=washingtonstory&sid=aGq2B3XeGKok.

107. Mark Pittman, "Fed Refuses to Disclose Recipients of $2 Trillion (Update 2)," Bloomberg, December 12, 2008, http://www.bloomberg.com/apps/news?pid=2060 1109&sid=apx7XNLnZZlc&refer=home.

108. Pittman, "Fed Refuses to Disclose Recipients of $2 Trillion (Update 2)."

109. FOXBusiness, "FOX Business Sues Treasury for Failure to Respond to Freedom of Information Act Requests," December 18, 2008, http://www.foxbusiness.com/story/markets/fox-business-sues-treasury-failure-respond-freedom-information-act-requests; Karey Wutkowski and Robert MacMillan, edited by Gerald E. McCormick, "Fox Business Sues Fed for Information on Bailouts," Reuters, January 12, 2009, http://www.reuters.com/article/bondsNews/idUSN1235009220090112.

110. U.S. House of Representatives, *Oversight of Implementation of the Emergency Economic Stabilization Act of 2008 and of Government Lending and Insurance Facilities: Impact on the Economy and Credit Availability, Hearing, November 18, 2008*, Serial No. 110–145, pp. 16–17, http://frwebgate.access.gpo.gov/cgi-bin/getdoc .cgi?dbname=110_house_hearings&docid=f:46593.pdf.

111. U.S. House of Representatives, *Statement of Ben S. Bernanke, Chairman Board of Governors of the Federal Reserve System before the Committee on Financial Services,*

February 10, 2009, p. 8, http://www.house.gov/apps/list/hearing/financialsvcs_dem/bernanke021009.pdf.

112. Board of Governors of the Federal Reserve System, *Chairman Ben S. Bernanke, Semiannual Monetary Policy Report to the Congress, before the Committee on Banking, Housing and Urban Affairs, Testimony, February 24, 2009*, http://www.federalreserve.gov/newsevents/testimony/bernanke20090224a.htm.

113. David Barstow and Mike McIntire, "Calls for Clarity in New Bailout for US Banks," *New York Times*, February 9, 2009, http://www.nytimes.com/2009/02/10/business/economy/10bank.html.

114. Board of Governors of the Federal Reserve System, *Chairman Ben S. Bernanke, Semiannual Monetary Policy Report to the Congress, before the Committee on Banking, Housing and Urban Affairs, Testimony, February 24, 2009*.

115. Board of Governors of the Federal Reserve System, H.4.1 Factors Affecting Reserve Balances of Depository Institutions and Condition Statement of Federal Reserve Banks, Federal Reserve Statistical Release, February 28, 2008, http://www.federalreserve.gov/releases/h41/20080228/h41.pdf.

116. Board of Governors of the Federal Reserve System, H.4.1 Factors Affecting Reserve Balances of Depository Institutions and Condition Statement of Federal Reserve Banks, Federal Reserve Statistical Release, February 19, 2009, http://www.federalreserve.gov/releases/H41/20090219/h41.pdf.

117. Board of Governors of the Federal Reserve System, "Federal Reserve Announces It Will Initiate a Program to Purchase the Direct Obligations of Housing-Related Government-Sponsored Enterprises and Mortgage-Backed Securities Backed by Fannie Mae, Freddie Mac, and Ginnie Mae," press release, November 25, 2008, http://www.federalreserve.gov/newsevents/press/monetary/20081125b.htm.

118. Board of Governors of the Federal Reserve System, "Federal Reserve Announces the Creation of the Term Asset-Backed Securities Loan Facility (TALF)," press release, November 25, 2008, http://www.federalreserve.gov/newsevents/press/monetary/20081125a.htm.

119. Paul Kasriel and Asha Bangalore, "SIVs Got Us into Trouble—SIVs to the Rescue?" Safe Haven, February 19, 2009, http://www.safehaven.com/article-12644.htm.

120. Ibid.

121. James Hamilton, phone conversation with the author, November 25, 2008.

122. U.S. Department of the Treasury, "Joint Statement by Treasury, Federal Reserve and FDIC," press release: HP-1206, October 14, 2008, http://www.treas.gov/press/releases/hp1206.htm.

123. Board of Governors of the Federal Reserve System, "Board Announces That It Will Begin to Pay Interest on Depository Institutions' Required and Excess Reserve Balances," press release, October 6, 2008, http://www.federalreserve.gov/newsevents/press/monetary/20081006a.htm.

124. Group of Thirty, *Financial Reform: A Framework for Financial Stability*, January 15, 2009, http://www.group30.org/pubs/recommendations.pdf.

125. David Goldman, "Volcker: Regulate to Prevent Future Crisis," CNNMoney.com, January 15, 2009, http://money.cnn.com/2009/01/15/news/economy/volcker_regulation.

126. Board of Governors of the Federal Reserve System, "Board Announces Final Rules Pertaining to the Asset-Backed Commercial Paper Money Market Fund Liquidity

Facility (AMLF), Regulations H, W, and Y," press release, January 30, 2009, http://www.federalreserve.gov/newsevents/press/monetary/20090130a.htm.

127. 24/7 Wall Street, "Bailout Moves Toward $2 Trillion," October 24, 2008, http://247wallst.com/2008/10/24/bailout-moves-t.

128. Charting Stocks, "Wall St Bailout Cost Now Exceeds $4 Trillion," November 18, 2008, http://www.chartingstocks.net/2008/11/wall-st-bailout-cost-now-exceeds-4-trillion.

129. Associated Press, "Bailout Tally Approaches $7 Trillion," *Boston Herald*, November 25, 2008, http://www.bostonherald.com/business/general/view/2008_11_25_Bailout_tally_approaches__7_trillion/srvc=home&position=recent.

130. Nomi Prins and Krisztina Ugrin, "Bailout Tally," June 2009, http://www.nomiprins.com/bailout.html.

131. Ibid.

132. Paul Kasriel, phone conversation with the author, November 24, 2008.

133. U.S. Department of the Treasury, "Joint Statement of Henry M. Paulson, Jr., Secretary of the Treasury, and Jim Nussle, Director of the Office of Management and Budget, on Budget Results for Fiscal Year 2008," press release: HP-1213, October 14, 2008, http://www.treasury.gov/press/releases/hp1213.htm.

134. Department of the Treasury Financial Management Service, *Monthly Treasury Statement of Receipts and Outlays of the United States Government*, February 2009, p. 3, http://www.fms.treas.gov/mts/mts0209.pdf.

135. Blythe McGarvie, phone conversation with the author, November 24, 2008.

Chapter 6. Everyone Saw This Coming

1. Howard Fine, "When the Markets Melt Down, Regulations Soon Follow," *Los Angeles Business Journal*, May 2, 2005.

2. Events, "Stock Market Crash of 1929," Ohio History Central, July 1, 2005, http://www.ohiohistorycentral.org/entry.php?rec=559.

3. Encyclopedia Britannica Online 2009, "Great Depression," *Encyclopedia Britannica*, http://www.britannica.com/EBchecked/topic/243118/Great-Depression/234442/Stock-market-crash.

4. United States Federal Deposit Insurance Corporation, "The 1920's," United States Federal Deposit Insurance Corporation Learning Bank, May 2, 2006, http://www.fdic.gov/about/learn/learning/when/1920s.html.

5. Microsoft Encarta Online Encyclopedia 2009, "Great Depression in the United States," Microsoft Network, http://encarta.msn.com/encyclopedia_761584403/great_depression_in_the_united_states.html.

6. "Does the Great Depression Hold the Answers for the Current Mortgage Distress?" Federal Reserve Bank of St. Louis press release, May 2, 2008, http://www.stlouisfed.org/news/releases/2008/05_02_08.html.

7. Andrew Jakabovics, "STATEMENT: Foreclosure Stats Say It's 1930 Again," Center for American Progress press release, August 14, 2008, http://www.americanprogress.org/pressroom/statements/2008/08/foreclosures.html.

8. "The Long Demise of Glass-Steagall," PBS *Frontline*, May 8, 2003, http://www.pbs.org/wgbh/pages/frontline/shows/wallstreet/weill/demise.html.

9. David C. Wheelock, "Regulation, Market Structure, and the Bank Failures of the Great Depression," *Federal Reserve Bank of St. Louis Review* (March–April 1995): 27–38.

10. Realtytrac, "Foreclosure Activity Increases 81 Percent in 2008," press release, January 15, 2009, http://www.realtytrac.com//ContentManagement/PressRelease .aspx?channelid=9&ItemID=5681.

11. Realtytrac, "Foreclosure Activity Increases 9 Percent in First Quarter," press release, April 16, 2009, http://www.realtytrac.com//ContentManagement/PressRelease.aspx? channelid=9&ItemID=6180.

12. Conrad Black, *Franklin Delano Roosevelt: Champion of Freedom* (New York: Public Affairs, 2003), p. 250.

13. The American Presidency Project, "Franklin D. Roosevelt: Inaugural Address," University of California Santa Barbara, http://www.presidency.ucsb.edu/ws/index. php?pid=14473.

14. Jean Edward Smith, *FDR* (New York: Random House, 2007; 2008). Citation is to the paperback edition.

15. United States Department of the Treasury, *History of the Treasury: Secretaries of the Treasury*, "William H. Woodin," www.ustreas.gov/education/history/secretaries/ whwoodin.shtml.

16. United States Department of the Treasury, *History of the Treasury, Secretaries of the Treasury*, http://www.ustreas.gov/education/history/secretaries/.

17. American President: An Online Reference Resource, "William H. Woodin (1933–1933): Secretary of the Treasury," University of Virginia Miller Center of Public Affairs, http://millercenter.org/academic/americanpresident/fdroosevelt/ essays/cabinet/524.

18. David J. Lynch, Sue Kirchhoff, and Barbara Hagenbaugh, "Obama to Tap Geithner for Treasury," *USA Today*, January 24, 2008, http://www.usatoday.com/money/ economy/2008-11-24-money-geithner_N.htm.

19. Smith, *FDR*, pp. 325–26.

20. Biographical Directory of the United States Congress, *Biography*, "Glass, Carter (1858–1946)," http://bioguide.congress.gov/scripts/biodisplay.pl?index=G000232; Biographical Directory of the United States Congress, *Biography*, "Steagall, Henry Bascom (1873–1943)," http://bioguide.congress.gov/scripts/biodisplay.pl?index=S000820.

21. Rob Chernow, "Where Is Our Ferdinand Pecora?" *New York Times*, January 5, 2009.

22. Senate Historical Office, *Major Senate Investigations: A Selected List*, May 2004, www.senate.gov/artandhistory/history/resources/pdf/Investigations.pdf.

23. Federal Reserve Archival System for Economic Research, Publications, *Stock Exchange Practices. Hearings before the Committee on Banking and Currency Pursuant to S.Res. 84 and S.Res. 56 and S.Res. 97*, http://fraser.stlouisfed.org/publications/sensep.

24. Investment Trusts: "An investment company that offers a fixed, unmanaged portfolio, generally of stocks and bonds, as redeemable 'units' to investors for a specific period of time. It is designed to provide capital appreciation and/or dividend income." Investopedia, "Unit Investment Trust," Forbes Digital, http://www.investopedia .com/terms/u/uit.asp.

25. Ron Chernow, "Where Is Our Ferdinand Pecora?"

26. *Securities Exchange Act of 1934, US Code* 15 (1934), § 4.

27. Public debt: Money raised to pay for the functioning of the federal government. Bureau of the Public Debt, "Who We Are," United States Department of the Treasury, http://www.publicdebt.treas.gov/whoweare/who_we_are.htm.

28. *Securities Exchange Act of 1934, US Code* 15 (1934); also see http://www.sec.gov/about/whatwedo.shtml#create.

29. *Securities Exchange Act of 1934, US Code* 15 (1934), 140.

30. Ferdinand Pecora, *Wall Street under Oath: The Story of Our Modern Money Changers* (New York: Simon and Schuster, 1939).

31. Testimony of Walter E. Sachs, New York City, Member of the Firm of Goldman, Sachs & Co., to the Senate Committee on Banking and Currency Investigation of Wall Street, 72nd Cong., 1st sess., 1932, part 2, 566.

32. Commercial Paper: "Short-term promissory notes issued primarily by corporations. Maturities range up to 270 days but average about 30 days. Many companies use commercial paper to raise cash needed for current transactions, and many find it to be a lower-cost alternative to bank loans"; United States Federal Reserve Banks, *Commercial Paper*, "About Commercial Paper," November 9, 2006, http://www.federalreserve.gov/releases/CP/about.htm.

33. "Cash & Comeback," *Time*, November 9, 1936, http://www.time.com/time/agazine/article/0,9171,770464-2,00.html.

34. Charles D. Ellis, *The Partnership: The Making of Goldman Sachs* (New York: Penguin Press, 2008).

35. "Insignificant," *Time*, June 9, 1930, http://www.time.com/time/magazine/article/0,9171,739487,00.html?promoid=googlep.

36. United States Federal Deposit Insurance Corporation, *Research & Analysis*, "The First Fifty Years," July 24, 2006, http://www.fdic.gov/bank/analytical/firstfifty/chapter3.html.

37. C. W Calomiris, "Runs on Banks and the Lessons of the Great Depression," The Cato Institute, *Regulation* (1999): 4–7.

38. "Roosevelt 'Won' to Bank Insurance; Republicans Publish Letter He Wrote in 1932 Opposing Such Legislation," *New York Times*, October 27, 1936.

39. United States Federal Deposit Insurance Corporation, *Research & Analysis*, "The First Fifty Years," United States Federal Deposit Insurance Corporation, July 24, 2006, http://www.fdic.gov/bank/analytical/firstfifty/chapter3.html.

40. United States Federal Deposit Insurance Corporation, *History of the Treasury: Chronology of Events*, "The 1930's," United States Federal Deposit Insurance Corporation Learning Bank, May 2, 2006, http://www.fdic.gov/about/learn/learning/when/1930s.html.

41. United States Federal Deposit Insurance Corporation, "Speeches and Testimony," *"Remarks by Ricki Helfer, Chairman, Federal Deposit Insurance Corporation, Before the Group of Thirty Conference on International Insolvency in the Financial Sector,"* United States Federal Deposit Insurance Corporation, May 14, 1997, http://www.fdic.gov/news/news/speeches/archives/1997/sp14may97.html.

42. United States Federal Deposit Insurance Corporation, "The 1980's," United States Federal Deposit Insurance Corporation Learning Bank, May 2, 2006, http://www.fdic.gov/about/learn/learning/when/1980s.html.

43. *Federal Deposit Insurance Reform Act of 2005*, Public Law 109-173, 109th Cong., 2nd sess. (February 15, 2006).

44. Federal Deposit Insurance Corporation, "Congress Extends $250,000 Insurance Coverage through 2013," press release, May 19, 2009.

45. United States Department of the Treasury, *History of the Treasury: Chronology of Events*, "1930–1939," http://www.ustreas.gov/education/history/events/1900-present .shtml#4.

46. United States Department of the Treasury, *History of the Treasury: Secretaries of the Treasury*, "Robert E. Rubin," http://www.treas.gov/education/history/secretaries/ rerubin.shtml.

47. "Rubin Calls for Modernization through Reform of Glass-Steagall Act," *Journal of Accountancy* (May 1, 1995), http://www.thefreelibrary.com/Rubin+calls+for+moder nization+through+reform+of+Glass-Steagall+Act-a016955462.

48. United States Department of the Treasury, "Treasury Secretary Robert E. Rubin Testimony before the Senate Banking Committee," press release, February 24, 1999, www.treas.gov/press/releases/rr2973.htm.

49. United States Senator Byron Dorgan (D-ND), "Dorgan Says Wall Street Bailout Plan Is 'Stampede in Wrong Direction,'" press release, September 22, 2008, http:// dorgan.senate.gov/newsroom/record.cfm?id=303365.

50. *Financial Services Modernization Act of 1999*, 106th Cong., 1st sess., *Congressional Record—Senate* (May 4, 1999): S 4632.

51. The White House, "Remarks by the President at Financial Modernization Bill Signing," press release, November 12, 1999, http://clinton4.nara.gov/WH/New/html/ 19991112_1.html.

52. United States Senate Committee on Banking, Housing and Urban Development, "Gramm's Statement at Signing Ceremony for Gramm-Leach-Bliley Act," press release, November 12, 1999, http://banking.senate.gov/prel99/1112gbl.htm.

53. Stephen Labaton, "Congress Passes Wide-Ranging Bill Easing Bank Laws," *New York Times*, November 5, 1999.

54. Walter Alarkon, "Clinton Rejects Blame for Financial Crisis," *The Hill*, September 25, 2008, http://thehill.com/leading-the-news/clinton-rejects-blame-for-financial-crisis-2008-09-25.html.

55. Nomi Prins and Krisztina Ugrin, "Bailout Tally," June 2009, http://www.nomiprins. com/bailout.html; Karey Wutkowski and Jonathan Stempel, "Bank of America to Need $34 Billion in Capital: Source," Reuters, May 6, 2009, http://www.reuters.com/ article/newsOne/idUSTRE5450C120090506.

56. The American Presidency Project, "William J. Clinton: Statement on Signing Legislation to Reform the Financial System," University of California Santa Barbara, http://www.presidency.ucsb.edu/ws/index.php?pid=56922.

57. Ibid.

58. Stephen Labaton, "Congress Passes Wide-Ranging Bill Easing Bank Laws," *New York Times*, November 5, 1999.

59. Broker-dealer: person or company engaged in securities transactions either for his/ her/itself or on behalf of others; United States Securities and Exchange Commission, *Guide to Broker-Dealer Registration*, May 9, 2008, http://www.sec.gov/divisions/ marketreg/bdguide.htm#II.

60. United States Senate Committee on Banking, Housing and Urban Development, *Prepared Testimony of Mr. Henry M. Paulson, Chairman and CEO, Goldman Sachs &*

Company: Hearing on the "Financial Marketplace of the Future," 106th Cong., 2nd sess., 2000.

61. Stephen Labaton, "Agency's '04 Rule Let Banks Pile Up New Debt," *New York Times*, October 2, 2008.

62. Julie Satow, "Ex-SEC Official Blames Agency for Blow-Up of Broker-Dealers," *New York Sun*, September 18, 2008, http://www.nysun.com/business/ex-sec-official-blames-agency-for-blow-up/86130.

63. Andrew Ross Sorkin, ed., comment on "As Goldman and Morgan Shift, a Wall St. Era Ends," Dealbook, comment posted September 21, 2008, http://dealbook.blogs .nytimes.com/2008/09/21/goldman-morgan-to-become-bank-holding-companies.

64. Structured Investment Vehicle: "A pool of investment assets that attempts to profit from credit spreads between short-term debt and long-term structured finance products such as asset-backed securities," Investopedia, "Structured Investment Vehicle," Forbes Digital, http://www.investopedia.com/terms/s/structured-investment-vehicle .asp; Sorkin, comment on "As Goldman and Morgan Shift, a Wall St. Era Ends."

65. Satow, "Ex-SEC Official Blames Agency for Blow-Up of Broker-Dealers," *New York Sun*, September 18, 2008.

66. Barry Ritholtz, "How SEC Regulatory Exemptions Helped Lead to Collapse," *RGE Monitor*, September 25, 2008, http://www.rgemonitor.com/financemarkets-monitor/ 253642/how_sec_regulatory_exemptions_helped_lead_to_collapse.

67. "Glass-Steagall Act," *American Law Encyclopedia, Vol. 5*, http://law.jrank.org/pages/ 7165/Glass-Steagall-Act.html.

68. Bernard Shull and Gerald A. Hanweck, *Bank Mergers in a Deregulated Environment* (Westport, CT: Quorum Books, 2001), p. 9.

69. Lynn S. Fox, chair, Publications Committee, et al., "The Federal Reserve System: Purposes & Functions," *Board of Governors of the Federal Reserve System*, June 2005.

70. Shull and Hanweck, *Bank Mergers in a Deregulated Environment*, p. 84.

71. Data from the Federal Reserve Board of Governors, compiled by the author and Clark Merrefield, http://www.federalreserve.gov.

72. Shull and Hanweck, *Bank Mergers in a Deregulated Environment*, p. 83.

73. Gary A. Dymski, "The Global Bank Merger Wave: Implications for Developing Countries," *The Developing Economies* (December 2002): 442.

74. Ibid., 446.

Chapter 7. Bonus Bonanza

1. Will Rogers Today Weekly Comments Archive, "Archived Issues," Will Rogers Today, http://www.willrogerstoday.com/weekly_comments/archive_issue.cfm?newsletterID=341.

2. House Committee on Oversight and Government Reform, *CEO Pay and the Mortgage Crisis, Hearing before the Committee on Oversight and Government Reform, House of Representatives*, 110th Cong., 2nd sess., March 7, 2008, serial no. 110–81, transcript, title page.

3. House Committee on Oversight and Government Reform, *Memorandum*, March 6, 2008, p. 1, http://www.shareholderforum.com/op/Library/20080306_House-memo.pdf.

4. House Committee on Oversight and Government Reform, *CEO Pay and the Mortgage Crisis*, title page.

5. Ibid., p. 2.
6. About Member of Congress Salaries, "History of Annual Salaries—Members of Congress and Leadership," Legistorm, http://www.legistorm.com/member_of_congress_salaries.html.
7. Bank of America, "Bank of America Agrees to Purchase Countrywide Financial Corp," press release, January 11, 2008, http://newsroom.bankofamerica.com/index.php?s=press_releases&item=7956.
8. House Committee on Oversight and Government Reform, *CEO Pay and the Mortgage Crisis*, p. 200.
9. Ibid., p. 268.
10. Charles E. Schumer letter to Ronald A. Rosenfeld, November 26, 2007, http://schumer.senate.gov/new_website/record.cfm?id=287914.
11. House Committee on Oversight and Government Reform, *CEO Pay and the Mortgage Crisis*, p. 234.
12. Ibid., p. 233.
13. Ibid., p. 265.
14. Ibid., p. 266.
15. E. Scott Reckard, "Countrywide Financial Chairman Angelo Mozilo's E-Mail Sets off a Furor," *Los Angeles Times*, May 21, 2008, http://articles.latimes.com/2008/may/21/business/fi-mozilo21.
16. News: Deals: Reports, "Countrywide Financial Corp. & Bank of America Corp.," CNN Money, January 23, 2009, http://money.cnn.tv/news/deals/mergers/reports/1142146020.html.
17. Bank of America "Bank of America Agrees to Purchase Countrywide Financial Corp.," press release, January 11, 2008, http://newsroom.bankofamerica.com/index.php?s=press_releases&item=7956.
18. Dina ElBoghdady, "Countrywide Loses $422 Million," *Washington Post*, January 30, 2008.
19. Philip van Doorn, "Countrywide Could Bring BofA Misery," *The Street*, July 1, 2008, http://www.thestreet.com/story/10424195/1/countrywide-could-bring-bofa-misery.html?puc=newshome.
20. Board of Governors of the Federal Reserve System, "Treasury, Federal Reserve, and the FDIC Provide Assistance to Bank of America," press release, January 16, 2009, http://www.federalreserve.gov/newsevents/press/bcreg/20090116a.htm; Eye on the Bailout, "Bailout Recipients," ProPublica, May 8, 2009, http://www.propublica.org/special/show-me-the-tarp-money; Google Finance, "Bank of America Corporation," http://www.google.com/finance?q=NYSE%3ABAC.
21. Riley McDermid, "B. of A. Says Merger on despite Countrywide Woes," Marketwatch, March 5, 2008, http://www.marketwatch.com/news/story/bank-america-says-merger-despite/story.aspx?guid={5F8BC85D-902E-4C85-9ADB-BB8DE35EF7B8}.
22. *Arkansas Teacher Retirement System, Fire & Police Pension Association of Colorado, and Louisiana Municipal Police Employees' Retirement System v. Angelo R Mozilo, et al. and Countrywide Financial* (9th Cir., 2007).
23. "Countrywide Sued Over 'Excessive' Fees on Defaults," Reuters, February 28, 2008, http://www.reuters.com/article/bondsNews/idUSN2749535120080228.
24. Office of the New York State Comptroller, "DiNapoli, Thompson to Lead Securities Fraud Suit," press release, November 30, 2008, http://www.osc.state.ny.us/press/releases/nov07/113007.htm.

25. California Office of the Attorney General, "Brown Sues Countrywide for Mortgage Deception," press release, June 25, 2008, http://ag.ca.gov/newsalerts/release.php?id=1582&year=2008&month=6.

26. Illinois Attorney General, "Illinois Attorney General Madigan Leads $8.7 Billion Groundbreaking Settlement of Lawsuit against Mortgage Giant Countrywide," press release, October 6, 2008, http://www.illinoisattorneygeneral.gov/pressroom/2008_10/20081006.html.

27. Dina ElBoghdady, "Bank of America to Modify Mortgages from Countrywide," *Washington Post*, October 7, 2008.

28. *Greenwich Financial Services Distressed Mortgage Fund 3 LLC et al. v. Country Financial Corporation et al.* (2nd Cir., 2008).

29. United States Securities and Exchange Commission, "SEC Files Securities Fraud Charges Against Former Countrywide Executives," press release, June 4, 2009, http://www.sec.gov/litigation/litreleases/2009/lr21068.htm.

30. House Committee on Oversight and Government Reform, *CEO Pay and the Mortgage Crisis*, p. 242.

31. Dan Wilchins, "Citigroup Gives ex-CEO Prince $40 Million Severance Package," *International Business Times*, November 10, 2007, http://in.ibtimes.com/articles/20071110/citigroup-charles-prince-robert-rubin-merrill-lynch-subprime-crisis-mortgage.htm.

32. David Ellis, "Citigroup to Cut More Than 50,000 Jobs," CNN Money, November 17, 2008, http://money.cnn.com/2008/11/17/news/companies/citigroup/index.htm.

33. Citigroup, *Citigroup Fourth Quarter 2008 Earnings Report*, January 16, 2008, http://www.citi.com/citi/fin/qer.htm.

34. Google Finance, "Citigroup," http://www.google.com/finance?q=NYSE%3AC.

35. Jeremy Smerd, "Citi Caps Severance Pay of Longtime Employees," *Financial Week*, December 3, 2008, http://www.financialweek.com/apps/pbcs.dll/article?AID=/20081203/REG/812039979/1028.

36. Citigroup, "Citi Reports First Quarter Revenues of $24.8 Billion," press release, April 17, 2009, http://www.citi.com/citi/press/2009/090417a.htm.

37. "Executive Incentives," *Wall Street Journal*, November 20, 2008, http://online.wsj.com/public/resources/documents/st_ceos_20081111.html.

38. Chris Palmeri, comment on "Bloodbath at Countrywide," Hot Property, comment posted September 7, 2007, http://www.businessweek.com/the_thread/hotproperty/archives/2007/09/bloodbath_at_co.html.

39. "Mozilo to Trim Retirement Package," *Los Angeles Times*, January 28, 2008, http://articles.latimes.com/2008/jan/28/business/fi-mozilo28.

40. Merrill Lynch, "Stan O'Neal Retires from Merrill Lynch; Alberto Cribiore to Serve as Interim Non-Executive Chairman and Chair Search Committee," press release, October 30, 2007, http://www.ml.com/index.asp?id=7695_7696_8149_74412_82725_84472.

41. "O'Neal's Exit Package Stirs Reaction: Senate May Revisit Say on Pay," *Directorship*, December 1, 2007, www.directorship.com/contentmgr/showdetails.php/id/10055.

42. Merrill Lynch, "Merrill Lynch Reports Third-Quarter 2007 Net Loss from Continuing Operations of $2.85 per Diluted Share," press release, October 24, 2007, http://ml.com/index.asp?id=7695_7696_8149_74412_82725_84064.

43. Merrill Lynch, "Merrill Lynch Reports Second-Quarter 2008 Net Loss from Continuing Operations of $4.6 Billion," press release, July 17, 2008, http://www.ml.com/index.asp?id=7695_7696_8149_88278_101366_102140; Edgar Online, "Merrill

Lynch & Co. (10K)," United States Securities and Exchange Commission, for the fiscal year ended December 26, 2008, http://www.sec.gov/Archives/edgar/data/6510 0/000095012309003322/y74695e10vk.htm.

44. House Committee on Oversight and Government Reform, *Corporate Accountability, Committee Holds Hearing on the Causes and Effects of the AIG Bailout*, October 7, 2008, http://oversight.house.gov/story.asp?ID=2211.

45. House Committee on Oversight and Government Reform, *Corporate Accountability, Committee Holds Hearing on the Causes and Effects of the AIG Bailout: Chairman Waxman's Opening Statement*, October 7, 2008, http://oversight.house .gov/story.asp?ID=2214.

46. Ibid.

47. Karina, comment on "Rep. Elijah Cummings: They Were Getting Manicures, Facials, Pedicures and Massages While American People Were Footing the Bill," The Gavel, comment posted October 7, 2008, http://www.speaker.gov/blog/?p=1539.

48. New York State Insurance Department, "About Us," http://www.ins.state.ny.us/ hp97wel.htm.

49. Matthew Karnitschnig, Deborah Solomon, Liam Pleven, and Jon E. Hilsenrath, "U.S. to Take Over AIG in $85 Billion Bailout; Central Banks Inject Cash as Credit Dries Up," *Wall Street Journal*, September 16, 2008.

50. CEO Pay, "Edward M. Liddy," *Forbes*, http://www.forbes.com/lists/2006/12/G0YE. html.

51. House Committee on Financial Services, "American International Group's Impact on the Global Economy: Before, during and after Federal Intervention," press release, March 18, 2009, http://www.house.gov/apps/list/hearing/financialsvcs_dem/ press031809.shtml.

52. Edgar Online, "Letter from Robert B. Willumstad: Exhibit 10.2," United States Securities and Exchange Commission, http://www.sec.gov/Archives/edgar/data/527 2/000095012308014821/y72212exv10w2.htm.

53. Edgar Online, "Letter Agreement: Exhibit 10.1," United States Securities and Exchange Commission, December 26, 2008, http://www.sec.gov/Archives/edgar/ data/5272/000095012308018575/y73613exv10w1.htm.

54. Daniel Golden, "Countrywide's Many 'Friends,'" *Portfolio*, June 12, 2008, http:// www.portfolio.com/news-markets/top-5/2008/06/12/Countrywide-Loan-Scandal.

55. Glenn R. Simpson, "Countrywide Made Home Loans to Gorelick, Mudd," *Wall Street Journal*, September 25, 2008.

56. Alex Viega, Associated Press, "Countrywide's Mozilo Forgoing $37.5M," *San Francisco Chronicle*, January 27, 2008, http://www.sfgate.com/cgi-bin/article/article?f=/n/ a/2008/01/27/financial/f211557S93.DTL.

57. Gretchen Morgenson, "After Huge Losses, a Move to Reclaim Executives' Pay," *New York Times*, February 21, 2009.

58. Senator Olympia J. Snow, "Snowe-Wyden Amendment to Recover Wall Street Bonuses Is Added to Economic Recovery Package," press release, February 9, 2009, http://snowe.senate.gov/public/index.cfm?FuseAction=PressRoom.PressReleases& ContentRecord_id=5bd29e96-802a-23ad-4a2c-3ef8f45e5168; *American Recovery and Reinvestment Act of 2009: Subtitle C—Excessive Bonuses* (Senate Amendment), 111th Cong., 1st sess.

59. *American Recovery and Reinvestment Act of 2009: Subtitle C—Excessive Bonuses*, Public Law 111-5, 111th Cong., 1st sess, February 17, 2009.

60. Matthew Daly, Associated Press, "Congress Kills Plan to Recover Wall Street Bonuses," ABC News, February 12, 2009, http://abcnews.go.com/Politics/WireStory?id=6866705&page=1.

61. Edmund L. Andrews and Peter Baker, "A.I.G. Planning Huge Bonuses after $170 Billion Bailout," *New York Times*, March 14, 2009.

62. Nomi Prins and Krisztina Ugrin, "Bailout Tally," June 2009, http://www.nomiprins .com/bailout.html.

63. Steve Turnham and Kathleen Johnston, "Analysis: Who Didn't Know about AIG Bonuses and Why Not?" CNN Politics, March 20, 2009, http://www.cnn.com/2009/POLITICS/03/20/aig.bonuses/index.html.

64. Ed Hornick, Ted Barrett, and Kristi Keck, "Dodd: Administration Pushed for Language Protecting Bonuses," CNN Politics, March 19, 2009, http://www.cnn .com/2009/POLITICS/03/18/aig.bonuses.congress/index.html.

65. Helene Cooper, "Obama Orders Treasury Chief to Try to Block A.I.G. bonuses," *New York Times*, March 16, 2009; House Committee on Financial Services, *Oversight of the Federal Government's Intervention at American International Group, Statement by Timothy F. Geithner*, 111th Cong., 1st sess., 2009.

66. Carl Hulse and David M. Herszenhorn, "House Approves 90% Tax on Bonuses after Bailouts," *New York Times*, March 19, 2009.

67. Govtrack, Legislation, *H.R. 1586: To Impose an Additional Tax on Bonuses Received from Certain TARP Recipients*, http://www.govtrack.us/congress/bill .xpd?bill=h111-1586.

68. House Committee on Oversight and Government Reform, *The Causes and Effects of the Lehman Brothers Bankruptcy, Statement of Richard S. Fuld, Jr.*, 110th Cong., 2nd sess., 2008, p. 3.

69. Executive Profile, "Richard S. Fuld Jr.," *Businessweek*, http://investing.businessweek .com/research/stocks/people/person.asp?personId=548100&symbol=LEHMQ.PK; House Committee on Oversight and Government Reform, *The Causes and Effects of the Lehman Brothers Bankruptcy, Statement of Richard S. Fuld, Jr.*, p. 3.

70. Executive Profile, "Richard S. Fuld Jr., *Businessweek*, http://investing.businessweek .com/research/stocks/people/person.asp?personId=548100&symbol=LEHMQ.PK.

71. House Committee on Oversight and Government Reform, *The Causes and Effects of the Lehman Brothers Bankruptcy, Statement of Richard S. Fuld, Jr.*, p. 3.

72. Andrew Ross Sorkin, "Lehman Files for Bankruptcy; Merrill Is Sold," *New York Times*, September 14, 2008.

73. House Committee on Oversight and Government Reform, *The Causes and Effects of the Lehman Brothers Bankruptcy*, 110th Cong., 2nd sess., 2008, p. 188.

74. Ibid., p. 187.

75. Luigi Zingales, "Curriculum Vitae," University of Chicago Booth School of Business, http://faculty.chicagobooth.edu/luigi.zingales/vita.

76. House Committee on Oversight and Government Reform, *The Causes and Effects of the Lehman Brothers Bankruptcy, Statement of Richard S. Fuld Jr.*, p. 62.

77. Louise Story and Ben White, "The Road to Lehman's Failure Was Littered with Lost Chances," *New York Times*, October 5, 2008.

78. Office of the New York State Comptroller, "DiNapoli: Wall Street Bonuses Fell 44% in 2008," press release, January 28, 2009, http://osc.state.ny.us/press/releases/jan09/012809.htm.

79. Jane Sasseen and Phil Mintz, "Obama Calls for Executive Pay Limits," *Businessweek*, February 4, 2009, http://www.businessweek.com/bwdaily/dnflash/content/feb2009/db2009024_052387.htm?chan=top+news_top+news+index+-+temp_top+story.

80. United States Department of the Treasury "Secretary Geithner Introduces Financial Stability Plan," press release, February 10, 2009, http://www.treas.gov/press/releases/tg18.htm.

81. Tomoeh Murakami Tse, "Congress Trumps Obama by Cuffing Bonuses for CEOs," *Washington Post*, February 14, 2009.

82. Office of the New York State Comptroller, "DiNapoli: Wall Street Bonuses Fell 44% in 2008."

83. Rob Cox and Richard Beales, Breakingviews.com, "Getting Around Smaller Bonuses," *New York Times*, May 25, 2009.

84. Sam Stein, comment on "Bailed-Out Firms Distributing Cash Rewards: 'Please Do Not Call It A Bonus,'" *Huffington Post*, comment posted February 11, 2009, http://www.huffingtonpost.com/2009/02/11/bailout-recipients-giving_n_165624.html.

85. Brian Wingfield and Josh Zumbrun, "Cautiously Capping Executive Pay," *Forbes*, February 4, 2009, http://www.forbes.com/2009/02/04/obama-geithner-tarp-biz-wash-0204_compensation.html.

86. Joe Bel Bruno, Associated Press, "Morgan Stanley, Merrill Chiefs Give Up Bonuses," *USA Today*, December 8, 2008, http://www.usatoday.com/money/companies/management/2008-12-08-wall-street-bonuses_N.htm.

87. Edgar Online, "The Goldman Sachs Group, Inc. (Schedule 14A) 2006," United States Security and Exchange Commission, http://www.sec.gov/Archives/edgar/data/886982/000119312506039420/ddef14a.htm.

88. Timothy Curry and Lynn Shibut, "The Cost of the Savings and Loan Crisis: Truth and Consequences," *FDIC Banking Review* 13, no. 2 (2002), http://www.fdic.gov/bank/analytical/banking/2000dec/brv13n2_2.pdf; Richard W. Stevenson, "G.A.O. Puts Cost of S.&L. Bailout at Half a Trillion Dollars," *New York Times*, July 13, 1996.

89. Office of the New York State Deputy Comptroller, "New York City Securities Industry Bonuses," press release, January 28, 2009, http://www.osc.state.ny.us/press/releases/jan08/bonus.pdf.

90. Frank Bass and Rita Beamish, Associated Press, "Study: $1.6B of Bailout Funds Given to Bank Execs," Finalcallnews.com, January 5, 2009, http://www.finalcall.com/artman/publish/article_5524.shtml.

91. Christine Harper, "Goldman Sachs's Tax Rate Drops to 1%, or $14 Million," Bloomberg, December 16, 2008, http://www.bloomberg.com/apps/news?pid=20601103&sid=a6bQVsZS2_18&refer=news.

92. Associated Press, "Citigroup Plans to Raise Employees' Base Pay," June 24, 2009.

93. Phillip Inman, "Goldman to Make Record Bonus Payout," June 21, 2009, *The Guardian;* Andrew Clark "Goldman Sachs Staff Set for Bumper Bonus as Bank Earns $39M per Day," *The Guardian*, July 14, 2009.

94. United States House of Representatives Committee on Financial Services, *Opening Statement of Congressman Paul E. Kanjorski*, 111th Cong., 1st sess., 2009.

95. Lloyd Blankfein, "Do Not Destroy the Essential Catalyst of Risk," *Financial Times*, February 8, 2009.

96. Goldman Sachs, About Us, "The Goldman Sachs Business Principles," http://www2 .goldmansachs.com/our-firm/about-us/business-principles.html.

97. "CEO Compensation: Kenneth D. Lewis," *Forbes*, April 30, 2008, http://www.forbes .com/lists/2008/12/lead_bestbosses08_Kenneth-D-Lewis_PAU6.html.

98. "Under New Ownership: Bank of America," *CBS News*, October 19, 2008, http:// www.cbsnews.com/stories/2008/10/19/60minutes/main4531244.shtml.

99. House Committee on Financial Services, *Oversight of the Federal Government's Intervention at American International Group, Statement by Timothy F. Geithner*.

100. House Committee on Financial Services, *Oversight of the Federal Government's Intervention at American International Group, Statement by Ben S. Bernanke, Chairman, Federal Reserve Board of Governors*, 111th Cong., 1st sess., 2009.

101. Todd Harrison, comment on "Surprise: AIG Bonuses More Than First Reported," Top Stocks, comment posted May 6, 2009, http://blogs.moneycentral.msn.com/top-stocks/archive/2009/05/06/surprise-aig-bonuses-more-than-first-reported.aspx.

Chapter 8. Big Banks Mean Trouble

1. Robert Andrews, *The Concise Columbia Dictionary of Quotations* (New York: Columbia University Press, 1989), p. 27.

2. Data compiled by Nomi Prins and Clark Merrefield from the Federal Reserve Board of Governors, www.federalreserve.gov.

3. Elmus Wicker, "Banking Panics in the US: 1873–1933," EH.Net Encyclopedia, edited by Robert Whaples, September 4, 2001, http://eh.net/encyclopedia/article/ wicker.banking.panics.us.

4. Jennifer 8. Lee, comment on "New York and the Panic of 1873," City Room, comment posted October 14, 2008, http://cityroom.blogs.nytimes.com/2008/10/14/ learning-lessons-from-the-panic-of-1873.

5. Sherman Anti-Trust Act (1890), "Approved July 2, 1890, the Sherman Anti-Trust Act was the first Federal act that outlawed monopolistic business practices," Our Documents, http://www.ourdocuments.gov/doc.php?flash=true&doc=51.

6. Eliot Jones, *The Trust Problem in the United States* (New York: Macmillan, 1921), pp. 20–21.

7. Sherman Anti-Trust Act (1890).

8. U.S. Constitution, art. 1, sec. 8.

9. Bernard Shull and Gerald A. Hanweck, *Bank Mergers in a Deregulated Environment* (Westport, CT: Quorum Books, 2001), p. 66.

10. Ibid., p. 80.

11. Bank of America, "CEO to Retire in April," press release, January 24, 2001, http:// newsroom.bankofamerica.com/index.php?s=43&item=5581.

12. Ross Yockey, *McColl: The Man with America's Money* (Marietta, GA: Longstreet Press, 1999), pp. 472–74.

13. "Bigger Footprints," *The Economist* (U.S. Edition), April 17, 2004.

14. "Goodbye to All That," *Daily Deal*, October 24, 2005.

15. Gary Dymski, *The Bank Merger Wave: The Economic Causes and Social Consequences of Financial Consolidation* (Armonk, NY: M. E. Sharpe, 1999), p. 69.

16. Saul Hansell, "Biggest Southeast Bank Buying Florida Giant for $15.5 Billion," *New York Times*, August 30, 1997.
17. Duke University, "North Carolina Case Study: Bank of America," *North Carolina in the Global Economy, Fall 2004*, http://www.soc.duke.edu/NC_GlobalEconomy/pdfs/banks/BankingCS_BankofAmerica.pdf.
18. Charles M. Becker, "The Post Merger Financial Position of NationsBank Corporation/BankAmerica Corporation," *Southwestern Economic Review* (Spring 2002): 85–96.
19. Data from Thomson Reuters/Freeman & Co., http://www.thomsonreuters.com.
20. Cyrus Sanati, comment on "Merging Banks Surge Past U.S. Deposit Caps," Dealbook, comment posted October 17, 2008, http://dealbook.blogs.nytimes.com/2008/10/17/merging-banks-surge-past-us-deposit-cap.
21. Ari Levy and Elizabeth Hester, "JPMorgan Buys WaMu Deposits; Regulators Seize Thrift," Bloomberg, September 26, 2008, http://www.bloomberg.com/apps/news?pid=20601087&refer=home&sid=aWxliUXHsOoA.
22. United States Federal Deposit Insurance Corporation, Federal Deposit Insurance Corporation Summary of Deposits: Deposits of FDIC-Insured Commercial Banks and Savings Institutions as of June 30: 1999–2008, June 30, 2008, http://www2.fdic.gov/sod/pdf/ddep_2008.pdf.
23. Monica Langley, *Tearing Down the Walls: How Sandy Weill Fought His Way to the Top of the Financial World—and Then Nearly Lost It All* (New York: Wall Street Journal Books, 2003), p. 288.
24. Binyamin Appelbaum, "Citi's Long History of Overreach, Then Rescue," *Washington Post*, March 11, 2009.
25. Langley, *Tearing Down the Walls*, p. 311.
26. Chris Suellentrop, "Sandy Weill: How Citigroup's CEO Rewrote the Rules so He Could Live Richly," Slate.com, November 20, 2002, http://www.slate.com/id/2074372.
27. Center for Responsive Politics, "Citigroup Inc. Client Profile: Summary, 1998," Opensecrets.org, http://www.opensecrets.org/lobby/clientsum.php?lname=Citigroup+Inc&year=1998.
28. Data from Thomson Reuters/Freeman & Co., http://www.thomsonreuters.com.
29. Associated Press, "Travelers Group to Buy Salomon for $9.3 Billion," *The Journal Record* (Oklahoma City), September 25, 1997, http://findarticles.com/p/articles/mi_qn4182/is_19970925/ai_n10112443.
30. About Citi, "Our Brands," Citigroup, http://www.citigroup.com/citi/business/brands.htm.
31. Mitchell Martin, "Citicorp and Travelers Plan to Merge in Record $70 Billion Deal," *International Herald Tribune*, April 7, 1998.
32. Forbes.com staff, "Sanford Weill to Step Down as CEO at 70," *Forbes*, July 16, 2003, http://www.forbes.com/2003/07/16/cx_ss_0716weillmini.html.
33. United States Securities and Exchange Commission, "SEC Sues Citigroup Global Markets, Formerly Known as Salomon Smith Barney, and Former Research Analyst Jack B. Grubman for Research Analyst Conflicts of Interest," press release, April 28, 2003, http://sec.gov/litigation/litreleases/lr18111.htm.
34. Daniel Dunaief, "Watchdog Labels Citi Board the Worst," *New York Daily News*, June 10, 2003.
35. Senior Advisers, "Sanford I. Weill," Citigroup, http://www.citigroup.com/citi/corporate governance/profiles/weill/index.htm.

36. Jonathan Stempel, "Sandy Weill to End Citigroup Consulting Job," Reuters, January 29, 2009, http://www.reuters.com/article/regulatoryNewsFinancialServicesAnd RealEstate/idUSN2929071720090129.

37. Morgan Stanley, "Morgan Stanley and Citi to Form Industry-Leading Wealth Management Business through Joint Venture," press release, January 13, 2009, http://www .morganstanley.com/about/press/articles/af3e409a-e1b7-11dd-84e6-b390c77322d3.html.

38. Eric Dash, "Buyers for a Citigroup Fire Sale Have Probably Been Singed, Too," *New York Times*, January 14, 2009.

39. Data from SGA Executive Tracker, http://www.sgaexecutivetracker.com/sga.html.

40. Center for Responsive Politics, "Bank of America Client Profile: Summary, 1998," Opensecrets.org, http://www.opensecrets.org/lobby/clientsum.php?year=1998&lna me=Bank+of+America&id=.

41. Center for Responsive Politics, "Bank of America Client Profile: Summary, 1999," Opensecrets.org, http://www.opensecrets.org/lobby/clientsum.php?year=1999&lna me=Bank+of+America&id=.

42. Center for Responsive Politics, "Bank of America Client Profile: Summary, 2008," Opensecrets.org, http://www.opensecrets.org/lobby/clientsum.php?year=2008&lna me=Bank+of+America&id=.

43. Data from Thomson Reuters/Freeman & Co., http://www.thomsonreuters.com.

44. Data from the U.S. Executive Compensation Database, http://www.lexis.com.

45. Bank of America, "Bank of America Buys Merrill Lynch Creating Unique Financial Services Firm," Bank of America press release, http://newsroom.bankofamerica .com/index.php?s=43&item=8255.

46. Heidi N. Moore, comment on "Bank of America-Merrill Lynch: A $50 Billion Deal From Hell," Deal Journal, comment posted January 22, 2009, http://blogs.wsj.com/ deals/2009/01/22/bank-of-america-merrill-lynch-a-50-billion-deal-from-hell.

47. Data from Thomson Reuters/Freeman & Co., http://www.thomsonreuters.com.

48. Dan Fitzpatrick, "Merrill Pay Scrutinized," *Wall Street Journal*, March 17, 2009, http://online.wsj.com/article/SB123732310146161443.html.

49. "Finger Interests Urges Bank of America Shareholders to Vote for Governance Changes," Business Wire (posted on Forbes.com), March 13, 2009, http://www .reuters.com/article/pressRelease/idUS155292+13-Mar-2009+BW20090313.

50. Dan Fitzpatrick and Marshall Eckblad, "Lewis Ousted as BofA Chairman," *Wall Street Journal*, April 30, 2009.

51. Bank of America, "Greg Curl Named Chief Risk Officer at Bank of America," press release, June 4, 2009, http://newsroom.bankofamerica.com/index.php?s=43&item=8472.

52. Louise Story and Eric Dash, "Bank of America Ousts Head of Risk Oversight," *New York Times*, June 4, 2009.

53. Members of the Board, "William B. Harrison, Jr.," JPMorgan Chase & Co., http:// www.jpmorganchase.com/cm/cs?pagename=Chase/Href&urlname=jpmc/about/ governance/members/harrisonHarrison.

54. Langley, *Tearing Down the Walls*, p. 50; Daniel Arnall and Charles Herman, "FDIC: WaMu the 'Largest Bank Failure Ever,'" ABC News, September 25, 2008, http:// abcnews.go.com/Business/Story?id=5889501&page=1.

55. Langley, *Tearing Down the Walls*, pp. 71–72, 88.

56. Ibid., p. 125.

57. Ibid., p. 317.

58. Data from Thomson Reuters/Freeman & Co., http://www.thomsonreuters.com.

59. People, "James S. Dimon," *Forbes*, http://people.forbes.com/profile/james-s-dimon/46630.

60. Data from the U.S. Executive Compensation Database, http://www.lexis.com.

61. David Ellis and Tami Luhby, "JPMorgan Scoops up Troubled Bear," CNN Money, March 17, 2008, http://money.cnn.com/2008/03/16/news/companies/jpmorgan_bear_stearns/index.htm.

62. United States Federal Deposit Insurance Corporation, "JPMorgan Chase Acquires Banking Operations of Washington Mutual," press release, September 25, 2008, http://www.fdic.gov/news/news/press/2008/pr08085.html.

63. Nomi Prins and Krisztina Ugrin, "Bailout Tally," June 2009, http://www.nomiprins.com/bailout.html.

64. Matthew Leising and Elizabeth Hester, "JPMorgan Said to Reap $5 Billion Derivatives Profit," Bloomberg, March 3, 2009, http://www.bloomberg.com/apps/news?pid=20601087&sid=a_v5DTUmYDbA&refer=home.

65. Daniel Macht, "Finance: Dimon Lashes Out at Critics," Crain's New York Business, February 4, 2009, http://futurenyc.crainsnewyork.com/2009/02/04/finance-dimon-lashes-out-at-critics.

66. Eric Dash, "Bankers Pledge Cooperation with Obama," *New York Times*, March 27, 2009, http://dealbook.blogs.nytimes.com/2009/03/27/bankers-promise-cooperation-with-obama.

67. Wells Fargo, "Wells Fargo, Wachovia Agree to Merge," press release, October 3, 2008, https://www.wellsfargo.com/press/2008/20081003.

68. McClatchy-Tribune Information Services, "Citigroup Battle Fallout Continues: Wells Fargo: No Plans for Major Layoffs at Wachovia," *The Decatur Daily*, October 12, 2008, http://www.tradingmarkets.com/.site/news/Stock%20News/1937180/?relatestories=1.

69. David Enrich and Dan Fitzpatrick, "Wachovia Chooses Wells Fargo, Spurns Citi," *Wall Street Journal*, October 4, 2008.

70. Business Briefing, "Bonuses Reined in at Wells Fargo," *Los Angeles Times*, February 28, 2009, http://articles.latimes.com/2009/feb/28/business/fi-briefs28; Compensation data from the U.S. Executive Compensation Database, http://www.lexis.com.

71. Marshall Eckblad and Mike Barris, "Wells Fargo Cuts Its Dividend 85%," *Wall Street Journal*, March 7, 2009, http://online.wsj.com/article/SB123634454649952469.html.

72. AIG, *The AIG Story*, "The AIG Financial Crisis: A Summary," www.aig.com/Our-Commitment_385_136429.html.

73. Gretchen Morgenson, "Behind Insurer's Crisis, Blind Eye to a Web of Risk," *New York Times*, September 27, 2008.

74. Michael Rapoport, Dow Jones Newswires, "Banks Protected again [sic] All risks in AIG Scandal," *The Australian*, March 20, 2009, http://www.theaustralian.news.com.au/business/story/0,,25214458-5017996,00.html?from=marketwatch_rss.

75. Liz Moyer, "Goldman on AIG: 'Don't Blame Us,'" *Forbes*, March 20, 2009, http://www.forbes.com/2009/03/20/goldman-sachs-aig-business-wall-street-goldman.html.

76. United States Department of the Treasury, "Statement by Secretary Henry M. Paulson, Jr. on Comprehensive Approach to Market Developments," press release, September 19, 2008, http://www.ustreas.gov/press/releases/hp1149.htm.

77. Senate Committee on Banking, Housing and Urban Affairs, Board of Governors of the Federal Reserve System, *Ben S. Bernanke Testimony: Turmoil in U.S. Credit*

Markets Recent Actions regarding Government Sponsored Entities, Investment Banks and Other Financial Institutions, 110th Cong., 2nd sess., 2008.

78. Board of Governors of the Federal Reserve System, press release, September 16, 2008, http://federalreserve.gov/newsevents/press/other/20080916a.htm.

79. John W. Schoen, "What Are 'Diluted' Shares?" MSNBC.com, http://www.msnbc.msn.com/id/7477469.

80. Barry Meier and Mary Williams Walsh, "A.I.G. to Get Additional $37.8 Billion," *New York Times*, October 8, 2008.

81. Board of Governors of the Federal Reserve System, press release, October 8, 2008, http://www.federalreserve.gov/newsevents/press/other/20081008a.htm.

82. AIG, "AIG Commercial Insurance," October 24, 2008, http://web.aig.com/2008/cig8454/cig8454_AIGCIFactSheet_102408.pdf.

83. Board of Governors of the Federal Reserve System, press release, November 10, 2008, http://federalreserve.gov/newsevents/press/other/20081110a.htm.

84. Carol D. Leonnig, "Government Again Expands AIG Rescue Plan," *Washington Post*, November 11, 2008.

85. Transcripts, "American International Group, Inc. Q4 2008 Earnings Call Transcript," Seekingalpha.com, March 3, 2009, http://seekingalpha.com/article/123915-american-international-group-inc-q4-2008-earnings-call-transcript.

86. AIG, "Results Reflect Ongoing Severe Market Disruption and Restructuring-Related Charges," press release, March 2, 2009, http://ir.aigcorporate.com/phoenix.zhtml?c=76115&p=irol-newsArticle&ID=1261312&highlight=.

87. AIG, "AIG Announces Chairman and CEO Edward M. Liddy to Step Down after Replacements Found," press release, May 21, 2009, http://phx.corporateir.net/phoenix.zhtml?c=76115&p=irol-newsArticle&ID=1291293&highlight=.

88. Nomi Prins and Krisztina Ugrin, "Bailout Tally," June 2009, http://www.nomiprins.com/bailout.html; House Financial Services Committee, Board of Governors of the Federal Reserve System, Ben S. Bernanke Testimony: oversight of the Federal Government's Intervention at American International Group, 111th Cong., 1st sess., 2009.

89. "Top Watchdog," *The Economist*, March 19, 2009.

90. House Financial Services Committee, Board of Governors of the Federal Reserve System, *Ben S. Bernanke Testimony: Oversight of the Federal Government's Intervention at American International Group*, 111th Cong., 1st sess., 2009.

91. AIG, "Code of Conduct," http://media.corporate-ir.net/media_files/irol/76/76115/AIGcoconduct.pdf.

92. Carrick Mollenkamp, Serena Ng, Liam Pleven, and Randall Smith, "Behind AIG's Fall, Risk Models Failed to Pass Real-World Test," *Wall Street Journal*, October 31, 2008.

93. Transcripts, "American International Group Q2 2007 Earnings Call Transcript," Seekingalpha.com, August 9, 2007, http://seekingalpha.com/article/44048-american-international-group-q2-2007-earnings-call-transcript?page=7.

94. Michael Daly, "Pin AIG Woes on Brooklyn Boy: Joseph Cassano Walked Away with $315 Million While Company Staggered," *New York Daily News*, March 17, 2009, http://www.nydailynews.com/money/2009/03/17/2009-03-17_pin_aig_woes_on_brooklyn_boy_joseph_cass-1.html.

95. American International Group, "Attachment A—Collateral Postings under AIGFP CDS: Direct Support to AIG from 9/16/08–12/31/08," http://www.aig.com/aigweb/internet/en/files/CounterpartyAttachments031809_tcm385-155645.pdf.

96. Eliot Spitzer, "The Real AIG Scandal," Slate.com, March 17, 2009, http://www.slate.com/id/2213942.

97. Eliot Spitzer, "The Real AIG Scandal, Continued!" Slate.com, March 22, 2009, http://www.slate.com/id/2214407.

Chapter 9. Change, Really?

1. Michael Lewis, "The End," *Portfolio*, December 2008, p. 1, http://www.portfolio.com/news-markets/national-news/portfolio/2008/11/11/The-End-of-Wall-Streets-Boom.

2. U.S. Department of the Treasury, *2007 Budget Receipts by Source*, Table 2, October 11, 2007, http://www.treas.gov/press/releases/reports/additionaltable2.pdf.

3. U.S. Department of the Treasury, "Opening Statement of Herbert M. Allison, Nominee for Assistant Secretary of the Treasury for Financial Stability before the Senate Committee on Banking, Housing, and Urban Affairs," press release, TG-157, June 4, 2009, http://www.treas.gov/press/releases/tg157.htm.

4. Reuters, "Fannie Mae CEO Takes over TARP," CNNMoney.com, April 17, 2009, http://money.cnn.com/2009/04/17/news/economy/tarp_director.reut/index.htm; Washington Post Company, "Herbert M. Allison," Who Runs Gov., n.d., http://www.whorunsgov.com/Profiles/Herbert_M._Allison_Jr.

5. Zachary A. Goldfarb, "Treasury Plans to Tap Fannie Mae Chief to Run Bailout," *Washington Post*, April 14, 2009, http://www.washingtonpost.com/wp-dyn/content/article/2009/04/13/AR2009041303257.html?hpid=topnews.

6. Washington Post Company, "Herbert M. Allison Jr."

7. Teachers Insurance and Annuity Association—"College Retirement Equities Fund, Who We Are," n.d., http://www.tiaa-cref.org/about/identity/index.html.

8. Jenny Anderson, "A Financial Veteran Brings Wall Street and Washington to Job at Fannie Mae," *New York Times*, September 7, 1008, http://www.nytimes.com/2008/09/08/us/08allison.html?_r=1.

9. Patrick McGeehan, "Openers: Suits; New in the Neighborhood," *New York Times*, May 7, 2006, http://query.nytimes.com/gst/fullpage.html?res=9E05E2DC1F3FF934A35756C0A9609C8B63.

10. GovTrack.us, *H.R. 1586: To Impose an Additional Tax on Bonuses Received From Certain TARP Recipients*, n.d., http://www.govtrack.us/congress/bill.xpd?bill=h111-1586.

11. Jeff Mason, "UPDATE 1—Obama Says Needs 'Ammunition' for Financial System," Reuters, January 13, 2009, http://in.reuters.com/article/governmentFilingsNews/idINN1235014120090112.

12. Nomi Prins and Krisztina Ugrin, "TARP Evaluation," June 2009, http://www.nomiprins.com/bailout.html.

13. U.S. Department of the Treasury, "Treasury Announces New Policy to Increase Transparency in Financial Stability Program," press release: TG-04, January 28, 2009, http://treas.gov/press/releases/tg04.htm.

14. U.S. Department of the Treasury, "Secretary Geithner Introduces Financial Stability Plan," press release: TG-18, February 10, 2009, http://www.treasury.gov/press/releases/tg18.htm.

15. Federal Deposit Insurance Corporation, *FDIC Quarterly*, vol. 3, no. 1 (2009), http://www.fdic.gov/bank/analytical/quarterly/2009_vol3_1/Quarterly_Vol3No1_entire_issue_FINAL.pdf.

16. U.S. Department of the Treasury, "Secretary Geithner Introduces Financial Stability Plan."

17. Ibid.

18. Fredreka Schouten, "Geithner Names Ex-Lobbyist as Treasury Chief of Staff," *USA Today*, January 27, 2009, http://www.usatoday.com/news/washington/2009-01-27-lobbyist_N.htm; Nomi Prins and Krisztina Ugrin, "Bailout Tally," June 2009, http://www.nomiprins.com/bailout.html.

19. The White House, *Executive Order—Ethics Commitments by Executive Branch Personnel*, January 21, 2009, http://www.whitehouse.gov/the_press_office/Executive Order-EthicsCommitments.

20. U.S. Department of the Treasury, "Secretary Tim Geithner Opening Statement—Senate Budget Committee Hearing Policies to Address the Crises in Financial and Housing Markets," press release: TG-02112009, February 11, 2009, http://www.treas.gov/press/releases/tg02112009.htm.

21. U.S. Department of the Treasury, "Treasury Secretary Tim Geithner Written Testimony, Congressional Oversight Panel," press release: TG-94, April 21, 2009, http://www.treas.gov/press/releases/tg94.htm.

22. United States Department of Labor, "Employment Situation Summary," press release, June 5, 2009, http://www.bls.gov/news.release/empsit.nr0.htm.

23. U.S. Department of the Treasury, "Secretary Geithner Introduces Financial Stability Plan."

24. Nomi Prins, "Obamanomics: The Good, the Bad, the Weak, *Mother Jones,* June 17, 2009, http://www.motherjones.com/bailout/2009/06/financial-regulation-good-bad-very-ugly? page 1; United States Department of the Treasury, "Financial Regulatory Reform: A New Foundation," white paper, June 17, 2009, http://www.financialstability.gov/docs/regs/Final Report_web.pdf.

25. Congressional Oversight Panel, *February Oversight Report, February 6, 2009*, p. 5, http://cop.senate.gov/documents/cop-020609-report.pdf; Nomi Prins and Krisztina Ugrin, "TARP Evaluation."

26. Wells Fargo, "Wells Fargo and Wachovia Merger Completed," press release, January 1, 2009, https://www.wellsfargo.com/press/2009/20090101_Wachovia_Merger.

27. Wells Fargo, *4th Quarter 2008 Earnings Release*, January 28, 2009, https://www.wellsfargo.com/pdf/press/4q08pr.pdf.

28. "JPMorgan Chase & Company," *New York Times*, April 21, 2009, http://topics.nytimes.com/topics/news/business/companies/morgan_j_p_chase_and_company/index.html.

29. Federal Reserve Bank of New York, "Summary of Terms and Conditions regarding the JPMorgan Chase Facility," press release, March 24, 2008, http://www.ny.frb.org/newsevents/news/markets/2008/rp080324b.html.

30. JPMorgan Chase, "3rd Quarter 2008 Earnings Release," press release, October 15, 2008, http://investor.shareholder.com/jpmorganchase/press/releasedetail.cfm?releaseid=340523&ReleaseType=Current; Eric Dash and Jonathan D. Glater, "Citigroup Says Judge Suspends Wachovia Deal," *New York Times*, October 4, 2008, http://www.nytimes.com/2008/10/05/business/05bank.html.

31. "Federal Reserve System," Microsoft Encarta Online Encyclopedia 2009, http://encarta.msn.com/encyclopedia_761574452/federal_reserve_system.html.

32. The White House, "Remarks by the President after Meeting with the Vice President and the Secretary of the Treasury," press release, January 29, 2009, http://www .whitehouse.gov/the_press_office/RemarksByThePresidentAfterMeeting WithTheVicePresidentAndTheSecretaryOfTheTreasury.

33. Stephen Labaton, "Wall Street Settlement: The Overview; 10 Wall St. Firms Reach Settlement in Analyst Inquiry," *New York Times*, April 29, 2003, http://query.nytimes .com/gst/fullpage.html?res=9F03E5D9103DF93AA15757C0A9659C8B63&sec=& spon=&pagewanted=all.

34. U.S. Securities and Exchange Commission, *Speech by SEC Chairman: Prepared for Delivery at SEC Press Conference Regarding Global Settlement, April 28, 2003,* http://www.sec.gov/news/speech/spch042803whd.htm.

35. Ximena Marinero, "SEC Chairman Nominee Committed to Agency Enforcement," Jurist Legal News and Research Services, January 16, 2009, http://jurist.law.pitt.edu/ paperchase/2009/01/sec-chairman-nominee-committed-to.php.

36. U.S. Securities and Exchange Commission, *Frequently Requested FOIA Document: Budget History—BA vs. Actual Obligations, March 05, 2008,* http://www.sec.gov/ foia/docs/budgetact.htm.

37. U.S. Securities and Exchange Commission, *Fiscal 2007 Appropriations Request by Chairman Christopher Cox, April 27, 2006,* http://www.sec.gov/news/testimony/ ts042706cc.htm.

38. Melissa Klein Aguilar, "Schapiro: Better Enforcement Is Job 1," *Compliance Week,* January 20, 2009, http://www.complianceweek.com/article/5236/embracing-502-the- new-hope-for-attorney-client-privilege.

39. Goldman Sachs, "Goldman Sachs to Become the Fourth Largest Bank Holding Company," press release, September 21, 2008, http://www2.goldmansachs.com/our- firm/press/press-releases/archived/2008/bank-holding-co.html.

40. Christine Harper, "Goldman Sachs Would Like to Repay Treasury, CFO Says (Update 1)," Bloomberg, February 4, 2009, www.bloomberg.com/apps/news?pid=2 0601087&refer=home&sid=a3xTcf52kEZM.

41. Goldman Sachs, "Goldman Sachs Announces $5 Billion Public Offering of Common Equity," press release, April 13, 2009, http://www2.goldmansachs.com/our-firm/ press/press-releases/current/public-stock-offering.print.html.

42. Nomi Prins, "10 Sleazy Ways That Goldman Sachs Distracted Us While Pocket- ing Billions from the Treasury," AlterNet, May 28, 2009, http://www.alternet.org/ story/140291; Nomi Prins and Krisztina Ugrin, "Bailout Tally," June 2009, http:// www.nomiprins.com/bailout.html.

43. Nomi Prins and Krisztina Ugrin, "CEO Compensation and Bonuses," June 2009, http://www.nomiprins.com/bailout.html.

44. U.S. Department of the Treasury, *TARP Transaction Report for Period Ending December 31, 2008,* January 13, 2009, http://www.financialstability.gov/docs/ transaction-reports/transaction_report_01132009.pdf.

45. Bank of International Settlements, Report, June 2008, http://www.bis.org/statistics/ otcder/dt1920a.pdf.

46. The Depository Trust & Clearing Corporation, "DTCC to Support All Central Coun- terparties for OTC Credit Derivatives," press release, January 12, 2009, http://www .dtcc.com/news/press/releases/2009/dtcc_supports_ccps.php.

47. Trade Information Warehouse (TIW), the central industry database and technology infrastructure implemented in November 2006 for the global, over-the-counter (OTC) derivatives market. The Depository Trust & Clearing Corporation, Trade Information Warehouse (TIW) Service Overview, n.d., http://www.dtcc.com/downloads/products/derivserv/TIW_Overview_On_Request.pdf; "CLS Bank International (CLS Bank) is an Edge corporation, a limited purpose institution regulated by the US Federal Reserve. CLS Bank observes the Core Principles for Systemically Important Payment Systems published by the BIS Committee on Payment and Settlement Systems of the Central Banks of the G10 countries (CPSS)." CLS Group, *About Us: What Is CLS?* n.d., http://www.cls-group.com/About/Pages/WhatIsCLS.aspx; The Depository Trust & Clearing Corporation, "DTCC to Support All Central Counterparties for OTC Credit Derivatives," press release, January 12, 2009, http://www.dtcc.com/news/press/releases/2009/dtcc_supports_ccps.php.

48. House Agriculture Committee, *Hearings and Opening Statements*, n.d., http://agriculture.house.gov/hearings/statements.html.

49. GovTrack, *H.R.977—111th Congress (2009): Derivatives Markets Transparency and Accountability Act of 2009*, GovTrack.us, http://www.govtrack.us/congress/bill.xpd?bill=h111-977.

50. Darla Mercado, "Regs for Swaps, Other Derivatives Debated," *InvestmentNews*, February 5, 2009, http://www.investmentnews.com/apps/pbcs.dll/article?AID=/20090205/REG/902059952.

51. credit default swap: A specific kind of counterparty agreement that allows the transfer of third-party credit risk from one party to the other. One party in the swap is a lender and faces credit risk from a third party, and the counterparty in the credit default swap agrees to insure this risk in exchange of regular periodic payments (essentially an insurance premium). If the third party defaults, the party providing insurance will have to purchase from the insured party the defaulted asset. In turn, the insurer pays the insured the remaining interest on the debt, as well as the principal. InvesterWords.com, "Credit Default Swap," n.d., http://www.investorwords.com/5876/credit_default_swap.html; MFA, Managed Funds Association, *Managed Funds Association, About MFA*, n.d., http://www.managedfunds.org/about-mfa.asp; U.S. House Committee on Agriculture, *Testimony of Stuart J. Kaswell for the Hearing on the Derivatives Markets Transparency and Accountability Act of 2009*, February 2, 2009, p. 8, http://agriculture.house.gov/testimony/111/h020409/Kaswell.pdf.

52. Mercado, "Regs for Swaps, Other Derivatives Debated."

53. Board of Governors of the Federal Reserve System, "The Federal Reserve Board on Sunday Approved, Pending a Statutory Five-Day Antitrust Waiting Period, the Applications of Goldman Sachs and Morgan Stanley to Become Bank Holding Companies," press release, September 21, 2008, http://www.federalreserve.gov/newsevents/press/bcreg/20080921a.htm.

54. *Gramm-Leach-Bliley Act, Public Law 106-102*, p. 113.

55. NPR, "Goldman Sachs CEO Defends Executive Pay," *All Things Considered*, April 8, 2009, http://www.npr.org/templates/story/story.php?storyId=102887296.

56. Nomi Prins and Krisztina Ugrin, "Bailout Tally," June 2009, http://www.nomiprins.com/bailout.html.

57. NPR, "Goldman Sachs CEO Defends Executive Pay."

58. David E. Sanger, "Nationalization Gets a New, Serious Look," *New York Times*, January 25, 2009, http://www.nytimes.com/2009/01/26/business/economy/26banks.html.

59. Nomi Prins and Krisztina Ugrin, "Bailout Tally," June 2009, http://www.nomiprins.com/bailout.html.

60. ABC News, "Transcript: Nancy Pelosi," *This Week*, January 25, 2009, p. 2, http://www.abcnews.go.com/ThisWeek/Story?id=6725512.

61. Jon Meacham and Evan Thomas, "We Are All Socialists Now," *Newsweek*, February 7, 2009, http://www.newsweek.com/id/183663.

62. Reuters, "'Bad Bank' Idea Heats Up, Financial Shares Soar," Reuters, January 28, 2009, http://www.reuters.com/article/newsOne/idUSTRE50R5XP20090128.

63. Alexandra Twin, "Stocks Stage Rally," CNNMoney.com, January 28, 2009, http://money.cnn.com/2009/01/28/markets/markets_newyork.

64. Tom Petruno, "Schumer Casts Doubt on 'Bad Bank' Plan for Toxic Loans," Bloomberg News through *Los Angeles Times*, February 3, 2009, http://latimesblogs.latimes.com/money_co/2009/02/bad-bank-financ.html.

65. Patrice Hill, "Investors Regroup after Wall Street Rout," *Washington Times*, January 1, 2009, p. 2, http://www.washingtontimes.com/news/2009/jan/01/wall-street-rout-reverberates-as-investors-regroup.

66. *Wall Street Journal*, "John Thain Office Final Budget Summary 1/15/2009," January 15, 2009, p. 3, http://online.wsj.com/public/resources/documents/thaindocuments2.pdf.

67. *Gramm-Leach-Bliley Act, Public Law 106-102*, p. 113.

68. Dean Baker, Phone conversation with the author, January 30, 2009.

69. Stanley Weiser, "*Wall Street*'s Message Was Not 'Greed Is Good,'" *Los Angeles Times*, October 5, 2008, http://www.latimes.com/la-ca-wallstreet5-2008oct05,0,3977968.story.

70. Ibid.

71. *Wall Street Journal*, "Merkel for the Fed," June 4, 2009, http://online.wsj.com/article/SB124407271719283173.html.

72. Rita Nazareth, "Global Stocks Gain, Led by Record U.S. Bank Rally; Bonds Fall," Bloomberg, April 9, 2009, http://www.bloomberg.com/apps/news?pid=20601087&sid=amWbPIx3pyb0&refer=home.

73. Wells Fargo, "Wells Fargo Expects Record First Quarter Earnings of Approximately $3 Billion," press release, April 9, 2009, https://www.wellsfargo.com/press/2009/20090409_Prelim_Earnings.

74. U.S. Department of the Treasury, "Speech by Secretary Geithner—The United States and China, Cooperating for Recovery and Growth," press release: TG-152, May 31, 2009, http://www.treas.gov/press/releases/tg152.htm.

75. Brett Philbin, "Merrill Lynch Turns Bullish On Hiring Brokers Again," *Wall Street Journal*, May 5, 2009, http://online.wsj.com/article_email/BT-CO-20090505-716372-kIyVDAtMEM5TzAtNjIwMDYwWj.html.

76. Evan Newmark, "Mean Street: It's Time to Enshrine Hank Paulson as National Hero," *Wall Street Journal*, June 3, 2009, http://blogs.wsj.com/deals/2009/06/03/mean-street-its-time-to-enshrine-hank-paulson-as-national-hero.

77. U.S. Department of the Treasury, "Treasury Announces $68 Billion in Expected CPP Repayments," press release, June 9, 2009, http://www.financialstability.gov/

latest/tg_06092009.html; Tim Ryan, "Wall Street Is a Willing Partner in Financial Reform," *Financial Times*, June 8, 2009, http://www.ft.com/cms/s/0/a3ea6b8c-5463-11de-a58d-00144feabdc0.html; Maya Jackson Randall, "Banks Get OK to Repay $68 Billion in Bailout Money," *Wall Street Journal*, June 9, 2009, http://online.wsj.com/article/SB124455528999797923.html.

78. Nomi Prins and Krisztina Ugrin, "Ten Bank TARP Payback," June 2009, http://www.nomiprins.com/bailout.html.

79. Peter S. Goodman and Jack Healy, "Job Losses Push Safer Mortgages to Foreclosure," *New York Times*, May 24, 2009, http://www.nytimes.com/2009/05/25/business/economy/25foreclose.html.

80. Standard & Poor's, "S&P/Case-Schiller U.S. National Home Price Values," May 26, 2009, http://www2.standardandpoors.com/portal/site/sp/en/us/page.article/2,3,4,0,1148433018483.html.

81. James J. Cramer, "Thank Bernanke," *New York*, June 5, 2009, http://www.nymag.com/news/businessfinance/bottomline/57177.

INDEX